FREE WILL AND DETERMINISM

SOURCES IN CONTEMPORARY PHILOSOPHY

FRANK A. TILLMAN, CONSULTING EDITOR

HARPER & ROW, PUBLISHERS NEW YORK AND LONDON

FREE WILL AND DETERMINISM

Edited
by

BERNARD BEROFSKY

Department of Philosophy
The University of Michigan

FREE WILL AND DETERMINISM

 For information address Harper & Row, Publishers, Incorporated, 49 East 33rd Street, New York, N. Y. 10016.

LIBRARY OF CONGRESS CATALOG CARD NUMBER: 66-11261

C-1

CONTENTS

PART TWO: TOPICS

EDITOR'S INTRODUCTION

No volume by a single scholar can recreate the incessant dialectic of contemporary philosophic inquiry; hence we are offering a series that is a collaboration of many hands. The present series is intended to provide students, teachers, and interested nonprofessionals with collections of essays in every major problem area of contemporary philosophy. Each volume is devoted to a single set of interconnected issues; each issue is currently the subject of intensc philosophic discussion. The editors have been uncompromising in their attempt to bring together essays of great clarity and high technical excellence. Most of the essays were written during the last ten years, some newly written for this series; a number have already become contemporary classics. Each collection is large enough to display a cumulative diversity of viewpoint and detail.

In making relatively inaccessible essays available, this series will enable teachers of philosophy to find strategic or supplementary materials for a wide range of courses. To the student it offers the luxury of possessing essays formerly buried in bound journals or closeted in library reserves. To readers other than teachers and students, the series offers an opportunity to explore contemporary philosophy at first hand. To all readers, it offers original formulations of new ideas and fresh insight into topics of ancient ancestry.

FRANK A. TILLMAN

PREFACE

The book is divided into two parts. In the first, four fundamentally different approaches are presented. In each section a position is defined and defended and at least one critique of the position, usually of the man whose defense of that view is presented, appears. The positions may now be sketchily defined.

Determinism. Although it is misleading to label the view presented here as "determinism" (for it asserts both that determinism[1] is true *and* that incompatibilism[1] is true) there is a strong historical precedent for this since determinists have been presented as people who not only espouse determinism, but who use this doctrine to show that people have no free will. They also argue that since people have no free will, they are never morally responsible for their actions.

Reconciliationism. This view maintains that determinism is true or there are good reasons to believe that it is and no compelling reason to reject it; but that incompatibilism is false. Thus, one must examine the content of the law accounting for some human action in order to discover whether or not the person could have done otherwise. Reconciliationists vary in their accounts of the characteristics a law must possess in order for us to say of some action governed by that law that the person could not have done otherwise.

Libertarianism. Some human actions are not determined and incompatibilism is true. Men have free will, but only when their behavior is not governed by any deterministic law. Moreover, one can distinguish between a genuine act of the person which is not lawfully linked to antecedents, and a mere chance occurrence or

[1] These notions are clarified in the General Introduction.

random happening of his body (or mind), usually by thinking of the self as an agent who can sometimes intrude into the causal order.

Action Theory. In recent years, many philosophers have been concerned with the notion of human action. This concept has, as a matter of fact, become the focal point for most current discussions in the philosophy of mind. But only some of the theses which have been advanced have a bearing on the free will issue. In particular, we are interested only if it is argued that there can be no deterministic explanations of action. For us, then, action theory necessarily includes a restriction on determinism along these lines.

The libertarian, although a bit worried that he might be wrong, denies *in fact* that deterministic accounts can be provided for all actions. The action theorist denies *in principle* the same proposition and is not, therefore, worried. He claims that, given the notion of "deterministic account of x" and "y is an action," it is conceptually impossible for x to be identical with y.

In the second part of the book, the essays are addressed specifically to three notions which are fundamental in free will debates: foreknowledge, power, and effort. The views in these chapters reflect, to some extent, the different positions outlined in the first part.

Foreknowledge. Competing answers are presented to the following questions: Can there be foreknowledge of a deliberately chosen act? and if there is foreknowledge of some action, could the action have been performed freely? The reasons for our concern about foreknowledge are discussed.

Power. Freedom as the power to perform several actions is the focus of interest. Differences between compatibilists and incompatibilists are reflected in competing analyses of "Although he did x, he could have done y."

Effort. There are discussions of the relationship between effort and free will. How central is the notion of effort or trying in our conception of freedom? The libertarian considers it quite central since he often views its appearance as the manifestation of self-activity and, hence, an instance of freedom. There is, therefore, a discussion of the possibility of deterministic accounts of effort of will.

BERNARD BEROFSKY

FREE WILL AND DETERMINISM

GENERAL INTRODUCTION

DETERMINISM

In discussions of human freedom it is not uncommon to omit a definition or clarification of the thesis of determinism, although reference to it may be made. This is quite serious if one considers (1) the fact that this thesis often plays a fundamental role in conceptions of human freedom and (2) the possibility that resolutions of fundamental questions about human freedom hinge upon clarification of the thesis of determinism. Since the serious accounts of determinism appear, on the whole, in the context of discussions, often technical, in the philosophy of science, we have not included any selections on determinism per se. A few words about it, therefore, are in order.

The conception of determinism which was being formulated and clarified between the times of Galileo and Laplace has, as an important historical predecessor, a doctrine more closely allied to religious outlooks. Rooted in ancient Greek thought was the conception of *Moira*, fate, or necessity—a force often conceived anthropomorphically which governs occurrences, especially the destiny of those who violate certain moral injunctions. Other cultures have similar conceptions and we shall use the term "fate" to refer to any of these conceptions. It was not common to conceive of fate as governing *all* occurrences though; whereas this universal aspect is a defining characteristic of determinism. The kinds of occurrences which fate was conceived typically to govern are (1) the outcome of human undertakings; (2) the occurrence of events which have an important effect on human beings; and (3) actions which we ordinarily believe to be under our own control. The homocentric character of fate is evident.

A more sophisticated predecessor of modern determinism appeared when Christian thinkers began to reflect upon God's characteristics and relationship to the world. One extreme conception, influenced strongly by neo-Platonism, views the world and everything that happens as the unraveling of God's essence, a process whose existence and character are necessary and immutable. This includes the act of creation and all human activity. The universal character of determinism—in this case, theological determinism—is evident in this type of conception, later to be espoused in its purely pantheistic form by Spinoza.

Whether or not a Christian thinker adopts the above view, the orthodox position maintained that God has foreknowledge of all that happens. This and similar doctrines (e.g., all events are capable of being foreknown) play a role in later formulations of determinism. This view about God has the extrinsic merit of conducing to a discussion of free will for, although it seems evident that there is no free will if what I do is done necessarily, it is not self-evident (although perhaps initially plausible) that I lack free will merely because God knows what I shall do. Thus we have St. Augustine's discussion of this issue (see Chapter 5). Free will seems to be necessary in this theological context since man is held morally responsible for some of his acts. This is implied in the doctrine of reward and punishment. The difficulty appears when we try to reconcile a free act of sin—for which God is to hold the person morally responsible—with the fact that God knew beforehand that the man was to sin.

God may be conceived to play an incidental role. For example, He may create a deterministic world; but our conception of its deterministic character may require no reference to Him or His nature. This position was taken in the seventeenth and eighteenth centuries by the deists. At that time, there were other thinkers among those who were presenting a conception of determinism based on the science of mechanics who took

God to be the First Cause, but gave Him a more important role. Robert Boyle, for example, conceived it necessary for God to sustain the harmony of the world through some form of permanent activity.

The more powerful and important God's role in the world is conceived, the more serious are the problems which are created for those who wish to retain a belief in human freedom.

But the most direct predecessors of modern determinism can be found by seeking out those thinkers who emphasized the unity or universal government of nature, while at the same time deemphasizing or eliminating in part the anthropomorphic form this conception took. One looks to Empedocles and the other mechanists for the suggestion that, in itself, matter is not alive. One looks to Heraclitus for a primitive conception of law as the fundamental fact about the world. And one finds the latter idea brought to prominence again by the Stoics. In each case, the view is surrounded and permeated by teleological and animistic intrusions; but the germ is present.

Passing now to the conception of determinism which received its eventual formulation by Laplace, we should note its dependence upon a particular scientific theory, viz., particle mechanics. For Laplace contends that a knowledge of the mechanical state of all particles at some particular time together with a knowledge of "all the forces acting in nature" at that instant would enable an intelligence to discover all future and all past states of the world. With this information, this intelligence can discover not only all future and past mechanical states, but all others as well, e.g., electromagnetic, chemical, psychological. Thus, Laplace's conception of determinism embodies the substantive idea that classical mechanics will turn out to be the universal science of nature.

Writers on psychology in the seventeenth and eighteenth centuries often held the same faith. They would, therefore, formulate the rudiments of a psychological theory in terms of the concepts and structure of classical mechanics. Hence, when a writer like Baron Holbach rejects the reality of free will, he does so often not on the grounds that human decisions and actions are governed by law, but on the grounds that such occurrences are governed by laws which are similar in some fundamental way to the laws of classical mechanics.

The fact that classical mechanics did not turn out to be the universal science of nature suggests that contemporary proponents of determinism do not ally themselves to this particular theory. Many ally themselves to no particular theory at all, but try to define determinism in such a way that its rejection is not necessitated by the rejection of any particular scientific theory. Let us turn to these now.

One may distinguish those positions which make reference to human powers, potentialities, and capabilities from those which do not. Within the first category fall all formulations which conceive of determinism in terms of the possibility of knowing, predicting, or explaining all that happens. When such views are examined, however, it is not difficult to show that such concepts are eliminable from the definition. For the basis upon which knowledge, prediction, and explanation of some event must rest for a definition of determinism is the lawful character of the event or the existence of a cause (in the sense of sufficient condition) of the event. Moreover, if the event is lawful or caused, it is thought of as determined, regardless of whether or not it is *humanly* possible to have sufficient information to know about, predict, or explain the event. Thus the apparent reference to human powers turns out to be an elliptical way of referring to the lawful or caused character of the event.

The second category of positions, then, defines determinism in terms of the concept of cause or law without referring to what it is (in principle) possible for human beings to do. Two problems initially face the determinist.

1. What is it that is determined? What are deterministic accounts about?[1] A traditional definition of determinism is "Every event has a cause." But if an event takes time and involves change, then many traditional determinists would argue

[1] Discussions with William P. Alston on this question have been very helpful in clarifying some of my ideas about the matter.

that the scope of the statement is too narrow since unchanges are determined too. A more serious difficulty is the following. Suppose it is determined that Jones eats lunch on Friday. The event of Jones's eating lunch on Friday is the same event as Jones's eating a grilled Edam cheese sandwich at 12 noon on Friday. It follows that Jones's eating a grilled Edam cheese sandwich at 12 noon is determined. But this consequence is false if there is no law which governs *what* Jones eats to such a degree of specificity. These two difficulties can be avoided by reverting to the language of facts or the language of states. With respect to the first problem, it is a fact that I have not moved or that my body is in a state of rest. Hence, deterministic accounts might be provided. As to the second problem, the fact that Jones eats lunch on Friday is a different fact from the fact that he eats a grilled Edam cheese sandwich at 12 noon on Friday. Although the language of states is not ordinary and may be cumbersome, it should not be that difficult to specify Jones's states on Friday, in which case the two distinct facts would be reflected as two distinct states. Those who opt for the language of events can offer rebuttal; but since the discussion can get quite involved, we shall say no more here.

2. Should we use the concept of cause or law, and how should the chosen concept be defined or perhaps restricted? For example, if the notion of cause is chosen, then the analysis of this concept must differ from one which remains as true as possible to ordinary usage. For it is rare that the cause of an event as specified in ordinary usage is a sufficient condition (e.g., "The action of the arsonist caused the fire"). Yet a deterministic account of some event (fact, state) must specify at least a sufficient condition in order to satisfy the traditional idea that the determining factors determine a unique outcome. As to the choice between cause and law, a Humean would argue that there is no problem since causal propositions involve a tacit reference to a law, or at least to the claim that there is a law of a certain kind. But many disagree with the Humean position. Even if the notion of (nonstatistical) law is chosen, it must be restricted. For example, there is a law which enables

us to ascribe a unique value to the length of a pendulum at a certain time if the period of the pendulum at that time is given. But this is compatible with the length of the pendulum's being "undetermined"—e.g., suppose its length varies in a purely random fashion. What we require then is a causal law or a law which shows that the event (fact, state) is determined. There are many other problems concerning the notion of law. But one requirement of the analysis (which some have used to define determinism) is that whenever a law is applied to some isolated system which is in state *S* and one may then deduce that this system will be in state *T*, *n* minutes later, then the same deduction will hold for any system of the same type which is in state *S*. This is the way in which laws show that "the past determines a unique future."

A determinist, then, is a person who believes that all events (facts, states) are lawful in the sense, roughly, that for any event *e*, there is a distinct event *d* plus a (causal) law which asserts, "Whenever *d*, then *e*."

The extremely general or universal character of this thesis has raised many questions, some of which concern the status of the thesis. Some have held the position as a necessary or a priori truth about the world. Others have insisted that determinism is itself a scientific theory, but much more general than most other scientific theories. This latter view has been criticized on the grounds that scientific theories are confirmed and disconfirmed; but there are difficulties on both scores for determinism. How can determinism be disconfirmed if the failure to find laws in a certain domain can always be explained by the determinist in terms of insufficient effort or intelligence, etc.? Thus determinism can always be saved and is not, therefore, like a legitimate scientific theory since the latter is open to possible rejection in the light of contrary evidence.

On the other hand, how can such a general view be confirmed? The only answer a determinist can provide requires him to construe each example in which a class of events is shown to be governed by law as indirect evidence for determinism. But even if we take physics as our model, we find the often cited deviation between experimentally ascertained values of the variables in laws and the values which are predicted from the laws. If it is implausible to ascribe all deviations which do not lead us to make revisions in the laws to "random experimental errors," then a determinist will have to acknowledge either that determinism is only "approximately true" or that its truth ought not entail that such a deviation does not exist. He may point out that there are criteria, perhaps vague, to decide whether or not deviations are sufficient to warrant rejection of the proposed law, and hence criteria which enable us to say that the event is governed by this law and one should not take this in such a way as to require perfect harmony between theory and experiment.

Because of the difficulties in construing determinism as a very general scientific theory and because of an antipathy to the view that it is an a priori truth, alternatives have been suggested. Some of these are (1) a maxim governing the conduct of scientific inquiry; (2) a statement of the goals of science; (3) an analytic consequence of the definition of key methodological concepts in science; (4) a postulate.

It is interesting to note that many of the problems revolving around a definition of determinism need not concern a person who is interested in determinism because of an interest in free will. We have seen that there are problems which arise because of the universal character of the thesis. Thus, it is possible to specify the meaning of "event *e*—a human action perhaps—is determined" without dealing with *those* problems. But this is all that is necessary for the free will issue since this is concerned with the relation between such propositions when *e* is some human action or decision and propositions ascribing free will and/or moral responsibility to the person performing the action or making the decision. The thesis of determinism is not to the point—only the claim that the action or decision is determined.

We may then construe the claim that a certain action (or decision) at time *t* is determined as the claim that there is a causal law which entails that the action takes place at *t*, given pertinent information about the individual and his environment which is completely specifiable independently of (and perhaps earlier than) *t*. (What information is pertinent can only be spelled out in the course of psychological inquiry.) This entails that any individual would perform the same action given the same pertinent information.

FREE WILL

We turn now to the question of the relationship between determinism and free will. It has been maintained that if an action is determined, then the person was not performing the action of his own free will. For surely, it is argued, if the antecedent conditions are such that they uniquely determine by law the ensuing result (the action), then it was not within the power of the person to do otherwise. And a person does *A* freely if, and only if, he could have done something other than *A*. Let us call this position "incompatibilism." Incompatibilists usually conclude as well that if a person's action is determined, then he is not morally responsible for having done it, since acting freely is a necessary condition of being morally responsible for the action.

Let us then discuss the notion of freedom or free will by distinguishing four sources from which the problem may arise.

Experiential

There are feelings that we have and activities that we engage in which are very commonplace. Each of them can, however, give rise to reflection on the free will issue.

Guilt or Remorse. That we sometimes feel guilty or remorseful for what we have done is a fact. We are then holding ourselves responsible in which case we must believe that we could have acted differently. Moreover, if we are incompatibilists, we shall also conclude that our action was not determined. Various positions can be outlined:

1. The belief in freedom is there, but illusory (i.e., the content of the belief is false).

2. It is impossible to believe that such a deep-seated feeling invariably gives rise to an erroneous belief. Thus we must sometimes be right in thinking that we could have done otherwise.

a) But incompatibilism is false. We believe that we could have done differently in a sense which does not entail that our action is not determined. We believe, for example, that we would have acted differently had we wanted (chosen, decided) to do differently, and this belief is compatible with the view that our action was determined since a difference in the result is conditioned upon a difference in antecedent factors.

b) Since incompatibilism is true, then our action was not determined. Therefore, determinism is false.

Choice or Decision. That we sometimes choose between alternatives or make decisions seems also to be the case. There is an analogy with guilt and remorse, for we do believe that our choice is free, up to us, that the alternatives are genuine, open possibilities. Views similar to those which appeared above concerning guilt and remorse may be outlined with one complication.

Due to differences of a methodological sort, philosophers have varied in their approaches to these problems. Some have tried to deal with them from a phenomenological standpoint, exploring the quality and nature of the experience and trying to discover what of importance is implicit therein. Others have been concerned to analyze the *notions* of choice and decision, trying to discover what of importance is implicit in these notions. Now the specific difference between these two approaches is difficult to state; but some philosophers engaged in the latter task have drawn the conclusion that choosing or deciding is an essentially undetermined activity. That is to say, nothing that is determined can be a genuine case of choosing or deciding. Hence, *if* we ever choose, determinism is false. Of course, these philosophers may then express skepticism or uncertainty as to whether or not we ever do actually choose because if what we call "choosing" is really determined, then it should not be so-called.

It is true that some philosophers have drawn the same conclusion from a phenomenological viewpoint; but this would be difficult to defend since it requires that we introspectively discover that what we are engaged in, e.g., choosing, is *not* determined. It is difficult to understand how one can discover this introspectively.

Effort. The notion of "making an effort" or "trying" assumes an importance in these matters when one reflects on the commonplace rebuttal to one who holds us morally responsible for doing *A*, viz., "I tried not to do *A*, but failed" or "Even if I had tried not to do *A*, I still would have done *A*." Some philosophers have suggested in this connection that the concept of freedom be defined in terms of the concept of trying. For example, "He could have done *A*" means "He would have done *A* if he had tried."

Again, the two approaches described above, the phenomenological and the conceptual, have both been employed with respect to the nature of effort or trying. But as far as I know, no one has drawn the conclusion that no one ever tries to do something or that this would be so if determinism were true. C. A. Campbell does, however, pose problems for determinists who wish to provide the outlines of a deterministic account of the peculiar effort involved in overcoming temptation (see Chapter 6).

Religious

Fate. Those who accept the existence of fate (as discussed earlier) would be more perturbed about its control over actions which we ordinarily believe to be under our control. For example, an oracle predicted that Oedipus was *fated* to slay his father, Laius, King of Thebes. Oedipus did; but he did not know at the time that the man he slew was his father. Given the notion of fate as it was employed, however, it is false that if he had known the man was his father he would not have killed him if fate had determined that he would kill his father. He would have done it at some time or another; and we might be able to offer what appears to be an ordinary explanation, e.g., ignorance, inadvertence, uncontrollable anger, when the act is performed. There are some interesting problems posed by this conception of fate. For example, it appears that what is not under Oedipus's control, what Oedipus is not free to refrain from doing, is an action of a certain kind, viz., slaying his father. But this notion of freedom is somewhat different from the one we have been talking about for we have been predicating freedom of particular actions. Can we say, for example, that Oedipus had to slay his father, but he did not have to slay him at the time and place he actually did? Or can we give meaning to the idea of fate's determining that something of a certain kind will come to pass without its setting up the machinery that would enable prediction that it would come to pass at a particular time and under specific conditions to be made. If not, then we shall have to say that when Oedipus did slay his father, he could not have refrained from so doing. It may be that he would have refrained from so doing if some condition had been absent; but fate determined that it would be present. Hence, Oedipus was powerless. We shall not get further embroiled in niceties, however, since the number of intelligent believers in this entity does not warrant detailed discussion.

God. God has been endowed with different powers by different thinkers, and, therefore, different problems which bear on free will are generated depending on the conception. If God is conceived in such a way as to require us to say of some person that he could not have done otherwise or that God *forced* him to do what he did, then the only question which is of interest to us is, "Is there a God like that?" Also, some attributes of God which raise problems about free will are such as to allow discussion of the problems without reference to God. Consider the following:

1. God may do something which causes us to decide or act in a certain way. But human beings have this power too,

and no special problems are raised by introducing God into the picture.

2. God may make us in a certain way in a deterministic world. But this problem can be discussed without reference to God by examining the implications of the assumption that determinism (a thesis that can be defined without reference to God) is true and that Jones's behavior, therefore, is completely determined (by heredity, environment, present situation, etc.).

3. God may know in advance all our decisions and actions. But with respect to some particular action, we can suppose that another human being knows beforehand that it will take place. If the term "knows" means the same in both cases, then the concept of God can again be eliminated, as nothing of interest is gained by retaining it in this context. But many have insisted that there are relevant differences between divine and human foreknowledge. Let us mention some.

A person's knowledge exists (is acquired) at a certain time. But since God is outside time, one cannot specify the time at which He knows something. Of course, one should not, then, speak of "foreknowledge" since God does not know that something will take place at *t prior to t.* From the vantage point of eternity, the whole temporal process is "non-temporally before God's eyes." If this can be rendered intelligible, it would appear that no incompatibility exists between divine foreknowledge and free will since God knows what I shall do in a way very similar to that in which Jones, *who is watching me do it,* knows. The problem of *fore*knowledge requires that we suppose the knowledge to exist prior to the event known; for it is only when this condition is satisfied that we become concerned. And when it is lacking, we do not feel that our free will is threatened.

Human beings know that propositions are true almost invariably on the basis of evidence for the propositions; but God never knows on this basis. One is naturally tempted to ask: "How does God know?" The usual answer to this question is that God's knowledge is intuitive or immediate. God knows things in the same way, roughly, that we know that $2 + 2 = 4$.

It may be argued, that is to say, that there are certain types of propositions which human beings know to be true not on the basis of evidence, but in some *immediate* way, and that this situation can serve as some kind of model for all of God's knowledge. The usual examples in the human sphere are (1) logico-mathematical propositions and (2) propositions like "I am in pain" and "It seems to me that there is a red object now before me."

Interestingly enough, though, in the human sphere it is the evidence for knowledge claims which ought really to induce concern about free will. It is true that people are concerned about free will because of other aspects of knowledge; but I think it can be shown that these concerns are not warranted.

In essence, what bothers people is the following: If Jones can at t be said truly to know that Smith will do A at $t + n$, then Jones is in a state at t which makes it necessary that Smith do A at $t + n$. But then, surely, when Smith does A at $t + n$, he was not acting of his own free will. Now this argument clearly depends on a feature of propositions of the form "J knows that p" which has often been cited. Since the falsity of p would make it impossible for anyone to say truly "I know that p," then "J knows that p" entails "p." (Some have disagreed; but for purposes of argument we shall assume that the entailment holds.) Thus if Jones knows at t that Smith will do A at $t + n$, it follows *logically* that Smith will do A at $t + n$. But this ought not in itself induce concern about Smith's free will since there are many true statements which might be made simultaneously with Jones's assertion "I know that Smith will do A at $t + n$" which entail that Smith will do A at $t + n$. One example is "$2 + 2 = 4$ and Smith will do A at $t + n$." If a person replies that there may be insufficient evidence for the latter assertion, then he is substantiating the point I am driving at, to wit, that what ought to concern us about "I know that Smith will do A at $t + n$" is the evidence Jones brings to bear to show that Smith will do A at $t + n$. Or perhaps one is still unconvinced because of the following line of thought:

Jones's true knowledge claim describes his state at t, viz., knowing that Smith will do A at $t + n$. Since he is *in* that state at t, and since a logical consequence of being in that state is Smith's doing A at $t + n$, then Smith is truly unfree for it is logically necessary for him to do A.

The confusion that engenders this line of thought involves the term "state." The argument requires that "*J* knows that *p*" logically entail "*p*" and, for that very reason, knowing cannot be a state like pain. That I am in pain now does not logically entail anything about the future. All that is asserted by "I am in pain now" is completely specified by my present psychological state. But for the very reason that "*J* knows that *p*" entails "*p*," one cannot say the same thing about knowing. If the nonoccurrence in the future of an event is logically conclusive evidence that I do not now know that the event will take place, then "knowing" does not simply describe my present state in the way that "being in pain" does. Thus the argument requires that two incompatible features be included in the scope of "knowing."

But if evidence of a certain kind, e.g., the specification of a deterministic account of the action, is the proper ground of concern about free will, and if God does not know on the basis of evidence, then it may be difficult to see how God's knowledge bears on free will. Let us turn for possible guidance to the two kinds of propositions which, it has been argued, human beings can know without evidence; (1) logico-mathematical propositions and (2) propositions known immediately, like "I am in pain now."

A necessary condition of our knowing logico-mathematical propositions in a special way is the status of the propositions as necessary truths. If we press this analogy, then we derive a picture of the world which was briefly described earlier as a system in which everything that takes place does so necessarily, a world which is virtually described as one in which free will is lacking. God, then, knows that there is no freedom and the only question before us concerns the truth of this view. Or if the world is described simply as a deterministic system which is laid out before God's eyes, then the question of the existence of free will is the same question debated by compatibilists and incompatibilists. No special problem is raised by the introduction of the concept of God.

With propositions known immediately, like "I am in pain now," my privileged position is of crucial importance. You must rely on evidence when you say (referring to me), "He is in pain." But I, presumably, do not rely on evidence. Using this as our analogy, God knows without evidence because of His special position. But what is His special position? If this refers to His nontemporal status, we have already dealt with that. If this refers to the fact that He really causes and knows that He causes everything to happen, we have seen that no special problems are raised here since we already have the problem of the relation between causation (or determinism) and human freedom.

God's knowledge is infallible; human knowledge is not. God cannot be mistaken; but human beings can. I cannot, however, think of any reasons for this difference which we have not already discussed as reasons for the nonevidential character of God's knowledge, e.g., the peculiar nontemporal position of God; and thus I have nothing to add in this connection. As to the *nature* of the difference, there is disagreement of a sort which would take us too far afield to discuss.

Insofar as any statement we have made concerning God's knowledge is criticized on the grounds that His knowledge is very different in nature from man's and this is not adequately taken into account, it is very much to the point to remind the critic that one cannot say anything very clear or definite about the relation between divine foreknowledge and free will unless a relatively clear conception of divine foreknowledge is presented. If human foreknowledge is not even a good starting point for the elucidation of the concept of divine foreknowledge, then the critic should be prepared to offer one, reject the whole discussion as pointless, or explain why the term "foreknowledge" is even used to characterize this divine attribute.

We conclude, then, that for the most part the introduction

of the concept of God is unnecessary in that the problems concerning the relation between certain divine attributes and free will can be formulated and handled without reference to the divine character and/or possession of these attributes.

Scientific

If there is evidence for determinism, it is provided by the success of deterministic scientific theories. Incompatibilists take any demonstration that actions of a certain kind are determined as an automatic demonstration that no one ever performs these actions freely. Moreover, incompatibilists (like Baron Holbach and the Marquis de Sade) who are sufficiently impressed by the results of classical mechanics to believe that the thesis of determinism is warranted conclude that free will does not exist.

In our own era, since the behavioral sciences have achieved independence, one must look to them for direct evidence that determinism holds in the sphere of human behavior. The evidence is, of course, slim; but some, like Clarence Darrow, have thought that this conclusion is warranted. One interesting debate which warrants comment has developed from an examination of psychological science.

Some compatibilists argue that if our actions are determined by our wants and volitions, then we are free. Thus, concern for the existence of free will can only be engendered by the results of psychology if its accepted theories turn out to be incompatible with our commonsense belief that we sometimes act in certain ways because of certain wants that we have. Some have argued that psychology *cannot* show this; others have said that psychology *will* not show this; and others are concerned that it may. Some who are impressed by the results of psychoanalysis assert that it has shown that much of our behavior is governed by unconscious motives and desires and that even if we are free if we act as the result of some conscious want, we are not free if we act as the result of an unconscious want or motive. It is, thus, important to see exactly what it is about a scientific theory of human behavior which makes a person concerned: (1) the fact that it is a deterministic theory; (2)

the fact that it explains behavior in terms of unconscious motives or desires; (3) the fact that it explains behavior without any reference to desires. Number (1) reflects incompatibilism; (2) reflects compatibilism with an implicit definition of a free act as one which proceeds from a conscious desire; (3) reflects compatibilism with an implicit definition of a free act as either one which proceeds from a conscious desire or as one which simply proceeds from some desire.

Philosophical

Although conclusions concerning free will based on the analysis of the concept of choice represents a clear case of philosophical activity, philosophers have drawn conclusions which bear on free will on the basis of premises which seem relatively divorced from human experience or other enterprises, like religion and science, which attempt to make sense out of experience.

For example, philosophers have argued that determinism must be true (is a priori) because (1) everything that happens must have a sufficient reason or (2) otherwise the world would be unintelligible (reason demands it) or (3) experience as we know it would be impossible. It is evident that these arguments are independent of the actual success (or lack of it) of science. Most philosophers are prone to reject these arguments on the grounds that it is impossible to know a priori that everything has a sufficient reason (in the sense of being completely determined). If it is argued that the world would otherwise be unintelligible, one must show (1) that one is not imposing some arbitrary criterion of intelligibility and (2) that the world is intelligible. (Number (2) is an essential premise if the truth of determinism is the conclusion.) Moreover, some would argue that quantum mechanics is an indeterministic theory and its acceptance does not *radically* alter our experience of the world.

Another example—one which has engaged the interest of many philosophers in recent years—concerns the alleged implications of the law of excluded middle. This law asserts that all propositions are true or false, and is presumably applicable, therefore, to propositions about the future. Some philosophers have concluded that the law entails that fatalism is true or that we have no free will or that we lack the power to affect the future. I shall briefly state the argument and let the reader pass on its merits.

It is certainly not within our power to affect the past. I could affect the past if I could bring it about that a certain necessary condition of some past event not take place. But this is not within my power. For suppose that a man's being buried is a necessary condition of his having died, i.e., if he is not buried, then he has not died. This is to say that his dying is a sufficient condition of his being buried. (Suppose all dead people are buried.) Suppose, moreover, that a man's not being buried is a necessary condition of his not having died, i.e., *only* dead people are buried. But either the man died or he did not. (Here is the application of the law of excluded middle.) If he died, then by hypothesis he will be buried. It is not, therefore, in my power to bring it about that he is not buried. (To suppose that it is, is to suppose that dying is not a sufficient condition of being buried.) If he did not die, then by hypothesis he will not be buried. It is not, therefore, in my power to bring it about that he is buried. (To suppose that it is, is to suppose that dying is not a necessary condition of being buried.) It is, therefore, not within my power to bring it about that a certain necessary condition of some actual past event not take place. I, therefore, cannot affect the past. But then nobody denies this conclusion.

The point is, however, that the very same argument can be applied to future occurrences. Assume again that dying is both necessary and sufficient for being buried. Now either Jones will be buried in a few days or he will not. (Here again is the application of the law.) If he will be, then he dies today. But if so, then it is not within my power to bring it about that he does not die today. If he will not be buried in a few days, then he does not die today. It is not, therefore, within my power to bring it about that he does die today. It is not, therefore, within my power to bring it about that a certain necessary condition of some actual future event not take place. I cannot, therefore, affect the future.

It is now argued that the only way to avoid a complete symmetry is to reject the application of the law of excluded middle to certain kinds of future occurrences. This requires philosophers to reject the common practice of conceiving truth as a timeless characteristic of propositions. Propositions describing occurrences *become* true when the occurrences take place—not before and not timelessly. Only then can our belief that it is within our power to affect the future be sustained.

PART ONE

ALTERNATIVE VIEWS

1

DETERMINISM

INTRODUCTION[1]

Baron Holbach's presentation of determinism in *System of Nature* (chapters XI and XII) may be considered the classic statement, although it is somewhat tied to the view that the true deterministic theory in the human sphere will look like classical mechanics. (This is to be distinguished from the view that human behavior is determined on the grounds that nonhuman behavior has been shown to be determined—a position which does not tie itself to a particular model or type of psychological theory.) In our own era, several psychological theories or types of theories have induced concern in many who harbor a belief in or a desire for the existence of free will. Behaviorism and neobehaviorism, especially as exemplified in the work of a man like B. F. Skinner, represent one source of concern. The other prominent source of concern is psychoanalysis; and Hospers' heavy reliance on examples described and explained by the use of its theories suggests that its success is at least part of the genesis of Hospers' concern.

On closer analysis, however, we see that Hospers is concerned about *any* deterministic theory in psychology. With respect to any neurotic act, he says that we would question the legitimacy of attributions of responsibility if we could show that it is governed by some deterministic law regardless of

[1] It may be advisable to reread this and subsequent introductions after the selections are read since the introductions contain remarks of a critical nature.

the content of the law. The only suggestion of a disclaimer here is his remark that the factors specified in the law determine results independently of the person's effort. But we are wrong if we conclude that Hospers' view is this: The person is responsible if it is true to say of him that he would have acted differently had he tried. This is made abundantly clear later when Hospers points out that the ability to overcome our early environment—for example, by the exertion of effort—is also determined by other aspects of our early environment and therefore we are not responsible in this case either.

A more obvious disclaimer appears when Hospers specifically disavows determinism. Notice that the reason given concerns a difficulty in the thesis of determinism, to wit, its alleged nondisconfirmable status. But as was pointed out in the general introduction, this does not preclude us from examining the implications of saying, "This event is determined," for we can know what would make this true. In any case, Hospers says here that even if some human action is not determined, it springs from our character and we have no control over the formation of our character. This is the reason that we are not responsible. Several comments are in order:

1. Hospers does not clearly distinguish (a) explanation of the development of character traits and abilities in terms of heredity and environment; (b) explanation of some human action in terms of character traits and abilities; and (c) explanation of some human action in terms of heredity and environment with or without the tacit stipulation that character traits and abilities play some kind of intermediary role. This is the source of much confusion.

2. If it is the fact that we have no control over the formative influences on character rather than the fact that these influences work deterministically that is of concern, it is difficult to understand Hospers' remark that we excuse a person from responsibility only after we have provided a *deterministic* account of the development of his character traits. (See Hospers' reply to his critic, p. 36.)

3. Little is said about the nature of explanations of actions in terms of character traits and abilities. It is not clear to many philosophers that these are or can be deterministic explanations. Hospers' primary concern with the formation of character leaves many questions about this other relation unanswered.

4. The clarity of the demand that we choose or shape our own character is taken up by Hook. Hook also points out alleged damaging consequences to the meaningfulness of the notion of "responsibility" if this demand is itself unclear or meaningless. The reader should also take cognizance of Hook's commitment to compatibilism in the particular form it takes.

In including Hospers in this section, we are presumably taking him as both a determinist and an incompatibilist. We have just seen that the applicability of the first label is dubious. He argues that the situation which he envisages as concern-inducing is not the truth of determinism in the human sphere. But we have seen that it is not that clear that this is not what he is concerned about. In any case, subtleties aside, Hospers certainly presents the kind of situation in the human sphere which orthodox determinists have cited as grounds for the claim that free will and moral responsibility do not exist.

Nor does Hospers reject compatibilism outright. On the level of action, he accepts it. Moreover, on the level of "springs of action," he claims that "can" (and "cannot") and "responsibility" do not apply. Thus he does not even accept incompatibilism on the level of springs of action; for he does not say, "We are not responsible for our character" but rather " 'responsible' has no meaning in this sphere." This view can be accommodated, however, by simply broadening the notion of incompatibilism.

Thus Hospers accepts Hook's charge that he has rendered the concept of responsibility vacuous. It is interesting then to reflect on Hook's further charge that Hospers' view is untenable in light of what Hospers wants to conclude, viz., it is not just to hold people morally responsible.

WHAT MEANS THIS FREEDOM?

JOHN HOSPERS

I am in agreement to a very large extent with the conclusions of Professor Edwards' paper, and am happy in these days of "soft determinism" to hear the other view so forcefully and fearlessly stated. As a preparation for developing my own views on the subject, I want to mention a factor that I think is of enormous importance and relevance: namely, unconscious motivation. There are many actions—not those of an insane person (however the term "insane" be defined), nor of a person ignorant of the effects of his action, nor ignorant of some relevant fact about the situation, nor in any obvious way mentally deranged—for which human beings in general and the courts in particular are inclined to hold the doer responsible, and for which, I would say, he should not be held responsible. The deed may be planned, it may be carried out in cold calculation, it may spring from the agent's character and be continuous with the rest of his behavior, and it may be perfectly true that he could have done differently *if* he had wanted to; nonetheless his behavior was brought about by unconscious conflicts developed in infancy, over which he had no control and of which (without training in psychiatry) he does not even have knowledge. He may even *think* he knows why he acted as he did, he may *think* he has conscious control over his actions, he may even *think* he is fully responsible for them; but he is not. Psychiatric casebooks provide hundreds of examples. The law and common sense, though puzzled sometimes by such cases, are gradually becoming aware that they exist; but at this early stage countless tragic blunders still occur because neither the law nor the public in general is aware

From John Hospers, "What Means This Freedom?," in *Determinism and Freedom in the Age of Modern Science*, edited by Sidney Hook. New York: Collier Books, 1961, pp. 126–142.

of the genesis of criminal actions. The mother blames her daughter for choosing the wrong men as candidates for husbands; but though the daughter thinks she is choosing freely and spends a considerable amount of time "deciding" among them, the identification with her sick father, resulting from Oedipal fantasies in early childhood, prevents her from caring for any but sick men, twenty or thirty years older than herself. Blaming her is beside the point; she cannot help it, and she cannot change it. Countless criminal acts are thought out in great detail; yet the participants are (without their own knowledge) acting out fantasies, fears, and defenses from early childhood, over whose coming and going they have no conscious control.

Now, I am not saying that none of these persons should be in jails or asylums. Often society must be protected against them. Nor am I saying that people should cease the practices of blaming and praising, punishing and rewarding; in general these devices are justified by the results—although very often they have practically no effect; the deeds are done from inner compulsion, which is not lessened when the threat of punishment is great. I am only saying that frequently persons we think responsible are not properly to be called so; we mistakenly think them responsible because we assume they are like those in whom no unconscious drive (toward this type of behavior) is present, and that their behavior can be changed by reasoning, exhorting, or threatening.

I

I have said that these persons are not responsible. But what is the criterion for responsibility? Under precisely what conditions is a person to be held morally responsible for an action? Disregarding here those conditions that have to do with a person's *ignorance* of the situation or the effects of his action, let us concentrate on those having to do with his "inner state." There are several criteria that might be suggested:

1. The first idea that comes to mind is that responsibility is

determined by the presence or absence of *premeditation*—the opposite of "premeditated" being, presumably, "unthinking" or "impulsive." But this will not do—both because some acts are not premeditated but responsible, and because some are premeditated and not responsible.

Many acts we call responsible can be as unthinking or impulsive as you please. If you rush across the street to help the victim of an automobile collision, you are (at least so we would ordinarily say) acting responsibly, but you did not do so out of premeditation; you saw the accident, you didn't think, you rushed to the scene without hesitation. It was like a reflex action. But you acted responsibly: unlike the knee jerk, the act was the result of past training and past thought about situations of this kind; that is why you ran to help instead of ignoring the incident or running away. When something done originally from conviction or training becomes habitual, it becomes *like* a reflex action. As Aristotle said, virtue should become second nature through habit: a virtuous act should be performed *as if* by instinct; this, far from detracting from its moral worth, testifies to one's mastery of the desired type of behavior; one does not have to make a moral effort each time it is repeated.

There are also premeditated acts for which, I would say, the person is not responsible. Premeditation, especially when it is so exaggerated as to issue in no action at all, can be the result of neurotic disturbance or what we sometimes call an emotional "block," which the person inherits from long-past situations. In Hamlet's revenge on his uncle (I use this example because it is familiar to all of us), there was no lack, but rather a surfeit, of premeditation; his actions were so exquisitely premeditated as to make Freud and Dr. Ernest Jones look more closely to find out what lay behind them. The very premeditation camouflaged unconscious motives of which Hamlet himself was not aware. I think this is an important point, since it seems that the courts often assume that premeditation is a criterion of responsibility. If failure to kill his uncle had been considered a crime, every court in the land would have convicted Hamlet. Again: a woman's decision to stay with her husband in spite of endless "mental cruelty" is, if she is the victim of an unconscious masochistic "will to punishment," one for which she is not responsible; she is the victim and not the agent, no matter how profound her conviction that she is the agent; she is caught in a masochistic web (of complicated genesis) dating back to babyhood, perhaps a repetition of a comparable situation involving her own parents, a repetition-compulsion that, as Freud said, goes "beyond the pleasure principle." Again: a criminal whose crime was carefully planned step by step is usually considered responsible, but as we shall see in later examples, the overwhelming impulse toward it, stemming from an unusually humiliating ego defeat in early childhood, was as compulsive as any can be.

2. Shall we say, then, that a person is not responsible for his act unless he can *defend it with reasons?* I am afraid that this criterion is no better than the previous one. First, intellectuals are usually better at giving reasons than nonintellectuals, and according to this criterion would be more responsible than persons acting from moral conviction not implemented by reasoning; yet it is very doubtful whether we should want to say that the latter are the more responsible. Second, the giving of reasons itself may be suspect. The reasons may be rationalizations camouflaging unconscious motives of which the agent knows nothing. Hamlet gave many reasons for not doing what he felt it was his duty to do: the time was not right, his uncle's soul might go to heaven, etc. His various "reasons" contradicted one another, and if an overpowering compulsion had not been present, the highly intellectual Hamlet would not have been taken in for a moment by these rationalizations. The real reason, the Oedipal conflict that made his uncle's crime the accomplishment of his own deepest desire, binding their fates into one and paralyzing him into inaction, was unconscious and of course unknown to him. One's intelligence and reasoning power do not enable one to escape from unconsciously motivated behavior; it only gives one greater facility in rationalizing that behavior; one's intelligence is simply

used in the interests of the neurosis—it is pressed into service to justify with reasons what one does quite independently of the reasons.

If these two criteria are inadequate, let us seek others.

3. Shall we say that a person is responsible for his action unless it is the *result of unconscious forces* of which he knows nothing? Many psychoanalysts would probably accept this criterion. If it is not largely reflected in the language of responsibility as ordinarily used, this may be due to ignorance of fact: most people do not know that there are such things as unconscious motives and unconscious conflicts causing human beings to act. But it may be that if they did, perhaps they would refrain from holding persons responsible for certain actions.

I do not wish here to quarrel with this criterion of responsibility. I only want to point out the fact that if this criterion is employed a far greater number of actions will be excluded from the domain of responsibility than we might at first suppose. Whether we are neat or untidy, whether we are selfish or unselfish, whether we provoke scenes or avoid them, even whether we can exert our powers of will to change our behavior—all these may, and often do, have their source in our unconscious life.

4. Shall we say that a person is responsible for his act unless it is *compelled?* Here we are reminded of Aristotle's assertion (*Nicomachean Ethics,* Book III) that a person is responsible for his act except for reasons of either ignorance or compulsion. Ignorance is not part of our problem here (unless it is unconsciously induced ignorance of facts previously remembered and selectively forgotten—in which case the forgetting is again compulsive), but compulsion is. How will compulsion do as a criterion? The difficulty is to state just what it means. When we say an act is compelled in a psychological sense, our language is metaphorical—which is not to say that there is no point in it or that, properly interpreted, it is not true. Our actions are compelled in a literal sense if someone has us in chains or is controlling our bodily movements. When we say that the storm compelled us to jettison

the cargo of the ship (Aristotle's example), we have a less literal sense of compulsion, for at least it is open to us to go down with the ship. When psychoanalysts say that a man was compelled by unconscious conflicts to wash his hands constantly, this is also not a literal use of "compel"; for nobody forced his hands under the tap. Still, it is a typical example of what psychologists call *compulsive* behavior: it has unconscious causes inaccessible to introspection, and moreover nothing can change it it is as inevitable for him to do it as it would be if someone were forcing his hands under the tap. In this it is exactly like the action of a powerful external force; it is just as little within one's conscious control.

In its area of application this interpretation of responsibility comes to much the same as the previous one. And this area is very great indeed. For if we cannot be held responsible for the infantile situations (in which we were after all passive victims), then neither, it would seem, can we be held responsible for compulsive actions occurring in adulthood that are inevitable consequences of those infantile situations. And, psychiatrists and psychoanalysts tell us, actions fulfilling this description are characteristic of all people some of the time and some people most of the time. Their occurrence, once the infantile events have taken place, is inevitable, just as the explosion is inevitable once the fuse has been lighted; there is simply more "delayed action" in the psychological explosions than there is in the physical ones.

(I have not used the word "inevitable" here to mean "causally determined," for according to such a definition every event would be inevitable if one accepted the causal principle in some form or other; and probably nobody except certain philosophers uses "inevitable" in this sense. Rather, I use "inevitable" in its ordinary sense of "cannot be avoided." To the extent, therefore, that adult neurotic manifestations *can* be avoided, once the infantile patterns have become set, the assertion that they are inevitable is not true.)

5. There is still another criterion, which I prefer to the previous ones, by which a man's responsibility for an act can

be measured: the degree to which that act can (or could have been) *changed by the use of reasons.* Suppose that the man who washes his hands constantly does so, he says, for hygienic reasons, believing that if he doesn't do so he will be poisoned by germs. We now convince him, on the best medical authority, that his belief is groundless. Now, the test of his responsibility is whether the changed belief will result in changed behavior. If it does not, as with the compulsive hand washer, he is not acting responsibly, but if it does, he is. It is not the *use* of reasons, but their *efficacy in changing behavior,* that is being made the criterion of responsibility. And clearly in neurotic cases no such change occurs; in fact, this is often made the defining characteristic of neurotic behavior: it is unchangeable by any rational considerations.

II

I have suggested these criteria to distinguish actions for which we can call the agent responsible from those for which we cannot. Even persons with extensive knowledge of psychiatry do not, I think, use any one of these criteria to the exclusion of the others; a conjunction of two or more may be used at once. But however they may be combined or selected in actual application, I believe we can make the distinction along some such lines as we have suggested.

But is there not still another possible meaning of "responsibility" that we have not yet mentioned? Even after we have made all the above distinctions, there remains a question in our minds whether we are, in the final analysis, *responsible for any of our actions at all.* The issue may be put this way: How can anyone be responsible for his actions, since they grow out of his character, which is shaped and molded and made what it is by influences—some hereditary, but most of them stemming from early parental environment—that were not of his own making or choosing? This question, I believe, still troubles many people who would agree to all the distinctions we have just made but still have the feeling that "this isn't all."

They have the uneasy suspicion that there is a more ultimate sense, a "deeper" sense, in which we are *not* responsible for our actions, since we are not responsible for the character out of which those actions spring. . . .

Let us take as an example a criminal who, let us say, strangled several persons and is himself now condemned to die in the electric chair. Jury and public alike hold him fully responsible (at least they utter the words "he is responsible"), for the murders were planned down to the minutest detail, and the defendant tells the jury exactly how he planned them. But now we find out how it all came about; we learn of parents who rejected him from babyhood, of the childhood spent in one foster home after another, where it was always plain to him that he was not wanted; of the constantly frustrated early desire for affection, the hard shell of nonchalance and bitterness that he assumed to cover the painful and humiliating fact of being unwanted, and his subsequent attempts to heal these wounds to his shattered ego through defensive aggression.

> The criminal is the most passive person in this world, helpless as a baby in his motorically inexpressible fury. Not only does he try to wreak revenge on the mother of the earliest period of his babyhood; his criminality is based on the inner feeling of being incapable of making the mother even feel that the child seeks revenge on her. The situation is that of a dwarf trying to annoy a giant who superciliously refuses to see these attempts. . . . Because of his inner feeling of being a dwarf, the criminotic uses, so to speak, dynamite. Of that the giant must take cognizance. True, the "revenge" harms the avenger. He may be legally executed. However, the primary inner aim of forcing the giant to acknowledge the dwarf's fury is fulfilled.[1]

The poor victim is not conscious of the inner forces that exact from him this ghastly toll; he battles, he schemes, he revels in pseudo-aggression, he is miserable, but he does not know

[1] Edmund Bergler, *The Basic Neurosis* (New York: Grune and Stratton, 1949), p. 305.

what works within him to produce these catastrophic acts of crime. His aggressive actions are the wriggling of a worm on a fisherman's hook. And if this is so, it seems difficult to say any longer, "He is responsible." Rather, we shall put him behind bars for the protection of society, but we shall no longer flatter our feeling of moral superiority by calling him personally responsible for what he did.

Let us suppose it were established that a man commits murder only if, sometime during the previous week, he has eaten a certain combination of foods—say, tuna fish salad at a meal also including peas, mushroom soup, and blueberry pie. What if we were to track down the factors common to all murders committed in this country during the last twenty years and found this factor present in all of them, and only in them? The example is of course empirically absurd; but may it not be that there is *some* combination of factors that regularly leads to homicide, factors such as are described in general terms in the above quotation? (Indeed the situation in the quotation is less fortunate than in our hypothetical example, for it is easy to avoid certain foods once we have been warned about them, but the situation of the infant is thrust on him; something has already happened to him once and for all, before he knows it has happened.) When such specific factors are discovered, won't they make it clear that it is foolish and pointless, as well as immoral, to hold human beings responsible for crimes? Or, if one prefers biological to psychological factors, suppose a neurologist is called in to testify at a murder trial and produces X-ray pictures of the brain of the criminal; anyone can see, he argues, that the *cella turcica* was already calcified at the age of nineteen; it should be a flexible bone, growing, enabling the gland to grow.[2] All the defendant's disorders might have resulted from this early calcification. Now, this particular explanation may be empirically false; but who can say that no such factors, far more complex, to be sure, exist?

[2] Meyer Levin, *Compulsion* (New York: Simon and Schuster, 1956), p. 403.

When we know such things as these, we no longer feel so much tempted to say that the criminal is responsible for his crime; and we tend also (do we not?) to excuse him—not legally (we still confine him to prison) but morally; we no longer call him a monster or hold him personally responsible for what he did. Moreover, we do this in general, not merely in the case of crime: "You must excuse Grandmother for being irritable; she's really quite ill and is suffering some pain all the time." Or: "The dog always bites children after she's had a litter of pups; you can't blame her for it: she's not feeling well, and besides she naturally wants to defend them." Or: "She's nervous and jumpy, but do excuse her: she has a severe glandular disturbance."

Let us note that the more *thoroughly* and *in detail* we know the causal factors leading a person to behave as he does, the more we tend to exempt him from responsibility. When we know nothing of the man except what we see him do, we say he is an ungrateful cad who expects much of other people and does nothing in return, and we are usually indignant. When we learn that his parents were the same way and, having no guilt feelings about this mode of behavior themselves, brought him up to be greedy and avaricious, we see that we could hardly expect him to have developed moral feelings in this direction. When we learn, in addition, that he is not aware of being ungrateful or selfish, but unconsciously represses the memory of events unfavorable to himself, we feel that the situation is unfortunate but "not really his fault." When we know that this behavior of his, which makes others angry, occurs more constantly when he feels tense or insecure, and that he now feels tense and insecure, and that relief from pressure will diminish it, then we tend to "feel sorry for the poor guy" and say he's more to be pitied than censured. We no longer want to say that he is personally responsible; we might rather blame nature or his parents for having given him an unfortunate constitution or temperament.

In recent years a new form of punishment has been imposed on middle-aged and elderly parents. Their children, now in

> their twenties, thirties or even forties, present them with a modern grievance: "My analysis proves that *you* are responsible for my neurosis." Overawed by these authoritative statements, the poor tired parents fall easy victims to the newest variations on the scapegoat theory.
>
> In my opinion, this senseless cruelty—which disinters educational sins which had been burned for decades, and uses them as the basis for accusations which the victims cannot answer—is unjustified. Yes "the truth loves to be centrally located" (Melville), and few parents—since they are human—have been perfect. But granting their mistakes, they acted as *their* neurotic difficulties forced them to act. To turn the tables and declare the children not guilty because of the *impersonal* nature of their own neuroses, while at the same time the parents are *personally* blamed, is worse than illogical; it is profoundly unjust.[3]

And so, it would now appear, neither of the parties is responsible: "they acted as their neurotic difficulties forced them to act." The patients are not responsible for their neurotic manifestations, but then neither are the parents responsible for theirs; and so, of course, for their parents in turn, and theirs before them. It is the twentieth-century version of the family curse, the curse on the House of Atreus.

"But," a critic complains, "it's immoral to exonerate people indiscriminately in this way. I might have thought it fit to excuse somebody because he was born on the other side of the tracks, if I didn't know so many bank presidents who were also born on the other side of the tracks." Now, I submit that the most immoral thing in this situation is the critic's caricature of the conditions of the excuse. Nobody is excused merely because he was born on the other side of the tracks. But if he was born on the other side of the tracks *and* was a highly narcissistic infant to begin with *and* was repudiated or neglected by his parents *and* . . . (here we list a finite number of conditions), and if this complex of factors is *regularly*

[3] Edmund Bergler, *The Superego* (New York: Grune and Stratton, 1952), p. 320.

followed by certain behavior traits in adulthood, and moreover *unavoidably* so—that is, they occur no matter what he or anyone else tries to do—then we excuse him morally and say he is not responsible for his deed. If he is not responsible for *A*, a series of events occurring in his babyhood, then neither is he responsible for *B*, a series of things he does in adulthood, provided that *B* inevitably—that is, unavoidably—follows upon the occurrence of *A*. And according to psychiatrists and psychoanalysts, this often happens.

But one may still object that so far we have talked only about neurotic behavior. Isn't nonneurotic or normal or not unconsciously motivated (or whatever you want to call it) behavior still within the area of responsibility? There are reasons for answering "No" even here, for the normal person no more than the neurotic one has caused his own character, which makes him what he is. Granted that neurotics are not responsible for their behavior (that part of it which we call neurotic) because it stems from undigested infantile conflicts that they had no part in bringing about, and that are external to them just as surely as if their behavior had been forced on them by a malevolent deity (which is indeed one theory on the subject); but the so-called normal person is equally the product of causes in which his volition took no part. And if, unlike the neurotic's, his behavior is changeable by rational considerations, and if he has the will power to overcome the effects of an unfortunate early environment, this again is no credit to him; he is just lucky. If energy is available to him in a form in which it can be mobilized for constructive purposes, this is no credit to him, for this too is part of his psychic legacy. Those of us who can discipline ourselves and develop habits of concentration of purpose tend to blame those who cannot, and call them lazy and weak-willed; but what we fail to see is that they literally *cannot* do what we expect; if their psyches were structured like ours, they could, but as they are burdened with a tyrannical superego (to use psychoanalytic jargon for the moment), and a weak defenseless ego whose energies are constantly consumed in fighting endless charges of the superego, they simply cannot do it, and it is irrational to expect it of them. We cannot with justification blame them for their inability, any more than we can congratulate ourselves for our ability. This lesson is hard to learn, for we constantly and naïvely assume that other people are constructed as we ourselves are.

For example: A child raised under slum conditions, whose parents are socially ambitious and envy families with money, but who nevertheless squander the little they have on drink, may simply be unable in later life to mobilize a drive sufficient to overcome these early conditions. Common sense would expect that he would develop the virtue of thrift; he would make quite sure that he would never again endure the grinding poverty he had experienced as a child. But in fact it is not so: the exact conditions are too complex to be specified in detail here, but when certain conditions are fulfilled (concerning the subject's early life), he will always thereafter be a spendthrift, and no rational considerations will be able to change this. He will listen to the rational considerations and see the force of these, but they will not be able to change him, even if he tries; he cannot change his wasteful habits any more than he can lift the Empire State Building with his bare hands. We moralize and plead with him to be thrifty, but we do not see how strong, how utterly overpowering, and how constantly with him, is the opposite drive, which is so easily manageable with us. But he is possessed by the all-consuming, all-encompassing urge to make the world see that he belongs, that he has arrived, that he is just as well off as anyone else, that the awful humiliations were not real, that they never actually occurred, for isn't he now able to spend and spend? The humiliation must be blotted out; and conspicuous, fleshy, expensive, and wasteful buying will do this; it shows the world what the world must know! True, it is only for the moment; true, it is in the end self-defeating, for wasteful consumption is the best way to bring poverty back again; but the person with an overpowering drive to mend a lesion to his narcissism cannot resist the avalanche of that drive with his puny rational consideration. A man with his back against the wall and a gun at his throat doesn't think of what may happen ten years hence. (Consciously, of course, he knows nothing of this drive; all that appears to consciousness is its shattering effects; he knows only that he must keep on spending—not why—and that he is unable to resist.) He hasn't in him the psychic capacity, the energy to stem the tide of a drive that at that moment is all-powerful. We, seated comfortably away from this flood, sit in judgment on him and blame him and exhort him and criticize him; but he, carried along by the flood, cannot do otherwise than he does. He may fight with all the strength of which he is capable, but it is not enough. And we, who are rational enough at least to exonerate a man in a situation of "overpowering impulse" when we recognize it to be one, do not even recognize this as an example of it; and so, in addition to being swept away in the flood that childhood conditions rendered inevitable, he must also endure our lectures, our criticisms, and our moral excoriation.

But, one will say, he could have overcome his spendthrift tendencies; some people do. Quite true: some people do. They are lucky. They have it in them to overcome early deficiencies by exerting great effort, and they are capable of exerting the effort. Some of us, luckier still, can overcome them with but little effort; and a few, the luckiest, haven't the deficiencies to overcome. It's all a matter of luck. The least lucky are those who can't overcome them, even with great effort, and those who haven't the ability to exert the effort.

But, one persists, it isn't a matter simply of luck; it *is* a matter of effort. Very well then, it's a matter of effort; without exerting the effort you may not overcome the deficiency. But whether or not you are the kind of person who has it in him to exert the effort is a matter of luck.

All this is well known to psychoanalysts. They can predict, from minimal cues that most of us don't notice, whether a person is going to turn out to be lucky or not. "The analyst," they say, "must be able to use the residue of the patient's unconscious guilt so as to remove the symptom or character trait that creates the guilt. The guilt must not only be present, but *available* for use, *mobilizable.* If it is used up (absorbed) in criminal activity, or in an excessive amount of self-damaging tendencies, then it cannot be used for therapeutic purposes, and the prognosis is negative." Not all philosophers will relish the analyst's way of putting the matter, but at least as a physician he can soon detect whether the patient is lucky or unlucky—and he knows that whichever it is, it *isn't the patient's fault.* The patient's conscious volition cannot remedy the deficiency. Even whether he will co-operate with the analyst is really out of the patient's hands: if he continually projects the denying-mother fantasy on the analyst and unconsciously identifies him always with the cruel, harsh forbidder of the nursery, thus frustrating any attempt at impersonal observation, the sessions are useless; yet if it happens that way, he can't help that either. That fatal projection is not under his control; whether it occurs or not depends on how his unconscious identifications have developed since his infancy. He can try, yes—but the ability to try enough for the therapy to have effect is also beyond his control; the capacity to try more than just so much is either there or it isn't—and either way "it's in the lap of the gods."

The position, then, is this: if we *can* overcome the effects of early environment, the ability to do so is itself a product of the early environment. We did not give ourselves this ability; and if we lack it we cannot be blamed for not having it. Sometimes, to be sure, moral exhortation brings out an ability that is there but not being used, and in this lies its *occasional* utility; but very often its use is pointless, because the ability is not there. The only thing that can overcome a desire, as Spinoza said, is a stronger contrary desire; and many times there simply is no wherewithal for producing a stronger contrary desire. Those of us who do have the wherewithal are lucky.

There is one possible practical advantage in remembering this. It may prevent us (unless we are compulsive blamers) from indulging in righteous indignation and committing the sin of spiritual pride, thanking God that we are not as this publican here. And it will protect from our useless moralizings those who are least equipped by nature for enduring them. As with responsibility, so with deserts. Someone commits a crime and is punished by the state; "he deserved it," we say self-righteously—as if we were moral and he immoral, when in fact we are lucky and he is unlucky—forgetting that there, but for the grace of God and a fortunate early environment, go we. Or, as Clarence Darrow said in his speech for the defense in the Loeb-Leopold case:

> I do not believe that people are in jail because they deserve to be. . . . I know what causes the emotional life. . . . I know it is practically left out of some. Without it they cannot act with the rest. They cannot feel the moral shocks which safeguard others. Is [this man] to blame that his machine is imperfect? Who is to blame? I do not know. I have never in my life been interested so much in fixing blame as I have in relieving people from blame. I am not wise enough to fix it.[4]

III

I want to make it quite clear that I have not been arguing for determinism. Though I find it difficult to give any sense to the term "indeterminism," because I do not know what it would be like to come across an uncaused event, let us grant indeterminists everything they want, at least in words—influences that suggest but do not constrain, a measure of acausality in an otherwise rigidly causal order, and so on—whatever these phrases may mean. With all this granted, exactly the same situation faces the indeterminist and the determinist; all we have been saying would still hold true. "Are our powers innate or acquired?"

> Suppose the powers are declared innate; then the villain may sensibly ask whether he is responsible for what he was born with. A negative reply is inevitable. Are they then acquired? Then the ability to acquire them—was *that* innate? or acquired? It is innate? Very well then. . . .[5]

[4] Levin, *op. cit.*, pp. 439–40, 469.

[5] W. I. Matson, "The Irrelevance of Free-will to Moral Responsibility," *Mind*, LXV (October 1956), p. 495.

The same fact remains—that we did not cause our characters, that the influences that made us what we are are influences over which we had no control and of whose very existence we had no knowledge at the time. This fact remains for "determinism" and "indeterminism" alike. And it is this fact to which I would appeal, not the specific tenets of traditional forms of "determinism," which seem to me, when analyzed, empirically empty.

"But," it may be asked, "isn't it your view that nothing ultimately *could* be other than it is? And isn't this deterministic? And isn't it deterministic if you say that human beings could never act otherwise than they do, and that their desires and temperaments could not, when you consider their antecedent conditions, be other than they are?"

I reply that all these charges rest on confusions.

1. To say that nothing *could* be other than it is, is, taken literally, nonsense; and if taken as a way of saying something else, misleading and confusing. If you say, "I can't do it," this invites the question, "No? Not even if you want to?" "Can" and "could" are power words, used in the context of human action; when applied to nature they are merely anthropomorphic. "Could" has no application to nature—unless, of course, it is uttered in a theological context: one might say that God *could* have made things different. But with regard to inanimate nature "could" has no meaning. Or perhaps it is intended to mean that the order of nature is in some sense *necessary*. But in that case the sense of "necessary" must be specified. I know what "necessary" means when we are talking about propositions, but not when we are talking about the sequence of events in nature.

2. What of the charge that we could never have acted otherwise than we did? This, I submit, is simply not true. Here the exponents of Hume-Mill-Schlick-Ayer "soft determinism" are quite right. I could have gone to the opera today instead of coming here; that is, if certain conditions had been different, I should have gone. I could have done many other things instead of what I did, if some condition or other had been

different, specifically if my desire had been different. I repeat that "could" is a power word, and "I could have done this" means approximately "I *should* have done this *if* I had wanted to." In this sense, all of us could often have done otherwise than we did. I would not want to say that I should have done differently even if *all* the conditions leading up to my action had been the same (this is generally not what we mean by "could" anyway); but to assert that I could have is empty, for if I *did* act different from the time before, we would automatically say that one or more of the conditions were different, whether we had independent evidence for this or not, thus rendering the assertion immune to empirical refutation. (Once again, the vacuousness of "determinism.")

3. Well, then, could we ever have, not acted, but *desired* otherwise than we did desire? This gets us once again to the heart of the matter we were discussing in the previous section. Russell said, "We can do as we please but we can't please as we please." But I am persuaded that even this statement conceals a fatal mistake. Let us follow the same analysis through. "I could have done *X*" means "I should have done *X* if I had wanted to." "I could have wanted *X*" by the same analysis would mean "I should have wanted *X* if I had wanted to"—which seems to make no sense at all. (What does Russell want? To please as he doesn't please?)

What does this show? It shows, I think, that the only meaningful context of "can" and "could have" is that of *action*. "Could have acted differently" makes sense; "could have desired differently," as we have just seen, does not. Because a word or phrase makes good sense in one context, let us not assume that it does so in another.

I conclude, then, with the following suggestion: that we operate on two levels of moral discourse, which we shouldn't confuse; one (let's call it the upper level) is that of actions; the other (the lower, or deeper, level) is that of the springs of action. Most moral talk occurs on the upper level. It is on this level that the Hume-Mill-Schlick-Ayer analysis of freedom fully applies. As we have just seen, "can" and "could" acquire their meaning on this level; so, I suspect, does "freedom." So does the distinction between compulsive and noncompulsive behavior, and among the senses of "responsibility," discussed in the first section of this paper, according to which we are responsible for some things and not for others. All these distinctions are perfectly valid on this level (or in this dimension) of moral discourse; and it is, after all, the usual one—we are practical beings interested in changing the course of human behavior, so it is natural enough that 99 per cent of our moral talk occurs here.

But when we descend to what I have called the lower level of moral discourse, as we occasionally do in thoughtful moments when there is no immediate need for action, then we must admit that we are ultimately the kind of persons we are because of conditions occurring outside us, over which we had no control. But while this is true, we should beware of extending the moral terminology we used on the other level to this one also. "Could" and "can," as we have seen, no longer have meaning here. "Right" and "wrong," which apply only to actions, have no meaning here either. I suspect that the same is true of "responsibility," for now that we have recalled often forgotten facts about our being the product of outside forces, we must ask in all seriousness what would be added by saying that we are not *responsible* for our own characters and temperaments. What would it mean even? Has it a significant opposite? What would it be like to be responsible for one's own character? What possible situation is describable by this phrase? Instead of saying that it is *false* that we are responsible for our own characters, I should prefer to say that the utterance is meaningless—meaningless in the sense that it describes no possible situation, though it *seems* to because the word "responsible" is the same one we used on the upper level, where it marks a real distinction. If this is so, the result is that *moral* terms—at least the terms "could have" and "responsible"—simply drop out on the lower level. What remains, shorn now of moral terminology, is the point we tried to bring out in Part II: whether or not we have personality disturbances, whether or not we have the ability to overcome deficiencies of early environment, is like the answer to the question whether or not we shall be struck down by a dread disease: "it's all a matter of luck." It is important to keep this in mind, for people almost always forget it, with consequences in human intolerance and unnecessary suffering that are incalculable.

NECESSITY, INDETERMINISM, AND SENTIMENTALISM

SIDNEY HOOK

. . .

The fatal error in the papers of Professors Hospers and Edwards, as read, is that they alternate between two conceptions of "moral responsibility"—one, a conception of moral responsibility as *empty* but meaningful, and the other as *vacuous* and meaningless. On the first conception, although it may be true *in fact* that no one is morally responsible, we can state the conditions under which one might be. We can differentiate between the two states. On the second, there are no possible conditions under which anyone can be declared "morally responsible." The expression has no intelligible opposite and thus makes no sense.

The force of most of their arguments, which gives them an air of high moral concern, is based on the assumption that under certain circumstances individuals are being *improperly* considered responsible. Hospers actually says that "frequently persons we think responsible are not properly to be called so," and Edwards implies the same thing. They explicitly appeal against the injustice of improperly blaming the morally innocent who, because their desires are determined, are the victims,

From Sidney Hook, "Necessity, Indeterminism, and Sentimentalism," in *Determinism and Freedom in the Age of Modern Science*, edited by Sidney Hook. New York: Collier Books, 1961, pp. 187–192.

not the agents, of misfortune. We eagerly await the description of the set of conditions under which an individual is properly held responsible, under which he is not a victim of circumstances. It then turns out that even if his desires were undetermined, even if circumstances were completely different, he would still not be responsible, would still be a morally innocent victim. The *empty* conception of moral responsibility becomes completely *vacuous*. This makes the whole procedure of Professors Hospers and Edwards methodologically self-defeating, and particularly their expressions of concern about the injustice of blaming the morally innocent. For to be morally innocent of having committed an evil deed entails that one is not responsible for its commission, and to be morally guilty entails that one is. *If moral responsibility is a vacuous expression, then moral innocence and guilt are too*. Were Hospers and Edwards consistent they could not plead for the innocent or condemn the guilty. Edwards in places suggests that a person would be responsible if he could *ultimately and completely shape or choose* his own character. But this is explaining an obscure notion by a still obscurer one. Since every decision to shape or choose one's character, to be responsible, must be one's own, and therefore already an indication of the kind of person one is, the notion that one can ultimately and completely shape or choose one's character is unintelligible. C. A. Campbell, to be sure, tries to distinguish between a choice that is the expression of a *formed character*, and therefore determined, and a choice of a *self*. But on Hospers' and Edwards' argument what is true of character must be true of self. Either the self has the power to mold character or it has not. In either case it cannot be held responsible for having or not having such a native power. And the same is true if we bring in a Self to explain the powers of the self and a Great Self to explain the powers of the Self, etc.

It is true that the notion of moral responsibility is often ambiguous and not clearly defined in ordinary experience. But if we follow Professor Hart's illuminating procedure, we can recognize certain actions in which we clearly admit the presence of excusing conditions—infancy, insanity, paralysis, duress, coercion, etc.—and actions in which we do not. We then try to formulate the principle we recognize in this distinction and apply it to more complicated and borderline cases. We find that we tend to hold individuals responsible for their voluntary or uncoerced actions, for knowingly doing or not doing what it was in their power to do or leave undone. All these terms are vague and need further specification. There are difficulties in ascertaining in particular instances what it was in one's power to do or leave undone. Nonetheless, no one can live in human society without learning to recognize the distinction between the actions he holds others and himself responsible for and the actions he does not.

For all its vagueness there is more agreement about how the distinction is to be applied than about the grounds of the distinction. No one blames a crawling infant who overturns a kerosene stove that starts a fire. Almost everybody would blame a man who, normal in every other way and by all known tests, insures a house beyond its value and then sets fire to it without even giving its occupants a chance to escape. If we make a list of the circumstances behind actions for which we hold individuals responsible and those for which we do not, we shall find that as a rule the first class consists of those in which evidence exists that praise and reward, blame and punishment, tend to influence the future conduct of those involved and/or those tempted. This is not the whole story. Campbell objects[1] that animals are not held responsible for their actions even though we can re-educate their desires and impulses by punishment. This is true, but it is also true that the higher the animal in the scale of intelligence, the more likely we are to blame it. If we believed that an animal could think like a man we would blame it like a man. The behavior of infants, too, is modifiable by appropriate reward and punishment even though we do not hold them morally responsible. But as the age of rationality approaches we gradually do. This suggests that in addition to suscepti-

[1] *Mind*, 1951.

bility to reward and punishment, we attribute responsibility where there is a tendency to respond to valid reasons, to behave rationally, to respond to human emotions in a human way. Perhaps a third element involved in the attribution of moral responsibility to voluntary action is the assumption that voluntary action is *approved* action. A man is morally responsible for an action he commits to the extent that he *approves* of it. If he sincerely disapproves of his action, regards it as wrong and condemns it as wrong, but still commits it we tend to regard him as ill, as acting under "compulsion." It is some such consideration as this that lies behind our extenuation of certain kinds of apparently voluntary action (as when we say: "He didn't mean to do it"), especially where ignorance is present.

There may be other elements involved in the complex notion of moral responsibility, but the foregoing explains an interesting phenomenological fact. Sickness, accident, or incapacity aside, one feels lessened as a human being if one's actions are always excused or explained away on the ground that despite appearances one is really not responsible for them. It means being treated like an object, an infant, or someone out of his mind. Our dignity as rational human beings sometimes leads us to protest, when a zealous friend seeks to extenuate our conduct on the ground that we were not responsible (we didn't know or intend what we were doing, etc.), that we really *are* responsible and that we are prepared to take the consequences of our responsibility. As bad as the priggishness of the self-righteous is the whine of the self-pitying.

The so-called "hard" determinism professed by Professors Hospers and Edwards, especially in the popular form defended by Darrow, whom Edwards so extravagantly praised, often leads to sentimentality, to so much pity for the criminal as a victim not of a special set of particular circumstances but of any circumstances in general (referred to as heredity and environment, the sway of the law of causality) that there is not sufficient pity or concern left for the criminal's victims—

not only for his past victims but his future ones and the victims of others his actions may inspire. To blame and to punish, of course, are two distinct things logically (except where blame is considered a form of punishment), but psychologically there is a great reluctance to punish if one believes there is no blame. Darrow as a "hard" determinist argued on a priori grounds that everyone was blameless and often won acquittals not on the evidence but despite it. If needless pain and cruelty are evils, then punishment that prevents or deters human beings from committing actions likely to result in much greater pain and cruelty than it imposes is sometimes the lesser evil.

It is argued by Professor Edwards that "hard" determinism, which, according to him, entails the belief that no one is morally responsible because no one ultimately shapes his own character, leads to the abandonment of retributive punishment. Even if this were so, it would not make the doctrine of "hard" determinism any more intelligible. But historically it is not so. From Augustine to Calvin to Barth the torment of eternal damnation is assigned and approved independently of moral responsibility. It is not related of the oft-quoted Puritan who piously observed to his son when they saw a man being led to the gallows, "There but for the grace of God go I," that he opposed retributive punishment. Nor can Edwards consistently with his own theory assert that "hard" determinists *should* repudiate retributive punishment, or morally blame them or anyone else, as he freely does, for approving of retributive punishment. For has he not told us that a man can't help having the character he has, no matter what kind of a character it is? Further, if retributive punishment is the enemy, there seems to me to be no necessary logical connection between a belief in moral responsibility and approval of retributive punishment. Certainly, "soft" determinists who assign responsibility to actions only when there is reason to believe that blame or punishment will modify future conduct are hardly likely to defend retributive punishment.

Why, after all, is retributive punishment evil? Not because

the wrongdoer "ultimately did not shape his own character"—whatever that may mean—but simply because the pain inflicted on him gratuitously adds to the sum total of suffering in the world without any compensating alleviation of anybody else's sufferings. Even if an individual were considered able "ultimately to shape his own character" and were held morally responsible for an evil act, punishment that would be purely retributive and that did not contribute to deterring him or others from evil doing, or did nothing toward rehabilitating him, would still be morally wrong. This is quite evident in situations in which the "hard" determinist who is not a fatalist, if there be any such, admits that a man is to some extent, not ultimately but proximately, responsible for some change in his character—for example, when his desire to gamble leads him to steal a beggar's portion. In such situations retributive punishment as such would be regarded as morally wrong. Directed only to the past, it would not give the beggar back his portion or wipe out his pain, and therefore the new sufferings it inflicts are futile and needlessly cruel. If one can oppose retributive punishment when one believes a person is proximately responsible for his action, one can oppose it even when one believes a person is ultimately responsible, whatever the cognitive content of that belief turns out to be. If retributive punishment is the target of their criticism, Hospers and Edwards are training their guns in the wrong direction.

Far from diminishing the amount of needless cruelty and suffering in the world, I am firmly convinced that the belief that nobody is ever morally responsible, in addition to being false, is quite certain to have a mischievous effect and to increase the amount of needless cruelty and suffering. For it justifies Smerdyakov's formula in *The Brothers Karamazov:* "All things are permissible." One of the commonest experiences is to meet someone whose belief that he can't help doing what he is doing (or failing to do) is often an excuse for not doing as well as he can or at least better than he is at present doing. What often passes as irremediable evil in this world, or inevitable suffering, is a consequence of our failure to act in time. We are responsible, whether we admit it or not, for what it is in our power to do; and most of the time we can't be sure what it is in our power to do until we attempt it. In spite of the alleged inevitabilities in personal life and history human effort can redetermine the direction of events, even though it cannot determine the conditions that make human effort possible. It is time enough to reconcile oneself to a secret shame or a public tyranny after one has done one's best to overcome it, and even then it isn't necessary.

To say, as Professor Hospers does, that "It's all a matter of luck" is no more sensible than saying: "Nothing is a matter of luck"—assuming "luck" has a meaning in a world of hard determinism. It is true that we did not choose to be born. It is also true that we choose, most of us, to keep on living. It is not true that everything that happens to us is like "being struck down by a dread disease." The treatment and cure of disease—to use an illustration that can serve as a moral paradigm for the whole human situation—would never have begun unless we believed that some things that were did not have to be, that they could be different, and that *we* could make them different. And what we can make different we are responsible for.

2

RECONCILIATIONISM

INTRODUCTION

Again, to offer a clear and intelligently argued presentation of reconciliationism, we have chosen two philosophers, Schlick and Hobart, neither of whom is prepared to commit himself completely to determinism (not, evidently, in the sense in which this entails incompatibilism). But we are primarily interested in the reconciliationist's defense of compatibilism and Schlick presents the classic arguments of the reconciliationist.

The incompatibilist, he tells us, holds his view because he has failed to draw certain distinctions. Once one sees clearly the difference between prescriptive law and descriptive law, and the difference between universality as a legitimate attribute of laws and necessity or compulsion as an anthropomorphic projection onto laws, one will no longer grant to incompatibilism its intuitive backing. But all that incompatibilism has to recommend it is this backing. And now this is gone.

Schlick then presents the reconciliationist conception of fieedom in terms of the absence of compulsion. But one concept appears in this account that is not sufficiently clarified. A man is compelled when he is hindered in the realization of his natural desires. But which desires are natural? The problem becomes acute when Schlick admits that the compulsion can come from "within" although it is thought of as external to the self. How is one to define the difference between desires which are "natural to me" or "mine" and compulsions which are "external to me"? This is not to say that we cannot identify many clear cases.

Schlick's discussion is also of interest insofar as he presents us with a typical utilitarian-educative conception of responsibility and punishment. This position together with the fundamental claim of the reconciliationist that the incompatibilist case rests upon the confusions cited above are examined by the libertarian, Campbell, in the next chapter. Broad too criticizes compatibilism; but we have included his selection in the next chapter for he presents a critique of libertarianism also.

We have omitted Schlick's defense of a view which reconciliationists typically advance, viz., that determinism is actually a necessary condition of free will and/or moral responsibility, for Hobart has presented what is perhaps the most extensive defense of this view. It is obviously an important claim; but one reason that it is important is not that evident—namely, that it implies the falsity of incompatibilism. The incompatibilist asserts that all determined acts are unfree or, if an act is free, then it is not determined. But Hobart's view is that if an act is free, then it is determined. There is no strict incompatibility between the two views; but their mutual retention requires us to conceive of freedom as a self-contradictory notion. If we are not prepared to do this, then Hobart's view entails the falsity of incompatibilism.

It is, therefore, important to examine closely Foot's attempt to refute this argument. She examines the arguments of Hobart and others who claim that what is not determined cannot be a full-blooded action and only full-blooded actions are free. Their grounds vary. It is argued that such events would be "undergone" rather than "done" by the person and that they are inexplicable. She also examines the argument that responsibility presupposes rationality which presupposes determinism. It is important to notice that, in her discussion, a common assumption of reconciliationists is undercut. Reconciliationists often say that if the libertarian or incompatibilist rejects determinism in some sphere of human behavior, then, in that sphere, people will not be doing what they want, will not be acting for a reason or from a motive or intentionally. But this is justified on the grounds that these explanations of actions are deterministic, i.e., that wants, reasons, motives, and intentions are antecedent conditions of action and therefore states which are specifiable independently of the resultant action. If it can be shown, as Foot tries to do, that some or all of these explanations are not deterministic, then the reconciliationist claim collapses. This debate is picked up later in the chapter on action theory.

WHEN IS A MAN RESPONSIBLE?

MORITZ SCHLICK

1. *The Pseudo-Problem of Freedom of the Will*

With hesitation and reluctance I prepare to add this chapter to the discussion of ethical problems. For in it I must speak of a matter which, even at present, is thought to be a fundamental ethical question, but which got into ethics and has become a much discussed problem only because of a misunderstanding. This is the so-called problem of the freedom of the will. Moreover, this pseudo-problem has long since been settled by the efforts of certain sensible persons; and, above all, the state of affairs just described has been often disclosed—with exceptional clarity by Hume. Hence it is really one of the greatest scandals of philosophy that again and again so much paper and printer's ink is devoted to this matter, to say nothing of the expenditure of thought, which could have been applied to more important problems (assuming that it would have sufficed for these). Thus I should truly be ashamed to write a chapter on "freedom." In the chapter heading, the word "responsible" indicates what concerns ethics, and designates the point at which misunderstanding arises. Therefore the concept of responsibility constitutes our theme, and if in the process of its clarification I also must speak of the concept of freedom I shall, of course, say only what others have already said

From Moritz Schlick, "When Is a Man Responsible?" in *Problems of Ethics,* translated by David Rynin. New York: Prentice-Hall, 1939, pp. 143–156.

better; consoling myself with the thought that in this way alone can anything be done to put an end at last to that scandal.

The main task of ethics . . . is to explain moral behavior. To explain means to refer back to laws: every science, including psychology, is possible only in so far as there are such laws to which the events can be referred. Since the assumption that *all* events are subject to universal laws is called the principle of causality, one can also say, "Every science presupposes the principle of causality." Therefore every explanation of human behavior must also assume the validity of causal laws; in this case the existence of psychological laws. (If for example our law of motivation . . . were incorrect, then human conduct would be quite unexplained.) All of our experience strengthens us in the belief that this presupposition is realized, at least to the extent required for all purposes of practical life in intercourse with nature and human beings, and also for the most precise demands of technique. Whether, indeed, the principle of causality holds universally, whether, that is, *determinism* is true, we do not know; no one knows. But we do know that it is impossible to settle the dispute between determinism and indeterminism by mere reflection and speculation, by the consideration of so many reasons for and so many reasons against (which collectively and individually are but pseudo-reasons). Such an attempt becomes especially ridiculous when one considers with what enormous expenditure of experimental and logical skill contemporary physics carefully approaches the question of whether causality can be maintained for the most minute intra-atomic events.

But the dispute concerning "freedom of the will" generally proceeds in such fashion that its advocates attempt to refute, and its opponents to prove, the validity of the causal principle, both using hackneyed arguments, and neither in the least abashed by the magnitude of the undertaking. (I can exclude only Bergson from this criticism, with whom, however, this whole question is not an ethical but a metaphysical problem. His ideas, which in my opinion will not stand epistemological analysis, are of no significance for us.) Others distinguish two realms, in one of which determinism holds, but not in the other. This line of thought (which was unfortunately taken by Kant) is, however, quite the most worthless (though Schopenhauer considered it to be Kant's most profound idea).

Fortunately, it is not necessary to lay claim to a final solution of the causal problem in order to say what is necessary in ethics concerning responsibility; there is required only an analysis of the concept, the careful determination of the meaning which is in fact joined to the words "responsibility" and "freedom" as these are actually used. If men had made clear to themselves the sense of those propositions, which we use in everyday life, that pseudo-argument which lies at the root of the pseudo-problem, and which recurs thousands of times within and outside of philosophical books, would never have arisen.

The argument runs as follows: "If determinism is true, if, that is, all events obey immutable laws, then my will too is always determined, by my innate character and my motives. Hence my decisions are necessary, not free. But if so, then I am not responsible for my acts, for I would be accountable for them only if I could do something about the way my decisions went; but I can do nothing about it, since they proceed with necessity from my character and the motives. And I have made neither, and have no power over them: the motives come from without, and my character is the necessary product of the innate tendencies and the external influences which have been effective during my lifetime. Thus determinism and moral responsibility are incompatible. Moral responsibility presupposes freedom, that is, exemption from causality."

This process of reasoning rests upon a whole series of confusions, just as the links of a chain hang together. We must show these confusions to be such, and thus destroy them.

2. Two Meanings of the Word "Law"

It all begins with an erroneous interpretation of the meaning of "law." In practice this is understood as a rule by which the state prescribes certain behavior to its citizens. These rules often contradict the natural desires of the citizens (for if they did not do so, there would be no reason for making them), and are in fact not followed by many of them; while others obey, but under *compulsion.* The state does in fact compel its citizens by imposing certain sanctions (punishments) which serve to bring their desires into harmony with the prescribed laws.

In natural science, on the other hand, the word "law" means something quite different. The natural law is not a *pre*scription as to how something should behave, but a formula, a *de*scription of how something does in fact behave. The two forms of "laws" have only this in common: both tend to be expressed in *formulae.* Otherwise they have absolutely nothing to do with one another, and it is very blameworthy that the same word has been used for two such different things; but even more so that philosophers have allowed themselves to be led into serious errors by this usage. Since natural laws are only descriptions of what happens, there can be in regard to them no talk of "compulsion." The laws of celestial mechanics do not prescribe to the planets how they have to move, as though the planets would actually like to move quite otherwise, and are only forced by these burdensome laws of Kepler to move in orderly paths; no, these laws do not in any way "compel" the planets, but express only what in fact planets actually do.

If we apply this to volition, we are enlightened at once, even before the other confusions are discovered. When we say that a man's will "obeys psychological laws," these are not civic laws, which compel him to make certain decisions, or dictate desires to him, which he would in fact prefer not to have. They are laws of nature, merely expressing which desires he *actually has* under given conditions; they describe the nature of the will in the same manner as the astronomical laws describe the nature of planets. "Complusion" occurs where man is prevented from realizing his natural desires. How could the rule according to which these natural desires arise itself be considered as "compulsion"?

3. Compulsion and Necessity

But this is the second confusion to which the first leads almost inevitably: after conceiving the laws of nature, anthropomorphically, as order imposed *nolens volens* upon the events, one adds to them the concept of "necessity." This word, derived from "need," also comes to us from practice, and is used there in the sense of inescapable compulsion. To apply the word with this meaning to natural laws is of course senseless, for the presupposition of an opposing desire is lacking; and it is then confused with something altogether different, which is actually an attribute of natural laws. That is, universality. It is of the essence of natural laws to be universally valid, for only when we have found a rule which holds of events without exception do we *call* the rule a law of nature. Thus when we say "a natural law holds necessarily" this has but one legitimate meaning: "It holds in *all* cases where it is applicable." It is again very deplorable that the word "necessary" has been applied to natural laws (or, what amounts to the same thing, with reference to causality), for it is quite superfluous, since the expression "universally valid" is available. Universal validity is something altogether different from "compulsion"; these concepts belong to spheres so remote from each other that once insight into the error has been gained one can no longer conceive the possibility of a confusion.

The confusion of two concepts always carries with it the confusion of their contradictory opposites. The opposite of the universal validity of a formula, of the existence of a law, is the nonexistence of a law, indeterminism, acausality; while the opposite of compulsion is what in practice everyone calls "freedom." Here emerges the nonsense, trailing through centuries, that freedom means "exemption from the causal principle," or "not subject to the laws of nature." Hence it is believed necessary to vindicate indeterminism in order to save human freedom.

4. Freedom and Indeterminism

This is quite mistaken. Ethics has, so to speak, no moral interest in the purely theoretical question of "determinism or indeterminism?," but only a theoretical interest, namely: in so far as it seeks the laws of conduct, and can find them only to the extent that causality holds. But the question of whether man is morally free (that is, has that freedom which, as we shall show, is the presupposition of moral responsibility) is altogether different from the problem of determinism. Hume was especially clear on this point. He indicated the inadmissible confusion of the concepts of "indeterminism" and "freedom"; but he retained, inappropriately, the word "freedom" for both, calling the one freedom of "the will," the other, genuine kind, "freedom of conduct." He showed that morality is interest only in the latter, and that such freedom, in general, is unquestionably to be attributed to mankind. And this is quite correct. Freedom means the opposite of compulsion; a man is *free* if he does not act under *compulsion*, and he is compelled or unfree when he is hindered from without in the realization of his natural desires. Hence he is unfree when he is locked up, or chained, or when someone forces him at the point of a gun to do what otherwise he would not do. This is quite clear, and everyone will admit that the everyday or legal notion of the lack of freedom is thus correctly interpreted, and that a man will be considered quite free and responsible if no such external compulsion is exerted upon him. There are certain cases which lie between these clearly described ones, as, say, when someone acts under the influence of alcohol or a narcotic. In such cases we consider the man to be more or less unfree, and hold him less accountable, because we rightly view the influence of the drug as "external," even though it is found within the body; it prevents him from making decisions in the manner peculiar to his nature. If he takes the narcotic of his own will, we make him completely responsible for *this* act and transfer a part of the responsibility to the consequences, making, as it were, an average or mean condemnation of the whole. In the case also of a person who is mentally ill we do not consider him free with respect to those acts in which the disease expresses itself, because we view the illness as a disturbing factor which hinders the normal functioning of his natural tendencies. We make not him but his disease responsible.

5. The Nature of Responsibility

But what does this really signify? What do we mean by this concept of responsibility which goes along with that of "freedom," and which plays such an important role in morality? It is easy to attain complete clarity in this matter; we need only carefully determine the manner in which the concept is used. What is the case in practice when we impute "responsibility" to a person? What is our aim in doing this? The judge has to discover who is responsible for a given act in order that he may *punish* him. We are inclined to be less concerned with the inquiry as to who deserves *reward* for an act, and we have no special officials for this; but of course the principle would be the same. But let us stick to punishment in order to make the idea clear. What is punishment, actually? The view still often expressed, that it is a natural *retaliation* for past wrong, ought no longer to be defended in cultivated society; for the opinion that an increase in sorrow can be "made good again" by further sorrow is altogether barbarous. Certainly the origin of punishment may lie in an impulse of retaliation or vengeance; but what is such an impulse except the instinctive desire to destroy the *cause* of the deed to be avenged, by the destruction of or injury to the malefactor? Punishment is concerned only with the institution of causes, of *motives* of conduct, and this alone is its meaning. Punishment is an educative measure, and as such is a means to the formation of motives, which are in part to prevent the wrongdoer from repeating the act (reformation) and in part to prevent others from committing a similar act (intimidation). Analogously, in the case of reward we are concerned with an incentive.

Hence the question regarding responsibility is the question: Who, in a given case, is to be punished? Who is to be considered the true wrongdoer? This problem is not identical with that regarding the original instigator of the act; for the great-grandparents of the man, from whom he inherited his character, might in the end be the cause, or the statesmen who are responsible for his social milieu, and so forth. But the "doer" is the one *upon whom the motive must have acted* in order, with certainty, to have prevented the act (or called it forth, as the case may be). Consideration of remote causes is of no help here, for in the first place their actual contribution cannot be determined, and in the second place they are generally out of reach. Rather, we must find the person in whom the decisive junction of causes lies. The question of who is responsible is the question concerning the *correct point of application of the motive*. And the important thing is that in this its meaning is completely exhausted; behind it there lurks no mysterious connection between transgression and requital, which is merely *indicated* by the described state of affairs. It is a matter only of knowing who is to be punished or rewarded, in order that punishment and reward function as such—be able to achieve their goal.

Thus, all the facts connected with the concepts of responsibility and imputation are at once made intelligible. We do not charge an insane person with responsibility, for the very reason that he offers no unified point for the application of a motive. It would be pointless to try to affect him by means of promises or threats, when his confused soul fails to respond to such influence because its normal mechanism is out of order. We do not try to give him motives, but try to heal him (metaphorically, we make his sickness responsible, and try to remove its causes). When a man is forced by threats to commit certain acts we do not blame him, but the one who held the pistol at his breast. The reason is clear: the act would have been prevented had we been able to restrain the person who threatened him; and this person is the one whom we must influence in order to prevent similar acts in the future.

6. The Consciousness of Responsibility

But much more important than the question of when a man is said to be responsible is that of when he *himself* feels responsible. Our whole treatment would be untenable if it gave no explanation of this. It is, then, a welcome confirmation of the view here developed that the subjective feeling of responsibility coincides with the objective judgment. It is a fact of experience that, in general, the person blamed or condemned is conscious of the fact that he was "rightly" taken to account—of course, under the supposition that no error has been made, that the assumed state of affairs actually occurred. What is this consciousness of having been the true doer of the act, the actual instigator? Evidently not merely that it was he who took the steps required for its performance; but there must be added the awareness that he did it "independently," "of his own initiative," or however it be expressed. This feeling is simply the consciousness of *freedom*, which is merely the knowledge of having acted of one's *own* desires. And "one's own desires" are those which have their origin in the regularity of one's character in the given situation, and are not imposed by an external power, as explained above. The absence of the external power expresses itself in the well-known feeling (usually considered characteristic of the consciousness of freedom) *that one could also have acted otherwise*. How this indubitable experience ever came to be an argument in favor of indeterminism is incomprehensible to me. It is of course obvious that I should have acted differently had I *willed* something else; but the feeling never says that I could also have willed something else, even though this is true, if, that is, other motives had been present. And it says even less that under *exactly the same* inner and outer conditions I could also have willed something else. How could such a feeling inform me of anything regarding the purely theoretical question of whether the principle of causality holds or not? Of course, after what has been said on the subject, I do not undertake to demonstrate the principle, but I do deny that from any such fact of consciousness the least follows regarding the principle's validity. This feeling is not the consciousness of the absence of a cause, but of something altogether different, namely, of *freedom*, which consists in the fact that I can act as I desire.

Thus the feeling of responsibility assumes that I acted freely, that my own desires impelled me; and if because of this feeling I willingly suffer blame for my behavior or reproach myself, and thereby admit that I might have acted otherwise, this means that other behavior was compatible with the laws of volition—of course, granted other motives. And I myself desire the existence of such motives and bear the pain (regret and sorrow) caused me by my behavior so that its repetition will be prevented. To blame oneself means just to apply motives of improvement to oneself, which is usually the task of the educator. But if, for example, one does something under the influence of torture, feelings of guilt and regret are absent, for one knows that according to the laws of volition no other behavior was possible—no matter what ideas, because of their feeling tones, might have functioned as motives. The important thing, always, is that the feeling of responsibility means the realization that one's self, one's own psychic processes constitute the point at which motives must be applied in order to govern the acts of one's body.

. . .

FREE WILL AS INVOLVING DETERMINATION AND INCONCEIVABLE WITHOUT IT

R. E. HOBART

The thesis of this article is that there has never been any ground for the controversy between the doctrine of free will and determinism, that it is based upon a misapprehension, that

From R. E. Hobart, "Free Will as Involving Determination and Inconceivable Without It," *Mind*, XLIII, No. 169 (January, 1934), pp. 1–27.

the two assertions are entirely consistent, that one of them strictly implies the other, that they have been opposed only because of our natural want of the analytical imagination. In so saying I do not tamper with the meaning of either phrase. That would be unpardonable. I mean free will in the natural and usual sense, in the fullest, the most absolute sense in which for the purposes of the personal and moral life the term is ever employed. I mean it as implying responsibility, merit and demerit, guilt and desert. I mean it as implying, after an act has been performed, that one "could have done otherwise" than one did. I mean it as conveying these things also, not in any subtly modified sense but in exactly the sense in which we conceive them in life and in law and in ethics. These two doctrines have been opposed because we have not realised that free will can be analysed without being destroyed, and that determinism is merely a feature of the analysis of it. And if we are tempted to take refuge in the thought of an "ultimate," an "innermost" liberty that eludes the analysis, then we have implied a deterministic basis and constitution for this liberty as well. For such a basis and constitution lie in the idea of liberty.

The thesis is not, like that of Green or Bradley, that the contending opinions are reconciled if we adopt a certain metaphysic of the ego, as that it is timeless, and identifies itself with a desire by a "timeless act." This is to say that the two are irreconcilable, as they are popularly supposed to be, except by a theory that delivers us from the conflict by taking us out of time. Our view on the contrary is that from the natural and temporal point of view itself there never was any need of a reconciliation but only of a comprehension of the meaning of terms. (The metaphysical nature of the self and its identity through time is a problem for all who confront memory, anticipation, etc.; it has no peculiar difficulties arising from the present problem.)

I am not maintaining that determinism is true; only that it is true in so far as we have free will. That we are free in willing is, broadly speaking, a fact of experience. That broad fact is more assured than any philosophical analysis. It is therefore surer than the deterministic analysis of it, entirely adequate as that in the end appears to be. But it is not here affirmed that there are no small exceptions, no slight undetermined swervings, no ingredient of absolute chance. All that is here said is that such absence of determination, if and so far as it exists, is no gain to freedom, but sheer loss of it; no advantage to the moral life, but blank subtraction from it.—When I speak below of "the indeterminist" I mean the libertarian indeterminist, that is, him who believes in free will and holds that it involves indetermination.

By the analytical imagination is meant, of course, the power we have, not by nature but by training, of realising that the component parts of a thing or process, taken together, each in its place, with their relations, are identical with the thing or process itself. If it is "more than its parts," then this "more" will appear in the analysis. It is not true, of course, that all facts are susceptible of analysis, but so far as they are, there is occasion for the analytical imagination. We have been accustomed to think of a thing or a person as a whole, not as a combination of parts. We have been accustomed to think of its activities as the way in which, as a whole, it naturally and obviously behaves. It is a new, an unfamiliar and an awkward act on the mind's part to consider it, not as one thing acting in its natural manner, but as a system of parts that work together in a complicated process. Analysis often seems at first to have taken away the individuality of the thing, its unity, the impression of the familiar identity. For a simple mind this is strikingly true of the analysis of a complicated machine. The reader may recall Paulsen's ever significant story about the introduction of a railway into Germany. When it reached the village of a certain enlightened pastor, he took his people to where a locomotive engine was standing, and in the clearest words explained of what parts it consisted and how it worked. He was much pleased by their eager nods of intelligence as he proceeded. But on his finishing they said: "Yes, yes, Herr Pastor, but there's a horse inside, isn't there?" They could not *realise* the analysis. They were wanting in the analytical imagination. Why not? They had never been trained to it. It is in the first instance a great effort to think of all the parts working together to produce the simple result that the engine glides down the track. It is easy to think of a horse inside doing all the work. A horse is a familiar totality that does familiar things. They could no better have grasped the physiological analysis of a horse's movements had it been set forth to them.

The reason for thinking that there is no occasion for the controversy lies exclusively in the analysis of the terms employed in it. But the several analyses must all be taken together, realised jointly, before the position can be fully understood.

Self and Character. We are not concerned with the total nature of the self, but only with the aspect of it strictly involved in our question. We are not dealing with the problem of knowledge and therefore not with the self as mere knower. It is clear that the self merely as knower in general (irrespective of just what particulars it knows) is similar in all men. The relation of subject to object, whatever it may be, is the same with you and with me. But the self as it interests ethics is not the same in different persons. It is the concrete, active self, existing through time and differing from others. The whole stress of morality arises because moral selves are not alike, because there is need of influencing some moral selves to make them refrain from certain acts or neglects, that is, in order to make them better moral selves. How do we express the difference? We call it a difference of moral qualities, traits, or character. We are having regard to the question what acts will come from these selves. By character we mean, do we not? the sum of a man's tendencies to action, considered in their relative strength; or that sum in so far as it bears upon morals.

Now the position of the indeterminist is that a free act of will is the act of the self. The self becomes through it the author of the physical act that ensues. This volition of the self causes the physical act but it is not in its turn caused, it is "spontaneous." To regard it as caused would be determinism.

The causing self to which the indeterminist here refers is to be conceived as distinct from character; distinct from temperament, wishes, habits, impulses. He emphasises two things equally: the physical act springs from the self through its volition, and it does not spring merely from character, it is not simply the result of character and circumstances. If we ask, "Was there anything that induced the self thus to act?" we are answered in effect, "Not definitively. The self feels motives but its act is not determined by them. It can choose between them."

The next thing to notice is that this position of the indeterminist is taken in defence of moral conceptions. There would be no fitness, he says, in our reproaching ourselves, in our feeling remorse, in our holding ourselves or anyone guilty, if the act in question were not the act of the self instead of a product of the machinery of motives.

We have here one of the most remarkable and instructive examples of something in which the history of philosophy abounds—of a persistent, an age-long deadlock due solely to the indisposition of the human mind to look closely into the meaning of its terms.

How do we reproach ourselves? We say to ourselves, "How negligent of me!" "How thoughtless!" "How selfish!" "How hasty and unrestrained!" "That I should have been capable even for a moment of taking such a petty, irritated view!" etc. In other words, we are attributing to ourselves at the time of the act, in some respect and measure, a bad character, and regretting it. And that is the entire point of our self-reproach. We are turning upon ourselves with disapproval and it may be with disgust; we wish we could undo what we did in the past, and, helpless to do that, feel a peculiar thwarted poignant anger and shame at ourselves that we *had it in us* to perpetrate the thing we now condemn. It is self we are reproaching, *i.e.*, self that we are viewing as bad in that it produced bad actions. Except in so far as what-it-is produced these bad actions, there is no ground for reproaching it (calling it bad) and no meaning in doing so. All self-reproach is self-judging, and all judging is imputing a character. We are blaming ourselves. If spoken, what we are thinking would be dispraise. And what are praise and dispraise? Always, everywhere, they are *descriptions* of a person (more or less explicit) with favourable or unfavourable feeling at what is described,—descriptions in terms of value comporting fact, or of fact comporting value, or of both fact and value. In moral instances they are descriptions of his character. We are morally characterising him in our minds (as above) with appropriate feelings. We are attributing to him the character that we approve and like and wish to see more of, or the contrary. All the most intimate terms of the moral life imply that the act has proceeded from *me,* the distinctive me, from the manner of man I am or was. And this is the very thing on which the libertarian lays stress. What the indeterminist prizes with all his heart, what he stoutly affirms and insists upon, is precisely what he denies, namely, that I, the concrete and specific moral being, am the author, the source of my acts. For, of course, that is determinism. To say that they come from the self is to say that they are determined by the self—the moral self, the self with a moral quality. He gives our preferrings the bad name of the machinery of motives, but they are just what we feel in ourselves when we decide. When he maintains that the self at the moment of decision may act to some extent independently of motives, *and is good or bad according as it acts in this direction or that,* he is simply setting up one character within another, he is separating the self from what he understands by the person's character as at first mentioned, only thereupon to attribute to it a character of its own, *in that he judges it good or bad.*

The whole controversy is maintained by the indeterminist in order to defend the validity of the terms in which we morally judge,—for example, ourselves. But the very essence of all judgment, just so far as it extends, asserts determination.

If in conceiving the self you detach it from all motives or tendencies, what you have is not a morally admirable or condemnable, not a morally characterisable self at all. Hence it is not subject to reproach. You cannot call a self good because of its courageous free action, and then deny that its action was determined by its character. In calling it good because of that action you have implied that the action came from its goodness (which means its good character) and was a sign thereof. By their fruits ye shall know them. The indeterminist appears to imagine that he can distinguish the moral "I" from all its propensities, regard its act as arising in the moment undetermined by them, and yet can then (for the first time, in his opinion, with propriety!) ascribe to this "I" an admirable quality. At the very root of his doctrine he contradicts himself. How odd that he never catches sight of that contradiction! He fights for his doctrine in order that he may call a man morally good, on account of his acts, with some real meaning; and his doctrine is that a man's acts (precisely so far as "free" or undetermined) do not come from his goodness. So they do not entitle us to call him good. He has taken his position in defence of moral conceptions, and it is fatal to all moral conceptions.

We are told, however, that it is under determinism that we should have no right any more to praise or to blame. At least we could not do so in the old sense of the terms. We might throw words of praise to a man, or throw words of blame at him, because we know from observation that they will affect his action; but the old light of meaning in the terms has gone out. Well, all we have to do is to keep asking what this old meaning was. We praise a man by saying that he is a good friend, or a hard worker, or a competent man of business, or a trusty assistant, or a judicious minister, or a gifted poet, or one of the noblest of men—one of the noblest of characters! In other words, he is a being with such and such qualities. If it is moral praise, he is a being with such and such tendencies to bring forth good acts. If we describe a single act, saying, for instance: "Well done!" we mean to praise the person for the act as being the author of it. It is he who has done well and proved himself capable of doing so. If the happy act is accidental we say that no praise is deserved for it. If a person is gratified by praise it is because of the estimate of him, in some respect or in general, that is conveyed. Praise (once again) means description, with expressed or implied admiration. If any instance of it can be found which does not consist in these elements our analysis fails. "Praise the Lord, O my soul, *and forget not all His benefits,*"—and the Psalm goes on to tell His loving and guarding acts toward human-kind. To praise the Lord is to tell His perfections, especially the perfections of His character. This is the old light that has always been in words of praise and there appears no reason for its going out.

Indeterminism maintains that we need not be impelled to action by our wishes, that our active will need not be determined by them. Motives "incline without necessitating." We choose amongst the ideas of action before us, but need not choose solely according to the attraction of desire, in however wide a sense that word is used. Our inmost self may rise up in its autonomy and moral dignity, independently of motives, and register its sovereign decree.

Now, *in so far* as this "interposition of the self" is undetermined, the act is not *its* act, it does not issue from any concrete continuing self; it is born at the moment, of nothing, hence it expresses no quality; it bursts into being from no source. The self does not register *its* decree, for the decree is not the product of just that "*it.*" The self does not rise up in *its* moral dignity, for dignity is the quality of an enduring being, influencing its actions, and therefore expressed by them, and that would be determination. *In proportion* as an act of volition starts of itself without cause it is exactly, so far as the freedom of the individual is concerned, as if it had been thrown into his mind from without—"suggested" to him—by a freakish demon. It is exactly like it in this respect, that in neither case does the volition arise from what the man is, cares for or feels allegiance to; it does not come out of him. *In proportion* as it is undetermined, it is just as if his legs should suddenly spring up and carry him off where he did not prefer to go. Far from constituting freedom, that would mean, in the exact measure in which it took place, the loss of freedom. It would be an interference, and an utterly uncontrollable interference, with his power of acting as he prefers. In fine, then, *just so far* as the volition is undetermined, the self can neither be praised nor blamed for it, since it is not the act of the self.

The principle of free will says: "*I* produce my volitions." Determinism says: "My volitions are produced by *me*." Determinism is free will expressed in the passive voice.

After all, it is plain what the indeterminists have done. It has not occurred to them that our free will may be resolved into its component elements. (Thus far a portion only of this resolution has been considered.) When it is thus resolved they do not recognise it. The analytical imagination is considerably taxed to perceive the identity of the free power that we feel with the component parts that analysis shows us. We are gratified by their nods of intelligence and their bright, eager faces as the analysis proceeds, but at the close are a little disheartened to find them falling back on the innocent supposition of a horse inside that does all the essential work. They forget that they may be called upon to analyse the horse. They solve the problem by forgetting analysis. The solution they offer is merely: "There is a self inside which does the deciding." Or, let us say, it is as if the *Pfarrer* were explaining the physiology of a horse's motion. They take the whole thing to be analysed, imagine a duplicate of it reduced in size, so to speak, and place this duplicate-self inside as an explanation—making it the elusive source of the "free decisions." They do not see that they are merely pushing the question a little further back, since the process of deciding, with its constituent factors, must have taken place within that inner self. Either it decided in a particular way because, on the whole, it preferred to decide in that way, or the decision was an underived event, a rootless and sourceless event. It is the same story over again. In neither case is there any gain in imagining a second self inside, however wonderful and elusive. Of course, it is the first alternative that the indeterminist is really imagining. If you tacitly and obscurely conceive the self as deciding *its own way*, *i.e.*, according to its preference, but never admit or recognise this, then you can happily remain a libertarian indeterminist; but upon no other terms. In your theory there is a heart of darkness.

Freedom. In accordance with the genius of language, free will means freedom of persons in willing, just as "free trade" means freedom of persons (in a certain respect) in trading. The freedom of anyone surely always implies his possession of a power, and means the absence of any interference (whether taking the form of restraint or constraint) with his exercise of that power. Let us consider this in relation to freedom in willing.

"Can." We say, "I can will this or I can will that, whichever I choose." Two courses of action present themselves to my mind. I think of their consequences, I look on this picture and on that, one of them commends itself more than the other, and I will an act that brings it about. I knew that I could choose either. That means that I had the power to choose either.

What is the meaning of "power"? A person has a power if it is a fact that when he sets himself in the appropriate manner to produce a certain event that event will actually follow. I have the power to lift the lamp; that is, if I grasp it and exert an upward pressure with my arm, *it will rise.* I have the power to will so and so; that is, if I want, that act of will will take place. That and none other is the meaning of power, is it not? A man's being in the proper active posture of body or of mind is the cause, and the sequel in question will be the effect. (Of course, it may be held that the sequel not only does but must follow, in a sense opposed to Hume's doctrine of cause. Very well; the question does not here concern us.)

Thus power depends upon, or rather consists in, a law. The law in question takes the familiar form that if something happens a certain something else will ensue. If A happens then B will happen. The law in this case is that if the man definitively so desires then volition will come to pass. There is a series, wish—will—act. The act follows according to the will (that is a law,—I do not mean an underived law) and the will follows according to the wish (that is another law). A man has the power (sometimes) to act as he wishes. He has the power (whenever he is not physically bound or held) to act as he wills. He has the power always (except in certain morbid states) to will as he wishes. All this depends upon the laws of his being. Wherever there is a power there is a law. In it the power wholly consists. A man's power to will as he wishes is simply the law that his will follows his wish.

What, again, does freedom mean? It means the absence of any interference with all this. Nothing steps in to prevent my exercising my power.[1]

All turns on the meaning of "can." "I can will either this or that" means, I am so constituted that if I definitively incline to this, the appropriate act of will will take place, and if I definitively incline to that, the appropriate act of will will take place. The law connecting preference and will exists, and there is nothing to interfere with it. My free power, then, is not an exemption from law but in its inmost essence an embodiment of law.

Thus it is true, after the act of will, that I could have willed otherwise. It is most natural to add, "if I had wanted to"; but the addition is not required. The point is the meaning of "could." I could have willed whichever way I pleased. I had the power to will otherwise, there was nothing to prevent my doing so, and I should have done so if I had wanted. If someone says that the wish I actually had prevented my willing otherwise, so that I could not have done it, he is merely making a slip in the use of the word "could." He means, that wish

[1] A word as to the relation of power and freedom. Strictly power cannot exist without freedom, since the result does not follow without it. Freedom on the other hand is a negative term, meaning the absence of something, and implies a power only because that whose absence it signifies is interference, which implies something to be interfered with. Apart from this peculiarity of the term itself, there might be freedom without any power. Absence of interference (of what would be interference if there were a power) might exist in the absence of a power; a man might be free to do something because there was nothing to interfere with his doing it, but might have no power to do it. Similarly and conveniently we may speak of a power as existing though interfered with; that is, the law may exist that would constitute a power if the interference were away.

could not have produced anything but this volition. But "could" is asserted not of the wish (a transient fact to which power in this sense is not and should not be ascribed) but of the person. And the person *could* have produced something else than that volition. He could have produced any volition he wanted; he had the power to do so.

But the objector will say, "The person as he was at the moment—the person as animated by that wish—could not have produced any other volition." Oh, yes, he could. "Could" has meaning not as applied to a momentary actual phase of a person's life, but to the person himself of whose life that is but a phase; and it means that (even at that moment) he had the power to will just as he preferred. *The idea of power, because it is the idea of a law, is hypothetical, carries in itself hypothesis as part of its very intent and meaning—"if he should prefer this, if he should prefer that,"—and therefore can be truly applied to a person irrespective of what at the moment he does prefer. It remains hypothetical even when applied.*[2] This very peculiarity of its meaning is the whole point of the idea of power. It is just because determinism is true, because a law obtains, that one "could have done otherwise."

Sidgwick set over against "the formidable array of cumulative evidence" offered for determinism the "affirmation of consciousness" "that I can now choose to do" what is right and reasonable, "however strong may be my inclination to act unreasonably."[3] But it is not against determinism. It is a true affirmation (surely not of immediate consciousness but of experience), the affirmation of my power to will what I deem right, however intense and insistent my desire for the wrong. I can will anything, and can will effectively anything that my body will enact. I can will it despite an inclination to the contrary of any strength you please—strength as felt by me before

[2] I am encouraged by finding in effect the same remark in Prof. G. E. Moore's *Ethics*, ch. vi., at least as regards what he terms one sense of the word "could." I should hazard saying, the only sense in this context.

[3] *Methods of Ethics*, 7th ed., 65.

decision. We all know cases where we have resisted impulses of great strength in this sense and we can imagine them still stronger. I have the power to do it, and shall do it, shall exercise that power, if I prefer. Obviously in that case (be it psychologically remarked) my solicitude to do what is right will have proved itself even stronger (as measured by ultimate tendency to prevail, though not of necessity by sensible vividness or intensity) than the inclination to the contrary, for that is what is meant by my preferring to do it. I am conscious that the field for willing is open; I can will anything that I elect to will. Sidgwick did not analyse the meaning of "can," that is all. He did not precisely catch the outlook of consciousness when it says, "I can." He did not distinguish the function of the word, which is to express the availability of the alternatives I see when, before I have willed, and perhaps before my preference is decided, I look out on the field of conceivable volition. He did not recognise that I must have a word to express my power to will as I please, quite irrespective of what I shall please, and that "can" is that word. It is no proof that I cannot do something to point out that I shall not do it if I do not prefer. A man, let us say, can turn on the electric light; but he will not turn it on if he walks away from it; though it is still true that he can turn it on. When we attribute power to a man we do not mean that something will accomplish itself without his wanting it to. That would never suggest the idea of power. We mean that if he makes the requisite move the thing will be accomplished. It is part of the idea that the initiative shall rest with him. The initiative for an act of will is a precedent phase of consciousness that we call the definitive inclination, or, in case of conflict, the definitive preference for it. If someone in the throes of struggle with temptation says to himself, "I can put this behind me," he is saying truth and precisely the pertinent truth. He is bringing before his mind the act of will, unprevented, quite open to him, that would deliver him from what he deems noxious. It may still happen that the noxiousness of the temptation does not affect him so powerfully as its allurement, and that he succumbs.

It is no whit less true, according to determinism, that he could have willed otherwise. To analyse the fact expressed by "could" is not to destroy it.

But it may be asked, "Can I will in opposition to my strongest desire at the moment when it is strongest?" If the words "at the moment when it is strongest" qualify "can," the answer has already been given. If they qualify "will," the suggestion is a contradiction in terms. Can I turn-on-the-electric-light-at-a-moment-when-I-am-not-trying-to-do-so? This means, if I try to turn on the light at a moment when I am not trying to, will it be turned on? A possible willing as I do not prefer to will is not a power on my part, hence not to be expressed by "I can."

Everybody knows that we often will what we do not want to will, what we do not prefer. But when we say this we are using words in another sense than that in which I have just used them. In *one* sense of the words, whenever we act we are doing what we prefer, on the whole, in view of all the circumstances. We are acting for the greatest good or the least evil or a mixture of these. In the *other* and more usual sense of the words, we are very often doing what we do not wish to do, *i.e.*, doing some particular thing we do not wish because we are afraid of the consequences or disapprove of the moral complexion of the particular thing we do wish. We do the thing that we do not like because the other thing has aspects that we dislike yet more. We are still doing what we like best on the whole. It is again a question of the meaning of words.

If the initiative for volition is not a wish, what is it? Indeterminism says that a moral agent sometimes decides against the more tempting course. He does so, let us say, because it is wrong, the other course is the right one. In other words, the desire to do right is at the critical moment stronger within him than the temptation. No, no, replies indeterminism, it is not that; he sometimes decides against the stronger desire. Very well; "can" meaning what it does, tell us what is the leaning or favourable disposition on the part of the ego, in a case of undetermined willing, toward the volition it adopts; what is that which constitutes the ego's initiative in that direction,—

since it is not a wish? Shall we say it is an approval or conscientious acceptance? Does this approval or acceptance arise from the agent's distinctive moral being? That is determinism, quite as much as if you called the initiative a wish. But the indeterminist has already answered in effect that there is no such initiative, or no effectual initiative. The act of will causes the physical act but is not itself caused. This is to deny the presence of power, according to its definition. How has it a meaning to say in advance that "I can" will this way or that? The self, considering the alternatives beforehand, is not in a position to say, "If I feel thus about it, this volition will take place, or if I feel otherwise the contrary will take place; I know very well how I shall feel, so I know how I shall will." The self now existing has not control over the future "free" volition, since that may be undetermined, nor will the self's future feelings, whatever they may be, control it. Hence the sense expressed by "I can," the sense of power inhering in one's continuous self to sway the volition as it feels disposed, is denied to it. All it is in a position to mean by "I can" is, "I do not know which will happen," which is not "I can" at all. Nay, even looking backward, it is unable to say: "I could have willed otherwise," for that clearly implies, "Had I been so disposed the other volition would have taken place," which is just what cannot, according to indeterminism, be said. Surely, to paraphrase a historic remark, our "liberty" does not seem to be of very much use to us. The indeterminist is in a peculiarly hapless position. The two things that he is most deeply moved to aver, that the free volition is the act of the self, and that the self can will one way or the other—these two things on his own theory fall utterly to pieces, and can only be maintained on the view that he opposes.

Compulsion. The indeterminist conceives that according to determinism the self is carried along by wishes to acts which it is thus necessitated to perform. This mode of speaking distinguishes the self from the wishes and represents it as under their dominion. This is the initial error. This is what leads the indeterminist wrong on all the topics of his problem. And the error persists in the most recent writings. In fact, the moral self is the wishing self. The wishes are its own. It cannot be described as under their dominion, for it has no separate predilections to be overborne by them; they themselves are its predilections. To fancy that because the person acts according to them he is compelled, a slave, the victim of a power from whose clutches he cannot extricate himself, is a confusion of ideas, a mere slip of the mind. The answer that has ordinarily been given is surely correct; all compulsion is causation, but not all causation is compulsion. Seize a man and violently force him to do something, and he is compelled—also caused—to do it. But induce him to do it by giving him reasons and his doing it is caused but not compelled.

Passivity. We have to be on our guard even against conceiving the inducement as a cause acting like the impact of a billiard ball, by which the self is precipitated into action like a second billiard ball, as an effect. The case is not so simple. Your reasons have shown him that his own preferences require the action. He does it of his own choice; he acts from his own motives in the light of your reasons. The sequence of cause and effect goes on within the self, with contributory information from without.

It is not clarifying to ask, "Is a volition free or determined?" It is the person who is free, and his particular volition that is determined. Freedom is something that we can attribute only to a continuing being, and he can have it only so far as the particular transient volitions within him are determined. (According to the strict proprieties of language, it is surely events that are caused, not things or persons; a person or thing can be caused or determined only in the sense that its beginning to be, or changes in it, are caused or determined.)

It is fancied that, owing to the "necessity" with which an effect follows upon its cause, if my acts of will are caused I am not free in thus acting. Consider an analogous matter. When I move I use ligaments. "Ligament" means that which binds, and a ligament does bind bones together. But *I* am not bound. *I* (so far as my organism is concerned) am rendered possible by the fact that my bones are bound one to another; that is part of the secret of my being able to act, to move about and work my will. If my bones ceased to be bound one to another I should be undone indeed. The human organism is detached, but it is distinctly important that its component parts shall not be detached. Just so my free power of willing is built up of tight cause-and-effect connections. The point is that when I employ the power thus constituted nothing determines the particular employment of it but *me*. Each particular act of mine is determined from outside itself, *i.e.*, by a cause, a prior event. But not from outside me. I, the possessor of the power, am not in my acts passively played upon by causes outside me, but am enacting my own wishes in virtue of a chain of causation within me. What is needed is to distinguish broadly between a particular effect, on the one hand, and, on the other, the detached, continuous life of a mental individual and his organism; a life reactive, but reacting according to its own nature.

What makes the other party uncontrollably reject all this —let us never forget—is the words. They smell of sordid detail, of unwinsome psychological machinery. They are not bathed in moral value, not elevated and glowing. In this the opponents' instinct is wholly right; only when they look for the value they fail to focus their eyes aright. It is in the whole act and the whole trait and the whole being that excellence and preciousness inhere; analysis must needs show us elements which, taken severally, are without moral expressiveness; as would be even the celestial anatomy of an angel appearing on earth. The analytic imagination, however, enables us to see the identity of the living fact in its composition with the living fact in its unity and integrity. Hence we can resume the thought of it as a unit and the appropriate feelings without fancying that analysis threatens them or is at enmity with them.

Spontaneity. The conception of spontaneity in an act or an utterance is the conception of its springing straight from the being himself, from his individuality, with naught to cause it but the freest impulse, the sheerest inclination, of that being. The term implies and requires but one causation, that from within. If we deny all causation behind the volition itself, even that from within his nature, we deny spontaneity on his part. We have emptied our formula of all human meaning.

Source. The indeterminist declares a man to be "the absolute source" of his acts. Let us scrutinise the term. The source of a stream is not a point where the water constituting the stream comes suddenly into existence, but on the contrary that from which it issues, that which supplies it because it has contained it. The stream—that particular stream—begins there, just as the action begins at its source, though the active energy flows from within it. The word "absolute" must mean true, genuine, complete, without reservation or qualification. Now such a genuine source a man in fact is; he knowingly and deliberately creates an act; the act issues forth from his chosen purpose, from his moral individuality. What the indeterminist, however, must mean by "absolute source" is a source that has in turn no source; a source, he thinks, cannot in the fullest and truest sense be such if it derives what it emits. This, as we see, certainly receives no support from the natural uses of the word, but is flatly incompatible with them. But the final objection is deeper. Will the indeterminist point out anything in the definition of the word "source" which implies that the thing defined is itself sourceless, or is imperfectly realised if it has a source? If he cannot, then the addition of the word "absolute" does not import that sourcelessness into the idea. Obviously "the man," as figuring in the indeterminist's conception here, would have to be the momentary man, not the enduring moral being. The truth clearly is that the indeterminist is confusing the idea of *flowing from this source and previously from another* with the quite distinct idea of *not flowing from this source but from another*. He feels that they cannot both be sources of the same act. And this is part of his confusion between causation and compulsion. If the agent were compelled to act as he does, not he but the compeller would be the intentional, the moral source of the act.

Prediction. If we knew a man's character thoroughly and the circumstances that he would encounter, determinism (which we are not here completely asserting) says that we could foretell his conduct. This is a thought that repels many libertarians. Yet to predict a person's conduct need not be repellent. If you are to be alone in a room with £1000 belonging to another on the table and can pocket it without anyone knowing the fact, and if I predict that you will surely *not* pocket it, that is not an insult. I say, I know you, I know your character; you will not do it. But if I say that you are "a free being" and that I really do not know whether you will pocket it or not, that is rather an insult. On the other hand, there are cases where prediction is really disparaging. If I say when you make a remark, "I knew you were going to say that," the impression is not agreeable. My exclamation seems to say that your mind is so small and simple that one can predict its ideas. That is the real reason why people resent in such cases our predicting their conduct; that if present human knowledge, which is known to be so limited, can foresee their conduct, it must be more naive and stereotyped than they like to think it. It is no reflection upon the human mind or its freedom to say that one who knew it through and through (a human impossibility) could foreknow its preferences and its spontaneous choice. It is of the very best of men that even we human beings say, "I am sure of him." It has perhaps in this controversy hardly been observed how much at this point is involved, how far the question of prediction reaches. The word "reliable" or "trustworthy" is a prediction of behaviour. Indeed, all judgment of persons whatever, in the measure of its definitude, is such a prediction.

Material Fate. The philosopher in the old story, gazing at the stars, falls into a pit. We have to notice the pitfall in our subject to which, similarly occupied, Prof. Eddington has succumbed.

"What significance is there in my mental struggle to-night whether I shall or shall not give up smoking, if the laws which govern the matter of the physical universe already pre-ordain for the morrow a configuration of matter consisting of pipe, tobacco, and smoke connected with my lips?" [4]

[4] *Philosophy*, Jan., 1933, p. 41.

No laws, according to determinism, pre-ordain such a configuration, unless I give up the struggle. Let us put matter aside for the moment, to return to it. Fatalism says that my morrow is determined no matter how I struggle. This is of course a superstition. Determinism says that my morrow is determined through my struggle. There is this significance in my mental effort, that it is deciding the event. The stream of causation runs through my deliberations and decision, and, if it did not run as it does run, the event would be different. The past cannot determine the event except through the present. And no past moment determined it any more truly than does the present moment. In other words, each of the links in the causal chain must be in its place. Determinism (which, the reader will remember, we have not here taken for necessarily true in all detail) says that the coming result is "pre-ordained" (literally, caused) at each stage, and therefore the whole following series for to-morrow may be described as already determined; so that did we know all about the struggler, how strong of purpose he was and how he was influenced (which is humanly impossible) we could tell what he would do. But for the struggler this fact (supposing it to be such) is not pertinent. If, believing it, he ceases to struggle, he is merely revealing that the forces within him have brought about that cessation. If on the other hand he struggles manfully he will reveal the fact that they have brought about his success. Since the causation of the outcome works through his struggle in either case equally, it cannot become for him a moving consideration in the struggle. In it the question is, "Shall I do this or that?" It must be answered in the light of what there is to recommend to me this or that. To this question the scientific truth (according to determinism) that the deliberation itself is a play of causation is completely irrelevant; it merely draws the mind delusively away from the only considerations that concern it.

As regards the rôle of matter in the affair, if, as Prof. Eddington on behalf of the determinists is here supposing, the behaviour of all matter, including the human organism, takes place according to a deterministic scheme of physical law, then we must conceive, according to the familiar formula, that the mental process is paralleled in the brain by a physical process. The whole psycho-physical occurrence would then be the cause of what followed, and the psychic side of it, the mental struggle proper, a concause or side of the cause. To-morrow's configuration of matter will have been brought about by a material process with which the mental process was inseparably conjoined. I make this supposition merely to show that supposing the existence of a physically complete mechanism through which all human action is caused and carried out has no tendency to turn determinism into fatalism. For the mental struggle must in that case be paralleled by a physical struggle which, so to speak, represents it and is in a manner its agent in the physical world; and upon this struggle the physical outcome will depend. (The determinist need not, but may of course, hold this doctrine of automatism, of a physically complete mechanism in human action.)

Self as Product and Producer. We can at this stage clearly see the position when a certain very familiar objection is raised. "How can any one be praised or blamed if he was framed by nature as he is, if heredity and circumstance have given him his qualities? A man can surely be blamed only for what he does himself, and he did not make his original character; he simply found it on his hands." A man is to be blamed only for what he does himself, for that alone tells what he is. He did not make his character; no, but he made his acts. Nobody blames him for making such a character, but only for making such acts. And to blame him for that is simply to say that he is a bad act-maker. If he thinks the blame misapplied he has to prove that he is not that sort of an act-maker. Are we to be told that we may not recognise what he is, with appropriate feelings for its quality, because he did not create himself—a mere contortion and intussusception of ideas? The moral self cannot be *causa sui.* To cause his original self a man must have existed before his original self. Is there something humiliating to him in the fact that he is not a contradiction in terms? If there were a being who made his "original character," and made a fine one, and we proceeded to praise him for it, our language would turn out to be a warm ascription to him of a still earlier character, so that the other would not have been original at all. To be praised or blamed you have to be; and be a particular person; and the praise or blame is telling what kind of a person you are. There is no other meaning to be extracted from it. Of course, a man does exist before his later self, and in that other sense he can be a moral *causa sui.* If by unflagging moral effort he achieves for himself better subsequent qualities, what can merit praise but the ingredient in him of aspiration and resolution that was behind the effort? If he should even remake almost his whole character, still there would be a valiant remnant that had done it. These are commonplaces, precisely of the moral outlook upon life. When we come to the moral fountainhead we come to what the man is, at a particular time, as measured by what he does or is disposed to do with his power of volition. It is fantastic to say that he finds his character on his hands. It is nothing but the moral description of himself. It is that self alone that wields his hands. The indeterminist is disquieted (through a mental confusion) by the discovery that the nature antedates the act, that virtue antedates the virtuous decision. (For that contains in itself the whole logical essence of the difficulty about origin.) And that lies in the signification of the terms. If we fancy that there would be any gain (or any meaning) in circumventing this order, we delude ourselves. The final fact we esteem or disesteem in a man is some subsisting moral quality. Morality has its eye upon acts, but an act is fleeting, it cannot be treasured and cherished. A quality can be, it lasts. And the reason why it is treasured and cherished is that it is the source of acts. Our treasuring and cherishing of it is (in part) our praise. It is the stuff certain people are made of that commands our admiration and affection. Where it came from is another question; it is precious in its own nature; let us be thankful when it is there. *Its origin cannot take away its value, and it is its value we are recognising when we praise.*

The peculiar importance that attaches to this "stuff" lies in its peculiar properties, so to speak. It is not a fixed "article of value," but lives, moves about in "this raging and confounding universe," this maze of unstable circumstances, yet can acquit itself with some fitness in face of all of them; reveals itself by choosing and rejecting with open eyes; steers its way through the dangers and complications, able to compare acts in advance, conscious of good and evil, allured to do otherwise but electing to do thus; good in a very special manner, in that it consciously cleaves to the good. A reliable character in the midst of unreliable circumstances. Consciousness, foresight, intelligence, moral consciousness, and sound choice. A unique "stuff."

The indeterminist, we noticed, requires a man to be "an absolute moral source" if we are to commend him. Well, if he were so, what could we say about him but what kind of a source he was? And he is so in fact. Suppose now that this source has in turn a source—or that it has not! Does that (either way) change what it is?

"But moral severity! How can we justly be severe toward a mere fact in nature—in human nature?" Because it is evil; because it must be checked. If somebody takes pleasure in torturing an innocent person, we spring to stop the act; to hold back the perpetrator, if need be with violence; to deter him from doing it again, if need be with violence; to warn any other possible perpetrators: "This shall not be done; we are the enemies of this conduct; this is evil conduct." At what could we be indignant but at a fact in somebody's human nature? Our severity and enmity are an active enmity to the evil; they are all part of that first spring to stop the act. "Society is opposed in every possible manner to such cruelty. You shall be made to feel that society is so, supposing that you cannot be made to feel yourself the vileness of the act." It does not remove our sense of its vileness to reflect that he was acting according to his nature. That is very precisely why we are indignant at him. We intend to make him feel that his nature is in that respect evil and its expression insufferable. We intend to interfere with the expression of his nature. That what he did proceeded from it is not a disturbing and pause-giving consideration in the midst of our conduct, but the entire basis of it. The very epithet "vile" assumes that his behaviour arose from an intention and a moral quality in the man. How can we justly be severe? Because he *ought* to be checked and deterred, made to feel the moral estimate of what he has been doing. This we consider more fully under the topic of Desert.

Compare a case where the wrongdoing, whatever it be, is one's own. Catch a man in a moment of fierce self-reproach, and bring the objection above before him. Would it relieve him of his feeling? It would be an irrelevant frivolity to him. He is shocked at a wrong that was done and at himself for doing it; he repents of the acts of will that brought it about; he would gladly so change himself as never to do the like again; he is ready to "beat himself with rods." With all that the metaphysical entanglement has simply nothing to do.

It would follow from the objector's way of thinking that if a man's moral state at one time was produced by himself through previous efforts, then our praise or blame must shift back to the earlier moral state and be applied to that alone; or, if that again was such a product, must shift still further back and be confined to the state that began the process. This is a vital misconception. The man in each of the moral states in the series may justly be characterised as good or bad, in this respect or that, in proportion as we truly know him; according to his decisions and intentions, or tendencies thereto, as compared with his then situation and knowledge of what he confronts, and of the effects that may fairly be expected from acts. This is implied whenever we make the remark that someone has deteriorated or improved in character; in other words, he is less or more to be praised now than he was formerly.

I say, "as compared with his then situation," for of course, in seeking to know what the forces of his character in themselves really are, we must take full account of the hardships, the exasperations, provocations to passion, causes of fatigue, etc., that enter into that situation. As regards the source of any moral degeneration, we cannot and do not call a person good because we can see that it is evil circumstances that have made him bad;

nor do we refrain from deeming him bad, since he is so; but we may have gained thereby a better insight into the hidden potential forces of his character, and see, in view of the previous circumstances, that it is at root less bad than we might have supposed. And while deeming him bad we may profoundly pity him in his wretched fortune.

"Still, does not determinism force us to face a fact in some sort new to us, that the offending person came to act so from natural causes; and does not that of necessity alter somewhat our attitude or state of mind about moral judgment?" Why, the fact is not new at all. In daily life we are all determinists, just as we are all libertarians. We are constantly attributing behaviour to the character, the temperament, the peculiarities of the person and expecting him to behave in certain fashions. The very words of our daily converse, as we have so amply observed, are full of determinism. And we see nothing inconsistent in being aware at the same time that he is free in choosing his course, as we know ourselves to be. We merely form expectations as to what he *will* freely choose. Nor do we see anything inconsistent in blaming him. At the very moment when we do so we often shake our heads over the environment or mode of life or ill-omened pursuits that have brought him to such ways and to being a blameworthy person. To be sure, in that economy of thought which is one of the salient traits of humanity, we seldom trouble ourselves to trace back with any attempt at thoroughness another's life, education, early temperament, etc. We do not go far back, but we are attentive, as we have to be, to his disposition and spirit in the present, at least as objectively expressed and thence imputed. And that is sufficient to include the whole point at issue. We recognise the one essential fact, that the nature precedes the act, and that the nature is simply a "given" fact in the world (not originally created by the agent himself—a would-be notion that visits the mind only in an attack of logical vertigo). Indeed, since blame is in itself the assertion of a particular nature existent in the world and father to an act, blame has contained in itself the truth in question from the beginning.

To be sure, determinism as a philosophic doctrine, determinism so named, may come as a new and repellent idea to us. We have been thinking in the right terms of thought all the while, but we did not identify them with terms of causation; when the philosophical names are put upon them we recoil, not because we have a false conception of the facts, but a false conception of the import of the philosophical terms. When we feel that somebody could have done otherwise but chose to do a wrong act knowingly, then we one and all feel that he is culpable and a proper object of disapproval, as we ought to feel. We merely have not been schooled enough in the application of general terms to call the course of mental events within him causation. So again, goodness consists in qualities, but the qualities express themselves in choosing, which is unfettered and so often trembles in the balance; when we are suddenly confronted with the abstract question, "Can we be blamed for a quality we did not choose?" the colours run and the outlines swim a little; some disentanglement of abstract propositions is required, though we think aright in practice on the concrete cases. So all that philosophic determinism "forces us to face" is the meaning of our terms.

No, it is the opposite doctrine that must revolutionise our attitude toward moral judgments. If it is true, we must come to see that no moral severity toward the helpless subject of an act of will that he suddenly finds discharging itself within him, though not emanating from what he is or prefers, can be deserved or relevant. To comprehend all is to pardon all—so far as it is undetermined. Or, rather, not to pardon but to acquit of all.

However, in face of the actual facts, there is something that does bring us to a larger than the usual frame of mind about indignation and punishment and the mood of severity. And that is thought, sympathetic thought, any thought that enters with humane interest into the inner lives of others and pursues in imagination the course of them. In an outbreak of moral indignation we are prone to take little cognizance of that inner life. We are simply outraged by a noxious act and a noxious trait (conceived rather objectively and as it concerns the persons affected) and feel that such act should not be and that such a trait should be put down. The supervening of a sympathetic mental insight upon moral indignation is not a displacement, but the turning of attention upon facts that call out other feelings too. To comprehend all is neither to pardon all nor to acquit of all; overlooking the disvalue of acts and intentions would not be comprehension; but it is to appreciate the human plight; the capacity for suffering, the poor contracted outlook, the plausibilities that entice the will. This elicits a sympathy or concern co-existing with disapproval. That which is moral in moral indignation and behind it, if we faithfully turn to it and listen, will not let us entirely wash our hands even of the torturer, his feelings and his fate; certainly will not permit us to take satisfaction in seeing him in turn tortured, merely for the torture's sake. His act was execrable because of its effect on sentient beings, but he also is a sentient being. The humanity that made us reprobate his crime has not ceased to have jurisdiction. The morality that hates the sin has in that very fact the secret of its undiscourageable interest in the sinner. We come, not to discredit indignation and penalty, nor to tamper with their meaning, but to see their office and place in life and the implications wrapped up in their very fitness. Of this more presently.

Amongst qualities none, of course, is higher than that which masters strong impulsive tendencies within ourselves that we decide not to tolerate. It is the possibility of this desperate inner struggle of self-overcoming, the genuine possibility of defying habit and weakness and asserting new life, which has caught and held the indeterminist's mind; but which he formulates loosely. He wishes to conceive of a self that need have no capital stock of qualities at all on which its volition depends. He thinks, or imagines that he thinks, of virtue as a thing nobly arising in the moment. In fact it is a thing nobly manifested in the moment; roused perhaps, brought to active life though it seemed dead, but still in some form pre-existing. What he admires is admirable, but he does not stop to think out its nature. To be "the author of novelties" is as possible, as fruitful for society, as challenging to the spirit as he deems it; but that author must exist as author, must have it in him to make a break for the new. The indeterminist would promptly retort that this is evidently not the sort of novelty he has in mind, that he means a moral act which is not an effect of anything pre-existing in the person. To which I answer: The novelty interesting to morality and to humanity is the escape from the spell of habit or ease or a straitened mental outlook, the leap of the soul with all its strength in a new direction; the question of causal nexus is of interest only to the philosophical analyst. The determinist's analysis leaves the escape from habit, etc., entirely possible and as creditable as it seems. On the indeterminist's account it would be a cosmological accident without moral significance.

Responsibility. Again, it is said that determinism takes from man all responsibility. As regards the origin of the term, a man is responsible when he is the person to respond to the question why the act was performed, how it is to be explained or justified. That is what he must answer; he is answerable for the act. It is the subject of which he must give an account; he is accountable for the act. The act proceeded from him. He is to say whether it proceeded consciously. He is to give evidence that he did or did not know the moral nature of the act and that he did or did not intend the result. He is to say how he justifies it or if he can justify it. If the act proceeded from him by pure accident, if he can show that he did the damage (if damage it was) by brushing against something by inadvertence, for example, then he has not to respond to the question what he did it for—he is not consciously responsible—nor how it is justified—he is not morally responsible, though of course he may have been responsible in these respects for a habit of carelessness.

But why does the peculiar moral stain of guilt or ennoblement of merit belong to responsibility? If an act proceeds from a man and not merely from his accidental motion but from his mind and moral nature, we judge at once that like acts may be expected from him in the future. The colour of the act for good or bad is reflected on the man. We see him now as a living source of possible acts of the same kind. If we must be on our guard against such acts we must be on our guard against such men. If we must take steps to defend ourselves against such acts we must take steps to defend ourselves against such men. If we detest such acts, we must detest that tendency in such men which produced them. He is guilty in that he knowingly did evil, in that the intentional authorship of evil is in him. Because the act proceeded in every sense from him, for that reason he is (so far) to be accounted bad or good according as the act is bad or good, and he is the one to be punished if punishment is required. And that is moral responsibility.

But how, it is asked, can I be responsible for what I will if a long train of past causes has made me will it—the old query asked anew in relation to another category, responsibility, which must be considered separately. Is it not these causes that are "responsible" for my act—to use the word in the only sense, says the objector, that seems to remain for it?

The parent past produced the man, none the less the man is responsible for his acts. We can truly say that the earth bears apples, but quite as truly that trees bear apples. The earth bears the apples by bearing trees. It does not resent the claim of the trees to bear the apples, or try to take the business out of the trees' hands. Nor need the trees feel their claim nullified by the earth's part in the matter. There is no rivalry between them. A man is a being with free will and responsibility; where this being came from, I repeat, is another story. The past finished its functions in the business when it generated him as he is. So far from interfering with him and coercing him the past does not even exist. If we could imagine it as lingering on into the present, standing over against him and stretching out a ghostly hand to stay his arm, then indeed the past would be interfering with his liberty and responsibility. But so long as it and he are never on the scene together they cannot wrestle; the past cannot overpower him. The whole alarm is an evil dream, a nightmare due to the indigestion of words. The past has created, and left extant, a free-willed being.

Desert. But we have not come to any final clearness until we see how a man can be said to *deserve* anything when his acts flow from his wishes, and his wishes flow from other facts further up the stream of his life. There is a peculiar element in the idea of deserving. This is the element of "ought." A man deserves punishment or reward if society ought to give it to him; he deserves the punishment or reward that he ought to receive. We cannot say universally that he deserves what he ought to receive, but only when it is a question of reward or punishment.

What treatment a man should receive from society as a result of wrongdoing is a question of ethics. It is widely held that an evildoer deserves punishment, not only for the defence of society but because there is an ultimate fitness in inflicting natural evil for moral evil. This, as we know, has been maintained by determinists. Since the idea of desert collapses altogether on the indeterminist's conception of conduct, this theory of the ground of desert cannot be said to be logically bound up with indeterminism. For my own part, however, owing to reasons for which I have no space here, I cannot hold the theory. I believe that the ideal ends of the administration of justice are (1) to see that all possible restitution is made, (2) to see as far as possible that the malefactor does not repeat the act, and (3) so far as possible to render the act less likely on the part of others. And these ends should be sought by means that will accomplish them. Morality is humane. It is animated by good-will toward humanity. Our instinctive impulse to retaliation must be interpreted with a view to its function in society, and so employed and regulated to the best purpose. Being a part of the defensive and fighting instinct, its functional aim is evidently to destroy or check the threatening source of evil—to destroy the culprit or change his temper. Our common and natural notion of desert is in harmony with either of these views; only on the second it receives a supplement, a purposive interpretation.

We discover punishment not only in combat but in nature at large. If a child puts its hand into flames it is burnt. After that it puts its hand into flames no more. Nature teaches us to respect her by punishments that deter. Society, to preserve itself, must find deterrents to administer to men. It must say, "I'll teach you not to do that." Already nature has taught it such deterrents. Society must shape men's actions or at least rough-hew them, to the extent of striking off certain jagged and dangerous edges, and the most obvious way to do so is by penalties. A secondary way is by rewards, and these nature has taught also.

When a man needlessly injures others, society by punishment injures him. It administers to him a specimen of what he has given to others. "This," it says, "is the nature of your act; to give men suffering like this. They rebel at it as you rebel at this. You have to be made more acutely conscious of the other side; the side of the feelings and the forces that you have outraged. You have to be made to feel them recoil upon you, that you may know that they are there. You have to be made to respect them in advance. And others like-minded to respect them in some degree better by seeing how they recoil upon you."

But this is only a method of working upon him and them; it is justified by effectiveness alone. It supposes two things; that society has been just in the first instance to these men themselves, that is, that they were not drawn by unjust conditions of life into the acts for which they are made to suffer; and that the suffering will in fact improve their conduct or that of others. The truth is that society often punishes when it is itself the greater malefactor, and that the penalty, instead of reforming, often confirms the criminality. It is due to nothing but the crude state of civilisation that we have added so little of a more sagacious and effectual mode of influencing criminals and preventing crime than the original and natural method of hitting back.

Out of this situation arises a subsidiary sense of deserving. A man may be said to deserve a punishment in the sense that, in view of the offence, it is not too severe to give him if it would work as above conceived; though if we believe it will not so work it ought not to be given him..

It is here that we confront the school that would sweep away all notions of desert, all indignation, whether against public or private offenders, on the ground that free will and responsibility are illusions, and would substitute the moral hospital for the prison. Tietjens, for example, would have us apply "de-suggestion" to rid ourselves of the heartburnings and disquiet that imputing moral responsibility brings upon us. It is a pity that a teaching which speaks to us in the name of advanced psychology should be founded on a hasty and crude analysis. If we did not acquire the idea of free will from our experience of the conditions of our own volition, how did we come by it at all? Under the laws of origin of our conceptions, how were we able to conceive an elementary type of volition that has no counterpart in real life? How could we fabricate the idea without any material for it? What these determinists do is, first, to make the unthinking concession to the indeterminists that they have a coherent theory and that it is one with the naive belief in free choice; having hastily conceded so much, they are constrained to call the naive notion an illusion. They do not see the strength of their own fundamental position.

Honour and dishonour will never be withdrawn from morals. We shall not cease to look out upon our world with appropriate emotions. But it behooves us to take care that they are appropriate. The moral emotions are often barbarously and with terrible effect misapplied; it shows what they could do if intelligence guarded their application. The Christian principle of hating the sin because it is in fact noxious, but bearing good-will to the sinner and preferring his reformation with a minimum of suffering to his punishment, is surely the root-principle. And here it is that the school of cool realism, of the medical, educational, and environmental treatment, brings fresh air and aid. It wants to discover effectual means to what is in truth a chief part of the moral end. We shall not be troubled by its shallow philosophy in so far as it can help to that end.

If the general view here taken, which seems forced upon us in the prosaic process of examining words, is correct, then as we look back over the long course of this controversy and the false antithesis that has kept it alive, how can we help exclaiming, "What waste!" Waste is surely the tragic fact above all in life; we contrast it with the narrow areas where reason and its economy of means to ends in some measure reign. But here is huge waste in the region of reasoning itself, the enemy in the citadel. What ingenuity, what resource in fresh shifts of defence, what unshaken loyalty to inward repugnances, what devotion to ideal values, have here been expended in blind opposition instead of analysis. The cause of determinism, seeming to deny freedom, has appeared as the cause of reason, of intelligence itself, and the cause of free will, seeming to exclude determination, has appeared that of morals. The worst waste is the clash of best things. In our subject it is time this waste should end. Just as we find that morality requires intelligence to give it effect and remains rudimentary and largely abortive till it places the conscience of the mind in the foreground, so we find that determinism and the faith in freedom meet and are united in the facts, and that the long enmity has been a bad dream.

FREE WILL AS INVOLVING DETERMINISM

PHILIPPA FOOT

The idea that free will can be reconciled with the strictest determinism is now very widely accepted. To say that a man acted freely is, it is often suggested, to say that he was not constrained, or that he could have done otherwise if he had chosen, or something else of that kind; and since these things could be true even if his action was determined it seems that there could be room for free will even within a universe completely subject to causal laws. Hume put forward a view of this kind in contrasting the "liberty of spontaneity . . . which is oppos'd to violence" with the nonexistent "liberty of indifference . . . which means a negation of necessity and causes."[1]

From Philippa Foot, "Free Will as Involving Determinism," *The Philosophical Review*, LXVI, No. 4 (October, 1957), pp. 439–450.

[1] *Treatise*, bk. II, pt. III, sec. 2.

A. J. Ayer, in his essay "Freedom and Necessity"[2] was summing up such a position when he said, "from the fact that my action is causally determined . . . it does not necessarily follow that I am not free"[3] and "it is not when my action has any cause at all, but only when it has a special sort of cause, that it is reckoned not to be free."[4]

I am not here concerned with the merits of this view but only with a theory which appears more or less incidentally in the writings of those who defend it. This is the argument that so far from being incompatible with determinism, free will actually requires it. It appears briefly in Hume's *Treatise* and was set out in full in an article by R. E. Hobart.[5] P. H. Nowell Smith was expressing a similar view when he said of the idea that determinism is opposed to free will that "the clearest proof that it is mistaken or at least muddled lies in showing that I could not be free to choose what I do *unless* determinism is correct. . . . Freedom, so far from being incompatible with causality implies it."[6] Ayer has taken up a similar position, arguing that the absence of causal laws governing action "does not give the moralist what he wants. For he is anxious to show that men are capable of acting freely in order to infer that they can be morally responsible for what they do. But if it is a matter of pure chance that a man should act in one way rather than another, he may be free but he can hardly be responsible."[7]

This argument is not essential to the main thesis of those who use it; their own account of free will in such terms as the absence of *constraining* causes might be correct even though there were no inconsistencies in the suggestion put forward by their libertarian opponents. But if valid the argument would be a strong argument, disposing of the position of any-

[2] *Polemic*, no. 5 (1946) ; reprinted in his *Philosophical Essays* (London, 1954).

[3] *Philosophical Essays*, p. 278.

[4] *Ibid.*, p. 281.

[5] "Freewill as Involving Determinism," *Mind*, XLIII (1934), 1–27.

[6] "Freewill and Moral Responsibility," *Mind*, LVII (1948), 46.

[7] *Philosophical Essays*, p. 275.

one who argued both that free will required the absence of determining causes and that free will was a possibility. That the argument is not valid, and indeed that it is singularly implausible, I shall now try to show. It is, I think, surprising that it should have survived so long; this is perhaps because it has not had to bear much weight. In any case the weapons which can be used against it are ones which are in general use elsewhere.

In discussing determinism and free will it is important to be clear about the sense which is given in this context to words such as "determined" and "caused." Russell gave this account:

> The law of universal causation . . . may be enunciated as follows: There are such invariable relations between different events at the same or different times that, given the state of the whole universe throughout any finite time, however short, every previous and subsequent event can theoretically be determined as a function of the given events during that time.[8]

This seems to be the kind of determinism which worries the defender of free will, for if human action is subject to a universal law of causation of this type, there will be for any action a set of sufficient conditions which can be traced back to factors outside the control of the agent.

We cannot of course take it for granted that whenever the word "determined" or the word "cause" is used this is what is implied, and what is intended may be in no way relevant to the question of free will. For instance, an action said to be determined by the desires of the man who does it is not necessarily an action for which there is supposed to be a sufficient condition. In saying that it is determined by his desires we may mean merely that he is doing something that he wants to do, or that he is doing it for the sake of something else that he wants. There is nothing in this to suggest determinism in Russell's sense. On the whole it is wise to be suspicious of expres-

[8] "On the Notion of Cause," in *Our Knowledge of the External World* (London, 1914), p. 221.

sions such as "determined by desire" unless these have been given a clear sense, and this is particularly true of the phrase "determined by the agent's character." Philosophers often talk about actions being determined by a man's character, but it is not certain that anyone else does, or that the words are given any definite sense. One might suppose that an action was so determined if it was *in* character, for instance the generous action of a generous man; but if this is so we will not have the kind of determinism traditionally supposed to raise difficulties for a doctrine of free will. For nothing has been said to suggest that where the character trait can be predicated the action will invariably follow; it has not been supposed that a man who can truly be said to be generous never acts ungenerously even under given conditions.

Keeping the relevant sense of "determinism" in mind, we may now start to discuss the view that free will requires determinism. The first version which I shall consider is that put forward by Hobart, who suggests that an action which is not determined cannot properly be called an *action* at all, being something that happened to the agent rather than something he *did*. Hobart says, "*In proportion* as it [the action] is undetermined, it is just as if his legs should suddenly spring up and carry him off where he did not prefer to go." To see how odd this suggestion is we have only to ask when we would say that a man's legs were carrying him where he did not prefer to go. One can imagine the scene: he is sitting quietly in his chair and has said that he is going to go on reading his book; suddenly he cries, "Good heavens, I can't control my legs!" and as he moves across the room, he hangs on to the furniture or asks someone else to hold him. Here indeed his legs are carrying him where he does not want to go, but what has this to do with indeterminism, and what has the ordinary case, where he walks across the room, to do with determinism? Perhaps Hobart thinks that when a man does something meaning to do it, he does what he wants to do, and so his action is determined by his desire. But to do something meaning to do it is to do it in a certain way, not to do it as the result of the operation of a causal law. When one means to do something, one does not call out for help in preventing the movement of one's limbs; on the contrary, one is likely to stop other people from interfering, saying, "I want to do this." It is by such factors that walking across the room is distinguished from being carried off by one's legs. It is to be explained in terms of the things said and done by the agent, not in terms of some force, "the desire," present before the action was done and still less in terms of some law telling us that whenever this "desire" is found it will be followed by the action. The indeterminist has no difficulty in distinguishing an action from something that happens to the agent; he can say exactly the same as anyone else.

Nowell Smith seems to be thinking along somewhat the same lines as Hobart when he attacks C. A. Campbell for saying that free will requires indeterminism:

> The essence of Campbell's account is that the action should not be predictable from a knowledge of the agent's character. But, if this is so, can what he does be called *his* action at all? Is it not rather a *lusus naturae*, an Act of God or a miracle? If a hardened criminal, bent on robbing the poor-box, suddenly and *inexplicably* fails to do so, we should not say that he *chose* to resist or deserves *credit* for resisting the temptation; we should say, if we were religious, that he was the recipient of a sudden outpouring of Divine Grace or, if we were irreligious, that his "action" was due to chance, which is another way of saying that it was inexplicable. In either case we should refuse to use the active voice.[9]

It is hard to see why a man who does something inexplicably does not really *do* it. Let us suppose that the hardened criminal's action really is inexplicable; we can only say, "He just turned away," and not why he did so; this does not mean that he did it by accident, or unintentionally, or not of his own free will, and I see no reason for refusing to use the active voice. In any case, to explain an action is not necessarily

[9] *Ethics* (London, 1954), pp. 281–282.

to show that it could have been predicted from some fact about the agent's character—that he is weak, greedy, sentimental, and so forth. We may if we like say that an action is never *fully* explained unless it has been shown to be covered by a law which connects it to such a character trait; but then it becomes even more implausible to say that an action must be explicable if we are to admit it as something genuinely *done*. In the ordinary sense we explain the criminal's action if we say, for instance, that a particular thought came into his mind; we do not also have to find a law about the way such thoughts do come into the minds of such men.

A rather different version of this argument runs as follows. We hold responsible only a man who is a rational agent; if someone were always to do things out of the blue, without having any reason to do them, we should be inclined to count him as a lunatic, one who could not be held responsible for his actions, so that even if he *did* things he would do things for which he could not be held responsible. And is it not through being determined by motives that actions are those of a rational agent whom we can praise or blame?

It certainly would be odd to suppose that free will required the absence of motives for action. We do not of course expect that everything that the rational man does should be done with a motive; if he gets up and walks about the room he need not be doing so in order to take exercise; it is quite usual for people to do this kind of thing without any particular purpose in view, and no one is counted irrational for doing so. And yet we do expect a man to have a motive for a great number of the things that he does, and we would count anyone who constantly performed troublesome actions without a motive as irrational. So it looks as if a moral agent is a man whose actions are in general determined, if determinism is involved in "having a motive" for what he does.

What does it mean to say that someone had a motive for doing what he did? Often this particular expression means that he did it with a particular intention, so we should first say something about intentions and the sense in which they can be said to determine action. We say that a man had a certain intention in acting when he aimed at a certain thing, and "his motive for such and such" often means "his aim in doing such and such," for instance, "His motive for going to the station was to take a train to London." But where motives are intentions it is clear that they cannot be determining causes; for intending to do *x* and being ready to take the steps thought necessary to do *x* are connected not empirically but analytically. A man cannot be said to have an intention unless he is reconciled to what he believes to be the intermediate steps. We cannot speak as if the intention were something which could be determined first, and "being ready to take the necessary steps" were a second stage following on the first.

It might be objected that this does not cover the case of "doing *y* because one wants *x*" where "wanting *x*" does not imply trying to get *x*. In one sense of "want" it is possible to say, "He wants *x*" without knowing whether he is prepared to take steps to get it. (One might, for instance, want to go to London but not be prepared to spend the money to get there.) So that *wanting* seems here to be a separate condition, which might in certain cases be connected by an empirical law to the adoption of particular courses of action. Certainly wanting is not an event, but one gets rid of wanting as a determining factor too easily if one merely says that desires are not causes because they are not occurrences.

We say "He wants" in this sense where he would adopt certain policies *if* there were no reasons for not doing so. We can say, "He wants to get to London," even when he is not prepared to take the necessary steps to get to London, provided he can say, "Trains are too expensive," or "Hitchhiking is too uncomfortable." If we offered him a spare railway ticket or otherwise disposed of his reasons against going, and he still did not go, we would have to say, "He didn't really want to go after all." So wanting in this sense is being prepared to act under certain conditions, though not being prepared to act under the given conditions. It is a description which could be applied to a man before we knew whether he was ready to act in a given situation, and it seems that there might then be a causal relation between the wanting and the acting where the latter took place. This is quite true; there could be a law to the effect that when the description "He wants x" applied at t_1, the description "He is taking the necessary steps to get x" applied at t_2. It would be possible to say this without making a mistake about what it is to *want* and inventing a hidden condition of body or mind. One could say, "Wanting in this sense just is being prepared to act under some conditions," and still maintain that there could be an empirical law connecting wanting with acting under a particular set of conditions. The mistake lies not in the idea that such laws are *possible* but in the thought that there is a reference to them in the statement that a man did one thing because he wanted something else.

So far we have been dealing only with cases in which a question about a motive was answered by specifying something aimed at or wanted. Now we should turn to the cases in which the motive is said to be kindness, vanity, ambition, meanness, jealousy, and so on, to see whether determinism is involved.

It is easy to show that a motive is not a cause in Russell's sense, for it is clearly not an antecedent cause. Professor Gilbert Ryle has pointed out that a man who acts out of vanity is not a man who had a feeling of vanity immediately before he acted, and if it is objected that the vanity which preceded the action need not have manifested itself in a feeling, one may ask what else *would* count as the vanity which was causing him to act. A man's motives are not given by what was happening to him immediately before he started to act. Nor do we discover some independent condition cotemporaneous with the action and a law linking the two, for again there is nothing which would count as vanity except the tendency to do this kind of thing.

So much is implied in what Ryle says about acting out of vanity, but his own account of what it is to do so still uses something which is objectionably like a causal model. The analogy which he thinks apt is that between saying a man acted out of vanity and saying a piece of glass broke because it was brittle: "To explain an act as done from a certain motive is not analogous to saying that the glass broke because a stone hit it, but to the quite different type of statement that the glass broke, when the stone hit it, because the glass was brittle."[10] The positive part of this statement seems to me mistaken. Acting out of vanity is not so closely connected with being vain as Ryle must suppose it to be. Let us suppose that his account of what it is to be vain is entirely correct; to say that a man is vain is to say that he tends to behave in certain ways, to feel aggrieved in particular situations, and so on.[11] It does not follow that ascribing vanity as a motive for an action is bringing this action under the "lawlike" proposition that the agent is a man who tends to do these things. For it makes sense to say that a man acts out of vanity on a particular occasion although he is not in general vain, or even vain about this kind of thing. It cannot therefore be true that when we speak of an agent's motive for a particular action we are explaining it in terms of his character, as Ryle suggests; we are not saying "he *would* do that." It is of course possible to give a motive *and* to say that the agent has the character trait concerned, but the latter cannot be included in an account of what it is to assign a motive to a particular action.

The explanation of why Ryle says what he does seems to lie in the fact that he has taken a false example of explaining an action by giving a motive. He considers as his example the explanation, "He boasted because he is vain," which is not in fact an explanation of the right type; considered as a statement assigning a motive to a particular action it would be uninformative, for except in very special cases *boasting is* acting out of vanity. It is not surprising that this particular sentence has a different function—that of relating this act of vanity to the character trait. What Ryle says about the example is correct, but it is not an example of the kind of thing he is trying to describe.

It might seem as if we could reformulate the theory to

[10] *Concept of Mind* (London, 1949), pp. 86–87.
[11] *Ibid.*, p. 86.

meet the objection about the man who acts out of vanity on one occasion by saying that a man's acting out of vanity is like glass breaking because of a brittleness which could be temporary. "He acted out of vanity" would then be explained as meaning that at that particular time he tended to react in the ways described by Ryle. (If he finds a chance of securing the admiration and envy of others, he does whatever he thinks will produce this admiration and envy.) This is wrong because, whereas glass which is even temporarily brittle has all the reactions which go by this name, a man who is temporarily acting out of vanity is not liable to do other things of this kind. To find concepts which this model would fit one must turn to such descriptions as "a boastful mood," "a savage frame of mind," or "a fit of bad temper."

Assigning a motive to an action is not bringing it under any law; it is rather saying something about the kind of action it was, the direction in which it was tending, or what it was done *as*. A possible comparison would be with the explanation of a movement in a dance which consisted in saying what was being danced. Often in diagnosing motives we should look to purposes—to what the action was done for. This we should discover if we found out what the agent was prepared to go without and what he insisted on having; the fact that visitors are made to admire a garden even in the rain is strong evidence that they were invited out of vanity rather than kindness. In other cases finding the motive will be better described as finding what was being done—finding, for instance, that someone was *taking revenge*. We should take it that a man's motive was revenge if we discovered that he was intentionally harming someone and that his doing so was conditional on his believing that that person had injured him. In the same way we should take it that someone was acting out of gratitude if he (1) intended to confer a benefit and (2) saw this as called for by a past kindness. The fact that it is only the character of the particular action which is involved shows how far we are from anything which could involve motives as determining causes.

We have now considered two suggestions: (1) that an undetermined action would not be one which could properly be attributed to an agent as something that he *did* and (2) that an undetermined action would not be the action of a *rational* agent. A third version, the one put forward by Hume, suggests that an undetermined action would be one for which it would be impossible to praise or blame, punish or reward a man, because it would be connected with nothing permanent in his nature.

> 'Tis only [Hume says] upon the principles of necessity, that a person acquires any merit or demerit from his actions. . . . Actions are by their very nature temporary and perishing; and where they proceed not from some cause in the characters and disposition of the person, who perform'd them, they infix not themselves upon him, and can neither redound to his honour, if good, nor infamy, if evil. The action in itself may be blameable. . . . But the person is not responsible for it; and as it proceeded from nothing in him, that is durable and constant, and leaves nothing of that nature behind it, 'tis impossible he can, upon its account, become the object of punishment or vengeance.[12]

Hume is surely wrong in saying that we could not praise or blame, punish or reward, a person in whose character there was nothing "permanent or durable." As he was the first to point out, we do not need any *unchanging* element in order to say that a person is the same person throughout a period of time, and our concept of merit is framed to fit our concept of personal identity. We honor people as well as nations for what they have done in the past and do not consider what has been done merely as an indication of what may be expected in the future. Moreover, it is perfectly rational to punish people for what they have done, even if there is no reason to think that they would be likely to do it again. The argument that it will be a different *me* who will be beaten tomorrow carries no weight, for "different" or not the back which will be beaten is the one about which I am concerned today. So we have no

[12] *Treatise*, bk. II, pt. III, sec. 2.

reason to invent something durable and constant underlying the actions which we punish or reward. And it is not in fact our practice to pick out for praise or blame only those actions for which something of the kind can be found. It would be possible, of course, that we should do this, punishing the cruel action of the cruel man but not that of one usually kind. But even in such a situation there would be no argument against the man who said that moral responsibility depended upon indeterminism; for a motive is not a determining cause, nor is an habitual motive. If we say that a man constantly acts out of cruelty, we no more say that his actions are determined than if we say that he acts out of cruelty on a particular occasion. There could of course be a law to the effect that no one who has been cruel for thirty years can turn to kindness after that, and this would throw responsibility back from the later to the earlier acts. But it is clear that this is a special assumption in no way involved in the statement that cruelty is a "durable and constant" element in someone's character.

I have already mentioned Ayer's argument that moral responsibility cannot be defended on the basis of indeterminism and will now consider his version in detail. Ayer says that the absence of a cause will not give the moralist what he wants, because "if it is a matter of pure chance that a man should act in one way rather than another, he may be free but he can hardly be responsible."[13] To the suggestion that "my actions are the result of my own free choice," Ayer will reply with a question about how I came to make my choice:

> Either it is an accident that I choose to act as I do or it is not. If it is an accident, then it is merely a matter of chance that I did not choose otherwise; and if it is merely a matter of chance that I did not choose otherwise, it is surely irrational to hold me morally responsible for choosing as I did. But if it is not an accident that I chose to do one thing rather than another, then presumably there is some causal explanation of my choice: and in that case we are led back to determinism.[14]

[13] *Philosophical Essays*, p. 275.
[14] *Ibid.*

The "presumably" seems to be the weak link in the argument, which assumes a straightforward opposition between causality and chance that does not in general exist. It is not at all clear that when actions or choices are called "chance" or "accidental" this has anything to do with the absence of causes, and if it has not we will not be saying that they are in the ordinary sense a matter of chance if we say that they are undetermined.

When should we say that it was a matter of chance that a man did what he did? A typical example would be the case in which a man killed someone with a bullet which glanced off some object in a totally unforseeable way; here he could disclaim responsibility for the act. But in this instance, and that of something done "by accident," we are dealing with what is done unintentionally, and this is not the case which Ayer has in mind. We may turn, as he does, to the actions which could be said to have been "chosen" and ask how the words "chance" and "accident" apply to choices. Ayer says, "Either it is an accident that I choose to act as I do, or it is not." The notion of choosing by accident to do something is on the face of it puzzling; for usually choosing to do something is opposed to doing it by accident. What does it mean to say that the choice itself was accidental? The only application I can think of for the words "I chose by accident" is in a case such as the following. I choose a firm with which to have dealings without meaning to pick on one run by an international crook. I can now rebut the charge of *choosing a firm run by an international crook* by saying that I chose it by accident. I cannot be held responsible for this but only for any carelessness which may have been involved. But this is because the relevant action —the one with which I am being charged—was unintentional; it is for this reason and not because my action was uncaused that I can rebut the charge. Nothing is said about my action being uncaused, and if it were, this could not be argued on my behalf; the absence of causes would not give me the same right to make the excuse.

Nor does it make any difference if we substitute "chance" for "accident." If I say that it was a matter of chance that I chose to do something, I rebut the suggestion that I chose it for this reason or for that, and this can be a plea against an accusation which has to do with my reasons. But I do not imply that there was no reason for my doing what I did, and I say nothing whatsoever about my choice being undetermined. If we use "chance" and "accident" as Ayer wants to use them, to signify the absence of causes, we shall have moved over to a totally different sense of the words, and "I chose it by chance" can no longer be used to disclaim responsibility.

3

LIBERTARIANISM

INTRODUCTION

The selections of Campbell and Broad are, to a certain extent, mutually supporting. After Campbell examines critically Schlick's analysis of responsibility, he undertakes to refute compatibilism. Both Campbell and Broad agree with reconciliationists that the conception of freedom which is relevant to moral responsibility is a conception according to which a person is free if, and only if, he could have acted differently. The two then agree that no analyses which are compatible with determinism (the various hypothetical analyses) are adequate. Campbell argues that the key question in cases in which one is considering the assignment of moral responsibility is, "Could the person have *chosen* otherwise?" Moreover, Campbell does not consider as damaging evidence from "ordinary usage" that people do not use the expression "could have acted differently" in such a way as to entail that the act is undetermined. What the "ordinary man" means and what a reflective, sophisticated person might mean are different and it is the latter's proposition which is to the point.

Campbell and Broad part ways, however, on the intelligibility of the requirement for freedom in addition to contra-causality. On the assumption that explanations of action in terms of character are deterministic, Campbell must, since he considers objections of the sort raised by Hobart to be germane, provide sense for the notion of an act which is the self's, but not the character's. It is important to see exactly what Campbell's introspective analysis of moral conflict accomplishes in this context. He wants to establish two points: (1) We believe in these cases that we can act either way (i.e., acquiesce to character or rise to duty). This is a categorical "can," one which is incompatible with determinism. We might, therefore, be wrong. (2) We believe in these cases that our selves are making the decision in a sense in which "self" is not replaceable by "character." Here, too, we might be wrong. But we at least understand what it is for an act to be ours, but not our character's.

Broad is sympathetic in believing that something like Campbell's libertarianism is necessary for moral responsibility; but he finds libertarianism an impossible position. Before one assesses Broad's critique, one must be sure that the conception of libertarianism he talks about is the same as that of Campbell's. This is not easy to determine for Campbell only gives us a brief, introspective report. Must Campbell's self be conceived as a continuant; i.e., as that which undergoes states and in which events occur? If so, can Campbell reply to Broad's objection that the total cause of an event must contain an event as a cause factor by conceiving of the self, which is not an event, as only a partial cause? (My heart, a continuant, is not an event, but its beatings are.) After all, character does admittedly have a bearing on the self's decision.

Mill denies that we do believe that we categorically could have chosen otherwise. If we examine matters closely, we always find a suppressed "if" clause, thereby rendering our belief compatible with determinism. But with formulations like Mill's, serious problems arise. For example, in considering that I might have chosen a red rather than a blue car, I might also be considering, contrary to fact, that I preferred red to blue. But unless my color preference is specifiable independently of the actual color choice, I am not providing a causal explanation of my choice, but rather, redescribing it in terms of the language of preference. And the apparently hypothetical "I could have chosen red if I had preferred it" turns out to mean no more than the categorical "I could have chosen red." Thus, Mill must show that in considering what could have been, we change in imagination some distinct antecedent. Mill's utilitarian account of responsibility is also of interest and should be considered in the light of the Schlick-Campbell debate on responsibility.

Whereas Campbell would be content to see freedom resident only in the limited sphere of moral conflict, Sartre extends it to the whole sphere of (intentional) action. Sartre's libertarianism is extreme and he does not shrink, as the final pages show, from the conception of moral responsibility he feels driven to by this set of views.

One of Sartre's basic criticisms of determinism merits a brief examination here. There is always a cause for some action, he says; but the cause only operates via our free concurrence. Jones will see his situation as "intolerable" and do something about it; whereas Smith will not view the same situation in this way and, therefore, do nothing. But why, one may ask, cannot this difference be accounted for by a determinist? The reason Sartre gives is this: In order for a person to have a purpose for acting, he must see a lack of some sort (wrong, inefficient, intolerable, etc.) in things. But any actual state of affairs is completely describable without reference to such notions. For example, one can completely describe Jones's salary as "$40 per week," and the fact that Jones considers this insufficient tells us no more about his salary. It may be relevant to note that his rent is $80 per month and his children are thin, etc.; but, again, all of this is fully describable without reference to concepts such as "insufficient." Let us call Jones's psychological state when he reflects upon his lot as his "consciousness seeing it as lacking." Sartre's claim is that this state cannot be sufficiently accounted for by earlier states and events since the latter are completely describable without reference to notions such as "lack" and "insufficiency." This would also be true of any action taken by Jones as a result of his "perception of a lack." Appeal to antecedent psychological states is of no use for they too are actual and completely describable without the use of negative terminology.

In the first place, the event described by "consciousness

seeing the situation as lacking in some way" is a real, actual, positive event. Hence, a person who believes that it is determined is not saddled with the absurd view that actual events cause nonactual or unreal events (whatever they may be). Secondly, one wonders whether Sartre is not confusing logical with causal relationships. I can completely describe the motion of the cue ball without referring to the motion of the eight ball although the former may cause the latter. Analogously, the fact that I can describe antecedent events without using negative terminology does not entail that these events do not cause other events which are so described.

It would perhaps be better to place Sartre in the next chapter as it certainly sounds as if he is rejecting the possibility that determinism is applicable to human action on the basis of analyses of the concepts of action and determinism. But we shall follow tradition and call him a "libertarian."

IS "FREEWILL" A PSEUDO-PROBLEM?

C. A. CAMPBELL

. . .

III

Here, then, in substance is Schlick's theory. Let us now examine it.

In the first place, it is surely quite unplausible to suggest that the common assumption that moral freedom postulates some breach of causal continuity arises from a confusion of two different types of law. Schlick's distinction between descriptive and prescriptive law is, of course, sound. It was no doubt worth pointing out, too, that descriptive laws cannot be said to compel human behaviour in the same way as prescriptive laws do. But it seems to me evident that the usual reason why it is held

From C. A. Campbell, "Is 'Freewill' a Pseudo-Problem?" *Mind*, LX, No. 240 (October, 1951), pp. 446–465.

that moral freedom implies some breach of causal continuity, is not a belief that causal laws 'compel' as civil laws 'compel,' but simply the belief that the admission of unbroken causal continuity entails a *further* admission which is directly incompatible with moral responsibility; *viz.* the admission that no man could have acted otherwise than he in fact did. Now it may, of course, be an error thus to assume that a man is not morally responsible for an act, a fit subject for moral praise and blame in respect of it, unless he could have acted otherwise than he did. Or, if *this* is not an error, it may still be an error to assume that a man could not have acted otherwise than he did, in the sense of the phrase that is crucial for moral responsibility, without there occurring some breach of causal continuity. Into these matters we shall have to enter very fully at a later stage. But the relevant point at the moment is that these (not *prima facie* absurd) assumptions about the conditions of moral responsibility have very commonly, indeed normally, been made, and that they are entirely adequate to explain why the problem of Free Will finds its usual formulation in terms of partial exemption from causal law. Schlick's distinction between prescriptive and descriptive laws has no bearing at all upon the truth or falsity of these assumptions. Yet if these assumptions are accepted, it is (I suggest) really inevitable that the Free Will problem should be formulated in the way to which Schlick takes exception. Recognition of the distinction upon which Schlick and his followers lay so much stress can make not a jot of difference.

As we have seen, however, Schlick does later proceed to the much more important business of disputing these common assumptions about the conditions of moral responsibility. He offers us an analysis of moral responsibility which flatly contradicts these assumptions; an analysis according to which the only freedom demanded by morality is a freedom which is compatible with Determinism. If this analysis can be sustained, there is certainly no problem of 'Free Will' in the traditional sense.

But it seems a simple matter to show that Schlick's analysis is untenable. Let us test it by Schlick's own claim that it gives us what we mean by 'moral responsibility' in ordinary linguistic usage.

We do not ordinarily consider the lower animals to be morally responsible. But *ought* we not to do so if Schlick is right about what we mean by moral responsibility? It is quite possible, by punishing the dog who absconds with the succulent chops designed for its master's luncheon, favourably to influence its motives in respect of its future behaviour in like circumstances. If moral responsibility is to be linked with punishment as Schlick links it, and punishment conceived as a form of education, we should surely hold the dog morally responsible? The plain fact, of course, is that we don't. We don't, because we suppose that the dog 'couldn't help it': that its action (unlike what we usually believe to be true of human beings) was simply a link in a continuous chain of causes and effects. In other words, we do commonly demand the contra-causal sort of freedom as a condition of moral responsibility.

Again, we do ordinarily consider it proper, in certain circumstances, to speak of a person no longer living as morally responsible for some present situation. But *ought* we to do so if we accept Schlick's essentially 'forward-looking' interpretation of punishment and responsibility? Clearly we cannot now favourably affect the dead man's motives. No doubt they could *at one time* have been favourably affected. But that cannot be relevant to our judgment of responsibility if, as Schlick insists, the question of who is responsible 'is a matter only of knowing who is to be punished or rewarded.' Indeed he expressly tells us, as we saw earlier, that in asking this question we are not concerned with a 'great-grand-parent' who may have been the 'original instigator,' because, for one reason, this 'remote cause' is 'out of reach.' We cannot bring the appropriate educative influence to bear upon it. But the plain fact, of course, is that we do frequently assign moral responsibility for present situations to persons who have long been inaccessible to any punitive action on our part. And Schlick's position is still more paradoxical in respect of our apportionment of responsibility for occurrences in the distant past. Since in these cases there is no agent whatsoever whom we can favourably influence by punishment, the question of moral responsibility here should have no meaning for us. But of course it has. Historical writings are studded with examples.

Possibly the criticism just made may seem to some to result from taking Schlick's analysis too much *au pied de la lettre*. The absurd consequences deduced, it may be said, would not follow if we interpreted Schlick as meaning that a man is morally responsible where his motive is such as can *in principle* be favourably affected by reward or punishment—whether or not we who pass the judgment are in a position to take such action. But with every desire to be fair to Schlick, I cannot see how he could accept this modification and still retain the essence of his theory. For the essence of his theory seems to be that moral responsibility has its whole meaning and importance for us in relation to our potential control of future conduct in the interests of society. (I agree that it is hard to believe that anybody *really* thinks this. But it is perhaps less hard to believe to-day than it has ever been before in the history of modern ethics.)

Again, we ordinarily consider that, in certain circumstances, the *degree* of a man's moral responsibility for an act is affected by considerations of his inherited nature, or of his environment, or of both. It is our normal habit to 'make allowances' (as we say) when we have reason to believe that a malefactor had a vicious heredity, or was nurtured in his formative years in a harmful environment. We say in such cases 'Poor chap, he is more to be pitied than blamed. We could scarcely expect him to behave like a decent citizen with *his* parentage or upbringing.' But this extremely common sort of judgment has no point at all if we mean by normal responsibility what Schlick says that we mean. On *that* meaning the degree of a man's moral responsibility must presumably be dependent upon the degree to which we can favourably affect his future motives, which is quite another matter. Now there is no reason to believe that the motives of a man with a bad heredity or a bad upbringing are either less or more subject to educative influence than those of his more fortunate fellows. Yet it is plain matter of fact that we do commonly consider the degree of a man's moral responsibility to be affected by these two factors.

A final point. The extremity of paradox in Schlick's identification of the question 'Who is morally blameworthy?' with the question 'Who is to be punished?' is apt to be partially concealed from us just because it is our normal habit to include in the meaning of 'punishment' an element of 'requital for moral transgression' which Schlick expressly denies to it. On that account we commonly think of 'punishment,' in its strict sense, as implying moral blameworthiness in the person punished. But if we remember to mean by punishment what Schlick means by it, a purely 'educative measure,' with no retributive ingredients, his identification of the two questions loses such plausibility as it might otherwise have. For clearly we often think it proper to 'punish' a person, in *Schlick's* sense, where we are not at all prepared to say that the person is morally blameworthy. We may even think him morally commendable. A case in point would be the unmistakably sincere but muddle-headed person who at the cost of great suffering to himself steadfastly pursues as his 'duty' a course which, in our judgment is fraught with danger to the common weal. We should most of us feel entitled, in the public interest, to bring such action to bear upon the man's motives as might induce him to refrain in future from his socially injurious behavior: in other words, to inflict upon him what Schlick would call 'punishment.' But we should most of us feel perfectly clear that in so 'punishing' this misguided citizen we are not proclaiming his moral blameworthiness or moral wickedness.

Adopting Schlick's own criterion, then, looking simply 'to the manner in which the concept is used,'[1] we seem bound to admit that constantly people do assign moral responsibility where Schlick's theory says they shouldn't, don't assign moral

[1] Moritz Schlick, "When Is a Man Responsible?" In *Problems of Ethics*, translated by David Rynin. New York: Prentice-Hall, 1939, Ch. VII, Section 5, p. 151.

responsibility where Schlick's theory says they should, and assign degrees of moral responsibility where on Schlick's theory there should be no difference in degree. I think we may reasonably conclude that Schlick's account of what we mean by moral responsibility breaks down.

The rebuttal of Schlick's arguments, however, will not suffice of itself to refute the pseudo-problem theory. The indebtedness to Schlick of most later advocates of the theory may be conceded; but certainly it does not comprehend all of significance that they have to say on the problem. There are recent analyses of the conditions of moral responsibility containing sufficient new matter, or sufficient old matter in a more precise and telling form, to require of us now something of a fresh start. In the section which follows I propose to consider some representative samples of these analyses—all of which, of course, are designed to show that the freedom which moral responsibility implies is not in fact a contra-causal type of freedom.

But before reopening the general question of the nature and conditions of moral responsibility there is a *caveat* which it seems to me worth while to enter. The difficulties in the way of a clear answer are not slight; but they are apt to seem a good deal more formidable than they really are because of a common tendency to consider in unduly close association two distinct questions: the question 'Is a contra-causal type of freedom implied by moral responsibility?' and the question 'Does a contra-causal type of freedom anywhere exist?' It seems to me that many philosophers (and I suspect that Moritz Schlick is among them) begin their enquiry with so firm a conviction that the contra-causal sort of freedom nowhere exists, that they find it hard to take very seriously the possibility that it is *this* sort of freedom that moral responsibility implies. For they are loath to abandon the commonsense belief that moral responsibility itself is something real. The implicit reasoning I take to be this. Moral responsibility is real. If moral responsibility is real, the freedom implied in it must be a fact. But contra-causal freedom is not a fact. Therefore contra-causal freedom is not the freedom implied in moral responsibility. I think we should be on our guard against allowing this or some similar train of reasoning (whose premises, after all, are far from indubitable) to seduce us into distorting what we actually find when we set about a direct analysis of moral responsibility and its conditions.

IV

The pseudo-problem theorists usually, and naturally, develop their analysis of moral responsibility by way of contrast with a view which, while it has enjoyed a good deal of philosophic support, I can perhaps best describe as the common view. It will be well to remind ourselves, therefore, of the main features of this view.

So far as the *meaning*, as distinct from the *conditions*, of moral responsibility is concerned, the common view is very simple. If we ask ourselves whether a certain person is morally responsible for a given act (or it may be just 'in general'), what we are considering, it would be said, is whether or not that person is a fit subject upon whom to pass moral judgment; whether he can fittingly be deemed morally good or bad, morally praiseworthy or blameworthy. This does not take us any great way: but (*pace* Schlick) so far as it goes it does not seem to me seriously disputable. The really interesting and controversial question is about the *conditions* of moral responsibility, and in particular the question whether freedom of a contra-causal kind is among these conditions.

The answer of the common man to the latter question is that it most certainly *is* among the conditions. Why does he feel so sure about this? Not, I argued earlier, because the common man supposes that causal law exercises 'compulsion' in the sense that prescriptive laws do, but simply because he does not see how a person can be deemed morally praiseworthy or blameworthy in respect of an act which he could not help performing. From the stand-point of moral praise and blame, he would say—though not necessarily from other stand-points—it is a matter of indifference whether it is by reason of some external constraint or by reason of his own given nature that the man could not help doing what he did. It is quite enough to make moral praise and blame futile that in either case there were no genuine alternatives, no open possibilities, before the man when he acted. He could not have acted otherwise than he did. And the common man might not unreasonably go on to stress the fact that we all, even if we are linguistic philosophers, do in our actual practice of moral judgment appear to accept the common view. He might insist upon the point alluded to earlier in this paper, that we do all, in passing moral censure, 'make allowances' for influences in a man's hereditary nature or environmental circumstances which we regard as having made it more than ordinarily difficult for him to act otherwise than he did: the implication being that if we supposed that the man's heredity and environment made it not merely very *difficult* but actually *impossible* for him to act otherwise than he did, we could not properly assign moral blame to him at all.

Let us put the argument implicit in the common view a little more sharply. The moral 'ought' implies 'can.' If we say that *A* morally ought to have done *X*, we imply that in our opinion, he could have done *X*. But we assign moral blame to a man only for failing to do what we think he morally ought to have done. Hence if we morally blame *A* for not having done *X*, we imply that he could have done *X* even though in fact he did not. In other words, we imply that *A* could have acted otherwise than he did. And that means that we imply, as a necessary condition of a man's being morally blameworthy, that he enjoyed a freedom of a kind not compatible with unbroken causal continuity.

V

Now what is it that is supposed to be wrong with this simple piece of argument?—For, of course, it must be rejected by all these philosophers who tell us that the traditional problem of Free Will is a mere pseudo-problem. The argument looks as though it were doing little more than reading off necessary implications of the fundamental categories of our moral thinking. One's inclination is to ask 'If one is to think morally at all, how else than this *can* we think?'.

In point of fact, there is pretty general agreement among the contemporary critics as to what is wrong with the argument. Their answer in general terms is as follows. No doubt *A*'s moral responsibility does imply that he could have acted otherwise. But this expression 'could have acted otherwise' stands in dire need of analysis. When we analyse it, we find that it is not, as is so often supposed, simple and unambiguous, and we find that in *some* at least of its possible meanings it implies *no* breach of causal continuity between character and conduct. Having got this clear, we can further discern that only in one of these *latter* meanings is there any compulsion upon our moral thinking to assert that if *A* is morally blameworthy for an act, *A* 'could have acted otherwise than he did.' It follows that, contrary to common belief, our moral thinking does *not* require us to posit a contra-causal freedom as a condition of moral responsibility.

So much of importance obviously turns upon the validity or otherwise of this line of criticism that we must examine it in some detail and with express regard to the *ipsissima verba* of the critics.

In the course of a recent article in *Mind*,[2] entitled 'Free Will and Moral Responsibility,' Mr. Nowell Smith (having earlier affirmed his belief that 'the traditional problem has been solved') explains very concisely the nature of the confusion which, as he thinks, has led to the demand for a contra-causal freedom. He begins by frankly recognising that "It is evident that one of the necessary conditions of moral action is that the agent 'could have acted otherwise' " and he adds "it is to this fact that the Libertarian is drawing attention."[3] Then, after showing (unexceptionably, I think) how the relationship of 'ought' to 'can' warrants the proposition which he has accepted as evident, and how it induces the Libertarian to assert the existence of action that is 'uncaused,' he proceeds to point out, in a crucial passage, the nature of the Libertarian's error:

[2] January, 1948.
[3] *Ibid.*, p. 49.

> The fallacy in the argument (he contends) lies in supposing that when we say 'A could have acted otherwise' we mean that A, *being what he was and being placed in the circumstances in which he was placed*, could have done something other than what he did. But in fact we never do mean this.[4]

What then *do* we mean here by '*A* could have acted otherwise'? Mr. Nowell Smith does not tell us in so many words, but the passage I have quoted leaves little doubt how he would answer. What we really mean by the expression, he implies, is not a *categorical* but a *hypothetical* proposition. We mean '*A* could have acted otherwise, *if he did not happen to be what he in fact was*, or *if he were placed in circumstances other than those in which he was in fact placed*.' Now, *these* propositions, it is easy to see, are in no way incompatible with acceptance of the causal principle in its full rigour. Accordingly the claim that our fundamental moral thinking obliges us to assert a contra-causal freedom as a condition of moral responsibility is disproved.

Such is the 'analytical solution' of our problem offered (with obvious confidence) by one able philosopher of to-day, and entirely representative of the views of many other able philosophers. Yet I make bold to say that its falsity stares one in the face. It seems perfectly plain that the hypothetical propositions which Mr. Nowell Smith proposes to substitute for the categorical proposition cannot express 'what we really mean' in this context by '*A* could have acted otherwise,' for the simple reason that these hypothetical propositions have no bearing whatsoever upon the question of the moral responsibility of *A*. And it is *A* whose moral responsibility we are talking about—a definite person *A* with a definitive character and in a definitive set of circumstances. What conceivable significance could it have for our attitude to *A*'s responsibility to know that someone with a *different* character (or *A* with a different character, if that collocation of words has any meaning), or *A* in a different set of circumstances from those in which *A* as we are concerned

[4] *Ibid.*, p. 49.

with him was in fact placed, 'could have acted otherwise'? No doubt this supposititious being *could* have acted otherwise than the definitive person *A* acted. But the point is that where we are reflecting, as we are supposed in this context to be reflecting, upon the question of *A*'s moral responsibility, our interest in this suppositious being is precisely *nil*.

The two hypothetical propositions suggested in Mr. Nowell Smith's account of the matter do not, however, exhaust the speculations that have been made along these lines. Another very common suggestion by the analysts is that what we really mean by '*A* could have acted otherwise' is '*A* could have acted otherwise *if he had willed, or chosen, otherwise*.' This was among the suggestions offered by G. E. Moore in the well-known chapter on Free Will in his *Ethics*. It is, I think, the suggestion he most strongly favoured: though it is fair to add that neither about this nor about any other of his suggestions is Moore in the least dogmatic. He does claim, for, I think, convincing reasons, that "we *very often* mean by 'could' merely 'would, *if* so-and-so had chosen.' "[5] And he concludes "I must confess that I cannot feel certain that this may not be all that we usually mean and understand by the assertion that we have Free Will."[6]

This third hypothetical proposition appears to enjoy also the support of Mr. C. L. Stevenson. Mr. Stevenson begins the chapter of *Ethics and Language* entitled 'Avoidability-Indeterminism' with the now familiar pronouncement of his School that 'controversy about freedom and determinism of the will . . . presents no permanent difficulty to ethics, being largely a product of confusions.' A major confusion (if I understand him rightly) he takes to lie in the meaning of the term 'avoidable,' when we say '*A*'s action was avoidable'—or, I presume, *A* could have acted otherwise.' He himself offers the following definition of 'avoidable'—" '*A*'s action was avoidable' has the meaning of 'If *A* had made a certain choice, which in fact he did not make, his action would not have occurred.' "[7] This I

[5] *Ethics*. London: Oxford University Press, 1912, p. 212.
[6] *Ibid.*, p. 217.
[7] *Ethics and Language*. New Haven: Yale University Press, 1944, p. 298.

think we may regard as in substance identical with the suggestion that what we really mean by '*A* could have acted otherwise' is '*A* could have acted otherwise *if* he had chosen (or willed) otherwise.' For clarity's sake we shall here keep to this earlier formulation. In either formulation the special significance of the third hypothetical proposition, as of the two hypothetical propositions already considered, is that it is compatible with strict determinism. If this be indeed all that we mean by the 'freedom' that conditions moral responsibility, then those philosophers are certainly wrong who hold that moral freedom is of the contra-causal type.

Now this third hypothetical proposition does at least possess the merit, not shared by its predecessors, of having a real relevance to the question of moral responsibility. If, *e.g.*, *A* had promised to meet us at 2 P.M., and he chanced to break his leg at 1 P.M., we should not blame him for his failure to discharge his promise. For we should be satisfied that he *could not* have acted otherwise, even if he had so chosen; or *could not*, at any rate, in a way which would have enabled him to meet us at 2 P.M. The freedom to translate one's choice into action, which we saw earlier is for Schlick the *only* freedom required for moral responsibility, is without doubt *one* of the conditions of moral responsibility.

But it seems easy to show that this third hypothetical proposition does not exhaust what we mean, and *some*times is not even *part* of what we mean, by the expression 'could have acted otherwise' in its moral context. Thus it can hardly be even part of what we mean in the case of that class of wrong actions (and it is a large class) concerning which there is really no question whether the agent could have acted otherwise, *if* he had chosen otherwise. Take lying, for example. Only in some very abnormal situation could it occur to one to doubt whether *A*, whose power of speech was evinced by his telling a lie, was in a position to tell what he took to be the truth *if* he had so chosen. Of *course* he was. Yet it still makes good sense for one's moral thinking to ask whether *A*, when lying, 'could have acted otherwise': and we still require an affirmative answer to this question if *A*'s moral blameworthiness is to be established. It seems apparent, therefore, that in this class of cases at any rate one does *not* mean by '*A* could have acted otherwise,' '*A* could have acted otherwise *if* he had so chosen.'

What then *does* one mean in this class of cases by '*A* could have acted otherwise'? I submit that the expression is taken in its simple, categorical meaning, without any suppressed 'if' clause to qualify it. Or perhaps, in order to keep before us the important truth that it is only as expressions of *will* or *choice* that acts are of moral import, it might be better to say that a condition of *A*'s moral responsibility is that he could have *chosen* otherwise. We saw that there is no real question whether *A* who told a lie could have acted otherwise *if* he had chosen otherwise. But there is a very real question, at least for any person who approaches the question of moral responsibility at a tolerably advanced level of reflexion, about whether *A* could have *chosen* otherwise. Such a person will doubtless be acquainted with the claims advanced in some quarters that causal law operates universally: or/and with the theories of some philosophies that the universe is throughout the expression of a single supreme principle; or/and with the doctrines of some theologians that the world is created, sustained and governed by an Omniscient and Omnipotent Being. Very understandably such world-views awaken in him doubts about the validity of his first, easy, instinctive assumption that there are genuinely open possibilities before a man at the moment of moral choice. It thus becomes for him a real question whether a man could have chosen otherwise than he actually did, and, in consequence, whether man's moral responsibility is really defensible. For how can a man be morally responsible, he asks himself, if his choices, like all other events in the universe, could not have been otherwise than they in fact were? It is precisely against the background of world-views such as these that for reflective people the problem of moral responsibility normally arises.

Furthermore, to the man who has attained this level of reflexion, it will in *no* class of cases be a sufficient condition of moral responsibility for an act that one could have acted otherwise *if* one had chosen otherwise—not even in these cases where there *was* some possibility of the operation of 'external constraint.' In these cases he will, indeed, expressly recognise freedom from external constraint as a *necessary condition,* but not as a *sufficient* condition. For he will be aware that, even granted *this* freedom, it is still conceivable that the agent had no freedom to choose otherwise than he did, and he will therefore require that the latter sort of freedom be added if moral responsibility for the act is to be established.

I have been contending that, for persons at a *tolerably advanced level of reflexion,* '*A* could have acted otherwise,' as a condition of *A*'s moral responsibility, means '*A* could have chosen otherwise.' The qualification italicised is of some importance. The unreflective or unsophisticated person, the ordinary 'man in the street,' who does not know or much care what scientists and theologians and philosophers have said about the world, sees well enough that *A* is morally responsible only if he could have acted otherwise, but in his intellectual innocence he will, very probably, envisage nothing capable of preventing *A* from having acted otherwise except some material impediment —like the broken leg in the example above. Accordingly, for the unreflective person, '*A* could have acted otherwise,' as a condition of moral responsibility, *is* apt to mean no more than '*A* could have acted otherwise *if* he had so chosen.'

It would appear, then, that the view now favoured by many philosophers, that the freedom required for moral responsibility is merely freedom from external constraint, is a view which they share only with the less reflective type of layman. Yet it should be plain that on a matter of this sort the view of the unreflective person is of little value by comparison with the view of the reflective person. There are some contexts, no doubt, in which lack of sophistication is an asset. But this is not one of them. The question at issue here is as to the kind of impediments which might have prevented a man from acting otherwise than he in fact did: and on this question knowledge and reflexion are surely prerequisites of any answer that is worth listening to. It is simply on account of the limitations of his mental vision that the unreflective man interprets the expression 'could have acted otherwise,' in its context as a condition of moral responsibility, solely in terms of external constraint. He has failed (as yet) to reach the intellectual level at which one takes into account the implications for moral choices of the world-views of science, religion, and philosophy. If on a matter of this complexity the philosopher finds that his analysis accords with the utterances of the uneducated he has, I suggest, better cause for uneasiness than for self-congratulation.

This concludes the main part of what it seems to me necessary to say in answer to the pseudo-problem theorists. My object so far has been to expose the falsity of those innovations (chiefly Positivist) in the way of argument and analysis which are supposed by many to have made it impossible any longer to formulate the problem of Free Will in the traditional manner. My contention is that, at least so far as these innovations are concerned, the simple time-honoured argument still holds from the nature of the moral ought to the conclusion that moral responsibility implies a contra-causal type of freedom. The attempts to avoid that conclusion by analysing the proposition '*A* could have acted otherwise' (acknowledged to be implied in *some* sense in *A*'s moral responsibility) into one or other of certain hypothetical propositions which are compatible with unbroken causal continuity, break down hopelessly when tested against the touchstone of actual moral thinking. It is, I think, not necessary to defend the procedure of testing hypotheses in the ethical field by bringing to bear upon them our actual moral thinking. If there is any other form of test applicable, I should be much interested to learn what it is supposed to be. Certainly 'logical analysis' *per se* will not do. That has a function, but a function that can only be ancillary. For what we are seeking to know is the meaning of the expression 'could have acted otherwise' not *in the abstract*, but in the context of the question of man's *moral responsibility*. Logical analysis *per se* is impotent to give us this information. It can be of value only in so far as it operates within the orbit of 'the moral consciousness.' One may admit, with some qualifications, that on a matter of this sort the moral consciousness without logical analysis is blind: but it seems to me to be true without any qualification whatsoever that, on the same problem, logical analysis without the moral consciousness is empty.

VI

There are times when what seems to a critic the very strength of his case breeds mistrust in the critic's own mind. I confess that in making the criticisms that have preceded I have not been altogether free from uncomfortable feelings of this kind. For the arguments I have criticised, and more particularly the analyses of the conditions of moral responsibility, seem to me to be in many cases quite desperately unplausible. Such a state of affairs ought, I think, to give the critic pause. The thought must at least enter his mind (unless he be a total stranger to modesty) that perhaps, despite his best efforts to be fair, he has after all misrepresented what his opponents are saying. No doubt a similar thought will enter, and perhaps find lodgment in, the minds of many readers.

In this situation there is, however, one course by which the critic may reasonably hope to allay these natural suspicions. He should consider whether there may not be certain predisposing influences at work, extrinsic to the specific arguments, which could have the effect of blinding the proponents of these arguments to their intrinsic demerits. If so, he need not be too much disquieted by the seeming weakness of the case against him. For it is a commonplace that, once in the grip of general prepossessions, even very good philosophers sometimes avail themselves of very bad arguments.

Actually, we can, I think, discern at least two such influences operating powerfully in the case before us. One is sympathy with the general tenets of Positivism. The other is the conviction already alluded to, that man does not in fact possess a contra-causal type of freedom; whence follows a strong presumption that no such freedom is necessary to moral responsibility.

About the first of these influences I propose to say very

little. I wish merely to indicate how strict adherence to Positivist tenets precludes one in principle from understanding moral responsibility as the ordinary man understands it, and how Positivists are therefore bound, when they attempt to define the conditions of moral responsibility, to say things that seem monstrously unplausible.

That the Positivist—who has certainly not been drawn initially to this way of philosophising by reflexion upon the phenomena of the moral life—should approach the problems of ethical analysis with certain strong prepossessions, is only to be expected. The most crucial of these is that (non-tautologous) statements in this field, as in every other field, can have no meaning—or at any rate no cognitive meaning—unless they are, at least in principle, sensibly verifiable. The consequence of that prepossession must be to close the mind in advance, more or less absolutely according to the extent to which the Verifiability principle is maintained as unshakeable dogma, against the common view of the moral ought—which happens also to be the view in terms of which the problem of moral responsibility historically and habitually arises. For on this view the moral ought as apprehended by the moral consciousness is most certainly an object neither of 'outer' nor of 'inner' sense. One need not wonder, therefore, that the Positivist should recommend analyses of the conditions of moral responsibility, such as the hypothetical propositions offered as the meaning of the expression 'could have acted otherwise,' which to anyone who understands the moral ought in the ordinary way seem little short of fantastic. By an *a priori* prejudice he has effectively debarred himself from appreciating what ordinary men mean by moral obligation and moral responsibility. I cannot forbear adding that in view of the doom which has so swiftly attended the very various attempts so far made to define moral obligation in Positivist terms, the case for at least a temporary suspension of belief in Positivist presuppositions in the ethical field would appear to be a strong one.

Of far wider and more permanent interest, in my judgment, is the second of the 'predisposing influences'—the conviction that there just *is* no contra-causal freedom such as is commonly alleged to be a condition of moral responsibility. A natural desire to 'save' moral responsibility issues, logically enough, in attempts to formulate its conditions in a manner compatible with unbroken causal continuity. The consequent analyses may be, as I have urged, very unsatisfactory. But there is no doubt that the conviction that motivates the analysis is supported by reasons of great weight: well-known arguments that are the property of no particular school and which most of us learned in our philosophical cradles. A very brief summary of what I take to be the most influential of these arguments will suffice for the comments I wish to make upon them.

A contra-causal freedom, it is argued, such as is implied in the 'categorical' interpretation of the proposition '*A* could have chosen otherwise than he did,' posits a breach of causal continuity between a man's character and his conduct. Now apart from the general presumption in favour of the universality of causal law, there are special reasons for disallowing the breach that is here alleged. It is the common assumption of social intercourse that our acquaintances will act 'in character'; that their choices will exhibit the 'natural' response of their characters to the given situation. And this assumption seems to be amply substantiated, over a wide range of conduct, by the actual success which attends predictions made on this basis. Where there should be, on the contra-causal hypothesis, chaotic variability, there is found in fact a large measure of intelligible continuity. Moreover, what is the alternative to admitting that a person's choices flow from his character? Surely just that the so-called 'choice' is not *that person's* choice at all: that, relatively to the person concerned, it is a mere 'accident.' Now we cannot really believe this. But if it *were* the case, it would certainly not help to establish *moral* freedom, the freedom required for *moral* responsibility. For clearly a man cannot be morally responsible for an act which does not express his own choice but is, on the contrary, attributable simply to chance.

These are clearly considerations worthy of all respect. It is not surprising if they have played a big part in persuading people to respond sympathetically to the view that 'Free Will,' in its usual contra-causal formulation, is a pseudo-problem. A full answer to them is obviously not practicable in what is little more than an appendix to the body of this paper; but I am hopeful that something can be said, even in a little space, to show that they are very far from being as conclusive against a contra-causal freedom as they are often supposed to be.

To begin with the less troublesome of the two main objections indicated—the objection that the break in causal continuity which free will involves is inconsistent with the predictability of conduct on the basis of the agent's known character. All that is necessary to meet this objection, I suggest, is the frank recognition, which is perfectly open to the Libertarian, that there is a wide area of human conduct, determinable on clear general principles, within which free will does not effectively operate. The most important of these general principles (I have no space to deal here with the others) has often enough been stated by Libertarians. Free will does not operate in these practical situations in which no conflict arises in the agent's mind between what he conceives to be his 'duty' and what he feels to be his 'strongest desire.' It does not operate here because there just is no occasion for it to operate. There is no reason whatever why the agent should here even contemplate choosing any course other than that prescribed by his strongest desire. In all such situations, therefore, he naturally wills in accordance with strongest desire. But his 'strongest desire' is simply the specific *ad hoc* expression of that system of conative and emotive dispositions which we call his 'character.' In all such situations, therefore, whatever may be the case elsewhere, his will is in effect determined by his character as so far formed. Now when we bear in mind that there are an almost immeasurably greater number of situations in a man's life that conform to *this* pattern than there are situations in which an agent is aware of a conflict between strongest desire and duty, it is apparent that a Libertarianism which accepts the limitation of free will to the *latter* type of situation is not open to the stock objection on the score of 'predictability.' For there still remains a vast area of human behaviour in which prediction on the basis of known character may be expected to succeed: an area which will accommodate without difficulty, I think, all these empirical facts about successful prediction which the critic is apt to suppose fatal to Free Will.

So far as I can see, such a delimitation of the field of effective free will denies to the Libertarian absolutely nothing which matters to him. For it is precisely that small sector of the field of choices which our principle of delimitation still leaves open to free will—the sector in which strongest desire clashes with duty—that is crucial for moral responsibility. It is, I believe, with respect to such situations, and in the last resort to such situations alone, that the agent himself recognises that moral praise and blame are appropriate. They are appropriate, according as he does or does not 'rise to duty' in the face of opposing desires; always granted, that is, that he is free to choose between these courses as genuinely open possibilities. If the reality of freedom be conceded *here*, everything is conceded that the Libertarian has any real interest in securing.

But, of course, the most vital question is, can the reality of freedom be conceded even here? In particular, can the standard objection be met which we stated, that if the person's choice does not, in these situations as elsewhere, flow from his *character*, then it is not *that person's* choice at all.

This is, perhaps, of all the objections to a contra-causal freedom, the one which is generally felt to be the most conclusive. For the assumption upon which it is based, *viz.*, that no intelligible meaning can attach to the claim that an act which is not an expression of the self's *character* may nevertheless be the *self's* act, is apt to be regarded as self-evident. The Libertarian is accordingly charged with being in effect an *In*determinist, whose 'free will,' in so far as it does not flow from the agent's character, can only be a matter of 'chance.' Has the Libertarian—who invariably repudiates this charge and claims to be a *Self*-determinist—any way of showing that, contrary to the assumption of his critics, we *can* meaningfully talk of an act as the self's act even though, in an important sense, it is not an expression of the self's 'character'?

I think that he has. I want to suggest that what prevents the critics from finding a meaning in this way of talking is that they are looking for it in the wrong way; or better, perhaps, with the wrong orientation. They are looking for it from the standpoint of the *external observer;* the standpoint proper to, because alone possible for, apprehension of the physical world. Now from the external standpoint we may observe processes of change. But one thing which, by common consent, *cannot* be observed from without is *creative activity*. Yet—and here lies the crux of the whole matter—it is precisely creative activity which we are trying to understand when we are trying to understand what is traditionally designated by 'free will.' For if there should be an act which is genuinely the self's act and is nevertheless not an expression of its character, such an act, in which the self 'transcends' its character as so far formed, would seem to be essentially of the nature of creative activity. It follows that to look for a meaning in 'free will' from the external standpoint is absurd. It is to look for it in a way that ensures that it will not be found. Granted that a creative activity of any kind is at least *possible* (and I know of no ground for its *a priori* rejection), there is one way, and one way only, in which we can hope to apprehend it, and that is from the *inner* standpoint of direct participation.

It seems to me therefore, that if the Libertarian's claim to find a meaning in a 'free' will which is genuinely the self's will, though not an expression of the self's character, is to be subjected to any test that is worth applying, that test must be undertaken from the inner standpoint. We ought to place ourselves imaginatively at the standpoint of the agent engaged in the typical moral situation in which free will is claimed, and ask ourselves whether from *this* standpoint the claim in question does or does not have meaning for us. That the appeal must be to introspection is no doubt unfortunate. But he would be a very doctrinaire critic of introspection who declined to make use of it when in the nature of the case no other means of apprehension is available. Everyone must make the introspective experiment for himself: but I may perhaps venture to report, though at this late stage with extreme brevity, what I at least seem to find when I make the experiment myself.

In the situation of moral conflict, then, I (as agent) have

before my mind a course of action *X*, which I believe to be my duty; and also a course of action *Y*, incompatible with *X*, which I feel to be that which I most strongly desire. *Y* is, as it is sometimes expressed, 'in the line of least resistance' for me—the course which I am aware I should take if I let my purely desiring nature operate without hindrance. It is the course towards which I am aware that my *character*, as so far formed, naturally inclines me. Now, as actually engaged in this situation, I find that I cannot help believing that I *can* rise to duty and choose *X*; the 'rising to duty' being effected by what is commonly called 'effort of will.' And I further find, if I ask myself just what it is I am believing when I believe that I 'can' rise to duty, that I cannot help believing that it lies with me here and now, quite absolutely, which of two genuinely open possibilities I adopt; whether, that is, I make the effort of will and choose *X*, or, on the other hand, let my desiring nature, my character as so far formed, 'have its way,' and choose *Y*, the course 'in the line of least resistance.' These beliefs may, of course, be illusory, but that is not at present in point. For the present argument all that matters is whether beliefs of this sort are in fact discoverable in the moral agent in the situation of 'moral temptation.' For my own part, I cannot doubt the introspective evidence that they are.

Now here is the vital point. No matter which course, *X* or *Y*, I choose in this situation, I cannot doubt, *qua* practical being engaged in it, that my choice is *not* just the expression of my formed character, and yet *is* a choice made by my *self*. For suppose I make the effort and choose *X* (my 'duty'). Since my very purpose in making the 'effort' is to enable me to act against the existing 'set' of desire, which is the expression of my character as so far formed, I cannot possibly regard the act itself as the expression of my *character*. On the other hand, introspection makes it equally clear that I am certain that it is *I* who choose; that the act is not an 'accident,' but is genuinely *my* act. Or suppose that I choose *Y* (the end of 'strongest desire'). The course chosen here is, it is true, in conformity with my 'character.' But since I find myself unable to doubt that

I *could* have made the effort and chosen X, I cannot possibly regard the choice of Y as *just* the expression of my character. Yet here again I find that I cannot doubt that the choice is *my* choice, a choice for which *I* am justly to be blamed.

What this amounts to is that I *can* and *do* attach meaning, *qua* moral agent, to an act which is not the self's character and yet is genuinely the self's act. And having no good reason to suppose that other persons have a fundamentally different mental constitution, it seems to me probable that anyone else who undertakes a similar experiment will be obliged to submit a similar report. I conclude, therefore, that the argument against 'free will' on the score of its 'meaninglessness' must be held to fail. 'Free Will' does have meaning; though, because it is of the nature of a creative activity, its meaning is discoverable only in an intuition of the practical consciousness of the participating agent. To the agent making a moral choice in the situation where duty clashes with desire, his 'self' is known to him as a creatively active self, a self which declines to be identified with his 'character' as so formed. Not, of course, that the self's character—let it be added to obviate misunderstanding—either is, or is supposed by the agent to be, devoid of bearing upon his choices, even in the 'sector' in which free will is held to operate. On the contrary, such a bearing is manifest in the empirically verifiable fact that we find it 'harder' (as we say) to make the effort of will required to 'rise to duty' in proportion to the extent that the 'dutiful' course conflicts with the course to which our character as so far formed inclines us. It is only in the polemics of the critics that a 'free' will is supposed to be incompatible with recognising the bearing of 'character' upon choice.

"But what" (it may be asked) "of the all-important question of the *value* of this 'subjective certainty'? Even if what you say is sound as 'phenomenology,' is there any reason to suppose that the conviction on which you lay so much stress is in fact *true?*" I agree that the question is important; far more important, indeed, than is always realised, for it is not always realised that the only direct evidence there *could* be for a creative activity like 'free will' is an intuition of the practical consciousness. But this question falls outside the purview of the present paper. The aim of the paper has not been to offer a constructive defence of free will. It has been to show that the problem as traditionally posed is a real, and not a pseudo, problem. A serious threat to that thesis, it was acknowledged, arises from the apparent difficulty of attaching meaning to an act which is not the expression of the self's character and yet *is* the self's own act. The object of my brief phenomenological analysis was to provide evidence that such an act *does* have meaning for us in the one context in which there is any sense in *expecting* it to have meaning.

VII

My general conclusion is, I fear, very unexciting. It is merely that it is an error to suppose that the 'Free Will' problem, when correctly formulated, turns out not to be a 'problem' at all. Labouring to reinstate an old problem is dull work enough. But I am disposed to think that the philosophic situation to-day calls for a good deal more dull work of a similar sort.

DETERMINISM, INDETERMINISM, AND LIBERTARIANISM

C. D. BROAD

The Implications of Obligability

We often make retrospective judgments about the past actions of ourselves or other people which take the form: 'You ought not to have done the action *X*, which you in fact did; you ought instead to have done the action *Y*, which in fact you

From C. D. Broad, "Determinism, Indeterminism, and Libertarianism," in *Ethics and the History of Philosophy*. London: Routledge & Kegan Paul, 1952, pp. 195–217.

did not.' If I make such a judgment about a person, and he wants to refute it, he can take two different lines of argument. (1) He may say: 'I could have done *Y* instead of *X*, but you are mistaken in thinking that *Y* was the action that I ought to have done. In point of fact, *X*, the action that I did, was the one that I ought to have done. If I had done *Y*, I should have done what I ought not to have done.' (2) He may say: 'I could not help doing *X*,' or he may say: 'Though I need not have done *X*, I could not possibly have done *Y*.'

If the accused person makes an answer of the first kind, he is admitting that the alternatives 'ought' and 'ought not' apply to the actions *X* and *Y*, but he is objecting to my applying 'ought' to *Y* and 'ought not' to *X*. He is saying that 'ought' applies to *X*, and 'ought not' to *Y*. It is as if two people, who agree that *X* and *Y* are each either black or white, should differ because one holds that *X* is black and *Y* white whilst the other holds that *X* is white and *Y* black. If the accused person makes an answer of the second kind, he is denying the applicability of the alternatives 'ought' and 'ought not.' If he says: 'I could not help doing *X*,' he assumes that his critic will admit that neither 'ought' nor 'ought not' has any application to an action which the agent could not help doing. If he says: 'Though I need not have done *X*, yet I could not possibly have done *Y*,' he assumes that his critic will admit that neither 'ought' nor 'ought not' has any application to an action which the agent could not have done. It is as if one person should say that *X* is black and *Y* is white, and the other should answer that at least one of them is unextended and therefore incapable of being either black or white.

Obligability Entails Substitutability

Now we are concerned here only with the second kind of answer. The essential point to notice is that it is universally admitted to be a *relevant* answer. We all admit that there is some sense or other of 'could' in which 'ought' and 'ought not' entail 'could.' We will now try to get clear about the connexion between these two notions.

Judgments of obligation about past actions may be divided into two classes, viz. (1) judgments about actions which were actually done, and (2) judgments about conceivable actions which were not done. Each divides into two sub-classes, and so we get the following fourfold division. (1 • 1) 'You did *X*, and *X* was the action that you ought to have done.' (1 • 2) 'You did *X*, and *X* was an action that you ought not to have done.' (2 • 1) 'You did not do *X*, and *X* was the action that you ought to have done.' And (2 • 2) 'You did not do *X*, and *X* was an action that you ought not to have done.' Now both judgments of the first class entail that you could have helped doing the action which you in fact did. If the action that you did can be said to be one that you ought to have done, or if it can be said to be one that you ought not to have done, it must be one that you *need not* have done. And, since you actually did it, it is obviously one that you *could have* done. Both judgments of the second class entail that you could have done an action which you did not in fact do. If a conceivable action which you did not do can be said to be one which you ought to have done, or if it can be said to be one that you ought not to have done, it must be one that you *could have* done. And, since you actually failed to do it, it is obviously one that you *need not* have done.

It is worth while to notice that the common phrases: 'You ought to have done so and so' and 'You ought not to have done so and so' are generally equivalent to our judgments (2 • 1) and (1 • 2) respectively. The former is generally used to mean: 'You did not do so and so, and that was an action which you ought to have done.' The latter is generally used to mean: 'You did so and so, and that was an action which you ought not to have done.' But we often need to express what is expressed by our judgments (1 • 1) and (2 • 2). We often want to say that a person did what he ought on a certain occasion, and we often want to say that a person avoided doing something which he ought not to have done on a certain occasion. For this is exactly the state of affairs which exists when a person has in fact done an unpleasant duty in face of a strong temptation to shirk it by lying.

Now the importance of this connexion between 'ought' and 'ought not,' on the one hand, and 'could,' on the other, is very great. People constantly make judgments of obligation of the four kinds which we have distinguished, and such judgments have constantly been made throughout the whole course of human history. Every single one of these judgments has been false unless there have been cases in which actions which *were* done could have been left undone and actions which *were not* done could have been done. And these judgments would all have been false in principle, and not merely in detail. They would have been false, not in the sense that they asserted 'ought' where they should have asserted 'ought not,' or *vice versa*. They would be false in the sense that nothing in the world has ever had that determinable characteristic of which 'ought to be done' and 'ought not to be done' are the determinate specifications. They would be false in the sense in which all judgments which predicated redness, blueness, etc., of any object would be false in a world which contained no objects except minds and noises.

It will be convenient to call an action 'obligable' if and only if it is an action of which 'ought to be done' or 'ought not to be done' can be predicated. It will be convenient to call an action 'substitutable' if, either it was done but could have been left undone, or it was left undone but could have been done. We may then sum up the situation by saying that an action is obligable if and only if it is, in a certain sense, substitutable; that, unless all judgments of obligations are false in principle, there are obligable actions; and therefore, unless all judgments of obligation are false in principle, there are actions which are, in this sense, substitutable.

Various Senses of 'Substitutable'

This is one aspect of the case. The other aspect is the following. There are several senses of 'could' in which nearly everyone would admit that some actions which were done could have been left undone, and some actions which were left undone could have been done. There are thus several senses of 'substitutable' in which it would commonly be admitted that some actions are substitutable. But, although an action which was *not* substitutable in these senses would *not* be obligable, it seems doubtful whether an action which was substitutable *only* in these senses *would be* obligable. It seems doubtful whether an action would be obligable unless it were substitutable in some further sense.

At this stage two difficulties arise. (i) It is extremely difficult to grasp and to express clearly this further sense of 'substitutable,' i.e. this further sense of 'could' in which an action that was done could have been left undone or an action which was not done could have been done. Many people would say that they can attach no meaning to 'substitutable' except those meanings in which it is insufficient to make an action obligable. (ii) Even if this other meaning of 'substitutable' can be grasped and clearly expressed, many people would say that no action is substitutable in this sense. They would claim to see that no action which has been done could have been left undone, and that no action which was not done could have been done, in that sense of 'could' which is required if an action is to be obligable.

Now anyone who holds these views is in a very awkward position. On the one hand, it is not easy to believe that every judgment of obligation is false, in the sense in which every judgment ascribing colour to an object would be false in a world containing only minds and noises. On the other hand, it is highly depressing to have to admit that there is a sense of 'could' which you can neither grasp nor clearly express. And it is equally unsatisfactory to have to believe that some actions *are* substitutable in a sense in which it seems to you self-evident that no action *could be* substitutable.

There are two problems to be tackled at this point. (i) To try to discover and state the sense of 'substitutable' in which being substitutable is the necessary and sufficient condition of being obligable. And (ii), if we can do this, to consider whether any action could be substitutable in this sense.

Voluntary Substitutability

Let us begin by considering an action which has actually been performed. In some cases we should say that the agent 'could not have helped' performing it. We should certainly say this if we had reason to believe that the very same act would have been performed by the agent in these circumstances even though he had willed that it should not take place. It is obvious that there are actions which are 'inevitable,' in this sense, since there are actions which take place although the agent is trying his hardest to prevent them. Compare, e.g., the case of a conspirator taken with an uncontrollable fit of sneezing.

Next consider a conceivable action which was not in fact performed. In some cases we should say that the agent 'could not possibly' have performed it. We should certainly say this if the act would not have taken place in these circumstances no matter how strongly the agent had willed it. It is obvious that there are conceivable acts which are 'impossible' in this sense, since there are cases where such an act fails to take place although the agent is trying his hardest to bring it about. Compare, e.g., the case of a man who is bound and gagged, and tries vainly to give warning to a friend.

We will call acts of these two kinds 'not voluntarily substitutable.' It is plain that an act which is not voluntarily substitutable is not obligable. No one would say that the conspirator ought not to have sneezed, or that the bound and gagged man ought to have warned his friend. At most we may be able to say that they ought or ought not to have done certain things in the past which are relevant to their present situation. Perhaps the conspirator ought to have sprayed his nose with cocaine before hiding behind the presumably dusty arras, and perhaps the victim ought not to have let himself be lured into the house in which he was gagged and bound. But these are previous questions.

We see then that to be voluntarily substitutable is a *necessary* condition for an action to be obligable. But is it a *sufficient* condition? Suppose I performed the action A on a certain occasion. Suppose that I should not have done *A* then if I had willed with a certain degree of force and persistence not to do it. Since I did *A*, it is certain that I *did not* will with this degree of force and persistence to avoid doing it. Now suppose that at the time I *could not* have willed with this degree of force and persistence to avoid doing *A*. Should we be prepared to say that I ought not to have done *A*?

Now take another case. Suppose that on a certain occasion I failed to do a certain conceivable action *B*. Suppose that I should have done *B* if I had willed with a certain degree of force and persistence to do it. Since I did not do *B*, it is certain that I *did not* will with this degree of force and persistence to do it. Now suppose that at the time I *could not* have willed with this degree of force and persistence to do *B*. Should we be prepared to say that I ought to have done *B*? It seems to me almost certain that, under the supposed conditions, we should not be prepared to say either that I ought not to have done *A* or that I ought to have done *B*.

Consider, e.g., the case of a man who gradually becomes addicted to some drug like morphine, and eventually becomes a slave to it. At the early stages we should probably hold that he could have willed with enough force and persistence to ensure that the temptation would be resisted. At the latest stages we should probably hold that he could not have done so. Now at every stage, from the earliest to the latest, the hypothetical proposition would be true: 'If he had willed with a certain degree of force and persistence to avoid taking morphine, he would have avoided taking it.' Yet we should say at the earlier stages that he ought to have resisted, whilst, at the final stages, we should be inclined to say that 'ought' and 'ought not' have ceased to apply.

Primary and Secondary Substitutability

An action which was in fact done, but would not have been done if there had been a strong and persistent enough desire in the agent not to do it, will be called 'primarily avoidable.' Suppose, in addition, that there could have been in the agent at the time a desire of sufficient strength and persistence to prevent the action being done. Then the action might be called 'secondarily avoidable.' If this latter condition is not fulfilled, we shall say that the action was 'primarily avoidable, but secondarily inevitable.' Similarly, an action which was not in fact done, but would have been done if there had been in the agent a strong and persistent enough desire to do it, will be called 'primarily possible.' Suppose, in addition, that there could have been in the agent at the time a desire of sufficient strength and persistence to ensure the action being done. Then the action may be called 'secondarily possible.' If this latter condition is not fulfilled, we shall say that the action is 'primarily possible, but secondarily impossible.' An action will be called 'primarily substitutable' if it is either primarily avoidable or primarily possible. It will be secondarily substitutable if it is either secondarily avoidable or secondarily possible. In order that an action may be obligable it is not enough that it should be primarily substitutable, it must be at least secondarily substitutable.

We are thus led on from the notion of voluntarily substitutable *actions* to that of substitutable *volitions*. Suppose that, on a certain occasion and in a certain situation, a certain agent willed a certain alternative with a certain degree of force and persistence. We may say that the volition was substitutable if the same agent, on the same occasion and in the same circumstances, could instead have willed a different alternative or could have willed the same alternative with a different degree of force and persistence. Now there is one sense of 'could' in which it might plausibly be suggested that many volitions are substitutable. It seems very likely that there are many occasions on which I *should* have willed otherwise than I did, *if* on previous occasions I had willed otherwise than I did. So it seems likely that many volitions have been voluntarily substitutable.

It is necessary to be careful at this point, or we may be inadvertently granting more than we are really prepared to admit. Obviously it is often true that, if I had willed otherwise than I did on certain earlier occasions, I should never have got into the position in which I afterwards made a certain decision. If, e.g., Julius Caesar had decided earlier in his career not to accept the command in Gaul, he would never have been in the situation in which he decided to cross the Rubicon. This, however, does not make his decision to cross the Rubicon substitutable. For a volition is substitutable only if a different volition could have occurred in the agent in the *same* situation. Again, it is often true that, if I had willed otherwise than I did on certain earlier occasions, my state of knowledge and belief would have been different on certain later occasions from what it in fact was. In that case I should have thought, on these later occasions, of certain alternatives which I did not and could not think of in my actual state of knowledge and belief. Suppose, e.g., that a lawyer has to decide what to do when a friend has met with an accident. If this man had decided years before to study medicine instead of law, it is quite likely that he would now think of, and perhaps choose, an alternative which his lack of medical knowledge prevents him from contemplating. This, however, does not make the lawyer's volition in the actual situation substitutable. For, although the external part of the total situation might have been the same whether he had previously decided to study medicine or to study law, the internal part of the total situation would have been different if he had decided to study medicine, instead of deciding, as he did, to study law. He would have become an agent with different cognitive powers and dispositions from those which he in fact has. No one would think of saying that the lawyer ought to have done a certain action, which he did not and could not contemplate, merely because he would have contemplated it and would have decided to do it if he had decided years before to become a doctor instead of becoming a lawyer.

Having cleared these irrelevances away, we can now come to the real point. A man's present conative-emotional dispositions, and what we may call his 'power of intense and persistent willing,' are in part dependent on his earlier volitions. If a person has repeatedly chosen the easier of the alternatives open to him, it becomes increasingly difficult for him to choose and to persist in pursuing the harder of two alternatives. If he has formed a habit of turning his attention away from certain kinds of fact, it will become increasingly difficult for him to attend fairly to alternatives which involve facts of these kinds. This is one aspect of the case. Another, and equally important, aspect is the following. If a man reflects on his own past decisions, he may see that he has a tendency to ignore or to dwell upon certain kinds of fact, and that this had led him to make unfair or unwise decisions on many occasions. He may decide that, in future, he will make a special effort to give due, and not more than due, weight to those considerations which he has a tendency to ignore or to dwell upon. And this decision may make a difference to his future decisions. On the other hand, he may see that certain alternatives have a specially strong attraction for him, and he may find that, if he pays more than a fleeting attention to them, he will be rushed into choosing them, and will afterwards regret it. He may decide that, in future, he will think as little as possible about such alternatives. And this decision may make a profound difference to his future decisions.

We can now state the position in general terms. Suppose that, if the agent had willed differently on earlier occasions, his conative-emotional dispositions and his knowledge of his own nature would have been so modified that he would now have willed differently in the actual external situation and in his actual state of knowledge and belief about the alternatives open to him. Then we can say that his actual volition in the present situation was 'voluntarily avoidable,' and that a volition of a different kind or of a different degree of force and persistence was 'voluntarily possible.' An action which took place was secondarily avoidable if the following two conditions are fulfilled. (i) That this action would not have been done if the agent had willed with a certain degree of force and persistence to avoid it. (ii) That, if he had willed differently in the past, his conative-emotional dispositions and his knowledge of his own nature would have been such, at the time when he did the action, that he would have willed to avoid it with enough force and persistence to prevent him doing it. In a precisely similar way we could define the statement that a certain conceivable action, which was not done, was secondarily possible. And we can thus define the statement that an action is secondarily substitutable.

Can we say that an action is obligable if it is secondarily substitutable, in the sense just defined, though it is not obligable if it is only primarily substitutable? It seems to me that the same difficulty which we noticed before reappears here. Suppose that the agent could not have willed otherwise than he did in the remoter past. It is surely irrelevant to say that, *if* he had done so, his conative dispositions *would* have been different at a later stage from what they in fact were then, and that he *would* have willed otherwise than he then did. One might, of course, try to deal with this situation by referring back to still earlier volitions. One might talk of actions which are not only primarily, or only secondarily, but are tertiarily substitutable. But it is quite clear that this is useless. If neither primary nor secondary substitutability, in the sense defined, suffice to make an action obligable, no higher order of substitutability, in this sense, will suffice. The further moves are of exactly the same nature as the second move. And so, if the second move does not get us out of the difficulty, none of the further moves will do so.

Categorical Substitutability

The kind of substitutability which we have so far considered may be called 'conditional substitutability.' For at every stage we have defined 'could' to mean 'would have been, if certain conditions had been fulfilled which were not.' Now I have concluded that merely conditional substitutability, of however high an order, is not a sufficient condition for obligability. If an action is to be obligable, it must be *categorically* substitutable. We must be able to say of an action, which was done, that it could have been avoided, in some sense of 'could' which is not definable in terms of 'would have, if.' And we must be able to say of a conceivable action, which was not done, that it could have been done, in some sense of 'could' which is not definable in terms of 'would have, if.' Unless there are some actions of which such things can truly be said, there are no actions which are obligable. We must therefore consider whether any clear meaning can be attached to the phrase 'categorically substitutable,' i.e. whether 'could' has any clear meaning except 'would have, if.' And, if we can find such a meaning, we must enquire whether any actions are categorically substitutable.

Various Senses of 'Obligable'

Before tackling these questions I must point out that the words 'ought' and 'ought not' are used in several different senses. In some of these senses obligability does not entail categorical substitutability.

(i) There is a sense of 'ought' in which we apply it even to inanimate objects. It would be quite proper to say: 'A car ought to be able to get from London to Cambridge in less than three hours,' or: 'A fountain-pen ought not to be constantly making blots.' We mean by this simply that a car which did take more than three hours would be a poor specimen of car, or would be in a bad state of repair. And similar remarks apply to the statement about the fountain-pen. We are comparing the behaviour of a certain car or fountain-pen with the average standard of achievement of cars or fountain-pens. We are not suggesting that *this* car or *this* pen, in its present state of repair, unconditionally could go faster or avoid making blots. Sometimes when we make such judgments we are comparing an individual's achievements, not with those of the *average* member, but with those of an *ideally perfect* member, of a certain class to which it belongs. We will call 'ought,' in this sense, 'the comparative ought.' And we can then distinguish 'the average-comparative ought' and 'the ideal-comparative ought.'

(ii) Plainly 'ought' and 'ought not' can be, and often are, used in this sense of human actions. But, in the case of human actions, there is a further development. Since a human being has the power of cognition, in general, and of reflexive cognition, in particular, he can have an idea of an average or an ideal man. He can compare his own achievements with those of the average, or the ideal, man, as conceived by him. And he will have a more or less strong and persistent desire to approximate to the ideal and not to fall below the average. Now it is part of the notion of an ideal man that he is a being who would have a high ideal of human nature and would desire strongly and persistently to approximate to his ideal. Obviously it is no part of the notion of an ideal horse or an ideal car that it is a being which would have a high ideal of horses or cars and a strong and persistent desire to live up to this. When we say that a man ought not to cheat at cards we often mean to assert two things. (*a*) That the average decent man does not do this, and that anyone who does falls in this respect below the average. And (*b*) that a man who does this either has a very low ideal of human nature or a very weak and unstable desire to approximate to the ideal which he has. So that, in this further respect, he falls below the average.

Now neither of these judgments implies that a particular person, who cheated on a particular occasion, categorically could have avoided cheating then; or that he categorically could have had a higher ideal of human nature; or that he categorically could have willed more strongly and persistently to live up to the ideal which he had. For an action to be obligable, in this sense, it is plain enough that it should be secondarily substitutable, in the sense already defined.

The Categorical Ought

Some philosophers of great eminence, e.g. Spinoza, have held that the sense of 'ought' which I have just discussed is the only sense of it. Plainly it is a very important sense, and it is one in which 'ought' and 'ought not' can be applied only to the actions of intelligent beings with power of reflexive cognition, emotion, and conation. I think that a clear-headed Determinist should hold either that this is the only sense; or that, if there is another sense, in which obligability entails *categorical* substitutability, it has no application.

Most people, however, would say that, although we often do use 'ought' and 'ought not' in this sense, we quite often use them in another sense, and that in this other sense they entail categorical substitutability. I am inclined to think that this is true. When I judge that I ought not to have done something which I in fact did, I do not as a rule seem to be judging merely that a person with higher ideals, or with a stronger and more persistent desire to live up to his ideals, would not have done what I did. Even when this is part of what I mean, there seems to be something more implied in my judgment, viz. that I *could* have had higher ideals or *could* have willed more strongly and persistently to live up to my ideals, where 'could' does not mean just 'would have, if.' Let us call this sense of 'ought' the 'categorical ought.' It seems to me then that we must distinguish between an action being obligable in the comparative sense and being obligable in the categorical sense; and that, if any action were categorically obligable, it would have to be categorically substitutable.

Analysis of Categorical Substitutability

We can now proceed to discuss the notion of categorical substitutability. It seems to me to involve a negative and a positive condition. I think that the negative condition can be clearly formulated, and that there is no insuperable difficulty in admitting that it may sometimes be fulfilled. The ultimate difficulty is to give any intelligible account of the positive condition. I will now explain and illustrate these statements.

Suppose that, on a certain occasion, I willed a certain alternative with a certain degree of force and persistence, and that, in consequence of this volition, I did a certain voluntary action which I should not have done unless I had willed this alternative with this degree of intensity and persistence. To say that I categorically could have avoided doing this action implies at least that the following negative condition is fulfilled. It implies that the process of my willing this alternative with this degree of force and persistence was not completely determined by the nomic, the occurrent, the dispositional, and the background conditions which existed immediately before and during this process of willing. In order to see exactly what this means it will be best to contrast it with a case in which we believe that a process is completely determined by such conditions.

Suppose that two billiard-balls are moving on a table, that they collide at a certain moment, and that they go on moving in modified directions with modified velocities in consequence of the impact. Let us take as universal premisses the general laws of motion and of elastic impact. We will call these 'nomic premisses.' Let us take as singular premisses the following propositions. (i) That each ball was moving in such and such a direction and with such and such a velocity at the moment of impact. We will call this an 'occurrent premiss.' (ii) That the masses and co-efficients of elasticity of the balls were such and such. We will call this a 'dispositional premiss.' (iii) That the table was smooth and level before, at, and after the moment of impact. We will call this a 'background premiss.' Lastly, let us take the proposition that the balls are moving, directly after the impact, in such and such directions with such and such velocities. Then this last proposition is a *logical consequence* of the conjunction of the nomic, the occurrent, the dispositional, and the background premisses. That is to say, the combination of these premisses with the denial of the last proposition would be *logically inconsistent*. It is so in exactly the sense in which the combination of the premisses of a valid syllogism with the denial of its conclusion would be so.

The Negative Condition

We can now work towards a definition of the statement that a certain event *e* was completely determined in respect of a certain characteristic. When we have defined this statement it will be easy to define the statement that a certain event was not completely determined in respect of a certain characteristic. I will begin with a concrete example, and will then generalize the result into a definition.

Suppose that a certain flash happened at a certain place and date. This will be a manifestation of a certain determinable characteristic, viz. colour, in a certain perfectly determinate form. It may, e.g., be a red flash of a certain perfectly determinate shade, intensity, and saturation. We may call shade, intensity, and saturation the three 'dimensions' of colour, and we shall therefore symbolize the determinable characteristic colour by a three-suffix symbol C_{123}. When we want to symbolize a certain perfectly determinate value of this we shall use the symbol C_{123}^{abc}. This means that the shade has the determinate value a, that the intensity has the determinate value b, and that the saturation has the determinate value c. Each *index* indicates the determinate value which the dimension indicated by the corresponding *suffix* has in the given instance.

Now the statement that this flash was completely determined in respect of colour has the following meaning. It means that there is a set of true nomic, occurrent, dispositional, and background propositions which together entail the proposition that a manifestation of colour, of the precise shade, intensity, and saturation which this flash manifested, would happen at the place and time at which this flash happened. To say that this flash was *not* completely determined in respect of colour means that there is *no* set of true nomic, occurrent, dispositional, and background propositions which together entail the proposition that a manifestation of colour, of the precise shade, intensity, and saturation which this flash manifested, would happen at the place and time at which this flash happened.

There are two remarks to be made at this point. (i) It seems to me that the second statement is perfectly *intelligible*, even if no such statement be ever true. (ii) It is a purely *ontological* statement, and not in any way a statement about the limitations of our knowledge. Either there is such a set of true propositions, or there is not. There may be such a set, even if no one knows that there is; and there may be no such set, even if everyone believes that there is.

We can now give a general definition. The statement that a certain event e was completely determined in respect of a certain determinable characteristic C_{123} is equivalent to the conjunction of the following two propositions. (i) The event e was a manifestation of C_{123} in a certain perfectly determinate form C_{123}^{abc} at a certain place and date. (ii) There is a set of true nomic, occurrent, dispositional, and background propositions which together entail that a manifestation of C_{123} in the form C_{123}^{abc} would happen at the place and date at which *e* happened. The statement that *e* was *not* completely determined in respect of C_{123} is equivalent to the conjoint assertion of (i) and denial of (ii).

The next point to notice is that an event might be partly determined and partly undetermined in respect of a certain characteristic. As before, I will begin with a concrete example. Our flash might be completely determined in respect of shade and saturation, but not in respect of intensity. This would be equivalent to the conjunction of the following two statements. (i) That there is a set of true propositions, of the kind already mentioned, which together entail that a flash, of precisely the shade and saturation which this flash had, would happen at the place and date at which this flash happened. (ii) There is no such set of true propositions which together entail that a flash, of precisely the intensity which this flash had, would happen at the time and place at which this flash happened. We thus get the notion of 'orders of indetermination' in respect of a given characteristic. If an event is undetermined in respect of one and only one dimension of a certain determinable characteristic, we say that it has 'indetermination of the first order' in respect of this characteristic. If it is undetermined in respect of two and only two dimensions of a certain determinable characteristic, we say that it has 'indetermination of the second order' in respect of this characteristic. And so on.

It is obvious that there is another possibility to be considered, which I will call 'range of indetermination in respect of a given dimension of a given characteristic.' Suppose that our flash is undetermined in respect of the intensity of its colour. There may be a set of true propositions, of the kind mentioned, which together entail that a flash, whose intensity falls within certain limits, would happen at the time and place at which this flash happened. This range of indetermination may be wide or narrow. Complete determination in respect of a given dimension of a given characteristic is the limiting case where the range of indetermination shuts up to zero about the actual value of this dimension for this event. Thus the 'extent of indetermination' of an event with respect to a given characteristic depends in general upon two factors, viz. (i) its order of indetermination with respect to the dimensions of this characteristic, and (ii) its range of indetermination with respect to those dimensions for which it is not completely determined.

We can now define the statement that a certain event *e* was completely determined. It means that *e* has zero range of indetermination for every dimension of every determinable characteristic of which it is a manifestation. The statement that a certain event *e* was *not* completely determined can now be defined. It means that *e* had a finite range of indetermination for at least one dimension of at least one of the characteristics of which it was a manifestation.

And now at last we can define 'Determinism' and 'Indeterminism.' Determinism is the doctrine that *every* event is completely determined, in the sense just defined. Indeterminism, is the doctrine that some, and it may be all, events are not completely determined, in the sense defined. Both doctrines are, *prima facie*, intelligible, when defined as I have defined them.

There is one other point to be noticed. An event might be completely determined, and yet it might have a 'causal ancestor' which was not completely determined. If *Y* is the total cause of *Z*, and *X* is the total cause of *Y*, I call both *Y* and *X* 'causal ancestors' of *Z*. Similarly, if *W* were the total cause of *X*, I should call *Y*, *X*, and *W* 'causal ancestors' of *Z*. And so on. If at any stage in such a series there is a term, e.g. *W*, which contains a cause-factor that is not completely determined, the series will stop there, just as the series of human ancestors stops with Adam. Such a term may be called the 'causal progenitor' of such a series. If Determinism be true, every event has causal ancestors, and therefore there are no causal progenitors. If Indeterminism be true, there are causal progenitors in the history of the world.

We can now state the negative condition which must be fulfilled if an action is to be categorically substitutable. Suppose that, at a certain time, an agent deliberated between two alternatives, *A* and *B*, and that he actually did *A* and not *B*. Suppose that the following conditions are fulfilled. (i) The doing of *A* by this agent at this moment was completely determined. (ii) The total cause of *A* being done contained as cause-factors a desire of a certain strength and persistence for *A* and a desire of a certain strength and persistence for *B*. (iii) These two desires were not completely determined in respect of strength and persistence. (iv) The range of indetermination was wide enough to include in it, as possible values, so strong and persistent a desire for *B* or so weak and fleeting a desire for *A* as would have determined the doing of *B* instead of the doing for *A*. Conditions (iii) and (iv) are the negative conditions which must be fulfilled if *B* is to be categorically substitutable for *A*. They amount to the following statement. It is consistent with (*a*) the laws of nature, including those of psychology, (*b*) the facts about the agent's dispositions and the dispositions of any other agent in the world at the moment of acting, (*c*) the facts about what was happening within and without the agent at that moment, and (*d*) the facts about the general background conditions at that moment, that the strength and persistence of the desires mentioned in (ii) should have any value that falls within the range mentioned in (iv).

Before we go further there is one point to be mentioned. Strictly speaking, what I have just stated are the negative conditions for *primary* categorical substitutability. For I have supposed the incomplete determination to occur at the *first* stage backwards, viz. in one of the cause-factors in the total cause of the action *A*. It would be quite easy to define, in a similar way, the negative conditions for secondary, or tertiary, or any other order of categorical substitutability. All that is needed is that, at *some* stage in the causal ancestry of *A*, there shall be a total cause which contains as factors desires of the agent answering to the conditions which I have stated. That is to say, all that is necessary is that *A* shall have a causal ancestor which is a causal progenitor, containing as a factor an incompletely determined desire of the agent's.

We come now to the final question. Supposing that this

negative condition were fulfilled, would this *suffice* to make an action categorically obligable? It seems to me plain that it would not. Unless some further and positive condition were fulfilled, all that one could say would be the following: 'The desire to do *A* happened to be present in me with such strength and persistence, as compared with the desire to do *B,* that I did *A* and avoided *B*. The desire to do *B* might have happened to be present in me with such strength and persistence, as compared with the desire to do *A,* that I should have done *B* and avoided *A*.' Now, if this is all, the fact that I did *A* and not *B* is, in the strictest sense, an *accident,* lucky or unlucky as the case may be. It may be welcomed or it may be deplored, but neither I nor anything else in the universe can properly be praised or blamed for it. It begins to look as if the categorical ought may be inapplicable, though for different reasons, both on the hypothesis that voluntary actions have causal progenitors and on the hypothesis that none of their causal ancestors are causal progenitors.

The Positive Condition

Let us now try to discover the positive conditions of categorical obligability. I think that we should naturally tend to answer the sort of objection which I have just raised in the following way. We should say: 'I deliberately identified myself with my desire to do *A,* or I deliberately threw my weight on the side of that desire. I might instead have made no particular effort in one direction or the other; or I might have identified myself with, and thrown my weight on the side of, my desire to do *B*. So my desire to do *A* did not just happen to be present with the requisite strength and persistence, as compared with my desire to do *B*. It had this degree of strength and persistence because, and only because, I *reinforced* it by a deliberate effort, which I need not have made at all and which I could have made in favour of my desire to do *B*.' Another way of expressing the same thing would be this: 'I forced myself to do *A*; but I need not have done so, and, if I had not done so, I should have done *B*.' Or again: 'I might have forced myself to do *B*; but I did not, and so I did *A*.'

It is quite plain that these phrases express a genuine positive experience with which we are all perfectly familiar. They are all, of course, metaphorical. It will be noticed that they all attempt to describe the generic fact by metaphors drawn from specific instances of it, e.g. deliberately pressing down one scale of a balance, deliberately joining one side in a tug-of-war, deliberately thrusting a body in a certain direction against obstacles, and so on. In this respect they may be compared with attempts to describe the generic facts about time and change by metaphors drawn from specific instances, such as flowing streams, moving spots of light, and so on. The only use of such metaphors is to direct attention to the sort of fact which one wants one's hearers to contemplate. They give no help towards analysing or comprehending this fact. A metaphor helps us to understand a fact only when it brings out an analogy with a fact of a *different* kind, which we already understand. When a generic fact can be described only by metaphors drawn from specific instances of itself it is a sign that the fact is unique and peculiar, like the fact of temporal succession and the change of events from futurity, through presentness, to pastness.

Granted that there is this unique and peculiar factor of deliberate effort or reinforcement, how far does the recognition of it help us in our present problem? So far as I can see, it merely takes the problem one step further back. My doing of *A* is completely determined by a total cause which contains as factors my desire to do *A* and my desire to do *B*, each of which has a certain determinate strength and persistence. The preponderance of my desire to do *A* over my desire to do *B*, in respect of strength and persistence, is completely determined by a total cause which contains as a factor my putting forth a certain amount of effort to reinforce my desire for *A*. This effort-factor is not completely determined. It is logically consistent with all the nomic, occurrent, dispositional, and background facts that no effort should have been made, or that it should have been directed towards reinforcing the desire for *B* instead of the desire for *A*, or that it should have been put forth more or less strongly than it actually was in favour of the desire for *A*. Surely then we can say no more than that it just happened to occur with a certain degree of intensity in favour of the desire for *A*.

I think that the safest course at this stage for those who maintain that some actions are categorically obligable would be the following. They should admit quite frankly what I have just stated, and should then say: 'However paradoxical it may seem, we do regard ourselves and other people as morally responsible for accidents of this unique kind, and we do not regard them as morally responsible, in the categorical sense, for anything but such accidents and those consequences of them which would have been different if the accidents had happened differently. Only such accidents, and their causal descendants in the way of volition and action, are categorically obligable.' If anyone should take up this position, I should not know how to refute him, though I should be strongly inclined to think him mistaken.

This is not, however, the position which persons who hold that some actions are categorically obligable generally do take at this point. I do not find that they ever state quite clearly what they think they believe, and I suspect that is because, if it were clearly stated, it would be seen to be impossible. I shall therefore try to state clearly what I think such people want to believe, and shall try to show that it is impossible. I suspect that they would quarrel with my statement that, on their view, the fact that one puts forth such and such an effort in support of a certain desire is, in the strictest sense, an accident. They would like to say that the putting forth of a certain amount of effort in a certain direction at a certain time *is* completely determined, but is determined in a unique and peculiar way. It is literally determined *by the agent or self*, considered as a substance or continuant, and not by a total cause which contains as factors *events in* and *dispositions of* the agent. If this could be maintained, our puttings-forth of effort would be completely determined, but their causes would neither be events nor contain events as cause-factors. Certain series of events would then originate from causal progenitors which are continuants and not events. Since the first event in such a series would be completely determined, it would not be an accident. And, since the total cause of such an event would not be an event and would not contain an event as a cause-factor, the two alternatives 'completely determined' and 'partially undetermined' would both be inapplicable to it. For these alternatives apply only to events.

I am fairly sure that this is the kind of proposition which people who profess to believe in Free Will want to believe. I have, of course, stated it with a regrettable crudity, of which they would be incapable. Now it seems to me clear that such a view is impossible. The putting-forth of an effort of a certain intensity, in a certain direction, at a certain moment, for a certain duration, is quite clearly an event or process, however unique and peculiar it may be in other respects. It is therefore subject to any conditions which self-evidently apply to every event, as such. Now it is surely quite evident that, if the beginning of a certain process at a certain time is determined at all, its total cause *must* contain as an essential factor another event or process which *enters into* the moment from which the determined event or process *issues*. I see no *prima facie* objection to there being events that are not completely determined. But, in so far as an event *is* determined, an essential factor in its total cause must be other *events*. How could an event possibly be determined to happen at a certain date if its total cause contained no factor to which the notion of date has any application? And how can the notion of date have any application to anything that is not an event?

Of course I am well aware that we constantly use phrases, describing causal transactions, in which a continuant is named as the cause and no event in that continuant is mentioned. Thus we say: 'The stone broke the window,' 'The cat killed the mouse,' and so on. But it is quite evident that all such phrases are elliptical. The first, e.g., expresses what would be more fully expressed by the sentence: 'The coming in contact of the moving stone with the window at a certain moment caused a process of disintegration to begin in the window at that moment.' Thus the fact that we use and understand such phrases casts no doubt on the general principle which I have just enunciated.

Let us call the kind of causation which I have just described and rejected 'non-occurrent causation of events.' We will call the ordinary kind of causation, which I had in mind when I defined 'Determinism' and 'Indeterminism,' 'occurrent causation.'

Now I think we can plausibly suggest what may have made some people think they believe that puttings-forth of effort are events which are determined by non-occurrent causation. It is quite usual to say that a man's putting-forth of effort in a certain direction on a certain occasion was determined by 'Reason' or 'Principle' or 'Conscience' or 'The Moral Law.' Now these impressive names and phrases certainly do not denote events or even substances. If they denote anything, they stand for propositions or systems of propositions, or for those peculiar universals or systems of universals which Plato called 'Ideas.' If it were literally true that puttings-forth of effort are determined by such entities, we should have causation of events in time by timeless causes. But, of course, statements like 'Smith's putting-forth of effort in a certain direction on a certain occasion was determined by the Moral Law' cannot be taken literally. The Moral Law, as such, has no causal efficacy. What is meant is that Smith's *belief* that a certain alternative would be in accordance with the Moral Law, and his *desire* to do what is right, were cause-factors in the total cause which determined his putting-forth of effort on the side of that alternative. Now this belief was an event, which happened when he began to reflect on the alternatives and to consider them in the light of the moral principles which he accepts and regards as relevant. And this desire was an event, which happened when his conative-emotional moral dispositions were stirred by the process of reflecting on the alternatives. Thus the use of phrases about action being 'determined by the Moral Law' may have made some people think they believe that some events are determined by non-occurrent causation. But our analysis of the meaning of such phrases shows that the facts which they express give no logical support to this belief.

Libertarianism

We are now in a position to define what I will call 'Libertarianism.' This doctrine may be summed up in two propositions. (i) Some (and it may be all) voluntary actions have a causal ancestor which contains as a cause-factor the putting-forth of an effort which is not completely determined in direction and intensity by occurrent causation. (ii) In such cases the direction and the intensity of the effort are completely determined by non-occurrent causation, in which the self or agent, taken as a substance or continuant, is the non-occurrent total cause. Thus, Libertarianism, as defined by me, entails Indeterminism, as defined by me; but the converse does not hold.

If I am right, Libertarianism is self-evidently impossible, whilst Indeterminism is *prima facie* possible. Hence, if categorical obligability entails Libertarianism, it is certain that no action can be categorically obligable. But if categorical obligability entails only Indeterminism, it is *prima facie* possible that some actions are categorically obligable. Unfortunately, it seems almost certain that categorical obligability entails more than Indeterminism, and it seems very likely that it entails Libertarianism. It is therefore highly probable that the notion of categorical obligability is a delusive notion, which neither has nor can have any application.

THE FREEDOM OF THE WILL

JOHN STUART MILL

. . .

His view of the controversy is peculiar, but harmonizes with his Philosophy of the Conditioned, which seems indeed to have been principally suggested to him by the supposed requirements of this question. He is of opinion that Free-will and

From John Stuart Mill, "The Freedom of the Will," in *An Examination of Sir William Hamilton's Philosophy*. New York: Holt, Rinehart and Winston, 1874, Vol. II, pp. 272–290.

Necessity are both inconceivable. Free-will, because it supposes volitions to originate without cause; because it affirms an absolute commencement, which, as we are aware, our author deems it impossible for the human mind to conceive. On the other hand, the mind is equally unable to conceive an infinite regress; a chain of causation going back to all eternity. Both the one and the other theory thus involve difficulties insurmountable by the human faculties. But, as Sir W. Hamilton has so often told us, the inconceivability of a thing by us, is no proof that it is objectively impossible by the laws of the universe; on the contrary, it often happens that both sides of an alternative are alike incomprehensible to us, while from their nature we are certain that the one or the other must be true. Such an alternative, according to Sir W. Hamilton, exists between the conflicting doctrines of Free-will and Necessity. By the law of Excluded Middle, one or other of them must be true; and inconceivability, as common to both, not operating more against one than against the other, does not operate against either. The balance, therefore, must turn in favor of the side for which there is positive evidence. In favor of Free-will we have the distinct testimony of consciousness; perhaps directly, though of this he speaks with some appearance of doubt;[1] but at all events, indirectly, freedom being implied in the consciousness of moral responsibility. As there is no corresponding evidence in favor of the other theory, the Free-will doctrine must prevail. "How[2] the will can possibly be free must remain to us, under the present limitation of our faculties, wholly incomprehensible. We cannot conceive absolute commencement; we cannot, therefore, conceive a free volition. But as little can we conceive the alternative on which liberty is denied, on which necessity is affirmed. And in favor of our moral nature, the fact that we are free is given us in the consciousness of an uncompromising law of Duty, in the consciousness of our moral accountability; and this fact of liberty cannot be redargued on the ground that it is incomprehensible, for the doctrine of the Conditioned

[1] Foot-notes to Reid, pp. 599, 602, 624.

[2] Lectures, ii. 412, 413.

proves, against the necessitarian, that something may, nay, must, be true, of which the mind is wholly unable to construe to itself the possibility, whilst it shows that the objection of incomprehensibility applies no less to the doctrine of fatalism than to the doctrine of moral freedom."

The inconceivability of the Free-will doctrine is maintained by our author, not only on the general ground just stated, of our incapacity to conceive an absolute commencement, but on the further and special ground, that the will is determined by motives. In rewriting the preceding passage for the Appendix to his "Discussions," he made the following addition to it:[3] "A determination by motives cannot, to our understanding, escape from necessitation. Nay, were we even to admit as true, what we cannot think as possible, still the doctrine of a motiveless volition would be only casualism; and the free acts of an indifferent, are, morally and rationally, as worthless as the preordered passions of a determined will.[4] *How*, therefore, I repeat, moral liberty is possible in man or God, we are utterly unable speculatively to understand. But . . . the scheme of freedom is not more inconceivable than the scheme of necessity. For whilst fatalism is a recoil from the more obtrusive inconceivability of an *absolute* commencement, on the fact of which commencement the doctrine of liberty proceeds, the fatalist is shown to overlook the equal, but less obtrusive, inconceivability of an *infinite* non-commencement, on the assertion of which non-commencement his own doctrine of necessity must ultimately rest." It rests on no such thing, if he believes in a First Cause, which a Necessitarian may. What is more, even if he does not believe in a First Cause, he

[3] Appendix to Discussions, pp. 624, 625.

[4] To the same effect in another passage: "That, though inconceivable, a motiveless volition would, if conceived, be conceived as morally worthless, only shows our impotence more clearly." (Appendix to Discussions, pp. 614, 615.) And in a foot-note to Reid (p. 602), "Is the person an *original undetermined* cause of the determination of his will? If he be not, then he is not a *free agent*, and the scheme of Necessity is admitted. If he be, in the first place, it is impossible to *conceive* the possibility of this; and, in the second, if the fact, though inconceivable, be allowed, it is impossible to see how a cause, undetermined by any motive, can be a rational, moral, and accountable cause."

makes no "assertion of non-commencement"; he only declines to make an assertion of commencement; a distinction of which Sir W. Hamilton, of all men, ought to recognize the importance. But to resume the quotation: "As equally unthinkable, the two counter, the two one-sided, schemes are thus theoretically balanced. But, practically, our consciousness of the moral law, which, without a moral liberty in man, would be a mendacious imperative, gives a decisive preponderance to the doctrine of freedom over the doctrine of fate. We are free in act, if we are accountable for our actions."

Sir W. Hamilton is of opinion that both sides are alike unsuccessful in repelling each other's attacks. The arguments against both are, he thinks, to the human faculties, irrefutable. "The champions[5] of the opposite doctrines are at once resistless in assault and impotent in defense. Each is hewn down, and appears to die under the home thrusts of his adversary; but each again recovers life from the very death of his antagonist, and, to borrow a simile, both are like the heroes in Valhalla, ready in a moment to amuse themselves anew in the same bloodless and interminable conflict. The doctrine of Moral Liberty cannot be made conceivable, for we can only conceive the determined and the relative. As already stated, all that can be done is to show, 1°. That, for the *fact* of Liberty, we have immediately or mediately, the evidence of Consciousness; and 2°. That there are among the phænomena of mind, many facts which we *must* admit as actual, but of whose possibility we are wholly unable to form any notion. I may merely observe that the fact of *Motion* can be shown to be impossible, on grounds not less strong than those on which it is attempted to disprove the fact of Liberty." These "grounds no less strong" are the mere paralogisms which we examined in a recent chapter, and with regard to which our author showed so surprising a deficiency in the acuteness and subtlety to be expected from the general quality of his mind.

Conformably to these views, Sir W. Hamilton, in his foot-notes on Reid, promptly puts an extinguisher on several of that

[5] Foot-note on Reid, p. 602.

philosopher's arguments against the doctrine of so-called Necessity. When Reid affirms that Motives are not causes—that they may influence to action, but do not act, Sir W. Hamilton observes,[6] "If Motives influence to action, they must co-operate in producing a certain effect upon the agent; and the determination to act, and to act in a certain manner, is that effect. They are thus, on Reid's own view, in this relation, *causes,* and *efficient* causes. It is of no consequence in the argument whether motives be said to determine a man to act, or to influence (that is, to determine) him to determine himself to act."[7] This is one of the neatest specimens in our author's writings of a fallacy cut clean through by a single stroke.

Again, when Reid says that acts are often done without any motive, or when there is no motive for preferring the means used, rather than others by which the same end might have been attained, Sir W. Hamilton asks,[8] "Can we conceive any act of which there was not a sufficient cause or concourse of causes why the man performed it and no other? If not, call this cause, or these concauses, the *motive,* and there is no longer a dispute."

Reid asks, "Is there no such thing as wilfulness, caprice, or obstinacy among mankind?" Sir W. Hamilton, *e contra:*[9] "But are not these all tendencies, and fatal tendencies, to act or not to act? By contradistinguishing such tendencies from motives strictly so called, or rational impulses, we do not advance a single step towards rendering liberty comprehensible."

According to Reid, the determination is made by the man, and not by the motive. "But," asks Sir W. Hamilton,[10] "was the *man* determined by no motive to that determination? Was his specific volition to this or to that without a cause? On the supposition that the sum of influences (motives, dispositions, and tendencies) to volition A, is equal to 12, and the sum of influences to counter-volition B equal to 8—can we conceive

[6] Foot-note on Reid, p. 608.

[7] To the same effect see Discussions, Appendix on Causality, p. 614.

[8] Foot-note on Reid, p. 609.

[9] Foot-note to Reid, p. 610.

[10] *Ibid.,* p. 611.

that the determination of volition A should not be necessary?—We can only conceive the volition B to be determined by supposing that the man *creates* (calls from non-existence into existence) a certain supplement of influences. But this creation as actual, or in itself, is inconceivable, and even to conceive the possibility of this inconceivable act, we must suppose some cause by which the man is determined to exert it. We thus, in *thought*, never escape determination and necessity. It will be observed that I do not consider this inability to the *notion*, any disproof of the *fact* of Free-will." Nor is it: but if, as our author so strongly inculcates, "every[11] effort to bring the fact of liberty within the compass of our conceptions only results in the substitution in its place of some more or less disguised form of necessity," it is a strong indication that some form of necessity is the opinion naturally suggested by our collective experience of life.[12]

Sir W. Hamilton having thus, as is often the case (and it is one of the best things he does), saved his opponents the trouble of answering his friends, his doctrine is left resting exclusively on the supports which he has himself provided for it. In examining them, let us place ourselves, in the first instance, completely at his point of view, and concede to him the coequal inconceivability of the conflicting hypotheses, an uncaused commencement, and an infinite regress. But this choice of inconceivabilities is not offered to us in the case of volitions only. We are held, as he not only admits but contends, to the same alternative in all cases of causation whatsoever. But we find our way out of the difficulty, in other cases, in quite a different manner. In the case of every other kind of fact, we do not elect the hypothesis that the event took place without a cause:

[11] Lectures, i. 34.

[12] So difficult is it to escape from this fact, that Sir W. Hamilton himself says (Lectures, i. 188), "Voluntary conation is a faculty which can only be determined to energy through a pain or pleasure—through an estimate of the relative worth of objects." If I am determined to prefer innocence to the satisfaction of a particular desire, through an estimate of the relative worth of innocence and of the gratification, can this estimate, while unchanged, leave me at liberty to choose the gratification in preference to innocence?

we accept the other supposition, that of a regress, not indeed to infinity, but either generally into the region of the Unknowable, or back to a Universal Cause, regarding which, as we are only concerned with it in relation to what it preceded, and not as itself preceded by anything, we can afford to make a plain avowal of our ignorance.

Now, what is the reason, which, in the case of all things within the range of our knowledge except volitions, makes us choose this side of the alternative? Why do we, without scruple, register all of them as depending on causes, by which (to use our author's language) they are determined necessarily, though, in believing this, we, according to Sir W. Hamilton, believe as utter an inconceivability as if we supposed them to take place without a cause? Apparently it is because the causation hypothesis, inconceivable as he may think it, possesses the advantage of having experience on its side. And how, or by what evidence, does experience testify to it? Not by disclosing any *nexus* between the cause and the effect, any Sufficient Reason in the cause itself why the effect should follow it. No philosopher now makes this supposition, and Sir W. Hamilton positively disclaims it. What experience makes known, is the fact of an invariable sequence between every event and some special combination of antecedent conditions, in such sort that wherever and whenever that union of antecedents exists, the event does not fail to occur. Any *must* in the case, any necessity, other than the unconditional universality of the fact, we know nothing of. Still, this à posteriori "does," though not confirmed by an à priori "must," decides our choice between the two inconceivables, and leads us to the belief that every event within the phænomenal universe, except human volitions, is determined to take place by a cause. Now, the so-called Necessitarians demand the application of the same rule of judgment to our volitions. They maintain that there is the same evidence for it. They affirm, as a truth of experience, that volitions do, in point of fact, follow determinate moral antecedents with the same uniformity, and (when we have sufficient knowledge of the circumstances) with the same certainty, as physical effects follow their physical causes. These moral antecedents are desires, aversions, habits, and dispositions, combined with outward circumstances suited to call those internal incentives into action. All these again are effects of causes, those of them which are mental being consequences of education, and of other moral and physical influences. This is what Necessitarians affirm: and they court every possible mode in which its truth can be verified. They test it by each person's observation of his own volitions. They test it by each person's observation of the voluntary actions of those with whom he comes into contact; and by the power which every one has of foreseeing actions, with a degree of exactness proportioned to his previous experience and knowledge of the agents, and with a certainty often quite equal to that with which we predict the commonest physical events. They test it further, by the statistical results of the observation of human beings acting in numbers sufficient to eliminate the influences which operate only on a few, and which on a large scale neutralize one another, leaving the total result about the same as if the volitions of the whole mass had been affected by such only of the determining causes as were common to them all. In cases of this description the results are as uniform, and may be as accurately foretold, as in any physical inquiries in which the effect depends upon a multiplicity of causes. The cases in which volitions seem too uncertain to admit of being confidently predicted, are those in which our knowledge of the influences antecedently in operation is so incomplete, that with equally imperfect data there would be the same uncertainty in the predictions of the astronomer and the chemist. On these grounds it is contended, that our choice between the conflicting inconceivables should be the same in the case of volitions as of all other phænomena; we must reject equally in both cases the hypothesis of spontaneousness, and consider them all as caused. A volition is a moral effect, which follows the corresponding moral causes as certainly and invariably as physical effects follow their physical causes. Whether it *must* do so, I acknowledge myself to be entirely ignorant, be the phænomenon moral or physical; and I condemn, accordingly, the word Necessity as applied to either case. All I know is, that it always *does*.

This argument from experience Sir W. Hamilton passes unnoticed, but urges, on the opposite side of the question, the argument from Consciousness. We are conscious, he affirms, either of our freedom, or at all events (it is odd that, on this theory, there should be any doubt) of something which implies freedom. If this is true, our internal consciousness tells us one thing, and the whole outward experience of the human race tells another. This is surely a very unfortunate predicament we are in, and a sore trial to the puzzled metaphysician. Philosophy is far from having so easy a business before her as our author thinks: the arbiter Consciousness is by no means invoked to turn the scale between two equally balanced difficulties; on the contrary, she has to sit in judgment between herself and a complete Induction from experience. Consciousness, it will probably be said, is the best evidence; and so it would be, if we were always certain what is Consciousness. But while there are so many varying testimonies respecting this; when Sir W. Hamilton can himself say,[13] "many philosophers have attempted to establish, on the principles of common sense, propositions which are not original data of consciousness, while the original data of consciousness from which these propositions were derived, and to which they owed all their necessity and truth, these same philosophers were (strange to say) not disposed to admit"; when M. Cousin and nearly all Germany find the Infinite and the Absolute in Consciousness, Sir W. Hamilton thinking them utterly repugnant to it; when philosophers, for many generations, fancied that they had Abstract Ideas—that they could conceive a triangle which was neither equilateral, isosceles, nor scalene,[14]

[13] Dissertations on Reid, p. 749.

[14] "Does it not require," says Locke (Essay on the Human Understanding, Book iv. chap. 7, sect. 9), "some pains and skill to form the general idea of a triangle (which yet is none of the most abstract, comprehensive, and difficult)? for it must be neither oblique nor rectangle, neither equilateral, equicrural, nor scalene; but all and none of these at once. In effect, it is something imperfect, that cannot exist; an idea wherein some parts of several different and inconsistent ideas are put together." Yet this union of contradictory elements such a philosopher as Locke was able to fancy that he conceived. I scarcely know a more striking example of the tendency of the human mind to believe that things can exist separately because they can be separately named; a tendency

which Sir W. Hamilton and all other people now consider to be simply absurd; with all these conflicting opinions respecting the things to which Consciousness testifies, what is the perplexed inquirer to think? Does all philosophy end, as in our author's opinion Hume believed it to do, in a persistent contradiction between one of our mental faculties and another? We shall find there is a solution, which relieves the human mind from this embarrassment: namely, that the question to which experience says yes, and that to which consciousness says no, are different questions.

Let us cross-examine the alleged testimony of consciousness. And, first, it is left in some uncertainty by Sir W. Hamilton whether Consciousness makes only one deliverance on the subject, or two; whether we are conscious only of moral responsibility, in which free-will is implied, or are directly conscious of free-will. In his Lectures, Sir W. Hamilton speaks only of the first. In the notes on Reid, which were written subsequently, he seems to affirm both, but the latter of the two in a doubtful and hesitating manner: so difficult, in reality, does he find it to ascertain with certainty what it is that Consciousness certifies. But as there are many who maintain, with a confidence far greater than his, that we are directly conscious of free-will,[15] it is necessary to examine that question.

To be conscious of free-will, must mean, to be conscious, be-

---

strong enough, in this case, to make a mind like Locke's believe itself to be conscious of that which by the laws of mind cannot be a subject of consciousness to any one.

[15] Mr. Mansel, among others, makes the assertion in the broadest form it is capable of, saying, "In every act of volition, I am fully conscious that I can at this moment act in either of two ways, and that, all the antecedent phænomena being precisely the same, I may determine one way to-day and another way to-morrow." (Prolegomena Logica, p. 152.) Yes, though the antecedent phænomena remain the same; but not if my judgment of the antecedent phænomena remains the same. If my conduct changes, either the external inducements or my estimate of them must have changed.

Mr. Mansel (as I have already observed) goes so far as to maintain that our immediate intuition of Power is given us by the ego producing its own volitions, not by its volitions producing bodily movements (pp. 139, 140, and 151).

fore I have decided, that I am able to decide either way. Exception may be taken *in limine* to the use of the word consciousness in such an application. Consciousness tells me what I do or feel. But what I am *able* to do, is not a subject of consciousness. Consciousness is not prophetic; we are conscious of what is, not of what will or can be. We never know that we are able to do a thing, except from having done it, or something equal and similar to it. We should not know that we were capable of action at all, if we had never acted. Having acted, we know, as far as that experience reaches, how we are able to act; and this knowledge, when it has become familiar, is often confounded with, and called by the name of, consciousness. But it does not derive any increase of authority from being misnamed; its truth is not supreme over, but depends on, experience. If our so-called consciousness of what we are able to do is not borne out by experience, it is a delusion. It has no title to credence but as an interpretation of experience, and if it is a false interpretation, it must give way.

But this conviction, whether termed consciousness or only belief, that our will is free—what is it? Of what are we convinced? I am told, that whether I decide to do or to abstain, I feel that I could have decided the other way. I ask my consciousness what I do feel, and I find, indeed, that I feel (or am convinced) that I could have chosen the other course *if I had preferred it;* but not that I could have chosen one course while I preferred the other. When I say preferred, I of course include with the thing itself, all that accompanies it. I know that I can, because I know that I often do, elect to do one thing, when I should have preferred another in itself, apart from its consequences, or from a moral law which it violates. And this preference for a thing in itself, abstractedly from its accompaniments, is often loosely described as preference for the thing. It is this unprecise mode of speech which makes it not seem absurd to say that I act in opposition to my preference; that I do one thing when I would rather do another; that my conscience prevails over my desires—as if conscience were not itself a desire—the desire to do right. Take any alternative: say, to murder or not to murder. I am told, that if I elect to murder, I am conscious that I could have elected to abstain: but am I conscious that I could have abstained if my aversion to the crime, and my dread of its consequences, had been weaker than the temptation? If I elect to abstain: in what sense am I conscious that I could have elected to commit the crime? Only if I had desired to commit it with a desire stronger than my horror of murder; not with one less strong. When we think of ourselves hypothetically as having acted otherwise than we did, we always suppose a difference in the antecedents: we picture ourselves as having known something that we did not know, or not known something that we did know; which is a difference in the external motives; or as having desired something, or disliked something, more or less than we did; which is a difference in the internal motives.

I therefore dispute altogether that we are conscious of being able to act in opposition to the strongest present desire or aversion. The difference between a bad and a good man is not that the latter acts in opposition to his strongest desires; it is that his desire to do right, and his aversion to doing wrong, are strong enough to overcome, and in the case of perfect virtue, to silence, any other desire or aversion which may conflict with them. It is because this state of mind is possible to human nature, that human beings are capable of moral government: and moral education consists in subjecting them to the discipline which has most tendency to bring them into this state. The object of moral education is to educate the will: but the will can only be educated through the desires and aversions; by eradicating or weakening such of them as are likeliest to lead to evil; exalting to the highest pitch the desire of right conduct and the aversion to wrong; cultivating all other desires and aversions of which the ordinary operation is auxiliary to right, while discountenancing so immoderate an indulgence of them, as might render them too powerful to be overcome by the moral sentiment, when they chance to be in opposition to it. The other requisites are, a clear intellectual standard of right and wrong, that moral desire and aversion may act in the proper places, and such general mental habits as shall prevent moral considerations from being forgotten or overlooked, in cases to which they are rightly applicable.

Rejecting, then, the figment of a direct consciousness of the freedom of the will, in other words, our ability to will in opposition to our strongest preference; it remains to consider whether, as affirmed by Sir W. Hamilton, a freedom of this kind is implied in what is called our consciousness of moral responsibility. There must be something very plausible in this opinion, since it is shared even by Necessitarians. Many of these —in particular Mr. Owen and his followers—from a recognition of the fact that volitions are effects of causes, have been led to deny human responsibility. I do not mean that they denied moral distinctions. Few persons have had a stronger sense of right and wrong, or been more devoted to the things they deemed right. What they denied was the rightfulness of inflicting punishment. A man's actions, they said, are the result of his character, and he is not the author of his own character. It is made *for* him, not *by* him. There is no justice in punishing him for what he cannot help. We should try to convince or persuade him that he had better act in a different manner; and should educate all, especially the young, in the habits and dispositions which lead to well-doing: though how this is to be effected without any use whatever of punishment as a means of education, is a question they have failed to resolve. The confusion of ideas, which makes the subjection of human volitions to the law of Causation seem inconsistent with accountability, must thus be very natural to the human mind; but this may be said of a thousand errors, and even of some merely verbal fallacies. In the present case there is more than a verbal fallacy, but verbal fallacies also contribute their part.

What is meant by moral responsibility? Responsibility means punishment. When we are said to have the feeling of being morally responsible for our actions, the idea of being punished for them is uppermost in the speaker's mind. But the feeling of liability to punishment is of two kinds. It may mean, expectation that if we act in a certain manner, punishment will actually be inflicted upon us, by our fellow-creatures or by a Supreme Power. Or it may only mean, being conscious that we shall deserve that infliction.

The first of these cannot, in any correct meaning of the term, be designated as a consciousness. If we believe that we shall be punished for doing wrong, it is because the belief has been taught to us by our parents and tutors, or by our religion, or is generally held by those who surround us, or because we have ourselves come to the conclusion by reasoning, or from the experience of life. This is not Consciousness. And, by whatever name it is called, its evidence is not dependent on any theory of the spontaneousness of volition. The punishment of guilt in another world is believed with undoubting conviction by Turkish fatalists, and by professed Christians who are not only Necessitarians, but believe that the majority of mankind were divinely predestined from all eternity to sin and to be punished for sinning. It is not, therefore, the belief that we shall be *made* accountable, which can be deemed to require or presuppose the free-will hypothesis; it is the belief that we ought so to be; that we are justly accountable; that guilt deserves punishment. It is here that the main issue is joined between the two opinions.

In discussing it, there is no need to postulate any theory respecting the nature or criterion of moral distinctions. It matters not, for this purpose, whether the right and wrong of actions depends on the consequences they tend to produce, or on an inherent quality of the actions themselves. It is indifferent whether we are utilitarians or anti-utilitarians; whether our ethics rest on intuition or on experience. It is sufficient if we believe that there is a difference between right and wrong, and a natural reason for preferring the former; that people in general, unless when they expect personal benefit from a wrong, naturally and usually prefer what they think to be right: whether because we are all dependent for what makes existence tolerable, upon the right conduct of other people, while their wrong conduct is a standing menace to our security, or for some more mystical and transcendental reason. Whatever be the cause, we are entitled to assume the fact; and its consequence is, that whoever cultivates a disposition to wrong, places his mind out of sympathy with the rest of his fellow-creatures, and if they are aware of his disposition, becomes a natural object of their active dislike. He not only forfeits the pleasure of their good will, and the benefit of their good offices, except when compassion for the human being is stronger than distaste towards the wrongdoer; but he also renders himself liable to whatever they may think it necessary to do in order to protect themselves against him; which may probably include punishment, as such, and will certainly involve much that is equivalent in its operation on himself. In this way he is certain to be made accountable, at least to his fellow-creatures, through the normal action of their natural sentiments. And it is well worth consideration, whether the practical expectation of being thus called to account, has not a great deal to do with the internal feeling of being accountable; a feeling, assuredly, which is seldom found existing in any strength in the absence of that practical expectation. It is not usually found that Oriental despots, who cannot be called to account by anybody, have much consciousness of being morally accountable. And (what is still more significant) in societies in which caste or class distinctions are really strong—a state so strange to us now, that we seldom realize it in its full force—it is a matter of daily experience that persons may show the strongest sense of moral accountability as regards their equals, who can make them accountable, and not the smallest vestige of a similar feeling towards their inferiors who cannot.

Another fact which it is of importance to keep in view, is, that the highest and strongest sense of the worth of goodness, and the odiousness of its opposite, is perfectly compatible with even the most exaggerated form of Fatalism. Suppose that there were two peculiar breeds of human beings,—one of them so constituted from the beginning, that however educated or treated, nothing could prevent them from always feeling and acting so as to be a blessing to all whom they approached; another, of such original perversity of nature that neither education nor punishment could inspire them with a feeling of duty, or prevent them from being active in evil doing. Neither of these races of human beings would have free-will; yet the former would be honored as demigods, while the latter would be regarded and treated as noxious beasts; not punished perhaps, since punishment would have no effect on them, and it might be thought wrong to indulge the mere instinct of vengeance: but kept carefully at a distance, and killed like other dangerous creatures when there was no other convenient way of being rid of them. We thus see that even under the utmost possible exaggeration of the doctrine of Necessity, the distinction between moral good and evil in conduct would not only subsist, but would stand out in a more marked manner than now, when the good and the wicked, however unlike, are still regarded as of one common nature. . . .

BEING AND DOING: FREEDOM

JEAN-PAUL SARTRE

Freedom: The First Condition of Action

It is strange that philosophers have been able to argue endlessly about determinism and free-will, to cite examples in favor of one or the other thesis without ever attempting first to make explicit the structures contained in the very idea of *action.* The concept of an act contains, in fact, numerous subordinate notions which we shall have to organize and arrange in a hierarchy: to act is to modify the *shape* of the world; it is to arrange means in view of an end; it is to produce an organized instrumental complex such that by a series of concatenations and connections the modification effected on one of the links causes modifications throughout the whole series and finally produces an anticipated result. But this is not what is important for us here. We should observe first that

From Jean-Paul Sartre, "Being and Doing: Freedom," in *Being and Nothingness*, translated by H. E. Barnes. New York: Philosophical Library, 1956, pp. 433–438; 439–445; 450–451; 553–556.

an action is on principle *intentional.* The careless smoker who has through negligence caused the explosion of a powder magazine has not *acted.* On the other hand the worker who is charged with dynamiting a quarry and who obeys the given orders has acted when he has produced the expected explosion; he knew what he was doing or, if you prefer, he intentionally realized a conscious project.

This does not mean, of course, that one must foresee all the consequences of his act. The emperor Constantine when he established himself at Byzantium, did not foresee that he would create a center of Greek culture and language, the appearance of which would ultimately provoke a schism in the Christian Church and which would contribute to weakening the Roman Empire. Yet he performed an act just in so far as he realized his project of creating a new residence for emperors in the Orient. Equating the result with the intention is here sufficient for us to be able to speak of action. But if this is the case, we establish that the action necessarily implies as its condition the recognition of a "desideratum"; that is, of an objective lack or again of a *négatité.* The intention of providing a rival for Rome can come to Constantine only through the apprehension of an objective lack: Rome lacks a counterweight; to this still profoundly pagan city ought to be opposed a Christian city which at the moment *is missing.* Creating Constantinople is understood as an act only if first the conception of a new city has preceded the action itself or at least if this conception serves as an organizing theme for all later steps. But this conception cannot be the pure representation of the city as *possible.* It apprehends the city in its essential characteristic, which is to be a *desirable* and not yet realized possible.

This means that from the moment of the first conception of the act, consciousness has been able to withdraw itself from the full world of which it is consciousness and to leave the level of being in order frankly to approach that of non-being. Consciousness in so far as it is considered exclusively in its being, is perpetually referred from being to being and can not find in being any motive for revealing non-being. The imperial system with Rome as its capital functions positively and in a certain real way which can be easily discovered. Will someone say that the taxes are collected badly, that Rome is not secure from invasions, that it does not have the geographical location which is suitable for the capital of a Mediterranean empire which is threatened by barbarians, that its corrupt morals make the spread of the Christian religion difficult? How can anyone fail to see that all these considerations are *negative;* that is, that they aim at what is not, not at what is. To say that sixty per cent of the anticipated taxes have been collected can pass, if need be for a positive appreciation of the situation *such as it is*. To say that they are *badly* collected is to consider the situation across a situation which is posited as an absolute end but which precisely *is not.* To say that the corrupt morals at Rome hinder the spread of Christianity is not to consider this diffusion for what it is; that is, for a propagation at a rate which the reports of the clergy can enable us to determine. It is to posit the diffusion in itself as insufficient; that is, as suffering from a secret nothingness. But it appears as such only if it is surpassed toward a limiting-situation posited *a priori* as a value (for example, toward a certain rate of religious conversions, toward a certain mass morality). This limiting-situation can not be conceived in terms of the simple consideration of the real state of things; for the most beautiful girl in the world can offer only what she *has,* and in the same way the most miserable situation can by itself be designated only as it *is* without any reference to an ideal nothingness.

In so far as man is immersed in the historical situation, he does not even succeed in conceiving of the failures and lacks in a political organization or determined economy; this is not, as is stupidly said, because he "is accustomed to it," but because he apprehends it in its plenitude of being and because he can not even imagine that he can exist in it otherwise. For it is necessary here to reverse common opinion and on the basis of what it is not, to acknowledge the harshness of a situation or the sufferings which it imposes, both of which are motives for conceiving of another state of affairs in which things would be better for everybody. It is on the day that we can conceive of a different state of affairs that a new light falls on our troubles and our suffering and that we *decide* that these are unbearable. A worker in 1830 is capable of revolting if his salary is lowered, for he easily conceives of a situation in which his wretched standard of living would be not as low as the one which is about to be imposed on him. But he does not represent his sufferings to himself as unbearable; he adapts himself to them not through resignation but because he lacks the education and reflection necessary for him to conceive of a social state in which these sufferings would not exist. Consequently *he* does not act. Masters of Lyon following a riot, the workers at Croix-Rousse do not know what to do with their victory; they return home bewildered, and the regular army has no trouble in overcoming them. Their misfortunes do not appear to them "habitual" but rather *natural; they are,* that is all, and they constitute the worker's condition. They are not detached; they are not seen in the clear light of day, and consequently they are integrated by the worker with his being. He suffers without considering his suffering and without conferring value upon it. To suffer and to *be* are one and the same for him. His suffering is the pure affective tenor of his non-positional consciousness, but he does not contemplate it. Therefore this suffering can not be in itself a *motive*[1] for his acts. Quite the contrary, it is after he has formed the project of changing the situation that it will appear intolerable to him. This means that he will have had to give himself room, to withdraw in relation to it, and will have to have effected a double nihilation: on the one hand, he must posit an ideal state of affairs as a pure *present* nothingness; on the other hand, he must posit the

[1] In this and following sections Sartre makes a sharp distinction between *motif* and *mobile.* The English word "motive" expresses sufficiently adequately the French *mobile,* which refers to an inner subjective fact or attitude. For *motif* there is no true equivalent. Since it refers to an external fact or situation, I am translating it by "cause." The reader must remember, however, that this carries with it no idea of determinism. Sartre emphatically denies the existence of any cause in the usual deterministic sense. Tr.

actual situation as nothingness in relation to this state of affairs. He will have to conceive of a happiness attached to his class as a pure possible—that is, presently as a certain nothingness—and on the other hand, he will return to the present situation in order to illuminate it in the light of this nothingness and in order to nihilate it in turn by declaring: "I *am not* happy."

Two important consequences result. (1) No factual state whatever it may be (the political and economic structure of society, the psychological "state," *etc.*) is capable by itself of motivating any act whatsoever. For an act is a projection of the for-itself toward what is not, and what is can in no way determine by itself what is not. (2) No factual state can determine consciousness to apprehend it as a *négatité* or as a lack. Better yet no factual state can determine consciousness to define it and to circumscribe it since, as we have seen, Spinoza's statement, "Omnis determinatio est negatio," remains profoundly true. Now every action has for its express condition not only the discovery of a state of affairs as "lacking in——," *i.e.*, as a *négatité*—but also, and before all else, the constitution of the state of things under consideration into an isolated system. There is a factual state—satisfying or not—only by means of the nihilating power of the for-itself. But this power of nihilation can not be limited to realizing a simple *withdrawal* in relation to the world. In fact in so far as consciousness is "invested" by being, in so far as it simply suffers what is, it must be included in being. It is the organized form—worker-finding-his-suffering-natural—which must be surmounted and denied in order for it to be able to form the object of a revealing contemplation. This means evidently that it is by a pure wrenching away from himself and the world that the worker can posit his suffering as unbearable suffering and consequently can *make of it the motive* for his revolutionary action. This implies for consciousness the permanent possibility of effecting a rupture with its own past, of wrenching itself away from its past so as to be able to consider it in the light of a non-being and so as to be able to confer on it the meaning which *it has* in terms of the project of a meaning which it *does not have.*

Under no circumstances can the past in any way by itself produce *an act;* that is, the positing of an end which turns back upon itself so as to illuminate it. This is what Hegel caught sight of when he wrote that "the mind is the negative," although he seems not to have remembered this when he came to presenting his own theory of action and of freedom. In fact as soon as one attributes to consciousness this negative power with respect to the world and itself, as soon as the nihilation forms an integral part of the *positing* of an end, we must recognize that the indispensable and fundamental condition of all action is the freedom of the acting being.

Thus at the outset we can see what is lacking in those tedious discussions between determinists and the proponents of free will. The latter are concerned to find cases of decision for which there exists no prior cause, or deliberations concerning two opposed acts which are equally possible and possess causes (and motives) of exactly the same weight. To which the determinists may easily reply that there is no action without a *cause* and that the most insignificant gesture (raising the right hand rather than the left hand, *etc.*) refers to causes and motives which confer its meaning upon it. Indeed the case could not be otherwise since every action must be *intentional;* each action must, in fact, have an end, and the end in turn is referred to a cause. Such indeed is the unity of the three temporal ekstases; the end or temporalization of my future implies a cause (or motive); that is, it points toward my past, and the present is the upsurge of the act. To speak of an act without a cause is to speak of an act which would lack the intentional structure of every act; and the proponents of free will by searching for it on the level of the act which is in the process of being performed can only end up by rendering the act absurd. But the determinists in turn are weighing the scale by stopping their investigation with the mere designation of the cause and motive. The essential question in fact lies beyond the complex organization "cause-intention-act-end"; indeed we ought to ask how a cause (or motive) can be constituted as such.

Now we have just seen that if there is no act without a

cause, this is not in the sense that we can say that there is no phenomenon without a cause. In order to be a *cause,* the *cause* must be *experienced* as such. Of course this does not mean that it is to be thematically conceived and made explicit as in the case of deliberation. But at the very least it means that the for-itself must confer on it its value as cause or motive. And, as we have seen, this constitution of the cause as such can not refer to another real and positive existence; that is, to a prior cause. For otherwise the very nature of the act as engaged intentionally in non-being would disappear. The motive is understood only by the end; that is, by the non-existent. It is therefore in itself a *négatité.* If I accept a niggardly salary it is doubtless because of fear; and fear is a motive. But it is *fear of dying from starvation;* that is, this fear has meaning only outside itself in an end ideally posited, which is the preservation of a life which I apprehend as "in danger." And this fear is understood in turn only in relation to the *value which I* implicitly give to this life; that is, it is referred to that hierarchal system of ideal objects which are values. Thus the motive makes itself understood as what it is by means of the ensemble of beings which "are not," by ideal existences, and by the future. Just as the future turns back upon the present and the past in order to elucidate them, so it is the ensemble of my projects which turns back in order to confer upon the *motive* its structure as a motive. It is only because I escape the in-itself by nihilating myself toward my possibilities that this in-itself can take on value as cause or motive. Causes and motives have meaning only inside a projected ensemble which is precisely an ensemble of non-existents. And this ensemble is ultimately myself as transcendence; it is Me in so far as I have to be myself outside of myself.

If we recall the principle which we established earlier—namely that it is the apprehension of a revolution as possible which gives to the workman's suffering its value as a motive—we must thereby conclude that it is by fleeing a situation toward our possibility of changing it that we organize this situation into complexes of causes and motives. The nihilation by which we achieve a withdrawal in relation to the situation is the same as the ekstasis by which we project ourselves toward a modification of this situation. The result is that it is in fact impossible to find an act without a motive but that this does not mean that we must conclude that the motive causes the act; the motive is an integral part of the act. For as the resolute project toward a change is not distinct from the act, the motive, the act, and the end are all constituted in a single upsurge. Each of these three structures claims the two others as its meaning. But the organized totality of the three is no longer explained by any particular structure, and its upsurge as the pure temporalizing nihilation of the in-itself is one with freedom. It is the act which decides its ends and its motives, and the act is the expression of freedom.

. . .

In our attempt to reach to the heart of freedom we may be helped by the few observations which we have made on the subject in the course of this work and which we must summarize here . . . we established the fact that if negation comes into the world through human-reality, the latter must be a being who can realize a nihilating rupture with the world and with himself; and we established that the permanent possibility of this rupture is the same as freedom. But on the other hand, we stated that this permanent possibility of nihilating what I am in the form of "having-been" implies for man a particular type of existence. We were able then to determine by means of analyses like that of bad faith that human reality is its own nothingness. For the for-itself, to be is to nihilate the in-itself which it is. Under these conditions freedom can be nothing other than this nihilation. It is through this that the for-itself escapes its being as its essence; it is through this that the for-itself is always something other than what can be said of it. For in the final analysis the for-itself is the one which escapes this very denomination, the one which is already beyond the name which is given to it, beyond the property which is recognized in it. To say that the for-itself has to be what it is, to say that it is what it is not while not being what it is, to say that in it existence precedes and conditions essence or inversely according to Hegel, that for it "Wesen ist was gewesen ist"—all this is to say one and the same thing: to be aware that man is free. Indeed by the sole fact that I am conscious of the causes which inspire my action, these causes are already transcendent objects for my consciousness; they are outside. In vain shall I seek to catch hold of them; I escape them by my very existence. I am condemned to exist forever beyond my essence, beyond the causes and motives of my act. I am condemned to be free. This means that no limits to my freedom can be found except freedom itself or, if you prefer, that we are not free to cease being free. To the extent that the for-itself wishes to hide its own nothingness from itself and to incorporate the in-itself as its true mode of being, it is trying also to hide its freedom from itself.

The ultimate meaning of determinism is to establish within us an unbroken continuity of existence in itself. The motive conceived as a psychic fact—*i.e.*, as a full and given reality—is, in the deterministic view, articulated without any break with the decision and the act, both of which are equally conceived as psychic givens. The in-itself has got hold of all these "data"; the motive provokes the act as the physical cause its effect; everything is real, everything is full. Thus the refusal of freedom can be conceived only as an attempt to apprehend oneself as being-in-itself; it amounts to the same thing. Human reality may be defined as a being such that in its being its freedom is at stake because human reality perpetually tries to refuse to recognize its freedom. Psychologically in each one of us this amounts to trying to take the causes and motives as *things*. We try to confer permanence upon them. We attempt to hide from ourselves that their nature and their weight depend each moment on the meaning which I give to them; we take them for constants. This amounts to considering the meaning which I gave to them just now or yesterday—which is irremediable because it is *past*—and extrapolating from it a character fixed still in the present. I attempt to persuade myself that the cause *is* as it was. Thus it would pass whole and untouched from my past consciousness to my present consciousness. It would inhabit my consciousness. This amounts to trying to give an essence to the for-itself. In the same way people will posit ends as transcendences, which is not an error. But instead of seeing that the transcendences there posited are maintained in their being by my own transcendence, people will assume that I encounter them upon my surging up in the world; they come from God, from nature, from "my" nature, from society. These ends ready made and pre-human will therefore define the meaning of my act even before I conceive it, just as causes as pure psychic givens will produce it without my even being aware of them.

Cause, act, and end constitute a *continuum*, a *plenum*. These abortive attempts to stifle freedom under the weight of being (they collapse with the sudden upsurge of anguish before freedom) show sufficiently that freedom in its foundation coincides with the nothingness which is at the heart of man. Human-reality is free because it *is not enough*. It is free because it is perpetually wrenched away from itself and because it has been separated by a nothingness from what it is and from what it will be. It is free, finally, because its present being is itself a nothingness in the form of the "reflection-reflecting." Man is free because he is not himself but presence to himself. The being which is what it is can not be free. Freedom is precisely the nothingness which *is made-to-be* at the heart of man and which forces human-reality *to make itself* instead of to be. As we have seen, for human reality, to be is to *choose oneself;* nothing comes to it either from the outside or from within which it can *receive or accept*. Without any help whatsoever, it is entirely abandoned to the intolerable necessity of making itself be—down to the slightest detail. Thus freedom is not *a* being; it is *the being* of man—*i.e.,* his nothingness of being. If we start by conceiving of man as a plenum, it is absurd to try to find in him afterwards moments or psychic regions in which he would be free. As well look for emptiness in a container which one has filled beforehand up to the brim! Man can not be sometimes slave and sometimes free; he is wholly and forever free or he is not free at all.

These observations can lead us, if we know how to use them, to new discoveries. They will enable us first to bring to light the relations between freedom and what we call the "will." There is a fairly common tendency to seek to identify free acts with voluntary acts and to restrict the deterministic explanation to the world of the passions. In short the point of view of Descartes. The Cartesian will is free, but there are "passions of the soul." Again Descartes will attempt a physiological interpretation of these passions. Later there will be an attempt to instate a purely psychological determinism. Intellectualistic analyses such as Proust, for example, attempts with respect to jealousy or snobbery can serve as illustrations for this concept of the passional "mechanism." In this case it would be necessary to conceive of man as simultaneously free and determined, and the essential problem would be that of the relations between this unconditioned freedom and the determined processes of the psychic life: how will it master the passions, how will it utilize them for its own benefit? A wisdom which comes from ancient times—the wisdom of the Stoics—will teach us to come to terms with these passions so as to master them; in short it will counsel us how to conduct ourselves with regard to affectivity as man does with respect to nature in general when he obeys it in order better to control it. Human reality therefore appears as a free power besieged by an ensemble of determined processes. One will distinguish wholly free acts, determined processes over which the free will has power, and processes which on principle escape the human-will.

It is clear that we shall not be able to accept such a conception. But let us try better to understand the reasons for our refusal. There is one objection which is obvious and which we shall not waste time in developing; this is that such a trenchant duality is inconceivable at the heart of the psychic unity. How in fact could we conceive of a being which could be *one* and which nevertheless on the one hand would be constituted as a series of facts determined by one another—hence existents in exteriority—and which on the other hand would be constituted as a spontaneity determining itself to be and revealing only itself? *A priori* this spontaneity would be capable of no action on a determinism already *constituted*. On what could it act? On the object itself (the present psychic fact)? But how could it modify an in-itself which by definition is and can be only what it is? On the actual law of the process? This is self-contradictory. On the antecedents of the process? But it amounts to the same thing whether we act on the present psychic fact in order to modify it in itself or act upon it in order to modify its consequences. And in each case we encounter the same impossibility which we pointed out earlier. Moreover, what instrument would this spontaneity have at its disposal? If the hand can clasp, it is because it can be clasped. Spontaneity, since by definition it is *beyond reach* can not in turn *reach;* it can produce only itself. And if it could dispose of a special instrument, it would then be necessary to conceive of this as of an intermediary nature between free will and determined passions—which is not admissible. For different reasons the passions could get no hold upon the will. Indeed it is impossible for a determined process to act upon a spontaneity, exactly as it is impossible for objects to act upon consciousness. Thus any synthesis of two types of existents is impossible; they are not homogeneous; they will remain each one in its incommunicable solitude. The only bond which a nihilating spontaneity could maintain with mechanical processes would be the fact that it *produces itself by an internal negation directed toward these existents.* But then the spontaneity will exist precisely only in so far as it denies concerning itself that it is these passions. Henceforth the ensemble of the determined πάθος will of necessity be apprehended by spontaneity as a pure transcendent; that is, as what is necessarily *outside,* as what *is* not it.[2] This internal negation would therefore have for its effect only the dissolution of the πάθος in the world, and the πάθος would exist as some sort of object in the midst of the world for a free spontaneity which would be simultaneously will and consciousness. This

[2] *I.e.,* is not spontaneity. Tr.

discussion shows that two solutions and only two are possible: either man is wholly determined (which is inadmissible, especially because a determined consciousness—*i.e.*, a consciousness externally motivated—becomes itself pure exteriority and ceases to be consciousness) or else man is wholly free.

. . .

But this is not all: the will, far from being the unique or at least the privileged manifestation of freedom, actually—like every event of the for-itself—must presuppose the foundation of an original freedom in order to be able to constitute itself as will. The will in fact is posited as a reflective decision in relation to certain ends. But it does not create these ends. It is rather a mode of being in relation to them: it decrees that the pursuit of these ends will be reflective and deliberative. Passion can posit the same ends. For example, if I am threatened, I can run away at top speed because of my fear of dying. This passional fact nevertheless posits implicitly as a supreme end the value of life. Another person in the same situation will, on the contrary, understand that he must remain at his post even if resistance at first appears more dangerous than flight; he "will stand firm." But his goal, although better understood and explicitly posited, remains the same as in the case of the emotional reaction. It is simply that the methods of attaining it are more clearly conceived; certain of them are rejected as dubious or inefficacious, others are more solidly organized. The difference here depends on the choice of means and on the degree of reflection and of making explicit, not on the end. Yet the one who flees is said to be "passionate," and we reserve the term "voluntary" for the man who resists. Therefore the question is of a difference of subjective attitude in relation to a transcendent end. But if we wish to avoid the error which we denounced earlier and not consider these transcendent ends as pre-human and as an *a priori* limit to our transcendence, then we are indeed compelled to recognize that they are the temporalizing projection of our freedom. Human reality can not receive its ends, as we have seen, either from outside or from a so-called inner "nature." It chooses them and by this very choice confers upon them a transcendent existence as the external limit of its projects. From this point of view—and if it is understood that the existence of the *Dasein* precedes and commands its essence—human reality in and through its very upsurge decides to define its own being by its ends. It is therefore the positing of my ultimate ends which characterizes my being and which is identical with the sudden thrust of the freedom which is mine. And this thrust is an *existence;* it has nothing to do with an essence or with a property of a being which would be engendered conjointly with an idea.

Thus since freedom is identical with my existence, it is the foundation of ends which I shall attempt to attain either by the will or by passionate efforts. Therefore it can not be limited to voluntary acts. Volitions, on the contrary, like passions are certain subjective attitudes by which we attempt to attain the ends posited by original freedom. By original freedom, of course, we should not understand a freedom which would be *prior* to the voluntary or passionate act but rather a foundation which is strictly contemporary with the will or the passion and which these *manifest,* each in its own way. Neither should we oppose freedom to the will or to passion as the "profound self" of Bergson is opposed to the superficial self; the for-itself is wholly selfness and can not have a "profound self," unless by this we mean certain transcendent structures of the psyche. Freedom is nothing but the *existence* of our will or of our passions in so far as this existence is the nihilation of facticity; that is, the existence of a being which is its being in the mode of having to be it. We shall return to this point. In any case let us remember that the will is determined within the compass of motives and ends already posited by the for-itself in a transcendent projection of itself toward its possibles. If this were not so, how could we understand deliberation, which is an evaluation of means in relation to already existing ends?

If these ends are already posited, then what remains to be decided at each moment is the way in which I shall conduct myself with respect to them; in other words, the attitude which

I shall assume. Shall I act by volition or by passion? Who can decide except me? In fact, if we admit that circumstances decide for me (for example, I can act by volition when faced with a minor danger but if the peril increases, I shall fall into passion), we thereby suppress all freedom. It would indeed be absurd to declare that the will is autonomous when it appears but that external circumstances strictly determine the moment of its appearance. But, on the other hand, how can it be maintained that a will which does not yet exist can suddenly decide to shatter the chain of the passions and suddenly stand forth on the fragments of these chains? Such a conception would lead us to consider the will as a *power* which sometimes would manifest itself to consciousness and at other times would remain hidden, but which would in any case possess the permanence and the existence "in-itself" of a property. This is precisely what is inadmissible. It is, however, certain that common opinion conceives of the moral life as a struggle between a will-thing and passion-substances. There is here a sort of psychological Manichaeism which is absolutely insupportable.

Actually it is not enough to will; it is necessary to will to will. Take, for example, a given situation: I can react to it emotionally. We have shown elsewhere that emotion is not a physiological tempest; [3] it is a reply adapted to the situation; it is a type of conduct, the meaning and form of which are the object of an intention of consciousness which aims at attaining a particular end by particular means. In fear, fainting and cataplexie[4] aim at suppressing the danger by suppressing the consciousness of the danger. There is an *intention* of losing consciousness in order to do away with the formidable world in which consciousness is engaged and which comes into being through consciousness. Therefore we have to do with magical behavior provoking the symbolic satisfactions of our desires

[3] *Esquisse d'une théorie phénoménologique des émotions,* Hermann, 1939. In English, *The Emotions: Outline of a Theory.* Tr. by Bernard Frechtman. Philosophical Library, 1948.

[4] A word invented by Preyer to refer to a sudden inhibiting numbness produced by any shock. Tr.

and revealing by the same stroke a magical stratum of the world. In contrast to this conduct voluntary and rational conduct will consider the situation scientifically, will reject the magical, and will apply itself to realizing determined series and instrumental complexes which will enable us to resolve the problems. It will organize a system of means by taking its stand on instrumental determinism. Suddenly it will reveal a technical world; that is, a world in which each instrumental-complex refers to another larger complex and so on. But what will make me decide to choose the magical aspect or the technical aspect of the world? It can not be the world itself, for this in order to be manifested waits to be discovered. Therefore it is necessary that the for-itself in its project must choose being the one by whom the world is revealed as magical or rational; that is, the for-itself must as a free project of itself give to itself magical or rational existence. It is responsible for either one, for the for-itself can *be* only if it has chosen itself. Therefore the for-itself appears as the free foundation of its emotions as of its volitions. My fear *is* free and manifests my freedom; I have put all my freedom into my fear, and I have chosen myself as fearful in this or that circumstance. Under other circumstances I shall exist as deliberate and courageous, and I shall have put all my freedom into my courage. In relation to freedom there is no privileged psychic phenomenon. All my "modes of being" manifest freedom equally since they are all ways of being my own nothingness.

. . .

Yet if the motive is transcendent, if it is only the irremediable being which we have to be in the mode of the "was," if like all our past it is separated from us by a breadth of nothingness, then it can act only if it is *recovered;* in itself it is without force. It is therefore by the very thrust of the engaged consciousness that a value and a weight will be conferred on motives and on prior causes. What they have been does not depend on consciousness, but consciousness has the duty of maintaining them in their existence in the past. I have willed this or that: here is what remains irremediable and which even constitutes my essence, since my essence is what I have been. But the meaning held for me by this desire, this fear, these objective considerations of the world when presently I project myself toward my futures—this must be decided by me alone. I determine them precisely and only by the very act by which I project myself toward my ends. The recovery of former motives—or the rejection or new appreciation of them—is not distinct from the project by which I assign new ends to myself and by which in the light of these ends I apprehend myself as discovering a supporting cause in the world. Past motives, past causes, present motives and causes, future ends, all are organized in an indissoluble unity by the very upsurge of a freedom which is beyond causes, motives, and ends.

The result is that a voluntary deliberation is always a deception. How can I evaluate causes and motives on which I myself confer their value before all deliberation and by the very choice which I make of myself? The illusion here stems from the fact that we endeavor to take causes and motives for entirely transcendent things which I balance in my hands like weights and which possess a weight as a permanent property. Yet on the other hand we try to view them as contents of consciousness, and this is self-contradictory. Actually causes and motives have only the weight which my project—*i.e.*, the free production of the end and of the known act to be realized—confers upon them. When I deliberate, the chips are down.[5] And if I am brought to the point of deliberating, this is simply because it is a part of my original project to realize motives by means of *deliberation* rather than by some other form of discovery (by passion, for example, or simply by action, which reveals to me the organized ensemble of causes and of ends as my language informs me of my thought). There is therefore a choice of deliberation as a procedure which will make known to me what I project and consequently what I am. And *the choice* of deliberation is organized with the ensemble motives-causes and end by free spontaneity. When the will intervenes,

[5] *Les jeux sont faits.* Sartre has written a novel by this title. Tr.

the decision is taken, and it has no other value than that of making the announcement.

. . .

The essential consequence of our earlier remarks is that man being condemned to be free carries the weight of the whole world on his shoulders; he is responsible for the world and for himself as a way of being. We are taking the word "responsibility" in its ordinary sense as "consciousness (of) being the incontestable author of an event or of an object." In this sense the responsibility of the for-itself is overwhelming since he[6] is the one by whom it happens that there is a world; since he is also the one who makes himself be, then whatever may be the situation in which he finds himself, the for-itself must wholly assume this situation with its peculiar coefficient of adversity, even though it be insupportable. He must assume the situation with the proud consciousness of being the author of it, for the very worst disadvantages or the worst threats which can endanger my person have meaning only in and through my project; and it is on the ground of the engagement which I am that they appear. It is therefore senseless to think of complaining since nothing foreign has decided what we feel, what we live, or what we are.

Furthermore this absolute responsibility is not resignation; it is simply the logical requirement of the consequences of our freedom. What happens to me happens through me, and I can neither affect myself with it nor revolt against it nor resign myself to it. Moreover everything which happens to me is *mine*. By this we must understand first of all that I am always equal to what happens to me *qua* man, for what happens to a man through other men and through himself can be only human. The most terrible situations of war, the worst tortures do not create a non-human state of things; there is no non-human

[6] I am shifting to the personal pronoun here since Sartre is describing the for-itself in concrete personal terms rather than as a metaphysical entity. Strictly speaking, of course, this is his position throughout, and the French "il" is indifferently "he" or "it." Tr.

situation. It is only through fear, flight, and recourse to magical types of conduct that I shall decide on the non-human, but this decision is human, and I shall carry the entire responsibility for it. But in addition the situation is *mine* because it is the image of my free choice of myself, and everything which it presents to me is *mine* in that this represents me and symbolizes me. Is it not I who decide the coefficient of adversity in things and even their unpredictability by deciding myself?

Thus there are no *accidents* in a life; a community event which suddenly bursts forth and involves me in it does not come from the outside. If I am mobilized in a war, this war is *my* war; it is in my image and I deserve it. I deserve it first because I could always get out of it by suicide or by desertion; these ultimate possibles are those which must always be present for us when there is a question of envisaging a situation. For lack of getting out of it, I have *chosen* it. This can be due to inertia, to cowardice in the face of public opinion, or because I prefer certain other values to the value of the refusal to join in the war (the good opinion of my relatives, the honor of my family, etc.). Anyway you look at it, it is a matter of a choice. This choice will be repeated later on again and again without a break until the end of the war. Therefore we must agree with the statement by J. Romains, "In war there are no innocent victims."[7] If therefore I have preferred war to death or to dishonor, everything takes place as if I bore the entire responsibility for this war. Of course others have declared it, and one might be tempted perhaps to consider me as a simple accomplice. But this notion of complicity has only a juridical sense, and it does not hold here. For it depended on me that for me and by me this war should not exist, and I have decided that it does exist. There was no compulsion here, for the compulsion could have got no hold on a freedom. I did not have any excuse; for as we have said repeatedly in this book, the peculiar character of human-reality is that it is without excuse. Therefore it remains for me only to lay claim to this war.

But in addition the war is *mine* because by the sole fact that

[7] J. Romains: *Les hommes de bonne volonté;* "Prélude à Verdun."

it arises in a situation which I cause to be and that I can discover it there only by engaging myself for or against it, I can no longer distinguish at present the choice which I make of myself from the choice which I make of the war. To live this war is to choose myself through it and to choose it through my choice of myself. There can be no question of considering it as "four years of vacation" or as a "reprieve," as a "recess," the essential part of my responsibilities being elsewhere in my married, family, or professional life. In this war which I have chosen I choose myself from day to day, and I make it mine by making myself. If it is going to be four empty years, then it is I who bear the responsibility for this.

Finally, as we pointed out earlier, each person is an absolute choice of self from the standpoint of a world of knowledges and of techniques which this choice both assumes and illumines; each person is an absolute upsurge at an absolute date and is perfectly unthinkable at another date. It is therefore a waste of time to ask what I should have been if this war had not broken out, for I have chosen myself as one of the possible meanings of the epoch which imperceptibly led to war. I am not distinct from this same epoch; I could not be transported to another epoch without contradiction. Thus *I am* this war which restricts and limits and makes comprehensible the period which preceded it. In this sense we may define more precisely the responsibility of the for-itself if to the earliér quoted statement, "There are no innocent victims," we add the words, "We have the war we deserve." Thus, totally free, undistinguishable from the period for which I have chosen to be the meaning, as profoundly responsible for the war as if I had myself declared it, unable to live without integrating it in *my* situation, engaging myself in it wholly and stamping it with my seal, I must be without remorse or regrets as I am without excuse; for from the instant of my upsurge into being, I carry the weight of the world by myself alone without anything or any person being able to lighten it.

Yet this responsibility is of a very particular type. Someone will say, "I did not ask to be born." This is a naive way of throwing greater emphasis on our facticity. I am responsible for everything, in fact, except for my very responsibility, for I am not the foundation of my being. Therefore everything takes place as if I were compelled to be responsible. I am *abandoned* in the world, not in the sense that I might remain abandoned and passive in a hostile universe like a board floating on the water, but rather in the sense that I find myself suddenly alone and without help, engaged in a world for which I bear the whole responsibility without being able, whatever I do, to tear myself away from this responsibility for an instant. For I am responsible for my very desire of fleeing responsibilities. To make myself passive in the world, to refuse to act upon things and upon others is still to choose myself, and suicide is one mode among others of being-in-the-world. Yet I find an absolute responsibility for the fact that my facticity (here the fact of my birth) is directly inapprehensible and even inconceivable, for this fact of my birth never appears as a brute fact but always across a projective reconstruction of my for-itself. I am ashamed of being born or I am astonished at it or I rejoice over it, or in attempting to get rid of my life I affirm that I live and I assume this life as bad. Thus in a certain sense I *choose* being born. This choice itself is integrally affected with facticity since I am not able not to choose, but this facticity in turn will appear only in so far as I surpass it toward my ends. Thus facticity is everywhere but inapprehensible; I never encounter anything except my responsibility. That is why I can not ask, "*Why* was I born?" or curse the day of my birth or declare that I did not ask to be born, for these various attitudes toward my birth—*i.e.*, toward the *fact* that I realize a presence in the world—are absolutely nothing else but ways of assuming this birth in full responsibility and of making it *mine*. Here again I encounter only myself and my projects so that finally my abandonment—*i.e.*, my facticity—consists simply in the fact that I am condemned to be wholly responsible for myself. I am the being which is in such a way that in its being its being is in question. And this "is" of my being *is* as present and inapprehensible.

Under these conditions since every event in the world can be revealed to me only as an *opportunity* (an opportunity made use of, lacked, neglected, *etc.*), or better yet since everything which happens to us can be considered as a *chance* (*i.e.,* can appear to us only as a way of realizing this being which is in question in our being) and since others as transcendences-transcended are themselves only *opportunities* and *chances,* the responsibility of the for-itself extends to the entire world as a peopled world. It is precisely thus that the for-itself apprehends itself in anguish; that is, as a being which is neither the foundation of its own being nor of the Other's being nor of the in-itselfs which form the world, but a being which is compelled to decide the meaning of being—within it and everywhere outside of it. The one who realizes in anguish his condition as *being* thrown into a responsibility which extends to his very abandonment has no longer either remorse or regret or excuse; he is no longer anything but a freedom which perfectly reveals itself and whose being resides in this very revelation. But as we pointed out at the beginning of this work, most of the time we flee anguish in bad faith.

4

ACTION THEORY

INTRODUCTION

Given some bit of human behavior, say, a leg movement, one cannot be sure that the person is really doing anything unless one is in a position (as one usually is) to eliminate other alternatives, e.g., hypnosis, sleepwalking, reflex behavior, etc. Moreover, one would want to distinguish between "intentionally moving one's leg" and "unintentionally (inadvertently, unknowingly) moving one's leg." At some point, the concept of action is introduced to distinguish what a man does—intentionally, perhaps—from what merely happens or comes to pass.

As was pointed out in the preface, only some of the conclusions of persons engaged in an analysis of the concept of action bear on free will. The central conclusion of Melden's which is of interest to us is as follows: (A) Determinism can have no bearing on freedom of action. Melden asserts or suggests a number of logically distinct theses along the way to this conclusion. The most important are the following: (B) Human action is not definable in terms of happenings or relationships between happenings. (C) No explanation of human action in terms of desire, motive, reason, or intention is causal (deterministic). (D) All causal (deterministic) explanation is of happenings. (E) There can be no causal explanation of action. (F) Some actions are done not by doing anything else.

Melden does not always distinguish these claims, and the reader must discover whether or not the actual logical relationships between them are correctly given by him.

(B) entails no other proposition and cannot, therefore, be

used alone to derive any of the others. The only proposition which entails it is (E) (under the obvious assumption that there can be causal explanation of happenings). (E) is entailed by the conjunction of (B) and (D) or the conjunction of (D) and a proposition somewhat weaker than (B); viz., no actions are happenings (G). (E) entails (A). (D) and (B) become, therefore, the central grounds for (A).

(F) is logically independent of (B) and (C); but its relationship to (D) is interesting. If "doing *x* by doing *y*" always describes a causal relationship, then (D) and (B) or (D) and (G) entails (F) because (D) and (B) or (D) and (G) entails that no actions are done by doing something else. But Melden believes that some actions are done by doing something else. Therefore, he cannot always construe "doing *x* by doing *y*" as the description of a causal relationship. ("I signaled by raising my arm" does not describe a causal relationship.) Moreover, he must say that it is *never* a description of a causal relationship if he is to retain (D) and (B) each of which he wants and needs. But then (F) is logically independent of all the others; and it cannot be used by itself, therefore, to derive any of them.

(C) entails no other proposition; but it is entailed by (A) in the sense that if, say, explanations of actions in terms of reasons are causal, then determinism might have a bearing on freedom of action (and does if incompatibilism is true). (C) is, therefore, entailed by (E) and by the conjunction of (D) and (B). Therefore, when Davidson rejects (C), his arguments bear on (A), (E), and the conjunction of (D) and (B) too. It is important to see that many of the arguments used by Davidson against (C) refer to grounds adduced by Melden which are independent of (D) and (B). In other words, Melden does not rely on (D) and (B), but cites facts like (1) the logical connection between wanting to do *x* and the doing of *x* and (2) the difficulty in construing reasons as events, in defense of (C). Some of these facts do have an indirect bearing on (B) though.

A very similar debate, but one in which the issues are

more specific and clearly focused, is provided by the second pair of articles.

It is interesting to see why MacIntyre's position is placed under action theory rather than libertarianism. A libertarian is one who grants the possibility in principle that all human behavior is determined, but for various reasons, believes that it is not. Melden argues that determinism does not apply in principle (for conceptual or logical reasons) to human action. Now, MacIntyre does not specifically endorse this last statement. But he does say that determinism does not in principle apply to "rational behavior" where the latter is defined as behavior which is (or can be) *rationally* influenced by reasons. Does MacIntyre reject in principle a deterministic account of the same behavior (I do not mean to assume in favor of MacIntyre that accounts in terms of reasons are not deterministic) in which case we could not call it rational? He says that "it seems impossible to give this kind of account of rational behavior without misdescribing it" and deterministic accounts "do violence to all our ordinary ways of talking about morality." This is about as close to a "rejection in principle" as one might want although, perhaps, not quite as strong as Melden's.

One incidental reason for the inclusion of the MacIntyre paper is its discussion of a position which was in vogue for a brief time, viz., the paradigm case argument as applied to the free will controversy.

FREE ACTION

A. I. MELDEN

Consider the following: Whenever I raise my arm (deliberately, let us say) I bring to pass certain muscle movements—I make these happen. Hence I raise my arm by moving (con-

From A. I. Melden, *Free Action*. London: Routledge & Kegan Paul, 1961, chaps. 5, 7, and 14, pp. 43–55; 66; 199–215.

tracting and expanding) certain muscles of my arm. This, then, is how I raise my arm.

This is a bad argument. We cannot identify what one does with what one makes happen. When I flex the biceps brachii of my arm very many things are brought to pass, made to happen. Nerve impulses are transmitted to the muscles, neural circuits in the brain are opened and closed, protein molecules in the brain are set into oscillation; and many many more things of which I have not the faintest intimation. But let us consider the conclusion on its own merits. Certainly I can contract certain muscles at will. If someone points to the biceps brachii and asks me to flex it, this I can easily do. So it is tempting to say that when I raise my arm, I do so by moving certain muscles *just as* when I signal, I do so by raising my arm.

But how do I move certain muscles? There is a difference between my biceps becoming flexed and *my* flexing my biceps just as there is a difference between my arm getting raised and *my* raising my arm. The flexing of my biceps may occur through no doing of mine (someone might raise my arm and in doing so cause my biceps to be flexed) just as my arm getting raised may be something that happens to me through the action of another person who raises my arm and not through anything I do. And what can the difference be, between the occurrence of a muscle movement in my arm and my moving that muscle, except this, that in the latter case it is by doing something that I bring the muscle movement to pass? In short, if it is sensible to say that I raise my arm by moving certain muscles, it is equally sensible to hold that one moves those muscles by doing something that brings those muscle movements to pass. And what can this latter doing be that has these muscle movements as effect?

Suppose someone points to the biceps brachii and says, 'Flex it!' What must I do in order to comply? Must I say to myself, 'Move, muscle, move!'? If I do this, nothing will happen. Does nothing happen because I do not *mean* it? Then how do I *mean* it? 'Meaning what I say'—is this something I do when I say whatever it is that I do say? Shall we say that I shall mean it only when I *want* my muscle to move? But if I want my biceps to move and stare at it again nothing will happen—I must do something about my want, *i.e.* get what it is that I want. Is it necessary that I set myself—to use Prichard's expression—to move my biceps?[1] But if 'setting myself' means getting ready, putting myself in a state of readiness, again nothing will happen. And if 'setting myself to do' means trying to do or exerting myself to do, then I need do nothing of the sort. I do not try to raise my arm, *e.g.*, it is held down—I simply raise it; and I do not try to flex my biceps unless there is some obstacle to be overcome or some chance of failure.

What then is the difference between my muscles being contracted and my contracting my muscles? A familiar doctrine is that in the latter case I *will* my muscles to move, whereas in the former case there are causes other than the act of volition. So I move my muscles by performing an act of volition which in turn produces a muscle movement.

Grant for a moment that an event labelled an 'act of volition' produces a muscle movement, there is a difference surely between an act of volition occurring and my performing such an act. We saw that there is a difference between the occurrence of a muscle movement and my moving that muscle, hence it was that the supposition of acts of volition was invoked. But equally there is a difference between the occurrence of an act of volition and my performing such an act—who can say that volitions may not occur through no doing of the subject, and in consequence, of interior mental events deep within the hidden recesses of the self? If so, willing the muscle movement is not enough, one must will the willing of the muscle movement, and so on *ad infinitum*. Here someone may retort impatiently: 'When I will a muscle movement, *I* will it and that is the end of the matter; there is no other doing by virtue of which this act of volition gets done—I simply will the movement of the muscle.' But even if this reply were correct it would not serve to explain what an action is as distinguished from a mere hap-

[1] Cf. the essay 'Duty and Ignorance of Fact' in *Moral Obligation*. Oxford, 1949.

pening—it explains the 'action' of raising the arm in terms of an internal action of willing, and hence all it does at best is to change the locus of action. Indeed it invites the view argued by Prichard that, strictly speaking and contrary to the notion conveyed by our ordinary ways of speaking, one does not raise one's arm at all—all one does or can do is *will* and by means of *this* action produce various effects such as the rising of one's arm. In any case if willing is some sort of doing one performs not by means of any other doing (one wills and that is the end of the matter), why not say the same about the movement of one's muscles—one tenses one's biceps and there is no doing by virtue of which the tensing gets done? But the troubles involved in the supposition that there are interior acts of willing go even deeper than this—the doctrine, familiar though it may be, is a mare's nest of confusions.

How shall we describe the alleged action of willing? Surely a description of *this* action independently of the consequence alleged for it—the production of a muscle movement—must be forthcoming. Let us call the act of willing A: then A produces B (a muscle movement), this being taken to be a causal sequence. Now in general if A causes B, a description of A other than that it has the causal property of producing B must be forthcoming, otherwise 'A causes B' degenerates into 'the thing that produces B produces B.' But what description of the act of volition can be offered? If something causes me to jump in fright, jerk my arm, or move my head, 'What caused you to . . . ?' is intelligible and answerable. It is no good saying, 'That which caused me to do it,' for this is no answer but a bit of rudeness or a feeble attempt at humour. How then shall one describe the act of willing?

It is at this point that the resort to indefinables appears attractive.[2] Willing is *sui generis*, indefinable, a bit of mental self-exertion in which we engage—an activity not capable of

[2] Indeed, this is the move made by Prichard in the essay 'Acting, Willing, Desiring,' written in 1945 and published posthumously in *Moral Obligation,* Oxford, The Clarendon Press, 1949. This essay is worth careful reading; in it Prichard abandons his earlier account of 'willing' as setting oneself to do.

further description but different from the wonderings, thinkings, supposings, expectings, picturings, etc. that comprise our mental activities. Yet the appeal to indefinables is a desperate defence that purchases immunity from further attack only at the expense of unintelligibility. Here the kind of objections raised by Wittgenstein against the doctrine of kinaesthetic sensations apply in full force. If all that can be said about the alleged act of volition, by virtue of which a muscle movement is produced, is that it is the sort of thing that produces a muscle movement, there is every uncertainty that anyone has understood what is meant by 'the act of volition.' And if an attempt to rescue this doctrine is made by appealing to something with which, it is alleged, each of us is intimately familiar and hence will have no difficulty in recognizing—the act of volition that produces the muscle movement—the retort must surely be '*What* do I recognize when I recognize an act of volition?' Unless I can recognize this act by having some description in mind that applies to such acts and only to these, it is at best a simple begging of the question to insist that all of us really understand what is being referred to; in fact it is an implied charge of dishonesty directed at those who refuse to give their assent. And in philosophy, when good manners alone stand in the way of the open parade of charges of this sort, there is something seriously amiss in one's thinking.

But the difficulty in this talk about acts of volition is not merely that some account of acts of volition in general is needed, failing which we can only conclude that the expression 'act of volition' can serve no rôle in our discourse, it is equally serious in other respects as well. Let us grant that there is some peculiar mental activity of willing, the causal consequence of which is that certain muscles are contracted and others relaxed as we perform our diverse bodily movements, and let us now ask first of all how it is that we are able to learn how to perform these bodily movements. Surely the act of volition involved in the production of one muscle movement must be distinguished from the act of volition involved in the production of any other. There will then be different acts of volition,

v_1, v_2, v_3, etc., which, respectively, move muscles m_1, m_2, m_3, etc. If $v_1 \rightarrow m_1$, $v_2 \rightarrow m_2$, $v_3 \rightarrow m_3$, etc. represent causal relations, then just as m_1, m_2, m_3, etc. are distinguishable, so v_1, v_2, v_3, etc. will needs be different in kind. And if I am to learn how to produce m_1 by performing the act of volition v_1, I must not only recognize the difference between v_1 and other acts of volition that have other effects, I must also recognize the causal relation holding between v_1 and m_1. Now this would seem to imply at least two things: (1) It must be possible to offer a set of characterizations of these acts of volition each different from the other, corresponding to the set of characterizations that can be given surely for the muscle movements m_1, m_2, m_3, m_4, etc. (2) I can only learn from experience that m_1 is produced by v_1, m_2 by v_2, m_3 by v_3, and soon, hence unless I suppose myself to have been endowed with superhuman prescience, I must have been surprised or astonished the first time I performed the act of volition v_1 to discover that muscle movement m_1 occurred; and antecedently I should have had no reason for ruling out the possibility that m_2 would not occur—I should have had no reason, for example, to suppose that when I performed that act of volition by which in fact my biceps became flexed, my right leg would not have been raised.

Consider the first of these consequences. Now I can certainly distinguish between muscle movements m_1 and m_2, say, the biceps of my right arm from that of my left arm. But how shall I distinguish between the acts of volition v_1 and v_2 by which these distinct muscle movements are produced? If I produce these muscle movements by performing these acts of volition, this at any rate is something I learn to do, an ability I come to acquire. But if I can learn to do this, I must be able to distinguish between the volitions v_1 and v_2. Surely it must be possible to describe the difference. And if this cannot be done, learning to produce m_1 by producing v_1 and learning to produce m_2 by producing v_2 is impossible. How then shall we describe v_1 as distinguished from v_2? Shall we say that not only are volitions in general indefinable, but that the difference between v_1 and v_2 is also something indefinable? At least, however, the difference must be recognizable. Is it that our vocabulary is inadequate? Then let us introduce words that will enable us to mark the distinction. And now that the words have been introduced, explain how they are to be employed! Is it that we can only *point*—v_1 is *this* thing, the one that one finds one performs when m_1 is produced, v_2 is *that* thing, the one that one finds that one performs when m_2 is produced? But this will do the trick only if I already know what sorts of things to look for and only if it is at least possible for me to go on and describe the difference between v_1 and v_2 independently of the considerations that v_1 produces m_1 and v_2 produces m_2. By pointing one can succeed in explaining the meaning of a term or expression, but only if by doing so one can help fill in a gap or supply the links missing in some initial background understanding we have of that term or expression. But here we do not know where to look or what to find. No background understanding is present. We are told that there are certain things—call them 'acts of volition'—that they are indefinable, and that nothing more can be said about them at all in explaining how this expression 'act of volition' is to be employed. Against *this* background, how can pointing serve to provide any explanation at all of the difference between act of volition_1 (call it $\text{mental-muscle-doing}_1$) and act of volition_2 ($\text{mental-muscle-doing}_2$)? To say at this point that the difference itself is indefinable is, surely, to carry philosophical pretension beyond all limits of credulity.

As far as I know philosophers are quite unwilling to pile indefinables upon indefinables in this fulsome manner. Prichard for one, despite his characteristic resort to indefinables, is admirable for an equally characteristic subtlety that leads him to reject such simple-minded answers even though, as he himself recognizes, he must accept a conclusion that is open to objections he cannot meet. Consider the second of the two consequences of the doctrine of acts of volition. That v_1 produces m_1 rather than m_2 is a causal fact; but if so, I should have no reason to suppose, when I first performed the act of volition v_1, that m_1 rather than m_2 would follow; for on this view the statement that, *e.g.*, I move the biceps brachii of my right arm by performing the act of volition v_1, rather than the biceps brachii of my left arm or the biceps femoris of my right leg, is justified only on the basis of inductive evidence. Now Prichard holds that an act of volition involves a desire to will whatever it is that one wills, and hence some idea of what the volition is likely to produce. This, however, is impossible since on the first occasions on which I performed v_1 and thereby produced m_1, v_1 would require the thought that I would be doing something that would produce m_1 and by hypothesis I should have no reason to expect what, if anything, v_1 would produce. Prichard is therefore led to the conclusion that an 'act of will requires an idea of something which we may cause if we perform the act,' a conclusion—indeed a difficulty—he is unable to avoid.[3]

Prichard's predicament involves a matter of central importance which can be stated quite independently of his insistence that if one is to perform an act of volition, one must be moved by a desire to perform that volition. The important issue is whether or not it is intelligible to speak of an act of volition where the very notion of such an act does not involve a reference to the relevant bodily event. Let the act of volition issue in a muscle movement; then as Prichard himself recognizes, the act must be the willing of that muscle movement, otherwise we should have only inductive grounds for supposing the act to issue in that particular muscle movement. Accordingly we are faced with the following dilemma: If in thinking of v_1 (some particular act of volition) we are of necessity to think of it as the willing of m_1 (some particular muscle movement), then v_1 cannot be any occurrence, mental or physiological, which is causally related to m_1, since the very notion of a causal sequence logically implies that cause and effect are intelligible without any logically internal relation of the one to the other. If on the other hand, we think of v_1 and m_1 as

[3] *Op cit.*, pp. 196–7. See also his second thoughts about his earlier notion of 'setting oneself' in the footnotes to his earlier essay, 'Duty and Ignorance of Fact,' which appear in the same volume on p. 38.

causally related in the way in which we think of the relation between the movements of muscles and the raising of one's arm, then we must conclude that when first we perform v_1 we should have absolutely no reason to suppose that m_1 would in fact ensue. If to avoid this latter consequence we maintain that the thought of the muscle movement enters into the very character of the act of volition (as Prichard puts it, 'the *thinking* enters into the character of the *willing*'[4]) no description of the act of volition can be given that does not involve an account of the muscle movement, and hence we must abandon the idea that the act of volition v_1 is a cause that produces m_1, the muscle movement. Prichard's predicament is that his conclusion that 'an act of will requires an idea of something which we may cause if we perform the act' is nothing less than self-contradictory.

This then is the logical incoherence involved in the doctrine of acts of volition: Acts of volition are alleged to be direct causes of certain bodily phenomena (whether these be brain occurrences, as Prichard supposed them to be, or muscle movements, as we have been assuming for the sake of argument, is of no matter), just as the latter are causes of the raising of one's arm. For, it is alleged, just as we raise our arms by moving our muscles, so we move our muscles by willing them to move. But no account of the alleged volitions is intelligible that does not involve a reference to the relevant bodily phenomena. And *no* interior cause, mental or physiological, can have this logical feature of acts of volition. Let the interior event which we call 'the act of volition' be mental or physical (*which* it is will make no difference at all), it must be logically distinct from the alleged effect—this surely is one lesson we can derive from a reading of Hume's discussion of causation. Yet nothing can be an act of volition that is not logically connected with that which is willed—the act of willing is intelligible only as the act of willing whatever it is that is willed. In short, there could not be such an interior event like an act of volition since (here one is reminded of Wittgenstein's famous remark about meaning) nothing of that sort could have the required logical consequences.

[4] *Ibid.*, p. 38.

Let me review the course of the argument in this chapter. The doctrine of acts of volition was introduced, it will be remembered, in order to elucidate the distinction between ones' arm rising and one's raising one's arm. The former need involve no doing or action performed by the agent, the latter surely does. But instead of rejecting the question, 'How does one raise one's arm?' by a 'One just does' retort, the reply we considered was 'One raises one's arm by moving certain muscles.' Here the same question arises again: How can one distinguish between 'moving certain muscles' and 'certain muscles getting moved'? The latter need involve no action on my part at all. And if it makes sense to ask, 'How does one raise one's arm?' surely it makes sense to ask, 'How does one move certain muscles?' Hence the doing required in order to preserve the distinction between 'moving certain muscles' and 'certain muscles getting moved' must be a doing other than the doing described as 'moving certain muscles.' At this point the philosophical doctrine of acts of volition—willings performed by an agent—appears attractive. By willing, we move certain muscles; by moving certain muscles we raise our arm. But the acts of volition in question are the ill-begotten offspring of the mating of two quite incompatible ideas: the supposition that such acts are causes, and the requirement that the volitions in question be the willings of the muscle movements. As causes, willings are events on a par with other events including muscle and other bodily movements, with respect to which the inevitable question must arise once more: 'How does one perform such an action?' since after all there is the distinction to be preserved between 'performing a willing' and 'a willing occurring.' But if to avoid the threatened regress of 'willing a willing' and 'willing the willing of a willing' and so on, one rejects the question and questions the intelligibility of such locutions as 'willing a willing,' the willing in question can only be understood as 'the willing of a muscle movement.' If so, the willing in question cannot be a cause of the muscle movement, since the reference to the muscle movement is involved in the very description of the willing. In that case to say that one moves certain muscles by willing them to move is not to give any causal account at all. But if this is so, what can it mean to say that one wills a muscle movement—since the willing in question cannot possibly be any interior occurrence in which one engages? If it is intelligible at all it means simply that one moves a muscle. In that case, the alleged elucidation of the statement that one moves certain muscles (in raising one's arm) by willing them to move degenerates into something that is no elucidation at all, namely, that one moves certain muscles by moving them. And if this is so, to say that one wills the movement of certain muscles is not to *answer* the question, 'How does one move those muscles?', it is in fact to *reject* it. If this is the outcome, why not refuse to plunge into the morass and reject the initial question, 'How does one raise one's arm?', by saying, 'One just does?' If, on the other hand, 'willing a muscle movement' does *not* mean 'moving a muscle,' what on earth can it possibly mean? Surely, it is an understatement to say that the philosophical talk about acts of volition involves a mare's nest of confusions!

. . .

It should be abundantly clear by now that the query 'How do I raise my arm?' is wholly misconceived. In raising my arm I am performing an action. There may be interior bodily occurrences that cause the arm to rise; indeed, if what physiologists tell us is true, this must be granted. But the elevation of the arm—the rising of the arm—is one thing, the doing or the action of raising the arm is something else again; and whatever the interior causes of the elevation of the arm may be, it is not by any interior doing, mental or bodily, that I succeed in raising my arm. 'How do I signal?' is a fair question, the answer to which is given by 'By raising my arm.' But in normal circumstances there is no doing of any sort by virtue of which I raise my arm. I simply raise my arm and, in doing this, exercise a primitive ability.

. . .

. . . In the argument just concluded I have attempted to show that it is a fundamental mistake to suppose that the causal model employed in the natural sciences will fit the everyday explanations of actions in terms of intentions, interests, desires, etc. It is not even our concern, in asking *how* someone did such-and-such, to inquire into the natural history of his action, to probe, as it were, behind the scene of human action itself, to discover events in an area that constitutes the general causal condition of action. For the answer to the question 'How did. . . . ?', does not remove us from the scene of human conduct; it specifies, rather, an *action* in the performance of which the agent was able to do what he did. Indeed, the action specified in the answer may even be the very same action as the one explained. Thus if I am asked how I signalled (or how I got into the house without a key), the reply that I did so by raising my arm (or by climbing through the window) refers the questioner to an action which in the given circumstances is the very same action as the one for which an explanation was sought. In any case, whether the question is 'Why?' or 'How?', the concern is not with logically self-contained events which stand in some empirically discovered causal relation to one another, but with human events. It is hardly necessary at this point to inquire into the logical features of our descriptions of the character of persons. Their logical connection with action, the interests, desires, motives, habits, etc., of agents is surely evident. It follows that there is a radical disparity between these two modes of explanation: causal explanations of events and our familiar explanations of human actions.

It is this radical disparity that accounts for the characteristic ambivalences and contradictions in current psychological discussions. Insofar as psychologists are obsessed with the desire to establish their inquiry on a parallel footing with the natural sciences, the search is on for mechanisms in terms of which explanations of conduct are to be given. Conduct viewed in this way becomes 'overt behaviour,' an ambiguous term that effectively obscures the all-important distinction between bodily movements or happenings and actions. As bodily movements, items of overt behaviour are physiological occurrences for which physiological occurrences would appear to be sufficient causal conditions. In that case psychology reduces to physiology, and the alleged explanations of human action have succeeded only in changing the subject, in substituting explanations of bodily movements for explanations of action. For absolutely nothing about any matter of human conduct follows logically from any account of the physiological conditions of bodily movement. If this gap between matters of physiological fact and matters of human action is to be bridged, at least some token concessions must be made to our everyday discourse about persons and their actions. Some mental terms must be retained in the speculations about the mechanism of human conduct. Not infrequently, however, and precisely in order to maintain the fiction of the application of the causal model, homely terms like 'desire,' 'person,' etc., are eschewed and instead the talk is about 'organism,' 'drive,' etc. And, not unexpectedly, fatal stresses and strains appear in the uses to which this jargon is put. The word 'drive' is a notorious example: as an interior movement—some sort of causal factor—a drive is blind, fully intelligible without reference to anything to which it might give rise; as something telic it is logically essential that it refer us to that to which the agent is driven—his action.

Does the rejection of the causal model imply that actions are uncaused, that freedom is to be purchased at the expense of a capricious indeterminism, or of a libertarianism that misrepresents every responsible action as an heroic effort that somehow thwarts the causal order? Quite the contrary, the argument is designed to show the logical incoherence involved in the supposition that actions, desires, intentions, etc., stand in causal relations, either in the Humean sense or in any sense in which the term 'causal' is employed in the natural sciences. And if the argument is correct, determinism, if it employs this sense of cause, is not false but radically confused. So it is with indeterminism and libertarianism which grant to determinism the intelligibility of employing the causal model—these seek to avoid the conclusion that each of us is the hapless victim of events, in the former case by viewing actions as causally indeterminate happenings, in the latter by viewing actions for which a person is responsible as events produced by extraordinary and mysterious self-exertions. The trouble in all these cases is that the applicability in principle of the causal model is taken for granted. Given this fatal blunder, actions degenerate into mere bodily happenings, produced or not as each of these doctrines would have it; and once this conceptual mistake has been made the way is open to a radical misunderstanding of desires, intentions, decisions, etc., as internal events that can operate in some sort of mechanism of the mind.

Notorious in this connection is the all too frequent talk about the causality of decision and choice, as if a decision or choice were some sort of inner 'oomph' that sparked something (but what?—an action, or a bodily movement?) into being. Surely it would be absurd to attempt to make out the distinction between bodily movement and action by reference to either decision or choice. For it is not true that agents decide or choose to do everything they do. If, for example, I go to the corner grocer to purchase a dozen eggs, it may well be that I have decided to do just that. But do I, when I pick up each egg and place it in a bag, then go on to make one decision or twelve—one for each egg? And if I pick up two eggs at a time, do I make one or two decisions? Must I, once I have decided to go to the grocer to purchase eggs, make any further decisions in the matter? Often, at least, I simply go to the grocer, and as a matter of course without giving the matter any further thought, pick up the eggs I see and put them in a bag. And if, say, I scratch my head or blow my nose, do I *decide* to do such things? So with choosing—must I choose to do everything I do? Perhaps I choose to purchase eggs rather than meat. But must I choose this egg rather than that egg when I pick up the former and not the latter? I might if I were selecting eggs for size; but often at least I do nothing of the sort—I just pick up each egg as it comes to hand. If I give my wallet to someone who holds a pistol to my head, *must* I have decided to do so, chosen to do so? It would be *a priorism* at its worst to say that, even when I am terrified—as indeed I would be in such a case—and act as I do, there must have been choice or decision. And, finally, deciding cannot possibly be an interior Humean cause of doing (and so too with choosing) for reasons that parallel precisely those given for the case of desire. If I decide to do X, the decision is intelligible only as the decision *to do X*. The reference to the doing is logically essential to the very thought of the decision. So too with choice, when in choosing between objects A and B, I choose to take A. Far from carrying us behind the scenes of action to events that somehow produce action, decisions and choices are intelligible only within the arena of action. By reference to them we may characterize, not bodily movements as actions (for that they are actions we already know when we ask whether a person has decided or chosen to act as he does), but actions as those the agent has decided or chosen to do and hence actions for which reasons of one sort or another can be given. It is, therefore, essential to decision and choice—no mere logical accident as it were—that there be agents, actions and reasons for doing.

Granted all this, do we not speak of the causes of a person's action? Do we not predict what persons will do, and if one can predict precisely and exactly what a person will do, must there not be causes of his doing which would justify such predictions? Again, some actions are voluntary, others involuntary; we say, as circumstances warrant, that a person could or could not have done otherwise; we recognize that some have and others do not have much will-power; and that some acts are and others are not performed of the agent's own free will. How can we avoid the irresistible conclusion that in various ways causal conditions of doings are applicable to human conduct?

It is certainly true that we use 'cause' in speaking about the actions of agents, but we can no more infer from this verbal consideration that actions are the Humean effects of events than we can from the etymological derivation of the term 'motive.' Earlier I discussed the impropriety in general of supposing that a motive is a Humean cause, but I examined in detail only the case of intention. 'Motive' covers a variety of items, not only the intention a person may have in doing something but also such items as anger, jealousy, revenge, etc. Consider the most likely candidate for Humean cause: the sudden flare-up of anger that causes a man to spank his child. Even here the Humean model will not fit in the way in which it fits the case of a blow on the patella which causes a man's leg to jerk up. In the latter case the person, his thoughts, his concerns, his intentions, reasons, etc., are wholly irrelevant to the occurrence thus produced. It is not that the blow causes *him* to jerk his leg, but rather that the blow caused, not something the man did, but a happening, the jerking of the leg. In the case of the angry man, the anger caused *the man* to act as he does. Anger indeed is no mere Humean impression of reflection; for it is logically essential to the concept of anger that the anger be about or over something. It is no more possible for a person to be angry about nothing than for a person to have a desire that is not a desire for something. And even here it is not causal knowledge that enables a man to say that he spanked his child because he was angry as it is in the case of one who explains the movement of the leg by a 'Because it was struck in the patellar region.' It is rather that the reference to his anger explains the action as that of an angry man—it enables us to describe *what* he did. And this by no means ends the matter, for anger may be justified or unjustified and the person in giving way to it may be blameable on account of it. Nothing of this sort applies to the jerk of the leg that results from the blow on the patella. Here we do not have an action of an agent but the action of the leg, namely, a bodily movement.

'Cause,' then, is one of the snare words in both ordinary and philosophical speech, and here every attention to the precise manner in which it is employed is essential. For even in cases in which we have an immediate response (*e.g.* the startled jump of a person when a fire-cracker suddenly explodes behind him, or the scream of terror at the sight of the apparition on the stairs, or the sudden withdrawal of the hand from the hot object one has touched), in which there is neither calculation nor any of the other evidences of reasoned or intentional conduct, the question is not 'What caused the action?' but 'What caused him (or her) to do . . . (to jump, scream, or withdraw the hand)?' Here the reference to the agent is essential in the way in which it is not in the case of the reflex jerk of the leg, the twitch of a muscle or the movement of the intestines. And here we have extreme cases which shade almost imperceptibly (when we consider the broad and varied spectrum of cases to which the question 'What caused him (or her) to . . . ?' is applicable) into the cases in which there is calculated and reasoned behaviour, in which the agent is getting what he wants for good and sufficient reasons. The important thing is not to be blinded by the fact that 'cause' may be used in all cases but to recognize just how it is applied and in what varied ways to cases that range from instinctive responses to reasoned, rational transactions of agents with one another. In none of these cases, varied though they may be, is causation in the sense in which this term applies to physical events applicable to the actions of agents. But a detailed inquiry into these uses of 'cause' is not possible within the limits of this essay.

Equally treacherous is the term 'prediction.' Granted that to predict is to say what will be the case, what does *this* mean? I can be said to say what will be by promising that I shall do such-and-such. By declaring that I shall hit the target, I can be said to say what will be, and then proving it by exhibiting my skill. I can be said to say what will be by contradicting someone's expression of intention, *e.g.* 'I won't let you harm that child!' and succeeding. I can be said to say what will be by saying that the coin will fall heads and having my guess come true. I can be said to say what will be by predicting the villainous act of someone I know to be a villain. I can be said to say what will be by predicting the path of a comet from its known velocity, direction of motion, etc. And so on. Here someone may object that after all there must be something common to all of these cases—saying what will be—whatever the differences between them might be. Certainly, in all of these and other cases of prediction this is common: something is said about the future. But to say this is only to say that these words apply. It is not to say that there is a common ingredient so that promising, for example, is saying what will be plus something else that makes the saying a promise and not, say, an expression of my resolution. What makes the promise a promise is not that there is one item—saying what will be—together with some other item. It is, rather, as I have argued elsewhere, that the saying what will be when it is done by an agent under such-and-such circumstances (and here it is no matter what goes on in the mind of the person speaking) is the very same thing as, and not part of, promising.[5] The formula 'saying what will be' is singularly unhelpful. It would be just as unilluminating to say that in all cases in which we use the term 'cause,' whether in speaking about the causes of the contractions of muscles or in speaking about the actions of agents (what caused him to do), there is something common to which we are referring—but of what and in what sense of 'cause' is the crucially important question. And if I predict that someone I know and fully understand—for I know the kind of person he is, the sorts of character traits he has, the things he wants and the goods with which he is concerned—will in such-and-such circumstances act in such-and-such a way, this is not at all like predicting the path of a satellite; nor does the reliability of my prediction rest upon hidden causal factors that operate in such a way as to make true what I say will be the case. For here the reliability of my prediction rests upon my understanding of the person—he is like an open book to me—not upon hidden Humean causal factors about which, if they were at all relevant, I can at best only speculate. Here nothing is hidden; it is because I understand him, not because I am aware of events transpiring in some alleged mechanism of his mind or body, that I am able to say what he will do.

Such predictions sometimes go wrong. Suppose, however, it were possible in principle to predict with perfect accuracy, how could one then maintain that the agent could do anything other than what he does, that his behaviour is not subject to causal factors in precisely the way in which this is admittedly true of the motions of some heavenly body, that a human being

[5] Cf. 'On Promising,' *Mind*, January 1956.

is not a helpless victim of circumstances within and without him? Here we have the picture of a human being reacting to stimuli from without in accordance with the precise character of his constitution—the pattern of events within his nervous system—an extraordinarily complex mechanical or electronic system no different in principle, but only in degree of complexity, from some of the self-regulating mechanisms of the laboratory which perform their perfectly predictable operations when suitably programmed.

This picture wholly misrepresents the character of agents and their actions. What would one predict—actions or bodily movements? Certainly, if one knew the state of the nervous system and musculature, then one could predict, given such-and-such stimulation, that, say, the arm would rise in the air. But our concern is not with the rising of the arm but with the person's raising of his arm; and with raising his arm, say, in order to signal, to get what he wants, and so on. Let it be that the nervous system of one who has been trained to drive and to give the signal that he is about to make a turn has been suitably 'conditioned'—that there are characteristic brain patterns present in these and only these cases at the time the arm is raised in order to give the signal—further conditions are required for the raising of the arm, and what can these be? It is no good saying that these conditions are the appropriate visual and auditory stimuli, the nervous excitation of the end-organs in the eye or ear. For so far all that such stimulations of the appropriately conditioned bodily mechanism can produce is the movement of the arm. In order that one might predict that the person will raise his arm in order to give the signal, one needs not only a knowledge of the central nervous system and of the appropriate stimulation of the end-organs, but also of the circumstances in which the *agent*—not the bodily mechanism—is placed and of what, in these circumstances, he will do. We need to know, in short, that we have an agent, a motorist, who is driving and whose action of raising the arm is to be understood in terms of the appropriate rule of the road as a case of signalling a turn as the cross-road comes into view. But in that case we have left behind all reference to hypothetical occurrences in the nervous system, for now we are back to the scene of human action. And the circumstances to which we must now attend, if we are to predict that he will raise his arm to signal, are not Humean causal conditions of his doing. They are rather circumstances in the context of which the bodily movement that does occur, and however it may be that it is produced, *is* understood as the specific action it is.

. . .

Here someone may object: granted that there is no one central nuclear experience that constitutes the intention of an agent, and similarly in the case of a desire or a decision or a choice, still these do make a difference to the character of a man's thoughts and feelings, *i.e.*, to his inner mental state. And if so, there must be corresponding sorts of neural events, however complex these may be, in each of these cases. So too with the circumstances in which a motorist finds himself and to which he attends as he performs his various actions. If he attends to these, if he has been trained, if he executes his skilful performances, there are characteristic states of the nervous system and characteristic exciting stimuli. Now if one knew enough about the nervous system, could we not 'interpret' or 'decode' such states and stimuli as the states and stimuli of such-and-such an agent doing such-and-such in the given sort of circumstances? And given a knowledge of the future stimuli, similarly 'decoded,' could we not infallibly predict such-and-such bodily movements, similarly decipherable as the bodily movements performed by the given sort of agent in doing such-and-such? No doubt such predictability would depend on our own status as agents who can understand cases of bodily movements as cases of actions and who can recognize that in given circumstances the actions in question would be of a given sort; but we could, given this understanding that would enable us to interpret neural data in the appropriate way, predict on the basis of such data what any given person will do. If so, could we still insist that any agent, even when he attends carefully to what he is doing, even when his behaviour is as calculated and as deliberate as it may be, could possibly have done otherwise? And since he in turn, equipped with the same ability, could discover, predict and interpret the neural data in *our* nervous systems, are we not equally helpless in all that we do—even in discussing these very matters? And if so, we seem to be on the brink of insanity—it is as if computing machines were to be programmed and decoded only by other machines of like sorts, as if work were being done in a laboratory without any person doing it.

What we know about the nervous system and the events transpiring in it as we think, feel and do is extraordinarily little, but the reply need not rest on such an appeal to our manifest ignorance. Indeed, one should hope and pray that it may be possible one day to know enough about the mechanism of the body to enable qualified persons to cure mental disorders by introducing the necessary changes in the central nervous system, perhaps by means of surgery. One may grant, in fact, that the development of the central nervous system goes hand-in-hand with the maturation of human beings as they acquire the varied skills which they exhibit in their reasoned and responsible thoughts and actions, that the latter is in some way dependent upon the former. But none of this implies the forbidding picture painted by the epiphenomenalist in which the status of a person reduces to the vaporous after-effects of physiological processes. For even if we could do the decoding, we should still have the central nervous system of a person who reasons, justifies, decides, chooses, intends, wants, and conducts himself as he does with other persons about him. Indeed, what our speculation implies is the requirement, for the thoughts and actions of such persons, of requisite states of the nervous system and this, far from reducing persons to hapless mechanisms, is only a more radical representation of the familiar view that persons are not disembodied spirits but persons who can be seen and touched and hurt, who use their arms, legs, etc. in the actions they perform, and who require for such employment of their limbs and other bodily parts certain general conditions and particular states of their nervous systems. Indeed, the alleged conclusion that each of us is a helpless victim of the events transpiring in the central nervous system is simply a logical howler. 'Could have done' and 'could not have done,' 'helpless,' etc.—these are expressions employed not with respect to events occurring in the mechanism of the body, nor to mental events, whether or not these are regarded as mere by-products of bodily processes—Humean effects of neural events—but to *persons*. We do not say that an itch or twitch, a feeling, thought or desire, however we understand these, is helpless. Neither do we say that the body is helpless in any sense in which we say this about a person. It is *persons* who are able or unable to do or to refrain from doing; to think or to refrain from thinking, etc. We need, in short, to recognize the necessary starting point for any elucidation of expressions of these sorts—persons who act, think, feel, in their commerce with the things about them and with each other. This is the language-game in which expressions like 'could have done,' 'could not have done,' 'helpless,' etc., are employed, in any sense in which they bear upon questions of the freedom of human action. To suppose that they can be employed, without radical distortion or change, in the account of the events within the body, or in any account of their Humean effects, is the confusion upon which the apparently disastrous consequences of our speculative assumption rests.

But still, if our speculation about the decoding were granted, would it not be possible, not merely to predict how human beings would behave, but also and without their knowledge to control them by altering the neural conditions within their bodies? Certainly. In point of fact, other devices are currently employed by politicians and others concerned to manipulate human beings—the difference is only one of degree in the success of the results; the methods currently employed are fortunately very crude and frequently inefficacious. And if by introducing an electrode into the brain of a person, I succeed in getting him to believe that he is Napoleon, that surely is not a rational belief that he has, nor is he responsible for what he does in consequence of this belief, however convinced he may be that he is fully justified in acting as he does. There would be no virtue in any philosophical doctrine which ruled out the possibility that human beings may be controlled, that by virtue of what we do to them we may render them incompetent, insane, devoid of responsibility. But here as before, we can understand terms like 'competence,' 'control,' 'responsible' only by keeping clearly in mind the contexts appropriate to their employment—human beings who are rational in and attentive to what they are doing in their transactions with one another and in their dealings with the things about them.

In short, even on our speculative assumption, nothing disastrous to our common beliefs about the freedom of human action would follow. Such knowledge might be dangerous—it might open the way to abuses in the management of human beings. But even if this knowledge were achieved, we should still employ our familiar discourse in describing persons and their conduct. Far from it being the case that the possibility of such knowledge implies the helplessness of human beings in all of their thoughts and actions, the achievement of such knowledge would enable us to understand, in a two-fold sense, why human beings think, desire, choose, decide and do as in fact they do. For one thing, we should have a knowledge of the neural conditions under which such human events occur; and, for another, since the neural states and events would be 'decoded,' these would be understood in terms that go beyond the purview of the physiologist. In effect, then, the knowledge of such decoded neural states and events would indeed give us a fuller understanding of the actions of responsible persons and hence a better basis for prediction than we now have; but it would do this *only* by revealing more fully their characters, interests, desires, hopes, social and moral rôles, choices, intentions, etc.—just those sorts of items in terms of which we do in fact explain and predict the actions of human beings. We should then be able, for one thing, to understand, explain and predict the quite rational, responsible actions of free agents; and we should then be able to understand and to predict that such agents would decide not to perform actions of various sorts, in circumstances to which they were attending, and which they could then and there have done, for this or that reason.

ACTIONS, REASONS, AND CAUSES

DONALD DAVIDSON

What is the relation between a reason and an action when the reason explains the action by giving the agent's reason for doing what he did? We may call such explanations *rationalizations,* and say that the reason *rationalizes* the action.

In this paper I want to defend the ancient—and commonsense—position that rationalization is a species of ordinary causal explanation. The defense no doubt requires some redeployment, but not more or less complete abandonment of the position, as urged by many recent writers.[1]

I

A reason rationalizes an action only if it leads us to see something the agent saw, or thought he saw, in his action—some feature, consequence, or aspect of the action the agent wanted, desired, prized, held dear, thought dutiful, beneficial, obligatory, or agreeable. We cannot explain why someone did what he did simply by saying the particular action appealed to him; we must indicate what it was about the action that appealed. Whenever someone does something for a reason, therefore, he can be characterized as (*a*) having some sort of pro attitude toward actions of a certain kind, and (*b*) believing (or knowing, perceiving, noticing, remembering) that his action is of that kind. Under (*a*) are to be included desires, wantings, urges, prompt-

From Donald Davidson, "Actions, Reasons, and Causes," *The Journal of Philosophy,* LX, No. 23 (November 7, 1963), pp. 685–700.

[1] Some examples: G. E. M. Anscombe, *Intention,* Oxford, 1959; Stuart Hampshire, *Thought and Action,* London, 1959; H. L. A. Hart and A. M. Honoré, *Causation in the Law,* Oxford, 1959; William Dray, *Laws and Explanation in History,* Oxford, 1957; and most of the books in the series edited by R. F. Holland, *Studies in Philosophical Psychology,* including Anthony Kenny, *Action, Emotion and Will,* London, 1963, and A. I. Melden, *Free Action,* London, 1961. Page references in parentheses will all be to these works.

ings, and a great variety of moral views, aesthetic principles, economic prejudices, social conventions, and public and private goals and values in so far as these can be interpreted as attitudes of an agent directed toward actions of a certain kind. The word 'attitude' does yeoman service here, for it must cover not only permanent character traits that show themselves in a lifetime of behavior, like love of children or a taste for loud company, but also the most passing fancy that prompts a unique action, like a sudden desire to touch a woman's elbow. In general, pro attitudes must not be taken for convictions, however temporary, that every action of a certain kind ought to be performed, is worth performing, or is, all things considered, desirable. On the contrary, a man may all his life have a yen, say, to drink a can of paint, without ever, even at the moment he yields, believing it would be worth doing.

Giving the reason why an agent did something is often a matter of naming the pro attitude (*a*) or the related belief (*b*) or both; let me call this pair the *primary reason* why the agent performed the action. Now it is possible to reformulate the claim that rationalizations are causal explanations, and give structure to the argument as well, by stating two theses about primary reasons:

1. For us to understand how a reason of any kind rationalizes an action it is necessary and sufficient that we see, at least in essential outline, how to construct a primary reason.
2. The primary reason for an action is its cause.

I shall argue for these points in turn.

II

I flip the switch, turn on the light, and illuminate the room. Unbeknownst to me I also alert a prowler to the fact that I am home. Here I do not do four things, but only one, of which four descriptions have been given.[2] I flipped the switch

[2] We would not call my unintentional alerting of the prowler an action, but it should not be inferred from this that alerting the prowler is therefore something different from flipping the switch, say just its con-

because I wanted to turn on the light, and by saying I wanted to turn on the light I explain (give my reason for, rationalize) the flipping. But I do not, by giving this reason, rationalize my alerting of the prowler nor my illuminating of the room. Since reasons may rationalize what someone does when it is described in one way and not when it is described in another, we cannot treat what was done simply as a term in sentences like 'My reason for flipping the switch was that I wanted to turn on the light'; otherwise we would be forced to conclude, from the fact that flipping the switch was identical with alerting the prowler, that my reason for alerting the prowler was that I wanted to turn on the light. Let us mark this quasi-intensional[3] character of action descriptions in rationalizations by stating a bit more precisely a necessary condition for primary reasons:

C 1. *R* is a primary reason why an agent performed the action *A* under the description *d* only if *R* consists of a pro attitude of the agent toward actions with a certain property, and a belief of the agent that *A*, under the description *d*, has that property.

---

sequence. Actions, performances, and events not involving intention are alike in that they are often referred to or defined partly in terms of some terminal stage, outcome, or consequence.

The word 'action' does not very often occur in ordinary speech, and when it does it is usually reserved for fairly portentous occasions. I follow a useful philosophical practice in calling anything an agent does intentionally an action, including intentional omissions. What is really needed is some suitably generic term to bridge the following gap: suppose '*A*' is a description of an action, '*B*' is a description of something done voluntarily, though not intentionally, and '*C*' is a description of something done involuntarily and unintentionally; finally, suppose $A = B = C$. Then *A*, *B*, and *C* are the same—what? 'Action,' 'event,' 'thing done,' each have, at least in some contexts, a strange ring when coupled with the wrong sort of description. Only the question "Why did you (he) do *A*?" has the true generality required. Obviously, the problem is greatly aggravated if we assume, as Melden does (*Free Action*, 85), that an action ("raising one's arm") can be identical with a bodily movement ("one's arm going up").

[3] "Quasi-intensional" because, besides its intensional aspect, the description of the action must also refer in rationalizations; otherwise it could be true that an action was done for a certain reason and yet the action not have been performed. Compare 'the author of *Waverley*' in 'George IV knew the author of *Waverley* wrote *Waverley*.'

How can my wanting to turn on the light be (part of) a primary reason, since it appears to lack the required element of generality? We may be taken in by the verbal parallel between 'I turned on the light' and 'I wanted to turn on the light.' The first clearly refers to a particular event, so we conclude that the second has this same event as its object. Of course it is obvious that the event of my turning on the light can't be referred to in the same way by both sentences, since the existence of the event is required by the truth of 'I turned on the light' but not by the truth of 'I wanted to turn on the light.' If the reference were the same in both cases, the second sentence would entail the first; but in fact the sentences are logically independent. What is less obvious, at least until we attend to it, is that the event whose occurrence makes 'I turned on the light' true cannot be called the object, however intensional, of 'I wanted to turn on the light.' If I turned on the light, then I must have done it at a precise moment, in a particular way—every detail is fixed. But it makes no sense to demand that my want be directed at an action performed at any one moment or done in some unique manner. Any one of an indefinitely large number of actions would satisfy the want, and can be considered equally eligible as its object. Wants and desires often are trained on physical objects. However, 'I want that gold watch in the window' is not a primary reason, and explains why I went into the store only because it suggests a primary reason—for example, that I wanted to buy the watch.

Because 'I wanted to turn on the light' and 'I turned on the light' are logically independent, the first can be used to give a reason why the second is true. Such a reason gives minimal information: it implies that the action was intentional, and wanting tends to exclude some other pro attitudes, such as a sense of duty or obligation. But the exclusion depends very much on the action and the context of explanation. Wanting seems pallid beside lusting, but it would be odd to deny that someone who lusted after a woman or a cup of coffee wanted her or it. It is not unnatural, in fact, to treat wanting as a genus including all pro attitudes as species. When we do this and when we know some action is intentional, it is empty to add that the agent wanted to do it. In such cases, it is easy to answer the question 'Why did you do it?' with 'For no reason,' meaning not that there is no reason but that there is no *further* reason, no reason that cannot be inferred from the fact that the action was done intentionally; no reason, in other words, besides wanting to do it. This last point is not essential to the present argument, but it is of interest because it defends the possibility of defining an intentional action as one done for a reason.

A primary reason consists of a belief and an attitude, but it is generally otiose to mention both. If you tell me you are easing the jib because you think that will stop the main from backing, I don't need to be told that you want to stop the main from backing; and if you say you are biting your thumb at me because you want to insult me, there is no point in adding that you think that by biting your thumb at me you will insult me. Similarly, many explanations of actions in terms of reasons that are not primary do not require mention of the primary reason to complete the story. If I say I am pulling weeds because I want a beautiful lawn, it would be fatuous to eke out the account with 'And so I see something desirable in any action that does, or has a good chance of, making the lawn beautiful.' Why insist that there is any *step*, logical or psychological, in the transfer of desire from an end that is not an action to the actions one conceives as means? It serves the argument as well that the desired end explains the action only if what are believed by the agent to be means are desired.

Fortunately, it is not necessary to classify and analyze the many varieties of emotions, sentiments, moods, motives, passions, and hungers whose mention may answer the question 'Why did you do it?' in order to see how, when such mention rationalizes the action, a primary reason is involved. Claustrophobia gives a man's reason for leaving a cocktail party because we know people want to avoid, escape from, be safe from, put distance between themselves and, what they fear. Jealousy is the motive in a poisoning because, among other things, the poisoner believes his action will harm his rival, remove the cause of his agony, or redress an injustice, and these are the sorts of things a jealous man wants to do. When we learn a man cheated his son out of greed, we do not necessarily know what the primary reason was, but we know there was one, and its general nature. Ryle analyzes 'he boasted from vanity' into "he boasted on meeting the stranger and his doing so satisfies the lawlike proposition that whenever he finds a chance of securing the admiration and envy of others, he does whatever he thinks will produce this admiration and envy" (*The Concept of Mind,* 89). This analysis is often, and perhaps justly, criticized on the ground that a man may boast from vanity just once. But if Ryle's boaster did what he did from vanity, then something entailed by Ryle's analysis is true: the boaster wanted to secure the admiration and envy of others, and he believed that his action would produce this admiration and envy; true or false, Ryle's analysis does not dispense with primary reasons, but depends upon them.

To know a primary reason why someone acted as he did is to know an intention with which the action was done. If I turn left at the fork because I want to get to Katmandu, my intention in turning left is to get to Katmandu. But to know the intention is not necessarily to know the primary reason in full detail. If James goes to church with the intention of pleasing his mother, then he must have some pro attitude toward pleasing his mother, but it needs more information to tell whether his reason is that he enjoys pleasing his mother, or thinks it right, his duty, or an obligation. The expression 'the intention with which James went to church' has the outward form of a description, but in fact it is syncategorematic and cannot be taken to refer to an entity, state, disposition, or event. Its function in context is to generate new descriptions of actions in terms of their reasons; thus 'James went to church with the intention of pleasing his mother' yields a new, and fuller, description of the action described in 'James went to church.' Essentially the same process goes on when I answer the question 'Why are you bobbing around that way?' with 'I'm knitting, weaving, exercising, sculling, cuddling, training fleas.'

Straight description of an intended result often explains

an action better than stating that the result was intended or desired. 'It will soothe your nerves' explains why I pour you a shot as efficiently as 'I want to do something to soothe your nerves,' since the first in the context of explanation implies the second; but the first does better, because, if it is true, the facts will justify my choice of action. Because justifying and explaining an action so often go hand in hand, we frequently indicate the primary reason for an action by making a claim which, if true, would also verify, vindicate, or support the relevant belief or attitude of the agent. 'I knew I ought to return it,' 'The paper said it was going to snow,' 'You stepped on *my* toes,' all, in appropriate reason-giving contexts, perform this familiar dual function.

The justifying role of a reason, given this interpretation, depends upon the explanatory role, but the converse does not hold. Your stepping on my toes neither explains nor justifies my stepping on your toes unless I believe you stepped on my toes, but the belief alone, true or false, explains my action.

III

In the light of a primary reason, an action is revealed as coherent with certain traits, long- or short-termed, characteristic or not, of the agent, and the agent is shown in his role of Rational Animal. Corresponding to the belief and attitude of a primary reason for an action, we can always construct (with a little ingenuity) the premises of a syllogism from which it follows that the action has some (as Miss Anscombe calls it) "desirability characteristic."[4] Thus there is a certain irreducible —though somewhat anemic—sense in which every rationaliza-

[4] Miss Anscombe denies that the practical syllogism is deductive. This she does partly because she thinks of the practical syllogism, as Aristotle does, as corresponding to a piece of practical reasoning (whereas for me it is only part of the analysis of the concept of a reason with which someone acted), and therefore she is bound, again following Aristotle, to think of the conclusion of a practical syllogism as corresponding to a judgment, not merely that the action has a desirable characteristic, but that the action is desirable (reasonable, worth doing, etc.).

tion justifies: from the agent's point of view there was, when he acted, something to be said for the action.

Noting that nonteleological causal explanations do not display the element of justification provided by reasons, some philosophers have concluded that the concept of cause that applies elsewhere cannot apply to the relation between reasons and actions, and that the pattern of justification provides, in the case of reasons, the required explanation. But suppose we grant that reasons alone justify in explaining actions; it does not follow that the explanation is not also—and necessarily—causal. Indeed our first condition for primary reasons (C1) is designed to help set rationalizations apart from other sorts of explanation. If rationalization is, as I want to argue, a species of causal explanation, then justification, in the sense given by C1, is at least one differentiating property. How about the other claim: that justifying is a kind of explaining, so that the ordinary notion of cause need not be brought in? Here it is necessary to decide what is being included under justification. Perhaps it means only what is given by C1: that the agent has certain beliefs and attitudes in the light of which the action is reasonable. But then something essential has certainly been left out, for a person can have a reason for an action, and perform the action, and yet this reason not be the reason why he did it. Central to the relation between a reason and an action it explains is the idea that the agent performed the action *because* he had the reason. Of course, we can include this idea too in justification; but then the notion of justification becomes as dark as the notion of reason until we can account for the force of that 'because.'

When we ask why someone acted as he did, we want to be provided with an interpretation. His behavior seems strange, alien, outré, pointless, out of character, disconnected; or perhaps we cannot even recognize an action in it. When we learn his reason, we have an interpretation, a new description of what he did which fits it into a familiar picture. The picture certainly includes some of the agent's beliefs and attitudes; perhaps also goals, ends, principles, general character traits, virtues or vices. Beyond this, the redescription of an action afforded by a reason may place the action in a wider social, economic, linguistic, or evaluative context. To learn, through learning the reason, that the agent conceived his action as a lie, a repayment of a debt, an insult, the fulfillment of an avuncular obligation, or a knight's gambit is to grasp the point of the action in its setting of rules, practices, conventions, and expectations.

Remarks like these, inspired by the later Wittgenstein, have been elaborated with subtlety and insight by a number of philosophers. And there is no denying that this is true: when we explain an action, by giving the reason, we do redescribe the action; redescribing the action gives the action a place in a pattern, and in this way the action is explained. Here it is tempting to draw two conclusions that do not follow. First, we can't infer, from the fact that giving reasons merely redescribes the action and that causes are separate from effects, that therefore reasons are not causes. Reasons, being beliefs and attitudes, are certainly not identical with actions; but, more important, events are often redescribed in terms of their causes. (Suppose someone was burned. We could redescribe this event "in terms of a cause" by saying he was burned.) Second, it is an error to think that, because placing the action in a larger pattern explains it, therefore we now understand the sort of explanation involved. Talk of patterns and contexts does not answer the question of how reasons explain actions, since the relevant pattern or context contains both reason and action. One way we can explain an event is by placing it in the context of its cause; cause and effect form the sort of pattern that explains the effect, in a sense of 'explain' that we understand as well as any. If reason and action illustrate a different pattern of explanation, that pattern must be identified.

Let me urge the point in connection with an example of Melden's. A man driving an automobile raises his arm in order to signal. His intention, to signal, explains his action, raising his arm, by redescribing it as signaling. What is the pattern that explains the action? Is it the familiar pattern of an action done for a reason? Then it does indeed explain the action, but only because it assumes the relation of reason and action that we want to analyze. Or is the pattern rather this: the man is driving, he is approaching a turn; he knows he ought to signal; he knows how to signal, by raising his arm. And now, in this context, he raises his arm. Perhaps, as Melden suggests, if all this happens, he does signal. And the explanation would then be this: if, under these conditions, a man raises his arm, then he signals. The difficulty, is, of course, that this explanation does not touch the question of why he raised his arm. He had a reason to raise his arm, but this has not been shown to be the reason why he did it. If the description 'signaling' explains his action by giving his reason, then the signaling must be intentional; but, on the account just given, it may not be.

If, as Melden claims, causal explanations are "wholly irrelevant to the understanding we seek" of human actions (184) then we are without an analysis of the 'because' in 'He did it because . . . ,' where we go on to name a reason. Hampshire remarks, of the relation between reasons and action, "In philosophy one ought surely to find this . . . connection altogether mysterious" (166). Hampshire rejects Aristotle's attempt to solve the mystery by introducing the concept of wanting as a causal factor, on the grounds that the resulting theory is too clear and definite to fit all cases and that "There is still no compelling ground for insisting that the word 'want' *must* enter into every full statement of reasons for acting" (168). I agree that the concept of wanting is too narrow, but I have argued that, at least in a vast number of typical cases, some pro attitude must be assumed to be present if a statement of an agent's reasons in acting is to be intelligible. Hampshire does not see how Aristotle's scheme can be appraised as true or false, "for it is not clear what could be the basis of assessment, or what kind of evidence could be decisive" (167). Failing a satisfactory alternative, the best argument for a scheme like Aristotle's is that it alone promises to give an account of the "mysterious connection" between reasons and actions.

IV

In order to turn the first 'and' to 'because' in 'He exercised *and* he wanted to reduce and thought exercise would do it,' we must, as the basic move,[5] augment condition C1 with:

C2. A primary reason for an action is its cause.

The considerations in favor of C2 are by now, I hope, obvious; in the remainder of this paper I wish to defend C2 against various lines of attack and, in the process, to clarify the notion of causal explanation involved.

A. The first line of attack is this. Primary reasons consist of attitudes and beliefs, which are states or dispositions, not events; therefore they cannot be causes.

It is easy to reply that states, dispositions, and conditions are frequently named as the causes of events: the bridge collapsed because of a structural defect; the plane crashed on takeoff because the air temperature was abnormally high; the plate broke because it had a crack. This reply does not, however, meet a closely related point. Mention of a causal condition for an event gives a cause only on the assumption that there was also a preceding event. But what is the preceding event that causes an action?

In many cases it is not difficult at all to find events very closely associated with the primary reason. States and dispositions are not events, but the onslaught of a state or disposition is. A desire to hurt your feelings may spring up at the moment you anger me; I may start wanting to eat a melon just when I see one; and beliefs may begin at the moment we notice, perceive, learn, or remember something. Those who have argued that there are no mental events to qualify as causes of actions have often missed the obvious because they have insisted that

[5] I say "as the basic move" to cancel the suggestion that C1 and C2 are jointly *sufficient* to define the relation of reasons to the actions they explain. I believe C2 can be strengthened to make C1 and C2 sufficient as well as necessary conditions, but here I am concerned only with the claim that both are, as they stand, necessary.

a mental event be observed or noticed (rather than an observing or a noticing) or that it be like a stab, a qualm, a prick or a quiver, a mysterious prod of conscience or act of the will. Melden, in discussing the driver who signals a turn by raising his arm, challenges those who want to explain actions causally to identify "an event which is common and peculiar to all such cases" (87), perhaps a motive or an intention, anyway "some particular feeling or experience" (95). But of course there is a mental event; at some moment the driver noticed (or thought he noticed) his turn coming up, and that is the moment he signaled. During any continuing activity, like driving, or elaborate performance, like swimming the Hellespont, there are more or less fixed purposes, standards, desires, and habits that give direction and form to the entire enterprise, and there is the continuing input of information about what we are doing, about changes in the environment, in terms of which we regulate and adjust our actions. To dignify a driver's awareness that his turn has come by calling it an experience, much less a feeling, is no doubt exaggerated, but whether it deserves a name or not, it had better be the reason why he raises his arm. In this case, and typically, there may not be anything we would call a motive, but if we mention such a general purpose as wanting to get to one's destination safely, it is clear that the motive is not an event. The intention with which the driver raises his arm is also not an event, for it is no thing at all, neither event, attitude, disposition, nor object. Finally, Melden asks the causal theorist to find an event that is common and peculiar to all cases where a man intentionally raises his arm, and this, it must be admitted, cannot be produced. But then neither can a common and unique cause of bridge failures, plane crashes, or plate breakings be produced.

The signaling driver can answer the question 'Why did you raise your arm when you did?', and from the answer we learn the event that caused the action. But can an actor always answer such a question? Sometimes the answer will mention a mental event that does not give a reason: 'Finally I made up my mind.' However, there also seem to be cases of intentional action where we cannot explain at all why we acted when we did. In such cases, explanation in terms of primary reasons parallels the explanation of the collapse of the bridge from a structural defect: we are ignorant of the event or sequence of events that led up to (caused) the collapse, but we are sure there was such an event or sequence of events.

B. According to Melden, a cause must be "logically distinct from the alleged effect" (52); but a reason for an action is not logically distinct from the action; therefore, reasons are not causes of actions.[6]

One possible form of this argument has already been suggested. Since a reason makes an action intelligible by redescribing it, we do not have two events, but only one under different descriptions. Causal relations, however, demand distinct events.

Someone might be tempted into the mistake of thinking that my flipping of the switch caused my turning on of the light (in fact it caused the light to go on). But it does not follow that it is a mistake to take 'My reason for flipping the switch was that I wanted to turn on the light' as entailing, in part, 'I flipped the switch, and this action is further describable as having been caused by my wanting to turn on the light.' To describe an event in terms of its cause is not to identify the event with its cause, nor does explanation by redescription exclude causal explanation.

The example serves also to refute the claim that we cannot describe the action without using words that link it to the alleged cause. Here the action is to be explained under the description: 'my flipping the switch,' and the alleged cause is 'my wanting to turn on the light.' What possible logical relation is supposed to hold between these phrases? It seems more plausible to urge a logical link between 'my turning on the light' and 'my wanting to turn on the light,' but even

[6] This argument can be found, in one or more versions, in Kenny, Hampshire, and Melden, as well as in P. Winch, *The Idea of a Social Science,* London, 1958, and R. S. Peters, *The Concept of Motivation,* London, 1958. In one of its forms, the argument was of course inspired by Ryle's treatment of motives in *The Concept of Mind.*

here the link turned out, on inspection, to be grammatical rather than logical.

In any case there is something very odd in the idea that causal relations are empirical rather than logical. What can this mean? Surely not that every true causal statement is empirical. For suppose '*A* caused *B*' is true. Then the cause of $B = A$; so, substituting, we have 'The cause of *B* caused *B*,' which is analytic. The truth of a causal statement depends on *what* events are described; its status as analytic or synthetic depends on *how* the events are described. Still, it may be maintained that a reason rationalizes an action only when the descriptions are appropriately fixed, and the appropriate descriptions are not logically independent.

Suppose that to say a man wanted to turn on the light *meant* that he would perform any action he believed would accomplish his end. Then the statement of his primary reason for flipping the switch would entail that he flipped the switch—"straightway he acts," as Aristotle says. In this case there would certainly be a logical connection between reason and action, the same sort of connection as that between 'It's water-soluble and was placed in water' and 'It dissolved.' Since the implication runs from description of cause to description of effect but not conversely, naming the cause still gives information. And, though the point is often overlooked, 'Placing it in water caused it to dissolve' does not entail 'It's water-soluble'; so the latter has additional explanatory force. Nevertheless, the explanation would be far more interesting if, in place of solubility, with its obvious definitional connection with the event to be explained, we could refer to some property, say a particular crystalline structure, whose connection with dissolution in water was known only through experiment. Now it is clear why primary reasons like desires and wants do not explain actions in the relatively trivial way solubility explains dissolvings. Solubility, we are assuming, is a pure disposition property: it is defined in terms of a single test. But desires cannot be defined in terms of the actions they may rationalize, even though the relation between desire and action is not simply empirical; there are other, equally essential criteria for desires —their expression in feelings and in actions that they do not rationalize, for example. The person who has a desire (or want or belief) does not normally need criteria at all—he generally knows, even in the absence of any clues available to others, what he wants, desires, and believes. These logical features of primary reasons show that it is not just lack of ingenuity that keeps us from defining them as dispositions to act for these reasons.

C. According to Hume, "we may define a cause to be an object, followed by another, and where all the objects similar to the first are followed by objects similar to the second." But, Hart and Honoré claim, "The statement that one person did something because, for example, another threatened him, carries no implication or covert assertion that if the circumstances were repeated the same action would follow" (52). Hart and Honoré allow that Hume is right in saying that ordinary singular causal statements imply generalizations, but wrong for this very reason in supposing that motives and desires are ordinary causes of actions. In brief, laws are involved essentially in ordinary causal explanations, but not in rationalizations.

It is common to try to meet this argument by suggesting that we do have rough laws connecting reasons and actions, and these can, in theory, be improved. True, threatened people do not always respond in the same way; but we may distinguish between threats and also between agents, in terms of their beliefs and attitudes.

The suggestion is delusive, however, because generalizations connecting reasons and actions are not—and cannot be sharpened into—the kind of law on the basis of which accurate predictions can reliably be made. If we reflect on the way in which reasons determine choice, decision, and behavior, it is easy to see why this is so. What emerges, in the *ex post facto* atmosphere of explanation and justification, as *the* reason frequently was, to the agent at the time of action, one consideration among many, *a* reason. Any serious theory for predicting action on the basis of reasons must find a way of evaluating the relative force of various desires and beliefs in the matrix of decision; it cannot take as its starting point the refinement of what is to be expected from a single desire. The practical syllogism exhausts its role in displaying an action as falling under one reason; so it cannot be subtilized into a reconstruction of practical reasoning, which involves the weighing of competing reasons. The practical syllogism provides a model neither for a predictive science of action nor for a normative account of evaluative reasoning.

Ignorance of competent predictive laws does not inhibit valid causal explanation, or few causal explanations could be made. I am certain the window broke because it was struck by a rock—I saw it all happen; but I am not (is anyone?) in command of laws on the basis of which I can predict what blows will break which windows. A generalization like 'Windows are fragile, and fragile things tend to break when struck hard enough, other conditions being right' is not a predictive law in the rough—the predictive law, if we had it, would be quantitative and would use very different concepts. The generalization, like our generalizations about behavior, serves a different function: it provides evidence for the existence of a causal law covering the case at hand.

We are usually far more certain of a singular causal connection than we are of any causal law governing the case; does this show that Hume was wrong in claiming that singular causal statements entail laws? Not necessarily, for Hume's claim, as quoted above, is ambiguous. It may mean that '*A* caused *B*' entails some particular law involving the predicates used in the descriptions '*A*' and '*B*,' or it may mean that '*A* caused *B*' entails that there exists a causal law instantiated by some true descriptions of *A* and *B*.[7] Obviously, both versions of Hume's

[7] We could roughly characterize the analysis of singular causal statements hinted at here as follows: '*A* caused *B*' is true if and only if there are descriptions of *A* and *B* such that the sentence obtained by putting these descriptions for '*A*' and '*B*' in '*A* caused *B*' follows from a true causal law. This analysis is saved from triviality by the fact that not all true generalizations are causal laws; causal laws are distinguished

doctrine give a sense to the claim that singular causal statements entail laws, and both sustain the view that causal explanations "involve laws." But the second version is far weaker, in that no particular law is entailed by a singular causal claim, and a singular causal claim can be defended, if it needs defense, without defending any law. Only the second version of Hume's doctrine can be made to fit with most causal explanations; it suits rationalizations equally well.

The most primitive explanation of an event gives its cause; more elaborate explanations may tell more of the story, or defend the singular causal claim by producing a relevant law or by giving reasons for believing such exists. But it is an error to think no explanation has been given until a law has been produced. Linked with these errors is the idea that singular causal statements necessarily indicate, by the concepts they employ, the concepts that will occur in the entailed law. Suppose a hurricane, which is reported on page 5 of Tuesday's *Times*, causes a catastrophe, which is reported on page 13 of Wednesday's *Tribune*. Then the event reported on page 5 of Tuesday's *Times* caused the event reported on page 13 of Wednesday's *Tribune*. Should we look for a law relating events of these *kinds?* It is only slightly less ridiculous to look for a law relating hurricanes and catastrophes. The laws needed to predict the catastrophe with precision would, of course, have no use for concepts like hurricane and catastrophe. The trouble with predicting the weather is that the descriptions under which events interest us—'a cool, cloudy day with rain in the afternoon'—have only remote connections with the concepts employed by the more precise known laws.

The laws whose existence is required if reasons are causes of actions do not, we may be sure, deal in the concepts in which rationalizations must deal. If the causes of a class of events (actions) fall in a certain class (reasons) and there is a law to

(though of course this is no analysis) by the fact that they are inductively confirmed by their instances and by the fact that they support counterfactual and subjunctive singular causal statements.

back each singular causal statement, it does not follow that there is any law connecting events classified as reasons with events classified as actions—the classifications may even be neurological, chemical, or physical.

D. It is said that the kind of knowledge one has of one's own reasons in acting is not compatible with the existence of a causal relation between reasons and actions: a person knows his own intentions in acting infallibly, without induction or observation, and no ordinary causal relation can be known in this way. No doubt our knowledge of our own intentions in acting will show many of the oddities peculiar to first-person knowledge of one's own pains, beliefs, desires, and so on; the only question is whether these oddities prove that reasons do not cause, in any ordinary sense at least, the actions that they rationalize.

You may easily be wrong about the truth of a statement of the form 'I am poisoning Charles because I want to save him pain,' because you may be wrong about whether you are poisoning Charles—you may yourself be drinking the poisoned cup by mistake. But it also seems that you may err about your reasons, particularly when you have two reasons for an action, one of which pleases you and one which does not. For example, you do want to save Charles pain; you also want him out of the way. You may be wrong about which motive made you do it.

The fact that you may be wrong does not show that in general it makes sense to ask you how you know what your reasons were or to ask for your evidence. Though you may, on rare occasions, accept public or private evidence as showing you are wrong about your reasons, you usually have no evidence and make no observations. Then your knowledge of your own reasons for your actions is not generally inductive, for where there is induction, there is evidence. Does this show the knowledge is not causal? I cannot see that it does.

Causal laws differ from true but nonlawlike generalizations in that their instances confirm them; induction is, therefore, certainly a good way to learn the truth of a law. It does not follow that it is the only way to learn the truth of a law. In any case, in order to know that a singular causal statement is true, it is not necessary to know the truth of a law; it is necessary only to know that some law covering the events at hand exists. And it is far from evident that induction, and induction alone, yields the knowledge that a causal law satisfying certain conditions exists. Or, to put it differently, one case is often enough, as Hume admitted, to persuade us that a law exists, and this amounts to saying that we are persuaded, without direct inductive evidence, that a causal relation exists.[8]

E. Finally I should like to say something about a certain uneasiness some philosophers feel in speaking of causes of actions at all. Melden, for example, says that actions are often identical with bodily movements, and that bodily movements have causes; yet he denies that the causes are causes of the actions. This is, I think, a contradiction. He is led to it by the following sort of consideration: "It is futile to attempt to explain conduct through the causal efficacy of desire—all *that* can explain is further happenings, not actions performed by agents. The agent confronting the causal nexus in which such happenings occur is a helpless victim of all that occurs in and to him" (128, 129). Unless I am mistaken, this argument, if it were valid, would show that actions cannot have causes at all. I shall not point out the obvious difficulties in removing actions from the realm of causality entirely. But perhaps it is worth trying to uncover the source of the trouble. Why on earth should a cause turn an action into a mere happening and a person into a helpless victim? Is it because we tend to assume, at least in the arena of action, that a cause demands a causer, agency an agent? So we press the question; if my action is caused, what caused it? If I did, then there is the absurdity of infinite regress; if I did not, I am a victim. But of course

[8] My thinking on the subject of this section, as on most of the topics discussed in this paper, has been greatly influenced by years of talk with Professor Daniel Bennett, now of Brandeis University.

the alternatives are not exhaustive. Some causes have no agents. Primary among these are those states and changes of state in persons which, because they are reasons as well as causes, make persons voluntary agents.

DETERMINISM

A. C. MACINTYRE

I

This paper has two aims. First I shall try to show that certain contemporary solutions offered to that cluster of logical puzzles traditionally known as 'the problem of free-will and determinism' not only do not shed light on them, but in some cases engender positive darkness. I shall then go on very tentatively to suggest the outline of a possible solution and to meet the more obvious difficulties that it presents. That this is an important problem no one presumably disputes, but it is perhaps not wholly superfluous to emphasise its precise contemporary importance. For it is paradoxical that refutations of theoretical determinism—of Laplace's dream, for example—which satisfy most contemporary philosophers have been propounded and accepted in a period in which for the first time there has been accomplished what the opponents of classical determinism most feared. The threat of classical determinism did not arise so much from its total programme as from that part of its programme which concerned human action in general and moral action in particular. Consequently it is not the physical sciences which should arouse the apprehension of the anti-determinist, but psychology and the social sciences. Sufficient has been already achieved in these sciences to make it clear that we can expect from them ever increasing success in explaining and predicting human behaviour.

From A. C. MacIntyre, "Determinism," *Mind*, LXVI, No. 261 (January, 1957), pp. 28–41.

If one considers, for example, the kind of correlation that Bowlby has claimed to establish between juvenile delinquency of a certain kind and the lack of a mother-figure at certain periods in early childhood (J. Bowlby, *Maternal Care and Mental Health*) ; or the Freudian hypotheses that certain adult traits are causally dependent on certain childhood failures and achievements; or some of the hypotheses advanced by learning theorists; one can hardly doubt that more and more of behaviour will be included in accounts which show such behaviour to be causally dependent on antecedent conditions. It does not in the least matter whether the particular hypotheses which I have mentioned turn out to be correct or not. What matters is that this type of explanation is firmly established. This means that the problem of determinism is not purely speculative, arising from philosophical enquiry, but arises from the very nature of the human sciences. Experience compels us to recognize that success in explaining behaviour is perhaps Janus-faced. For success in explaining and predicting can never be divorced from success in manipulating and controlling. The traditional cheer-leaders of the natural sciences have been wont to emphasise causal explanation as the key to freedom and to offer such examples as medicine and psychotherapy. But successful totalitarian propaganda and social conditioning derive equally from a knowledge of how to predict and manipulate human behaviour. *Brave New World* and *1984* are not baseless fantasies.

So there appears a dilemma, either horn of which seems intolerable. The discovery of causal explanations for our actions, preferences and decisions shows that we could not have done other than we have done, that responsibility is an illusion and the moral life as traditionally conceived a charade. It makes praise and blame irrelevant, except in so far as we discover these to be causally effective, and while the moral judgments of agents might therefore retain some point, those of spectators and critics would be pointless. But even the moral judgments of agents would be affected by such discoveries, since in considering what I ought to do my whole assessment of alternatives presupposes that there are alternatives. The gradual establishment of determinism suggests a Spinozistic elimination of distinctively moral terms. Yet we find it difficult to believe that moral praise and blame are appropriate only because and in so far as we are ignorant; or rather, that they are not, but only seem appropriate. But to react against this is to discover that the other horn of the dilemma is equally menacing. For the only possible alternative seems to be a pious hope that psychological and sociological explanation should in fact prove impossible. To believe that human behaviour is inexplicable is to offend against all that we have learned from the successive victories of the sciences. Kant was right in seeing in this dilemma a genuine conflict between moral and scientific interests.

II

Some contemporary philosophers, however, have tried to show that there is no real problem here and that if we only remove certain misconceptions the whole dilemma will be resolved. These alleged misconceptions fall into two classes. There is first the view that what misleads us into taking determinism seriously is the belief that universal causal determinism might be proved. But, it is argued, it can be shown that this is not so and hence we need not worry about determinism. The arguments adduced to support this view seem to me for the most part undeniably valid. It is argued first that any thesis of the form "Every event has a cause" fails by being overgeneral; and secondly, that some events are in principle unpredictable. But while I am convinced of the truth of these two contentions, I find myself puzzled as to their relevance to our present problem. For both contentions are compatible with the thesis that some events are caused, and the second does not go any way towards showing that any event is uncaused. To say of an event that it is unpredictable is by no means to deny that it has sufficient determining causes. The question of predictability and the question of causality may be connected but are certainly distinct. What is more important is that even if we could show that some events were uncaused we should have done nothing to the point in our present dilemma. For to say that any given event is uncaused is surely to say that such an event is random. What is random is no more free than what is caused. The correct moral to be drawn no doubt from Professor Popper's arguments, for example, that some events are unpredictable is that some events are random and this is certainly a refutation of classical determinism. But it does not take us a step nearer a justification of the belief that we are responsible for our actions, that there are times when we could have done other than we have done and when we therefore merit praise and blame. For, granted that some events are caused, if the evidence goes to show, as the evidence from psychology and the social sciences may well go to show, that human action is for the most part among the caused events, the dilemma which is our problem remains as sharp as ever.

There have been those, however, who have taken a bolder line. They have attempted to show that our dilemma is simply non-existent, that an act can be free and praise- or blame-worthy and at the same time causally determined. This has been recently argued by Professor A. G. N. Flew in a paper on "Divine Omnipotence and Human Freedom" (*New Essays in Philosophical Theology*, 1955), somewhat as follows. First Flew cites what he regards as a paradigm case of 'acting freely.' His example is that of two young people who decide to marry. They are not under pressure of any kind and they weigh up possible courses of action before coming to a decision. The importance of the paradigm case is that it is regarded as the kind of example by means of which the expression 'acting freely' would have to be taught. If someone questioned whether such a decision to marry was genuinely free, the correct response would be to ask what could be meant by a free act if not just such a decision. Secondly, Flew argues that if this is what we mean by a free act there is nothing about such an act which is incompatible with its being the predictable outcome of a causal sequence. That the young man, given the state of his glands or the facts of his upbringing, was manifestly going to marry the particular young woman that he did in fact marry does not make his decision any the less a free act. Thirdly, Flew asserts that to say that someone could have helped doing what he did is not to deny that there were determining causes of his action; it is rather to assert 'that *if* he had chosen to do otherwise he would have been able to do so; that there were alternatives within the capacities of one of his physical strength, of his I.Q., with his knowledge and open to a person in his situation.' Once again the notion of the paradigm case is brought in to substantiate this analysis of 'could have helped it.' I hope that this summary of Flew's argument does not do it injustice because I now want to argue that it fundamentally misrepresents what is ordinarily meant by the expression 'free act.'

Let us suppose that Flew's young man has visited a hypnotist who has successfully made three suggestions to him while he is in a mesmerised state: that he shall consider the merits of his female acquaintances, that after due reflection he shall choose one particular young woman for his proposal, and that he shall forget his visit to the hypnotist. The young man's decision is still surely a free act on all Flew's criteria. He considered the possible alternatives before deciding; and if he had chosen otherwise, he would have been able, in Flew's sense, to implement his decision. So that we should have to say that he could have helped acting as he did. (The assumption in my extension of Flew's example, of course, is that the young man was hypnotised entirely against his will; whether this could in fact happen is irrelevant.) The only possible way of avoiding this conclusion without abandoning Flew's premisses would be to include hypnotic suggestion among those factors the presence of which is to be explicitly excluded in the paradigm case. But Flew does not wish to exclude the presence of other causal factors such as glandular states. Indeed, his argument is designed to show that their presence is perfectly compatible with the young man's decision being a free act. There is no relevant difference in logical status between explanations in terms of endocrine glands and those which refer us to hypnotic suggestion. We are forced to the conclusion that it is a necessary consequence of Flew's argument that we denominate the young man's proposal a 'free act.' This is paradoxical in the extreme. For if the young man's marriage turned out unhappily and we blamed him for his unwise choice, the discovery that he had been hypnotised would surely be held to exculpate him. Actions which are the effects of hypnotic suggestion or glandular states are notably among those cases where neither praise nor blame is in place and hence—as Aristotle pointed out—cannot be rightly called voluntary. Our dissatisfaction with Flew's argument is heightened because the kind of case we have imagined might have been adduced as a paradigm case to explain what is meant by 'acting unfreely.' This surely is conclusive.

The logical root of the trouble is this. Flew tries to show that determinism is necessarily false. For on his view the determinist would be arguing that what is a *prima facie* free act is really unfree, whereas what we mean by 'a free act' is 'an act that is *prima facie* free.' The resemblance between his position and that of the introspectionist defenders of free will is striking. Both wish to say that to assert that an act is free is to assert that it possesses some observable feature or features by which it can be identified. Both thereby try to make our belief that an act is free independent of all discoveries about its causal antecedents and indeed of all experimental investigation. If they were right as to how we use the expressions 'free act,' 'acting freely' and their logical kith and kin, it could never happen that we should revise our opinion of a *prima facie* free act in the light of psychological or sociological evidence. But the history of these sciences is in part a history of just such revisions of opinion. We cannot then take a 'high priori road' out of our dilemma, by defining 'free' in terms of paradigm cases.

It is also worth noting that protagonists of this view, such as Professor Flew, and more markedly Mr. Nowell Smith (*Ethics*, pp. 273–278), are forced to do violence to ordinary linguistic usage in order to uphold their case. For both of them say in effect that 'He could have done otherwise' means 'If he had chosen otherwise, he would not have been frustrated by want of ability or circumstances.' This is surely false. For, first, it is simply not the case that by ordinary rules of English syntax the first sentence can be translated into the second. 'He could have done otherwise,' if it refers to purposive action, means 'He could have chosen to do otherwise and he could have acted on his choice.' If his choice was determined, 'He could have done otherwise' is false, even though if he had chosen to do otherwise, he would have been able to do so. Secondly, this interpretation of 'He could have done otherwise' relies on a particular interpretation of 'If he had chosen, he would have been able.' Clearly 'if he had chosen' states a causal condition on this interpretation. Is the 'if' in 'He could have done so, if he had chosen' or in 'He can, if he chooses' a causal 'if?' I do not think so. If I say 'He can if he chooses' this normally entails 'He can, even if he does not choose.' I can think of no other way of using this expression which would make sense in ordinary English. What I am offering here is not perhaps so much an additional argument against Flew's position as an indication of the lengths that one has to go to make plausible a thesis which violates not only our ordinary beliefs about freedom and causal determination, but some of the most deeply rooted conventions in our language. To note this is to be brought sharply up against the question what we do mean when we call an act 'free' or 'unfree,' 'responsible' or the opposite.

III

We call an act 'free' when certain criteria are satisfied. Some of these criteria refer to positive features of free acts, and of these only a selection need to be, or indeed can be, satisfied in any one particular case. Thus a free act may be reflective, and that the agent reflected before acting might be part of the evidence that his act was free. But a free act need not be reflective, for it might be impulsive, as jumping in a river to rescue a drowning man can be. In spite of the attempts of legal reformers to use the notion of 'acting on impulse' in formulating criteria to decide when a man is or is not responsible for his acts, there is no contradiction in saying that a man on a particular occasion acted freely, responsibly and on impulse. Others of these criteria must always be satisfied for an act to be called 'free.' These are the criteria which list those features which an act must not possess to be called 'free.' The resemblances between this list and the list of defences which can be offered to defeat a claim in the courts as to the existence of a valid contract have been pointed out by Professor Hart in his paper on "The Ascription of Responsibility and Rights" (*Logic and Language*, vol. ii, ed. Flew). But there is a crucial difference between the two lists. The legal list could in principle be added to, but its items can be enumerated exhaustively. The list of features which must be absent from a free act is indefinitely long. Aristotle gives us some of the most important items on it, but we must go to Freud for others and the neurophysiologists may yet make their additions. The determinist claims that one of these features will always be present in any *prima facie* free act. This is sometimes asserted with a metaphysical generality that is self-condemning, but it need not be. The logically unsophisticated determinist may seek to put his views beyond refutation by asking how we can be certain in any given case that some one of these features will not be discovered or does not go undiscovered. But this question only has force, so long as we use the word 'certain' in such a way that we mean by a 'certain proposition' a proposition that we can have no reason to doubt; whereas in empirical discourse we mean, or ought to mean, by a 'certain proposition,' not one that we can have no reason to doubt, but one that we *do* have no reason to doubt. This kind of determinist then can be answered by saying that a given act is free, if on reasonable inspection we find that none of the relevant features are present. To say just this, however, is to betray our weakness in the face of a more moderate determinism. For the case of such a determinism would be that such a reasonable inspection has not yet been made. The sciences of human behaviour have so much more to tell us that we must always be prepared for the area of human freedom to be still further delimited.

I want to suggest that we can meet this case by means of a

concept which will allow us to admit both the indefinite possibilities of psychological and physiological discovery and the fact that such discoveries may be legitimately added to our list of negative criteria without, however, conceding that we may see the area of human freedom dwindle indefinitely. This is the concept of 'rational behaviour.' Behaviour is rational—in this arbitrarily defined sense—if, and only if, it can be influenced, or inhibited by the adducing of some logically relevant consideration. This definition must now be expanded. The expression 'logically relevant consideration' is vague, but not, I think, fatally so. What is logically relevant will necessarily vary from case to case. If Smith is about to give generously to someone who appears to be in need, the information that this man is only disguised as a beggar, but has in fact ample means, will be logically relevant. And of course the scope of the concept of rational behaviour is far wider than the area of moral choice. The scholar dating a document is behaving rationally in so far as, and only in so far as, he admits only logically relevant considerations. Indeed the task of philosophy might almost be defined as the task of defining 'logical relevance.' The 'can' in the definition of 'rational behaviour' means 'can in principle,' for an impulsive action can in this sense be rational. There may in fact be no time to adduce any considerations at all, but we can in principle distinguish the man who would leap in any way from the man who would be stopped by the information that what was in the water was a log and not a man, or that the man was a suicide and that he, the rescuer, had always upheld the right to suicide. Rational behaviour is thus by no means co-extensive with reflective behaviour. Indeed, behaviour can be reflective without being, in this sense, rational. For a man may spend a great deal of time thinking about what he should do, and yet refuse to entertain a great many logically relevant considerations. This brings us to what is crucial in the definition. Rational behaviour is defined with reference to the possibility of altering it. A man who is behaving rationally will alter his behaviour if, and only if, logically relevant considerations are adduced. Thus in principle we can always verify whether or not a man is behaving rationally. But this means that if a man's behaviour is rational it cannot be determined by the state of his glands or any other antecedent causal factor. For if giving a man more or better information or suggesting a new argument to him is a both necessary and sufficient condition for, as we say, changing his mind, then we exclude, for this occasion at least, the possibility of other sufficient conditions. All that we need to know is that the other factors in the situation, glandular states and the like, remain more or less constant. We do in fact possess sufficient evidence to be sure enough of this. Thus to show that behaviour is rational is enough to show that it is not causally determined in the sense of being the effect of a set of sufficient conditions operating independently of the agent's deliberation or possibility of deliberation. So the discoveries of the physiologist and psychologist may indefinitely increase our knowledge of why men behave irrationally but they could never show that rational behaviour in this sense was causally determined.

There are certain important differences to be stressed between this position, and that of the introspectionists on the one hand and of Flew on the other. First, on this view there will be a great many situations where we will not in practice be able to say whether an action was free, that is 'rational,' or not. This arises from the fact that for both Flew and the introspectionist all you need to do to know whether an act is free is to observe a segment of the agent's biography, whereas on this view there are tests which cannot always in practice be applied. But this position is closer to Flew's than to that of the introspectionists in that these tests, like Flew's observations, are public and not private to the agent. Indeed on this view the agent may be in a less good position to speak of his acts than others are. This will be anathema to introspectionists, but is surely closer to experience. Also, we can now see why Flew's example was unfortunate. For the choice of wife is certainly not always free: love, as they do say, is blind. Who cares? But it is important to see that to define free behaviour as rational behaviour, as I have done, does not lead to the paradox that a free act is never a foolish act. To say that a man's behaviour is open to alteration by logically relevant considerations is not to say that he alters his behaviour in actual fact.

The arguments that I have so far advanced suggest a sense in which the agent's choice can be called uncaused. But to say that rational behaviour is uncaused is misleading. What can be called uncaused is the agent's particular decision, conclusion or deed, in that only the adducing of logically relevant considerations played a part in determining them. But obviously rational behaviour is caused in that there are necessary conditions for its occurrence. Thus there is a sense in which the psychologist can rightly be said to provide explanations of rational behaviour, and in which non-rational devices may be employed in order that people may behave rationally. This of course is what psychotherapists do, and I have suggested elsewhere that there are important logical differences between those psycho-therapeutic methods, such as insulin treatment, which operate solely by means of non-rational, causal devices, and those such as psycho-analysis, in which the treatment extends into the field of rational behaviour and in which the adducing of logically relevant considerations plays an essential part. But if there are conditions necessary for rational behaviour, there are also conditions sufficient for the fomenting of non-rational behaviour. These we have seen created deliberately in Nazi Germany and the Soviet Union. They can also be studied in the techniques of mass advertisement. In an important sense you can be said to *make* men irrational, but you cannot be said to make them rational in the same sense. This is surely the logical ground for the distinction between education and indoctrination.

It should be noted that this analysis of rationality and freedom allows us to speak of complex behaviour patterns as more or less free or rational. Distinctively moral behaviour enjoys no privileges. Some introspectionists have tried to maintain that over moral behaviour the agent could not be deceived as he was elsewhere; but on this analysis we call moral behaviour free, in so far as it is a sub-class of rational behaviour, and we can be deceived or mistaken about it, exactly in the same way as with other kinds of potentially rational behaviour.

There is one other sense in which rational behaviour can be explained. Because most kinds of rational behaviour involve references to principles, and references to principles involves some degree of consistency in acting, rational behaviour will often be predictable. This predictability has nothing to do with causal determination. Nowell Smith has pointed out that very often we want to say that an act is both voluntary and predictable; when, for example a good man acts, as we say, 'in character.' But the moral of this is not that Flew is right in seeing no contradiction in saying that an action is at once causally determined and voluntary. The correct moral is that actions are predictable in two different senses. In the first sense we may predict successfully how a man will behave from knowledge of factors other than and antecedent to his own present and past decisions, preferences and consciously motivated behaviour. Such is the prediction than an infant deprived at a certain age of maternal care will prove in later life incapable of genuine love-relationships. But other predictions may be of a kind that can only be made on the basis of data that include knowledge of a man's decisions, preferences and so on. Such, at any rate at the present time, are the predictions as to how votes will be cast at elections. Predictability in this second sense is not only compatible with, but up to a point required by, rational behaviour.

IV

Against the case that I have argued so far a powerful counter-attack may be launched by the determinist. This attack may be mounted in three stages and as each is met new and more threatening moves may be developed. The first stage is to point out that in the widest sense of the word 'cause' the giving of a reason may function as a cause. This is not to lose sight of the logical distinction between reasons and causes. It is to note that the giving of a reason is not a reason, is always in fact a physical event of a certain kind, the uttering of sounds or the writing of letters, and is therefore admirably adapted to function as a cause. If we allow that this is so, if the giving of reasons is sufficient to alter a man's behaviour, then it may be argued we have found causal conditions sufficient to account for rational behaviour, and not merely necessary conditions, as I suggested earlier. To meet this first stage of the attack one has only to note that this contention can be made effective only at the cost of being made tautological. For in terms of the concept of rational behaviour we can certainly discriminate between a giving of reasons which is causally and a giving of reasons which is rationally effective. You may act as a result of my reasoning with you, but it may be on account of the passion in my tone or as a result of forgotten associations of the words that I used that you were moved to act. A little ingenuity could furnish us with tests for discriminating between such occasions and occasions when you accepted and acted on the reasons I offered you. So that in the sense in which I have maintained it earlier, to act because you were given reasons to act would not necessarily be to act in a causally determined way. It would only be necessarily the case that to act as a result of being given reasons to act was to act as a result of determining causes, if we counted as a cause of behaviour anything which influenced behaviour at all. If we understood the expression 'cause of behaviour' in this way, to say that our giving of reasons supplied a sufficient determining cause of behaviour would be to utter an empty tautology.

The second stage of the determinist argument would run as follows. It might be suggested that there are empirical grounds for believing that we can always be mistaken about rational behaviour, that it may on the surface be influenced by rational considerations and yet be in fact wholly determined by antecedent causes. The evidence for this, it might be suggested, is drawn from an examination of the phenomena of post-hypnotic suggestion. If one suggests to the subject that he shall behave in a particular way—walk out of the room, for example—ten minutes after he has regained normal consciousness, he will not only do this, but he will unhesitatingly produce, if questioned, an ingenious set of reasons to explain why he acts as he does. This is certainly strong evidence that being able to give a rational justification of one's behaviour in no way precludes that one's behaviour is wholly causally determined. But it provides an opportunity for, rather than a case against, the use of the concept of rational behaviour, in the sense defined. If, as a result of post-hypnotic suggestion, a man walked out of the room, producing as he did so a reason for so acting, what would be crucial would be to observe his reaction if we offered him a better reason for staying in the room. If, no matter how good the reasons we offered him, he persisted in leaving it, we should have to say that his behaviour was wholly causally determined; but, if the adducing of reasons could change his behaviour, we should have to say that the hypnotic suggestion was not a sufficient condition *per se* of his walking out of the room, but was only sufficient in the absence of a good reason for staying in the room. To say this would be to say that in fact the suggestion did not determine his behaviour apart from his own rational processes.

It is at this point that the determinist might produce what is certainly his strongest argument. He might suggest that advances in learning theory, for example, might teach us that rational, intelligent behaviour was nothing more than well-drilled behaviour, of which a complete causal account could be given, only provided that that account was sufficiently complex. Given a detailed knowledge of the subject's learning history and achievements we might be able to predict that when the subject was confronted with the exciting causes of rational behaviour that is, the offering of good reasons for behaving in a particular way, we should be able to predict on the basis of laws covering both predisposing and exciting causes how the subject would react. So all rational behaviour would be predictable in detail. I find two different kinds of difficulty in this suggestion. The first is that it seems impossible to give this kind of account of rational behaviour without misdescribing it. Consider examples from two different fields. If a man confronts a moral problem, weighing up the pros and cons of a situation, to depict his judgment on it as the effect of a causal impact made by the situation would do violence to all our ordinary ways of talking about morality. For we normally want to contrast sharply the irrational reaction of feeling and the carefully scrutinised moral appraisal. It was the error of the emotive theory in ethics to blur this contrast and its restoration has been central to more recent discussion. Likewise someone undergoing psycho-analysis may start by reacting to a particular kind of situation by compulsive and non-rational actions, such as those manifested in claustrophobia or kleptomania. But as his analysis progresses and he becomes aware of unconscious fantasies, desires and motives, he will tend to appraise and to weigh up alternatives and the compulsiveness of his original reaction will fall away. As in moral situations, it must seem that to classify both compulsive and non-compulsive behaviour under the heading of reaction to exciting causes determined in its form by certain predisposing causes is to obliterate important distinctions which emerge in simply trying to describe the differences between the two kinds of behaviour. Terms such as 'appreciation' and 'appraisal' and 'weighing of pros and cons' which certainly do not express any causal relationship must inevitably find their way into such descriptions.

Secondly, if determinism rests its hopes on this complex pattern of explanation I find it difficult to see how determinism could ever be verified or falsified. For suppose that the determinist is able to supply a complete explanation of my behaviour in causal terms. Suppose also that my behaviour is rational, that whatever strong reasons are adduced for acting in a certain way I act in that way, that I am infinitely flexible and resourceful in meeting new contingencies. Then no test will be available to decide whether I act as I do because it is the rational way to act or because it is the way in which my deeds are causally determined. For on either supposition I will do the same things. To try and include my reasonableness in a story about causal factors is to try and produce a story about my behaviour sufficiently comprehensive to include everything.

This means that whereas the contention that my behaviour is determined by causal factors is normally taken to mean 'determined by causal factors as contrasted with rational appreciation, etc.,' here 'causal factors' have nothing to be contrasted with and hence the expression 'determined by causal factors' has been evacuated of its customary meaning.

V

What I am trying to argue is easily epitomised. I have claimed in effect that the determinist must either interpret his own thesis in a wide or in a narrow sense. If he interprets it in a narrow sense, then we can contrast 'causally determined behaviour' and 'rational behaviour' in such a way that we can in principle enquire of a piece of behaviour into which category it falls. Here I would add to what I said above. For there I merely claim that we could in principle draw this distinction. Now I want to add to this the claim that we do in fact in everyday experience find evidence for the occurrence of rational behaviour. Constantly, when there are no grounds for believing that there has been any change in causal factors, people decide to act differently because they have adduced reasons for so acting and, if they find that they were mistaken about those reasons, they will once again alter their plans and projects. It is because we so often do experience behaviour responsible in that it is rational that we all feel with Dr. Johnson that, no matter how cogent determinist arguments may seem, 'We are free and there's an end on 't.'

If the determinist however interprets his thesis in a wide sense, then he obliterates that contrast between determined behaviour and rational, responsible behaviour on which his case essentially rests. No doubt the convinced determinist can produce other and better arguments than I have put into his mouth; but I am certain that if the determinist case is to be met at all it must be met in some such way as I have suggested. There is no way out in arguing that determinism and a belief in human responsibility are really compatible. Whatever else is uncertain in this area of argument, of the genuine existence of the conflict that creates the whole problem there can be no doubt whatever.

A NOTE ON MR. MACINTYRE'S DETERMINISM

M. C. BRADLEY

Mr. MacIntyre (*Mind*, January 1957), pointing out the growing success of science in explaining human action, argues that this is relevant to the problem of Free Will, and cannot be discounted simply by arguments (*e.g.* those of Professor Flew) derived from paradigm usages of terms like 'free.' Insisting in this way that there is an incompatibility between the growing evidence for Determinism in human action and the notion of Free Will, he then proceeds to give an *a priori* argument against Determinism as applied to human action.

While I accept the incompatibility which Mr. MacIntyre argues for, I wish now to argue that his *a priori* way with Determinism will not do. He suggests (p. 34); "that we can meet this case [the case of the sciences' having continued success in the explanation of behaviour] by means of a concept which will allow us to admit both the indefinite possibilities of psychological and physiological discovery and the fact that such discoveries may be legitimately added to our list of negative criteria without, however, conceding that we may see the area of human freedom dwindle indefinitely. This is the concept of 'rational behaviour.' Behaviour is rational—in this arbitrarily defined sense—if, and only if, it can be influenced, or inhibited by the adducing of some logically relevant consideration." Certain areas of action are, by this argument, brought under what even Mr. MacIntyre admits to be an arbitrarily defined notion; from the terms of the definition it is then inferred that this class of actions must

From M. C. Bradley, "A Note on Mr. MacIntyre's *Determinism*," *Mind*, LXVIII, No. 272 (October, 1959), pp. 521–525.

be uncaused. How is this inference defended? It is held (p. 35) that it follows from the definition of rational behaviour "that if a man's behaviour is rational it cannot be determined by the state of his glands *or any other antecedent causal factor* [my italics]. For if giving a man more or better information or suggesting a new argument to him is a both necessary and sufficient condition for . . . changing his mind, then we exclude, for this occasion at least, the possibility of other sufficient conditions. . . . Thus to show that behaviour is rational is enough to show that it is not causally determined in the sense of being the effect of a set of sufficient conditions operating independently of the agent's deliberation or possibility of deliberation."

Now it is clearly the case that if it is true that someone acts solely as a consequence of deliberating logically relevant considerations, then it is not true that he acts either solely or partly as a consequence of the state of his glands, etc., etc. But this has not the least tendency to show that if someone acts rationally then his behaviour "cannot be determined by the state of his glands *or* any other antecedent causal factor." For obviously the Determinist will not deny that people often act as a result of deliberation, *i.e.* rationally in Mr. MacIntyre's sense; but will hold that "deliberation" marks out a process in which each earlier state causally determines each later state, and which in turn causally determines those actions which are performed as a result of deliberation.

It should be noted that even this answer would not be necessary in many cases which Mr. MacIntyre would class as rational. For "rational behaviour is defined with reference to the possibility of altering it [by logically relevant considerations]" (p. 35). Thus, as Mr. MacIntyre fully admits, there are many instances in which the agent does not deliberate at all, but acts on the spur of the moment; yet nonetheless still acts rationally. Now in such cases as these Mr. MacIntyre cannot hold that the action proceeds from no antecedent causal factor, for since *ex hypothesi* it does not proceed from deliberation either it would then be random, and he admits[1] the cogency of the arguments aimed at showing that random behaviour, if it occurred, would not be free, nor hence, in his sense, rational behaviour. He must therefore allow that sub-class of rational behaviour in which no deliberation *in fact* occurs to have causal antecedents, in which case it drops out of the argument against Determinism; or else he must admit that it is random, in which case the premiss that it is rational, in his sense, is defeated. So it is only necessary for the Determinist to concentrate his attention on those cases where deliberation *does in fact* occur.

So let us return to Mr. MacIntyre's main case in which rational behaviour *does* proceed from deliberation. He takes full cognizance of the Determinist reply I suggest above; ". . . in the widest sense of the word 'cause' the giving of a reason may function as a cause" (p. 37). But he rejects the argument on the following grounds; there is a difference, he argues, between "a giving of reasons which is causally and a giving of reasons which is rationally effective" (p. 38). My reasons might persuade you because they were propounded in a convinced tone, but this would not be a case of rational behaviour. From this fact Mr. MacIntyre infers that "to act because you were given reasons to act would not necessarily be to act in a causally determined way. It would only be necessarily the case that to act as a result of being given reasons to act was to act as a result of determining causes, if we counted as a cause of behaviour anything which influenced behaviour at all. If we understood the expression 'cause of behaviour' in this way, to say that our giving of reasons supplied a sufficient determining cause of behaviour would be to utter an empty tautology" (p. 38).

Now while it is true that there is a distinction between reasons which are *merely* causally effective and reasons which are rationally effective, this fact goes no way to meet the De-

[1] ". . . to say that any given event is uncaused is surely to say that such an event is random. What is random is no more free than what is caused." (p. 30).

terminist argument that rationally effective reasons are also causally effective. Let us hold with MacIntyre that for the Determinist to classify as causal factors the giving and deliberation of logically relevant reasons, *if* he did not also think it possible to describe completely such giving and deliberation as *causally* effective, would involve him in making his case by a definition of *anything* influencing behaviour as a cause of behaviour. But even on this assumption, the argument must fail, for it is precisely what the Determinist *is* suggesting that what happens when someone gives reasons, and when someone else deliberates them and acts on them, is that a sequence of causes and effects occurs, in which the last term is the action in question. (This *seems* to require a discussion of the mind-body problem, and the establishing of some sort of Epiphenomenalist or Behaviourist view, in which physical causes are the only causes of behaviour. But I do not think this is so. For even if Interactionism were true, which I think highly unlikely, the Determinist could still maintain that those mental occurrences which are postulated as occasional determinants of behaviour *were* determinants of behaviour, *ex hypothesi*, in the same sense as physical determinants of behaviour.) And this seems to me to be a very likely suggestion. For I see no reason to believe that the series of events marked out by such a description as "He acted in such and such a way because he had taken to heart the cogent reasons advanced by his friend" cannot be redescribed, without loss, in terms of causally determined sequences of events. It may be urged that two utterly disparate ways of speaking are in question. No doubt; but why should precisely the same situation not be described in two utterly disparate ways?

Mr. MacIntyre returns to say why with this argument; "if a man confronts a moral problem, weighing up the pros and cons of a situation, to depict his judgement on it as the effect of a causal impact made by the situation would do violence to all our ordinary ways of talking about morality" (p. 39). That is, it is normal to *contrast* unthinking action, or action proceeding from emotion alone,[2] with action proceeding from careful and calm consideration of the factors of a situation. Mr. MacIntyre adduces as analogous the progress possible under psychotherapy from stubborn compulsive reaction to awareness of compulsiveness and its undesirability by comparison with other more rational techniques for decision-making. Mr. MacIntyre's argument, then, so well as I can understand it, is that the Determinist position is involved in assimilating what we ordinarily seek to distinguish. It is hard for me to see what force, suasive or demonstrative, it possesses. For if any piece of deliberative behaviour, of no matter what complexity, can also be represented as a strict causal sequence, then that's that, and so much the worse for "all our ordinary ways of talking about morality." And that it can be so represented seems not unlikely. There is a great difference between the machine which shoots out a chocolate when a sixpence is put in it, and the machine which calculates, on the basis of range, direction and velocity of target, velocity of gun, wind-speed and direction, barometric pressure, etc., etc., where a shell must fall, fired from a moving gun, to strike a moving target. But this vast difference in complexity has no bearing whatsoever on the question whether in each case the end-product is or is not strictly determined by a series of steps, themselves all strictly determined. I intend the analogy in a double sense; first as showing that the difference between a largely automatic response to a stimulus and a response involving manipulation, according to prescribed rules, of a variety of highly complex data does not touch on the question of Determinism or Indeterminism; second to draw attention, in passing, to a well established scientific hypothesis concerning the causation of deliberative behaviour—I mean the hypothesis of Cybernetics. The very difference between the sixpence-in-the-slot machine, and the gun-laying computer, *viz.* that between a purely Newtonian

[2] That Mr. MacIntyre should make such a distinction, implying that there is no objection to assigning causes to the first sort of action, lends further importance to my earlier argument aimed at showing that unreflective action cannot be rational in his sense.

machine, and one embodying the feed-back principle, may well prove to be roughly the difference between a reflex or habitual or impulsive action and a carefully deliberated action.

That is one sort of reply to Mr. MacIntyre's argument; but a different sort is also possible. For he suggests that the distinction (between unreflective and reflective behaviour) on which his present argument rests would somehow be broken down, or shown to be unreal, by a successful causal account of the latter type of behaviour ("would violate . . ."). He seems to strengthen his case by speaking of a successful Determinist account of deliberative behaviour as depicting the "judgement [of a man who has weighed pros and cons] as the effect *of a causal impact made by the situation* [my italics]" (p. 39). This last is in fact a complete misdescription of the sort of causal account of deliberative action that I have suggested—a Determinist *au fait* with modern science would not maintain that the "causal impact of the situation" is of some simple S-R sort *both* in the case of reflex or drilled *and* in that of deliberative action. But by improperly suggesting that this is so, Mr. MacIntyre seems to strengthen his argument that somehow a causal account of deliberative action *would* break down the distinction between it and reflex or drilled or impulsive action. There *is* a difference between responding unthinkingly on the one hand, and carefully weighing all the relevant data on the other. This difference could be finally established merely by a full description of the two sorts of activity; but that we should be able to make it is a fact which is untouched by any causal account we find can be given, even if it were a purely S-R account, as Mr. MacIntyre incorrectly suggests it is or must be. *Even if* the S-R account were the correct one—that is, when the argument is at its most persuasive—I do not see that this would in any way break down the ordinary distinction that is in question. In fact, however, if the feed-back hypothesis, or something like it, is correct, then the distinction is reflected in the quite different explanatory principles required for the two sorts of action.

As against Mr. MacIntyre, then, I have argued that even if a causal account of both types of behaviour *did* break down the ordinary distinction between them, that would not be an argument against the correctness of the causal accounts. I then argued that there was anyway no reason to think that *any* causal account *would* break down that distinction.

A further argument is proposed against the Determinist programme of assigning causes to rational action, but I find it equally unconvincing. It is the alleged difficulty in seeing "how determinism could ever be verified or falsified" (pp. 39–40). Suppose, runs the argument, a complete causal explanation of my behaviour given. Suppose too my behaviour to be fully rational, in the defined sense. "Then no test will be available to decide whether I act as I do because it is the rational way to act or because it is the way in which my deeds are causally determined. . . . Whereas the contention that my behaviour is determined by causal factors is normally taken to mean 'determined by causal factors as contrasted with rational appreciation, etc.,' here 'causal factors' have nothing to be contrasted with and hence the expression 'determined by causal factors' has been evacuated of its customary meaning" (p. 40).

But the argument does not support its conclusion. The antithesis Mr. MacIntyre points to between behaviour proceeding from causal factors and behaviour proceeding from rational appreciation is presumably co-extensive with that between behaviour proceeding from non-rational and behaviour proceeding from rational sources. (This seems to follow from his willingness to allow that all non-rational (in his sense) behaviour can very probably be assigned causes.) So that whatever the "customary meaning" of "causal factors" is, the meaning is *not* the same when (1) Mr. MacIntyre contrasts caused and rational behaviour, and (2) when the Determinist asserts that *all* behaviour, including rational, is caused (susceptible to a causal explanation). For the Determinist does *not* mean "non-rational," but "caused" in the prescribed general metaphysical sense, which stands in contrast to the sense of that cluster of Indeterminist positions which hold in one way or another that some stretches of behaviour are *uncaused*. The Determinist is therefore not committed to the absurdity of holding that all behaviour is caused in a sense which would involve that even paradigmly *un*caused behaviour was caused. This means in turn that the general conclusion that Determinism would be neither verifiable nor falsifiable is unsupported, since the required supporting argument that "caused" in the Determinist sense has been emptied of meaning cannot be made good.

Mr. MacIntyre describes, to reject, another Determinist argument aimed at showing that rational behaviour might also be caused behaviour. It is the argument, suggested by psychoanalysis, that all behaviour is irrational, only *appearing* rational in the required sense, and hence probably susceptible to causal explanation. I do not wish to defend this argument.

In this paper I have been arguing that Mr. MacIntyre's *a priori* way with Determinism will not do. I do not want, in this note, to describe in detail what I think is a correct approach to the problem. I should like, however, to make the following suggestions.

(1) Arguments, like those of Professor Flew, quoted by Mr. MacIntyre, show that Determinism is compatible with *ordinary* and *juridical* notions of freedom, in so far as these must provide ways of deciding the *practical* question of where reward and punishment must fall.

(2) It cannot be the case that advances in science, showing more and more areas of action where detailed causes are assignable, should indefinitely narrow the field of free action, in the ordinary sense. This because it is beyond doubt that many actions, caused or not, can be influenced according to our requirements by reward and punishment.

(3) There is, however, a metaphysical notion of freedom which consists, roughly, in the beliefs that (*a*) certain actions cannot be explained entirely in terms of preceding states of the agent, and (*b*) that such actions are fully responsible and the paradigm cases of moral choice. This metaphysical notion of freedom is incompatible with the hypothesis of Determinism. Hence continuing success in explanation of behaviour means an indefinitely narrowing field of free actions in this sense. It is this

sense of freedom that makes philosophers' attempts to show Freedom and Determinism to be compatible seem always unsatisfactory.

(4) Arguments of a Humean sort designed to show that actions, free in this sense, could not also be responsible, may (or may not) work. They do not, however, show that this is not the generating model of the Free Will problem.

If a conflict rises from a powerfully fixed pre-scientific view of human nature, it can only be resolved by looking that view full in the face; then discarding it.

PART TWO

TOPICS

5

FOREKNOWLEDGE AND FREE WILL

INTRODUCTION

Since the general problem of the relationship between foreknowledge and free will was discussed in the general introduction, we shall turn immediately to the next two selections.

St. Augustine finds nothing unique in the problem of foreknowledge, for the problem arises when we recognize that foreknowledge of event *e* entails an order of causes leading to *e*, and it is really the latter fact that might lead one to accept fatalism. But if fatalism entails the lack of causal efficacy of our wills, it is certainly not entailed by a causal order leading to *e* since willing might be a member of this order. Moreover, there is every good reason to believe that some things we do or that happen to us are causally dependent on our wills, i.e., they are in our power.

But do we have freedom *to* will? Necessarily, replies St. Augustine. For x is in our power if and only if x would not happen if we will not. Hence, willing is in our power if and only if willing would not happen if we will not. But "willing would not happen if we will not" is a necessary truth. Willing, therefore, is necessarily in our power. Thus, it is necessary that we have free will if we have a will at all.

One may raise doubts about the validity of this argument, though. Anything we do is in our power to do. We wonder whether something we did not do was in our power to do. With respect to willing, then, we wonder whether it was in our power to will x if, as a matter of fact, we willed y. There is no doubt that willing *generally* is in our power, since we do will. On St. Augustine's analysis, we had the power to will x if and only if "willing x would not have happened had we willed the willing of x not to happen" is true. Although the quoted statement may in some or most cases be true, its necessary character seems to vanish once we distinguish, as we apparently must on St. Augustine's own analysis, the willing of x from the willing to will x. Now, if St. Augustine can show that the willing to will x is nothing but the willing of x, then he will have reestablished the necessity of the quoted statement. The status of "willing to will" becomes, then, the crux of the issue.

Taylor's paper is a good example of action theory as applied to the problem of foreknowledge. It is, as he says, "from the very nature of a deliberately chosen act" that no one, including God, can have foreknowledge of it. It is chosen not only as a contrast to St. Augustine's view that there is divine foreknowledge of all, but also as a contrast to St. Augustine's view that there is no conceptual absurdity in the notion of foreknowledge of a deliberately chosen act. The contrast is sharpened when one notices that both have the same notion of foreknowledge in mind. In both cases, (1) "*J* knows that *p*" entails "*p*"; (2) one knows future events via a string of sufficient conditions; and (3) problems concerning the relationship between foreknowledge and free will arise via (2), and not via some mysterious connection between the state of the knower and the event foreknown.

In assessing Taylor's arguments, one must distinguish them for there are several. One argument is a *reductio ad absurdum:*

Assume: Jones knows that Smith will deliberate and decide in favor of *A* (*K*). Therefore, there is a sufficient condition of *A* (the way Jones knows). Therefore, the sufficient condition can be revealed to Smith (why not?). Therefore, Smith will not deliberate and decide in favor of *A*. But (*K*) also entails that Smith will deliberate and decide in favor of *A*. (*K*), therefore, entails a contradiction and cannot be true.

The argument is invalid as it stands for the sufficient condition must actually be revealed to Smith in order for him not to deliberate and decide in favor of *A*. The reader must decide whether or not Taylor bridges the gap between "can be revealed" and "is revealed."

Taylor asserts that deliberation entails that the person does not believe that the outcome has a sufficient condition. This claim, however, is distinct from his further claim that the presence of a sufficient condition entails that the decision is no longer up to the individual and, hence, that deliberation is ineffective. For I may deliberate, not knowing that deliberation is ineffective.

As to the latter thesis, it is not clear that deliberation is ineffective if its course is determined. Might one not argue that had Smith not assessed that consideration in that way (assessment is a part of deliberation), he would have decided differently even though one can also show that the assessment is determined? This would be St. Augustine's argument and Taylor would have to reply to it.

THE FREEDOM OF THE WILL

ST. AUGUSTINE

The manner in which Cicero addresses himself to the task of refuting the Stoics, shows that he did not think he could effect anything against them in argument unless he had first demolished divination.[1] And this he attempts to accomplish by denying that there is any knowledge of future things, and maintains with all his might that there is no such knowledge either in God or man, and that there is no prediction of events. Thus he both denies the foreknowledge of God, and attempts by vain arguments, and by opposing to himself certain oracles very easy to be refuted, to overthrow all prophecy, even such as

From St. Augustine, "The Freedom of the Will," in *The City of God*, translated and edited by Marcus Dods. London: Edinburgh House, 1892, Book V, pp. 164–169.

[1] *De Divinat.* ii.

is clearer than the light (though even these oracles are not refuted by him).

But, in refuting these conjectures of the mathematicians, his argument is triumphant, because truly these are such as destroy and refute themselves. Nevertheless, they are far more tolerable who assert the fatal influence of the stars than they who deny the foreknowledge of future events. For, to confess that God exists, and at the same time to deny that He has foreknowledge of future things, is the most manifest folly. This Cicero himself saw, and therefore attempted to assert the doctrine embodied in the words of Scripture, "The fool hath said in his heart, There is no God."[2] That, however, he did not do in his own person, for he saw how odious and offensive such an opinion would be; and, therefore in his book on the nature of the gods,[3] he makes Cotta dispute concerning this against the Stoics, and preferred to give his own opinion in favour of Lucilius Balbus, to whom he assigned the defense of the Stoical position, rather than in favour of Cotta, who maintained that no divinity exists. However, in his book on divination, he in his own person most openly opposes the doctrine of the prescience of future things. But all this he seems to do in order that he may not grant the doctrine of fate, and by so doing destroy free will. For he thinks that, the knowledge of future things being once conceded, fate follows as so necessary a consequence that it cannot be denied.

But, let these perplexing debatings and disputations of the philosophers go on as they may, we, in order that we may confess the most high and true God Himself, do confess His will, supreme power, and prescience. Neither let us be afraid lest, after all, we do not do by will that which we do by will, because He, whose foreknowledge is infallible, foreknew that we would do it. It was this which Cicero was afraid of, and therefore opposed foreknowledge. The Stoics also maintained that all things do not come to pass by necessity, although they contended that all things happen according to destiny. What is

[2] Ps. xiv. 1.
[3] Bk. iii.

it, then, that Cicero feared in the prescience of future things? Doubtless it was this,—that if all future things have been foreknown, they will happen in the order in which they have been foreknown; and if they come to pass in this order, there is a certain order of things foreknown by God; and if a certain order of things, then a certain order of causes, for nothing can happen which is not preceded by some efficient cause. But if there is a certain order of causes according to which everything happens which does happen, then by fate, says he, all things happen which do happen. But if this be so, then is there nothing in our own power, and there is no such thing as freedom of will; and if we grant that, says he, the whole economy of human life is subverted. In vain are laws enacted. In vain are reproaches, praises, chidings, exhortations had recourse to; and there is no justice whatever in the appointment of rewards for the good, and punishments for the wicked. And that consequences so disgraceful, and absurd, and pernicious to humanity may not follow, Cicero chooses to reject the foreknowledge of future things, and shuts up the religious mind to this alternative, to make choice between two things, either that something is in our own power, or that there is foreknowledge,—both of which cannot be true; but if the one is affirmed, the other is thereby denied. He therefore, like a truly great and wise man, and one who consulted very much and very skilfully for the good of humanity, of those two choose the freedom of the will, to confirm which he denied the foreknowledge of future things; and thus, wishing to make men free, he makes them sacrilegious. But the religious mind chooses both, confesses both, and maintains both by the faith of piety. But how so? says Cicero; for the knowledge of future things being granted, there follows a chain of consequences which ends in this, that there can be nothing depending on our own free wills. And further, if there is anything depending on our wills, we must go backwards by the same steps of reasoning till we arrive at the conclusion that there is no foreknowledge of future things. For we go backwards through all the steps in the following order:—If there is free will, all things do not happen according to fate; if all things do not happen according to fate, there is not a certain order of causes; and if there is not a certain order of causes, neither is there a certain order of things foreknown by God,—for things cannot come to pass except they are preceded by efficient causes, —but, if there is no fixed and certain order of causes foreknown by God, all things cannot be said to happen according as He foreknew that they would happen. And further, if it is not true that all things happen just as they have been foreknown by Him, there is not, says he, in God any foreknowledge of future events.

Now, against the sacrilegious and impious darings of reason, we assert both that God knows all things before they come to pass, and that we do by our free will whatsoever we know and feel to be done by us only because we will it. But that all things come to pass by fate, we do not say; nay we affirm that nothing comes to pass by fate; for we demonstrate that the name of fate, as it is wont to be used by those who speak of fate, meaning thereby the position of the stars at the time of each one's conception or birth, is an unmeaning word, for astrology itself is a delusion. But an order of causes in which the highest efficiency is attributed to the will of God, we neither deny nor do we designate it by the name of fate, unless, perhaps, we may understand fate to mean that which is spoken, deriving it from *fari*, to speak; for we cannot deny that it is written in the sacred Scriptures, "God hath spoken once; these two things have I heard, that power belongeth unto God. Also unto Thee, O God, belongeth mercy: for Thou wilt render unto every man according to his works."[4] Now the expression, "Once hath He spoken," is to be understood as meaning "immovably," that is, unchangeably hath He spoken, inasmuch as He knows unchangeably all things which shall be, and all things which He will do. We might, then, use the word fate in the sense it bears when derived from *fari*, to speak, had it not already come to be understood in another sense, into which I am unwilling that the hearts of men should unconsciously slide. But it does not follow that, though there is for God a certain order of all causes,

[4] Ps. lxii. 11, 12.

there must therefore be nothing depending on the free exercise of our own wills, for our wills themselves are included in that order of causes which is certain to God, and is embraced by His foreknowledge, for human wills are also causes of human actions; and He who foreknew all the causes of things would certainly among those causes not have been ignorant of our wills. For even that very concession which Cicero himself makes is enough to refute him in this argument. For what does it help him to say that nothing takes place without a cause, but that every cause is not fatal, there being a fortuitous cause, a natural cause, and a voluntary cause? It is sufficient that he confesses that whatever happens must be preceded by a cause. For we say that those causes which are called fortuitous are not a mere name for the absence of causes, but are only latent, and we attribute them either to the will of the true God, or to that of spirits of some kind or other. And as to natural causes, we by no means separate them from the will of Him who is the author and framer of all nature. But now as to voluntary causes. They are referable either to God, or to angels, or to men, or to animals of whatever description, if indeed those instinctive movements of animals devoid of reason, by which, in accordance with their own nature, they seek or shun various things, are to be called wills. And when I speak of the wills of angels, I mean either the wills of good angels, whom we call the angels of God, or of the wicked angels, whom we call the angels of the devil, or demons. Also by the wills of men I mean the wills either of the good or of the wicked. And from this we conclude that there are no efficient causes of all things which come to pass unless voluntary causes, that is, such as belong to that nature which is the spirit of life. For the air or wind is called spirit, but, inasmuch as it is a body, it is not the spirit of life. The spirit of life, therefore, which quickens all things, and is the creator of every body, and of every created spirit, is God Himself, the uncreated spirit. In His supreme will resides the power which acts on the wills of all created spirits, helping the good, judging the evil, controlling all, granting power to some, not granting it to others. For, as He is the creator of all natures, so also is

He the bestower of all powers, not of all wills; for wicked wills are not from Him, being contrary to nature, which is from Him. As to bodies, they are more subject to wills: some to our wills, by which I mean the wills of all living mortal creatures, but more to the wills of men than of beasts. But all of them are most of all subject to the will of God, to whom all wills also are subject, since they have no power except what He has bestowed upon them. The cause of things, therefore, which makes but is not made, is God; but all other causes both make and are made. Such are all created spirits, and especially the rational. Material causes, therefore, which may rather be said to be made than to make, are not to be reckoned among efficient causes, because they can only do what the wills of spirits do by them. How, then, does an order of causes which is certain to the foreknowledge of God necessitate that there should be nothing which is dependent on our wills, when our wills themselves have a very important place in the order of causes? Cicero, then, contends with those who call this order of causes fatal, or rather designate this order itself by the name of fate; to which we have an abhorrence, especially on account of the word, which men have become accustomed to understand as meaning what is not true. But, whereas he denies that the order of all causes is most certain, and perfectly clear to the prescience of God, we detest his opinion more than the Stoics do. For he either denies that God exists,—which, indeed, in an assumed personage, he has laboured to do, in his book *De Natura Deorum*,—or if he confesses that He exists, but denies that He is prescient of future things, what is that but just "the fool saying in his heart there is no God"? For one who is not prescient of all future things is not God. Wherefore our wills also have just so much power as God willed and foreknew that they should have; and therefore whatever power they have, they have it within most certain limits; and whatever they are to do, they are most assuredly to do, for He whose foreknowledge is infallible foreknew that they would have the power to do it, and would do it. Wherefore, if I should choose to apply the name of fate to anything at all, I should rather say that fate belongs to the weaker of two parties, will to the stronger, who has the other in his power, than that the freedom of our will is excluded by that order of causes, which, by an unusual application of the word peculiar to themselves, the Stoics call *Fate*.

Wherefore, neither is that necessity to be feared, for dread of which the Stoics laboured to make such distinctions among the causes of things as should enable them to rescue certain things from the dominion of necessity, and to subject others to it. Among those things which they wished not to be subject to necessity they placed our wills, knowing that they would not be free if subjected to necessity. For if that is to be called *our necessity* which is not in our power, but even though we be unwilling, effects what it can effect,—as, for instance, the necessity of death,—it is manifest that our wills by which we live uprightly or wickedly are not under such a necessity; for we do many things which, if we were not willing, we should certainly not do. This is primarily true of the act of willing itself,—for if we will, it *is;* if we will not, it *is* not,—for we should not will if we were unwilling. But if we define necessity to be that according to which we say that it is necessary that anything be of such or such a nature, or be done in such and such a manner, I know not why we should have any dread of that necessity taking away the freedom of our will. For we do not put the life of God or the foreknowledge of God under necessity if we should say that it is necessary that God should live for ever, and foreknow all things; as neither is His power diminished when we say that He cannot die or fall into error,—for this is in such a way impossible to Him, that if it were possible for Him, He would be of less power. But assuredly He is rightly called omnipotent on account of His doing what He wills, not on account of His suffering what He wills not; for if that should befall Him, He would by no means be omnipotent. Wherefore, He cannot do some things for the very reason that He is omnipotent. So also, when we say that it is necessary that, when we will, we will by free choice, in so saying we both affirm what is true beyond doubt, and do not still subject our wills thereby to a necessity which destroys liberty. Our wills, therefore, *exist* as *wills*, and do themselves whatever we do by willing, and which would not be done if we were unwilling. But when any one suffers anything, being unwilling, by the will of another, even in that case will retains its essential validity,—we do not mean the will of the party who inflicts the suffering, for we resolve it into the power of God. For if a will should simply exist, but not be able to do what it wills, it would be overborne by a more powerful will. Nor would this be the case unless there had existed will, and that not the will of the other party, but the will of him who willed, but was not able to accomplish what he willed. Therefore, whatsoever a man suffers contrary to his own will, he ought not to attribute to the will of men, or of angels, or of any created spirit, but rather to His will who gives power to wills. It is not the case, therefore, that because God foreknew what would be in the power of our wills, there is for that reason nothing in the power of our wills. For he who foreknew this did not foreknow nothing. Moreover, if He who foreknew what would be in the power of our wills did not foreknow nothing, but something, assuredly, even though He did foreknow, there is something in the power of our wills. Therefore we are by no means compelled, either retaining the prescience of God, to take away the freedom of the will, or, retaining the freedom of the will, to deny that He is prescient of future things, which is impious. But we embrace both. We faithfully and sincerely confess both. The former, that we may believe well; the latter, that we may live well. For he lives ill who does not believe well concerning God. Wherefore, be it far from us, in order to maintain our freedom, to deny the prescience of Him by whose help we are or shall be free. Consequently, it is not in vain that laws are enacted, and that reproaches, exhortations, praises, and vituperations are had recourse to; for these also He foreknew, and they are of great avail, even as great as He foreknew that they would be of. Prayers, also, are of avail to procure those things which He foreknew that He would grant to those who offered them; and with justice have rewards been appointed for good deeds, and punishments for sins. For a man does not therefore sin because

God foreknew that he would sin. Nay, it cannot be doubted but that it is the man himself who sins when he does sin, because He, whose foreknowledge is infallible, foreknew not that fate, or fortune, or something else would sin, but that the man himself would sin, who, if he wills not, sins not. But if he shall not will to sin, even this did God foreknow.

DELIBERATION AND FOREKNOWLEDGE

RICHARD TAYLOR

Deliberation is often confused, particularly in discussions of free will, with speculation and reasoning concerning one's future behavior. It has even been suggested that unless one could infer from certain things—e.g., from his intentions or whatnot—what he was going to do and unless, accordingly, determinism were true, then one would have no way of knowing what he was going to do—as if statements of the form "I am going to do A" were all just predictions.[1]

I want to make clear the great difference between deliberation, on the one hand, and speculation and inference, on the other, by eliciting some of the things that are involved in the former but not in the latter. Some of these appear to have important consequences for the "free will" controversy. It is not, however, my purpose to defend any theory of free will.

I shall go about this by listing some of the things that appear to be involved in deliberation and which distinguish it from everything else, illustrating these with examples as I go along. I shall begin with the more obvious things and conclude with the more controversial.

From Richard Taylor, "Deliberation and Foreknowledge," *American Philosophical Quarterly*, I, No. 1 (January, 1964), pp. 73–80.

[1] See e.g., J. M. E. McTaggart, *Some Dogmas of Religion* (London, Edward Arnold and Co., 1930), pp. 182–184, and R. E. Hobart, "Freewill as Involving Determination and Inconceivable Without It," *Mind*, XLIII, No. 169 (January, 1934), pp. 1–27.

I

One cannot deliberate about anything except his own possible future actions, though one can speculate or make inferences about almost anything he likes.

With respect to acts of other people, for instance, one can speculate about them, try to predict them, or to infer what they are going to be; but, one cannot deliberate about them. A statement such as "I am deliberating whether Jones will do E" cannot be true, unless it means "I am deliberating whether I shall have Jones do E," in which case it expresses deliberation about one's own possible future act. The reason for this is that one can deliberate only about what he believes to be within his own power. Thus, "I am deliberating whether Smith shall be reprieved" entails "I believe it to be within my power alone to reprieve Smith." If I believe this to be within the power of another—the governor, for example—then I can speculate about what he will do, or I can deliberate about what I would do if I were the governor; but I cannot deliberate about what will be done.

Even in case of my own acts, moreover, I cannot deliberate about what I have already done or am already doing. I can deliberate only about my possible *future* acts. With respect to things I have already done, I can regret them, take satisfaction in them, and so on. If I have forgotten what those acts were, I can try to find out, infer, or guess; but I cannot deliberate about them. Though I may not know, for example, whether I took my vitamin pill yesterday, I can no longer deliberate about whether or not to take it *then*. There is simply nothing there to decide and, besides, past and present things, even if they are my own acts, are not within my power to do or to forego, and I can deliberate only about things which are. Similarly, if I am sitting, I cannot deliberate about whether to be sitting. I can only deliberate about whether to remain sitting; and this has to do with the future.

Now it would not, to be sure, be outrageously incongruous for one to say that he is deliberating or (synonymously) trying to decide whether he ought to have done something which he has in fact done, which might seem to render doubtful the claim that deliberation is concerned only with the future. Deliberation in this sense, however, is both logically and psychologically different from what I am here concerned with. It is essentially no different from what a meteorologist would be doing if, studying his data and charts, he truly said that he was trying to *decide* what tomorrow's weather is going to be, or what a moralist would be doing if he truly said he was deliberating or trying to decide whether, say, Socrates should have taken the hemlock. In such cases one is, obviously, doing nothing more than trying to resolve a question or doubt of one kind or another. The meteorologist, unless he happens also to be a rainmaker, is not trying to decide whether to have it rain tomorrow, since this is not within his power, nor is the moralist trying to decide whether to have Socrates drink the hemlock. Similarly, in deliberating or trying to decide whether I ought to have done what I in fact did, I am not trying to decide whether to do it or not, it being no longer within my power to alter that fact. I am trying only to resolve a doubt, which in this case happens to be a moral one, and what I am doing is essentially no different from what the moralist, pondering Socrates' behavior, is doing. Thoughts and reflections which are aimed merely at the resolution of doubt, however, are essentially speculative rather than deliberative. When, unlike such cases, I am deliberating whether I ought *to do* something, which it is within my power to do or to forego, I am *not* merely trying to resolve a doubt or settle my opinion about something. Unlike the meteorologist who reflects about the weather, or the moralist who reflects upon the moral implications of Socrates' behavior, I *am* trying to decide whether to do something, or whether to leave it undone. I am trying, not merely to settle upon certain opinions, moral or otherwise, concerning what I do, but to decide just what it is that I shall do. Whatever may be the permissiveness of "ordinary usage," it is *this* which I prefer to call deliberation, in the strict sense, just to distinguish it from all those thoughts and reflections which are essentially intellectual and speculative.

Again, one cannot deliberate about such things as the future behavior of some heavenly body, even though this may be unknown to him, though he may make inferences or speculations concerning such things. One reason for this is that such things occur by necessity, as Aristotle pointed out, and are not within anyone's power to control. But that is not the only reason. One could no more deliberate about, say, the outcome of the spin of a roulette wheel, even if he assured this to be causally undetermined. He could only guess, make bets on it, and so on—unless, of course, he thought he could influence this outcome. But then he would be deliberating on his own future activity—namely, whether or not to try influencing this outcome.

Finally, I have said that deliberation is concerned with one's *possible* future actions, and this is a qualification that is dictated by the pre-conditions of deliberation as well as by logic. As we shall see shortly, an action which is believed to be inevitable can be no subject of deliberation nor, by the same token, can one which is believed to be impossible. Beyond that, however, if one is deliberating concerning certain *alternative* actions, then not all of them can be, simply, his future actions. Each can be no more than a *possible* action. If, for example, I am deliberating whether to leave the room or to stay, then not both of these can be my future actions, for on the supposition that either of them is my future action, it logically follows that the other is not.

II

One cannot deliberate about his own future act, in case he believes the act in question is already inevitable.

This is, again, a consequence of the fact that one can deliberate only about what he believes to be within his power to do and to forego, and the very point in calling anything inevitable is to deny that this condition exists. Thus, one cannot deliberate about whether to (eventually) die; he can only deliberate on how to make the best of it, with insurance and so on. The husband of a pregnant woman cannot deliberate on whether to become a father, unless this is a question of whether to terminate the pregnancy. A passenger in an airplane cannot deliberate about whether or not to return to earth; he well knows that he will, in one way or another. He cannot even deliberate about when or where to come down, unless he is the pilot—i.e., unless this is up to him, or within his power. In case such things are thought not to be "acts," we can add that a soldier cannot deliberate about whether or not to arm himself, in case he knows that there is a regulation requiring him to do so, and that the regulation will be enforced. What to do is, in this case, not up to him.

Now of course one can deliberate whether to do this or that *if* a certain condition is fulfilled, not knowing whether that condition will be fulfilled but believing that it has already been rendered inevitable that it will be, or that it will not. One might, for example, deliberate whether to study in France or in Italy in case he gets a certain award, knowing that the awards have already been finally decided but not yet announced. In that case he can only guess, speculate, or even try by secret intelligence to find out whether he has won an award. But without doing any of this he can still deliberate about whether to go to France or to Italy, in case he does get it. In that case, however, he must believe that neither of these two alternatives is likewise already rendered inevitable, in case he has won the award. He cannot, for example, believe that the award, in case he has won it, will turn out to be one permitting him to study only in Italy, or only in France, and still deliberate about where to study on the award. At most he can then only deliberate about whether or not to accept the award, in case he turns out to have won it.

III

One cannot deliberate about what he is going to do, even though this may be something that is up to him, at the same time knowing what he is going to do.[2]

[2] This point is derived from Carl Ginet's paper, "Can the Will be Caused?" *Philosophical Review*, vol. 71 (1962), pp. 49–55. See also Stuart Hampshire and H. L. A. Hart, "Decision, Intention and Certainty," *Mind*, vol. 67 (1958), pp. 1–12, referred to by Ginet.

This is one thing that deliberation has in common with speculation, inference, and guesswork; namely, that all presuppose ignorance, in the absence of which they can only be shammed. Inference about things future, however, has for its purpose the *discovery* of what is *going* to happen, whereas deliberation, which is necessarily about things future, has for its purpose a *decision* or "making up one's mind" about what to *make* happen, and in this respect the two are utterly different.

There seem, in fact, to be only these two ways in which one could know what he is going to do; namely, by *inferring* what he is going to do, or by *deciding* what he is going to do. In neither case can one deliberate about what he is going to do.

Thus, if a governor said "I am, as a result of my forthcoming deliberations, going to reprieve Smith," he would indicate that his mind was already made up, and hence, that he was not going to deliberate about it—unless, of course, with a view to possibly changing his mind. But in that case he could not know that his statement was true. He could, of course, pretend to deliberate about it, discuss the matter with his assistants, perhaps publicly review the pros and cons once again, but if he did so he would be shamming deliberation. His purpose would not be to arrive at a decision, this having been already arrived at, but something else—perhaps that of conveying a desirable public image of himself.

Similarly, if any one said "I see, by reliable signs and portents, that I am about to do E, so I shall deliberate about it," he could not possibly be expressing himself accurately. If he does already know what he is going to do, there is nothing there for him to decide, and hence nothing to deliberate about.

For example, it might be possible for a group of observers to infer reliably from certain signs that a certain man is about to be married. They see the flowers, witnesses assembled, preacher waiting, music playing, groom suitably attired, and so on. From the same evidence, which is apparent to the groom himself, he too can gather that he is about to be married, though for him, unless he doesn't realize what he has gotten himself into, such signs and portents are superfluous. If, however, he regards these signs as reliable evidence of what he is about to do, he cannot deliberate about what to do—he is past deliberation, and the die is cast. If, on the other hand, he still does deliberate about whether to get married—if he has last minute misgivings and second thoughts—then he obviously does not regard the signs as reliable evidence of what he is going to do. He is, in fact, contemplating confuting the very thing those signs point to, by walking right out of the church.

Of course deliberation is seldom if ever so pure as this. More commonly one finds himself partly trying to decide what to do, partly trying to predict what he is going to do, partly deliberating about what to do if the predictions turn out right and, perhaps in addition, partly deliberating about whether to hold to a decision that has been at least tentatively made, and so on. Mixed with our governor's deliberations, for instance, might be all sorts of attempts at predicting what his opponents will do, what he will be forced to do in response, and what, in the light of these, he ought to do about this reprieve, and so on. Still, deliberation about what *to* do is essentially different, both logically and psychologically, from prediction about what one is *going* to do, or what other people or things are going to do. One can deliberate, but not predict, about what to *make* happen, and one can predict, but not really deliberate, about what *is going* to happen. The fact that both can occur together and have significant connections with each other, and are for this and other reasons often confused in the minds of philosophers and others, does not obliterate the essential differences at all.

IV

If one's act is caused, in the usual sense—i.e., is the inevitable consequence of certain conditions existing antecedently—then he can, simply by his awareness of those causes, know by inference what his act is going to be.[3]

Under such circumstances—i.e., the awareness of such causes and knowledge of their consequences—one cannot, of

[3] Ginet, *op. cit.*, p. 50.

course, deliberate whether to do the thing in question, for he already knows that he will. Examples are supplied by compulsions, addictions, solemn agreements, and the like. Or consider some such act as sneezing, which is ordinarily performed involuntarily but which can be done deliberately. If one feels a sneeze coming on, in the sense that he is forewarned of this impending convulsion by a certain familiar nasal tickle, then he cannot deliberate whether to sneeze or not; he can only prepare for it. The only exception would be in case he thought he might be able to repress the sneeze; but in that case he would not, obviously, consider the felt irritation to be causally sufficient to make him sneeze. One might, on the other hand, have some occasion to deliberate whether to sneeze, if he were considering ways of attracting someone's attention, for example, or perhaps of feigning illness in order to avoid some irksome chore. His deliberation would have to cease, however, the moment he became aware of any condition sufficient either for his sneezing, or for his not sneezing, for he would then know what he was going to do.

From this it of course follows that one's deliberate acts cannot be caused, in the usual sense, or, if they are, then he cannot know that those causes exist at the time he deliberates. Like speculation about what is going to happen, then, deliberation about what is going to happen, or, more precisely, about what one is going to make happen, rests upon ignorance.

But now the question arises whether deliberation rests upon anything more; that is, whether it presupposes only an *ignorance* of the causes of one's deliberate act, or the actual *absence* of such causes. We shall return to this important question shortly, but here we can note that it is quite possible for one to deliberate about whether to do a certain thing even in the presence of conditions causally sufficient for his doing what he contemplates doing, provided, of course, that he is ignorant of the existence of such conditions. One might, for instance, be deliberating whether to sneeze, thinking that this might be an effective way of feigning illness, not knowing that a sneezing powder has been liberated into the room, the inevitable effect of which will soon be to cause everyone in the room to begin sneezing. Or one might be deliberating whether to leave a certain house, wholly unaware that the house is on fire and he will shortly be forced to leave. One can hardly help noting, however, that in such cases one's deliberation is otiose and pointless, since what one then does is not the *result* of his deliberation at all. There was really nothing for him to decide; he only thought there was.

V

If one does not know what he is going to do, but knows that conditions already exist sufficient for his doing whatever he is going to do, then he cannot deliberate about what to do, even though he may not know what those conditions are.

One can, in such a case, only guess or speculate about what he will do, or try to find out what it is that he will be forced to do. This is a consequence of the fact that one can deliberate whether to do a certain act only if he believes it is up to him whether to do it or not, or, that it is within his power equally to do it, and to forego it.

For example, consider a soldier who knows that daily orders regarding the bearing of arms are enforced, and that he has no choice but to obey them. Suppose he does not know whether or not he shall be required to arm himself today, though he knows that the order has been posted. He cannot deliberate about whether to arm himself today. He can only check to see what order has been posted and, until then, perhaps try to guess. Of course he might deliberate whether to comply with his order; but if he did he would not be assuming that such orders are really *enforced*. He would be assuming only that there are strong, but perhaps insufficient, inducements for obedience.

Or consider a man—we'll call him Adam—who has spent the evening at the distant home of a friend and is then invited by his host to spend the night. This might call for careful consideration of the pros and cons on Adam's part, for weighing in his mind the pleasures of staying over as against considerations of his responsibilities at home, and so on. Suppose further, however, that another guest—we'll call him Brown—knows that there exist conditions which render it causally impossible for Adam to go home. He knows, for instance, that the last train has left, and that there is no other way for Adam to get home. Now clearly, Adam can still deliberate about whether to remain or not, in ignorance of what Brown knows. But now suppose Brown announces that he knows what Adam is going to do, without giving any hint as to what this is, and that he knows it on the basis of certain unnamed conditions which are causally sufficient for Adam's doing what Brown knows he will do. If Adam *believes* this, he cannot any longer deliberate about what to do, even though he does not know what he is going to do and is not himself aware of any conditions sufficient for his doing either the one thing or the other. All he can do is speculate, guess, and wait to see what he will have to do, meanwhile exhorting Brown to tell him. He can no longer deliberate about the matter because, if he believes Brown, then he believes it is not up to him what he does; the matter has already been "decided," one way or the other, and there is no decision for Adam to make.

It is no good here, incidentally, to introduce such vague and familiar slogans as "Deliberation might, after all, be a natural process," or "Deliberation is only the way some, perhaps psychological, causes work themselves out," and so on. If such remarks are unpacked, and "natural processes" are found to be nothing but causal chains, and "causes" are understood to be causes of the usual kind—namely, antecedent conditions, psychological or other, which are sufficient for, and thus render inevitable, whatever it is that they cause—then far from being rejoinders to what has been said they only illustrate something that is painfully well known; namely, that philosophers, no less than the vulgar, are perfectly capable of holding speculative opinions that are inconsistent with some of their own beliefs of common sense.[4]

Now I believe the principle involved here can be general-

[4] A well-known philosopher is alleged to have announced to an audience that he was a solipsist, and that he could not understand why they were not all solipsists too, and I once heard a philosopher claim

ized, such that if a man believes that there are, or ever will be, conditions, not themselves within his control, sufficient for his doing whatever it is that he is going to do, then he cannot deliberate about what to do, even though he may not have the slightest idea what this is, or the slightest idea what those conditions are, or will be, or what they will be sufficient for.

Consider a man at a cocktail party, for instance, who knows, in a cognitive sense of "knows" which entails that what he knows is true, that he will accept any standard cocktail that is offered provided it is made with gin, but that he will drink nothing alcoholic otherwise, having a nausea for any other type of spiritous beverage. Now this man cannot deliberate about whether to drink gin, for he already knows that he will, *if* it is offered. There is, then, nothing there for him to decide. Nor can he deliberate about whether to drink at all, for he already knows that he will not, *unless* gin is offered, so there is nothing there to be decided. All he can do is try to speculate, or guess, whether gin will be served, this being, we are supposing, something that is not up to him. And it should be noted that under the conditions assumed it is impossible for him to deliberate, even though he may not know what he is going to do, and may even doubt that conditions already exist which are sufficient for his doing whatever he is going to do.

This example is imperfect, however, for one can justly wonder how anyone could have such knowledge. One can "know" what he is going to do under certain and as yet undecided alternative circumstances, in the sense of having firmly made up his mind—and still, for instance, fall dead before having a chance to do it, showing that his "knowledge" was not of the kind that entails that what was thus "known" was true. This

---

that he knew nothing at all, not even that he was enunciating that opinion to me. These are extreme examples of the kind of muddle some philosophers have appeared to me to be involved in when they have said that they are determinists who deliberate—as if this were some sort of challenge or rejoinder to something. Merely pointing out that certain views are held, even by philosophers, or even by oneself, does not prove that the views are consistent and is sometimes a *prima facie* reason for suspecting they are not.

observation does not really affect the argument, but since the doubt raised about the illustration can easily transfer itself to the argument we should perhaps supply a better example. Consider, then, a man who is watching the spinning of a roulette wheel, and who knows (and has not merely resolved) that he will take the purse in case it stops on an even number, but that he will have to surrender his own stake in case it stops on an odd number. Now he cannot deliberate about whether to take the purse or surrender his own, even though this has not been at all determined. And, it should be noted, this is still true, even if he believes the behavior of the wheel to be causally undetermined with respect to where it stops, and hence believes that his own act will have been causally undetermined as well, such that there are not yet any conditions sufficient either for his doing the one thing, or for his doing the other. The reason for this is obvious; namely, that having got this far into the game it is no longer up to him what he does. It is entirely up to the roulette wheel, and there is nothing for him to decide. All he can do is guess, and hope.

Now we can, I believe, extend this principle still farther, and say that if a man knows that there will at any future time be some condition sufficient for his having done a certain act in the meantime, then he cannot deliberate whether to do that act, even though he does not know what his act will be or what that condition will be.

This is, of course, plainly false on one natural interpretation, for one sometimes knows that, whichever of two alternative things he does, there will then be traces from which it can be certainly inferred what he has done, and he can, nevertheless, deliberate about which thing to do.

Nevertheless, if one were to learn that there was going to be a certain condition, as yet unspecified, for his doing a certain act in the meantime, then he could not deliberate about that act, even though he did not yet know which act it is. He knows, or can infer, that he can act only in whatever way is necessary for the occurrence of that condition, whatever it is.

For example, suppose a man knows that if he is found

in a certain place at some given future time, this will be sufficient for his having gone there in the meantime, whereas if he is found in another place at that time, this will be sufficient for his having gone to that other place. He does not know where he will be found, and hence, where he will have gone in the meantime. There is nothing so far, then, that prevents his deliberating, with a view to making up his mind, where to go, and where, accordingly, to be found. But now suppose he learns that some other person does somehow already know where he will be found—not that this other person has a fair idea or can make a more or less educated guess, but that, somehow or other, he actually knows. Now I believe the first man cannot, if he knows that another man is in possession of such knowledge, any longer deliberate about where to go; he can only wait and see where he is going. It is not within the power of any man to render false what another man knows to be true.[5] To the extent that he *can* deliberate about where to go, to that extent he must consider it doubtful that anyone could already know where he will subsequently be found. One deliberates, not about what *will* happen, but about what to *make* happen; and if it is up to him what he shall make happen, then it is also up to him what shall eventually be true about what has happened.

VI

No one can know what another is going to do as a result of forthcoming deliberation, nor could God have such foreknowledge.

One can, of course, know what another is going to do as a result of deliberation that is already concluded, for that person can then simply announce what he is going to do. But one can make no such announcement while still deliberating,

[5] There is room for endless misunderstanding in this statement, but one must try to resist the temptation to say that while it is within a man's *power* to render false what another knows to be true—meaning by that only that what is known to be true could be false—no man ever *does* render false what another knows to be true. That familiar modal fallacy, taught to all philosophy students early in the game, is not involved here.

for he could not himself know that it was true. There is no way that he could possibly know, before he has decided, nor is there any way that anyone else could know.

If someone knew what another was going to do as a result of forthcoming deliberation, then he would know on the basis of some kind of evidence; that is, on the basis of his knowledge of certain conditions that were sufficient for the agent's doing the thing in question, and from which it could be inferred that he would do that. But if there were such conditions, then they could also be known by, or made known to, the agent himself, such that he too could infer what he was going to do. This, however, is impossible, so long as the agent has not yet himself decided what to do. Indeed, the agent cannot even believe that any such conditions, known or unknown, exist, and at the same time believe that it is within his power both to do, and to forego doing, the thing in question. This, as we have seen, appears to be a necessary condition of deliberation.

The foregoing is not to be confused with a familiar type of fallacy, whereby one truly asserts what cannot happen in case something else happens, and then, ignoring this qualification, draws some categorical conclusion about what cannot happen. The point is rather, that no one can know by inference that a certain event is going to happen, except on the basis of his knowledge of certain conditions sufficient to produce that event. If no such conditions exist, then it obviously cannot be known by inference that the event in question is going to happen, and if it is so known, then there must be such conditions. If the event in question is the act of some agent, however, then that agent cannot deliberate about whether to do it, believing that any such conditions already exist, even though he may not know what they are; for the fact that *any* such conditions already exist would entail that it is no longer up to him what he is going to do. And moreover, if another person knows by inference what his act will be, then he cannot know that this act will be the result of deliberation still forthcoming. He will, on the contrary, know that it will be the result of conditions, known by him, sufficient to produce it.

Suppose, for example, that I feel confident that a certain man, now deliberating whether to go to Boston or to New York, is going to decide to go to New York. Now if I am really confident of this, and my confidence rests upon something more than a mere feeling or hunch, then I cannot believe that he is really deliberating with a view to deciding where to go. I must instead believe that the matter is already fairly settled in his own mind, and that he is, at best, only reviewing the pros and cons of what he has already fairly decided. If, on the other hand, I believe that he is really deliberating about where to go, in the sense which presupposes that it is up to him where he goes, then I cannot feel confident that he will go to either place rather than the other. What he finally decides is something that is up to him, if his decision is really the result of his deliberation.

Now I might, to be sure, know a person and his habits well enough to know that, whenever he is confronted with a certain choice—say, that of going to New York or to Boston—then he invariably decides the same way—say, by going to New York. And it is possible to suppose that, before deciding, he always or often deliberates about the matter. In that case I could predict with confidence what he was going to do, and this would be consistent with his always deliberating first. But then I would know what he was going to do, *not* as a result of his deliberation, but as a result of something else—of habit, for example. If, as a result of sheer habit, or as a result of some other condition that is always present when such a decision is made, the man invariably decides in the same way, then his decision is not the result of his deliberation, and not something that is really up to him. It is the result, or causal consequence, of something else; of habit, for example, or of whatever other condition we are supposing determines the matter.[6]

If, moreover, I know that another person is deliberating about a certain choice that is before him, and know what his decision is going to be, on the basis of some consideration

[6] See John Canfield, "Knowing about Future Decisions," *Analysis*, vol. 22 (1962), pp. 127–129

that is known to me and which must sooner or later also come to his attention and certainly decide the matter, then I know what he is going to do, not as a result of his deliberation, but as a result of this further consideration, which will terminate his deliberation. If, for instance, I know that someone is deliberating whether to remain in the room or leave, and I know, further, that the room is on fire, and that he will shortly notice this himself, and leave as a consequence of this, then I know what he is going to do. But I know this only because I know that what he is going to do will *not* be the result of his deliberation, but of his knowledge of the circumstances. What he does is not up to him at all, assuming the fire to be of such a nature as leaves him no real alternative.

From the foregoing it becomes apparent that the inability of anyone to know what someone is going to do, as a result of deliberation, does not result from any limitations of human sagacity, but from the very nature of a deliberately chosen act. God, accordingly, can have no more such foreknowledge than any man; and it is no rejoinder to this simply to *define* God as an omniscient being.

If God had foreknowledge of the deliberate act of some man, then that knowledge could be shared with that man himself. At least, there is no reason why it could not. But that is impossible, for no man can continue to deliberate about whether to do something, if he already knows or can know what he is going to do. There is an absurdity in the conception of a man learning (as contrasted with merely hearing) from God that he is going to deliberate about whether to do or forego doing a certain act, and then, as a result of his deliberation, that he is going to forego it. Nor is this just a consequence of the fact that, if a man is deliberating about what to do, then it would be a contradiction to say that he already knows what he is going to do. The fact that a man is deliberating is no *obstacle* to his knowing, or learning, anything whatever, any more than a man's being a bachelor is an obstacle to his marrying someone. The fact that a man knows or can find out by inquiry what he is going to do, on the other hand, is an obstacle to his deliberating about it and then doing it as a result of such deliberation, just as the fact that a man has a wife is an obstacle to his having still another.[7]

Even if such supposed divine knowledge could not, for some reason, be shared with men, it still could not exist, even for God. For to the extent that a man can deliberate whether to do one act or another, to that extent he believes that each act is equally within his power. Hence, on the supposition that God believes the man will do the first of these acts and not the second, or that he will do the second and not the first—whichever of these suppositions one chooses—the man must also *believe* it to be within his power to confute God's belief, which is absurd. This is not, it should be noted, to say that foreknowledge, whether human or divine, is ever any cause by itself, or that it exerts any compulsion on anything whatever.

VII

There can be no truth or falsity in any assertion about what any man's future deliberate act will be.

This, combined with the supposition of God's omniscience, is a consequence of what has already been said. For if God is omniscient, then he knows everything that can be known, which is for God exactly coextensive with everything that is true. Hence, if as between the assertion and the denial that a man will, as a result of deliberation still forthcoming, do a certain act, God cannot know which is true, it follows that neither is true, and accordingly, that neither is false.

[7] Any reader to whom the point of this analogy is unclear may ignore it.

6

POWER AND EFFORT

INTRODUCTION

We have seen how fundamental differences among the various schools turn on, or perhaps are reflected in different positions on, the analysis of certain key concepts. In *Ethics* (Penguin, 1954) P. H. Nowell Smith defended an analysis of "He could have done otherwise" which became for a while the standard reconciliationist view on the subject. He opposed his analysis to Campbell's categorical analysis. The discussion reached a deeper and subtler level with the publication in 1956 of Austin's famous paper, reprinted here. Although Austin sets out neither to defend nor to attack compatibilism, his paper, on the whole, turns out to be critical of it. Nowell Smith feels, in his rebuttal, that Austin's criticisms can be accounted for without rejecting a hypothetical analysis—indeed, he still believes that a hypothetical analysis is essential.

It is interesting that both Nowell Smith and Chisholm attempt to follow through on Austin's suggestion that "can" be analyzed as "will, if tries" although Austin does not believe that the suggestion is really tenable. Chisholm eventually agrees with Austin, for even if the analysis is made more sophisticated, it must run afoul of the incompatibilist objection that the hypothetical is true even when "he can" is false if he cannot try.

Nowell Smith's suggestion that some of the difficulties in these discussions arise from a failure to consider analyses in the context of ascriptions of moral responsibility is interesting. Although Austin may not have been interested in the problem of moral responsibility in *Ifs and Cans*, it is surely relevant to notice that his golfer, who misses a short putt knowing full well that he could have holed it, would not be considered morally responsible if he had tried as hard as he could to hole it. Thus even if the golfer believes that he (categorically) could have holed it, we do not consider him morally responsible for failing to hole the putt. Thus his "freedom" here does not make him morally responsible. We cannot, therefore, ignore moral questions if we are really looking for *the* freedom which is requisite for moral responsibility.[1]

The final two selections are concerned with the concept of trying or effort. Campbell's paper points to difficulties which psychologists have faced and must face in an effort to present a deterministic account of what Campbell calls "effort of will." We have omitted Campbell's brief description at the end of his own positive theory of self-activity since it appears in the *Mind* selection. Nowell Smith, on the other hand, suggests serious difficulties for libertarian analyses of trying in general and Campbell's in particular.

IFS AND CANS

J. L. AUSTIN

Are *cans* constitutionally iffy? Whenever, that is, we say that we can do something, or could do something, or could have done something, is there an *if* in the offing—suppressed, it may be, but due nevertheless to appear when we set out our sentence in full or when we give an explanation of its meaning?

Again, if and when there *is* an *if*-clause appended to a main clause which contains a *can* or *could* or *could have*, what sort of an *if* is it? What is the meaning of the *if*, or what is the effect or the point of combining this *if*-clause with the main clause?

From J. L. Austin, "Ifs and Cans," in *Philosophical Papers*. London: Oxford University Press, 1961, pp. 153–180.

Reprinted from the *Proceedings of the British Academy*, 1956, by courtesy of the editor.

[1] The same general point has been made by Arnold Kaufman.

These are large questions, to which philosophers, among them some whom I most respect, have given small answers: and it is two such answers, given recently by English philosophers, that I propose to consider. Both, I believe, are mistaken, yet something is to be learned from examining them. In philosophy, there are many mistakes that it is no disgrace to have made: to make a first-water, ground-floor mistake, so far from being easy, takes one (*one*) form of philosophical genius.[1]

Many of you will have read a short but justly admired book written by Professor G. E. Moore of Cambridge, which is called simply *Ethics*. In it, there is a point where Moore, who is engaged in discussing Right and Wrong, says that if we are to discuss whether any act that has been done was right or wrong then we are bound to discuss what the person concerned *could have* done instead of what he did in fact do. And this, he thinks, may lead to an entanglement in the problem, so-called, of Free Will: because, though few would deny, at least expressly, that a man could have done something other than what he did actually do *if he had chosen*, many people would deny that he *could* (absolutely) have done any such other thing. Hence Moore is led to ask whether it is ever true, and if so in what sense, that a man could have done something other than what he did actually do. And it is with his answer to this question, not with its bearings upon the meanings of *right* and *wrong* or upon the problem of Free Will, that we are concerned.

With his usual shrewdness Moore begins by insisting that there is at least *one* proper sense in which we can say that a man can do something he does not do or could have done something he did not do—even though there may perhaps be *other* senses of *can* and *could have* in which we cannot say such things. This sense he illustrates by the sentence 'I could have walked a mile in 20 minutes this morning, but I certainly could not have run two miles in 5 minutes': we are to take it that in fact the speaker did not do either of the two things mentioned, but this in no way hinders us from drawing the very common and necessary distinction between undone acts that we could have done

[1] Plato, Descartes, and Leibniz all had this form of genius, besides of course others.

and undone acts that we could not have done. So it is certain that, at least in *some* sense, we often could have done things that we did not actually do.

Why then, Moore goes on to ask, should anyone try to deny this? And he replies that people do so (we may call them 'determinists') because they hold that everything that happens has a *cause* which precedes it, which is to say that once the cause has occurred the thing itself is *bound* to occur and *nothing* else *could* ever have happened instead.

However, on examining further the 20-minute-mile example, Moore argues that there is much reason to think that 'could have' in such cases simply means 'could have *if* I had chosen,' or, as perhaps we had better say in order to avoid a possible complication (these are Moore's words), simply means '*should* have if I had chosen.' And if this *is* all it means, then there is after all no conflict between our conviction that we often could have, in this sense, done things that we did not actually do and the determinist's theory: for he certainly holds himself that I often, and perhaps even always, should have done something different from what I did do *if I had chosen* to do that different thing, since my choosing differently would constitute a change in the causal antecedents of my subsequent act, which would therefore, on his theory, naturally itself be different. If, therefore, the determinist nevertheless asserts that in *some* sense of 'could have' I could *not* ever have done anything different from what I did actually do, this must simply be a second sense[2] of 'could have' different from that which it has in the 20-minute-mile example.

In the remainder of his chapter, Moore argues that quite possibly his first sense of 'could have,' in which it simply means 'could or should have if I had chosen,' is all we need to satisfy our hankerings after Free Will, or at least is so if conjoined in some way with yet a third sense of 'could have' in which sense 'I could have done something different' means 'I might, for all anyone could know for certain beforehand, have done something different.' This third kind of 'could have' might, I think, be held to be a vulgarism, 'could' being used incorrectly for

[2] About which Moore has no more to tell us.

'might': but in any case we shall not be concerned with it here.

In the upshot, then, Moore leaves us with only one important sense in which it can be said that I could have done something that I did not do: he is not convinced that any other sense is necessary, nor has he any clear idea what such another sense would be: and he is convinced that, on his interpretation of 'could have,' even the determinist can, and indeed must, say that I could very often have done things I did not do. To summarize his suggestions (he does not put them forward with complete conviction) once again:

1. 'Could have' simply means 'could have if I had chosen.'
2. For 'could have if I had chosen' we may substitute 'should have if I had chosen.'
3. The *if*-clauses in these expressions state the causal conditions upon which it would have followed that I could or should have done the thing different from what I did actually do.

Moore does not state this third point expressly himself: but it seems clear, in view of the connexions he alleges between his interpretation of 'could have' and the determinist theory, that he did believe it, presumably taking it as obvious.

There are then three questions to be asked:

1. Does 'could have if I had chosen' mean the same, in general or ever, as 'should have if I had chosen'?
2. In either of these expressions, is the *if* the *if* of causal condition?
3. In sentences having *can* or *could have* as main verb, are we required or entitled always to supply an *if*-clause, and in particular the clause 'if I had chosen'?

It appears to me that the answer in each case is No.

1. Anyone, surely, would admit that in general *could* is very different indeed from *should* or *would*.[3] What a man *could*

[3] Since Moore has couched his example in the first person, he uses 'should' in the apodosis: but of course in the third person, everyone would use 'would.' For brevity, I shall in what follows generally use 'should' to do duty for both persons.

do is not at all the same as what he *would* do: perhaps he could shoot you if you were within range, but that is not in the least to say that he would. And it seems clear to me, in our present example, that 'I could have run a mile if I had chosen' and 'I should have run a mile if I had chosen' mean quite different things, though unfortunately it is not so clear exactly what either of them, especially the latter, does mean. 'I should have run a mile in 20 minutes this morning if I had chosen' seems to me an unusual, not to say queer, specimen of English: but if I had to interpret it, I should take it to mean the same as 'If I had chosen to run a mile in 20 minutes this morning, I should (jolly well) have done so,' that is, it would be an assertion of my strength of character, in that I put my decisions into execution (an assertion which is, however, more naturally made, as I have now made it, with the *if*-clause preceding the main clause). I should certainly not myself understand it to mean that if I had made a certain choice my making that choice would have caused me to do something. But in whichever of these ways we understand it, it is quite different from 'I *could* have walked a mile in 20 minutes this morning if I had chosen,' which surely says something rather about my opportunities or powers. Moore, unfortunately, does not explain why he thinks we are entitled to make this all-important transition from 'could' to 'should,' beyond saying that by doing so we 'avoid a possible complication.' Later I shall make some suggestions which may in part explain why he was tempted to make the transition: but nothing can justify it.

2. Moore, as I pointed out above, did not discuss what sort of *if* it is that we have in 'I can if I choose' or in 'I could have if I had chosen' or in 'I should have if I had chosen.' Generally, philosophers, as also grammarians, have a favourite, if somewhat blurred and diffuse, idea of an *if*-clause as a 'conditional' clause: putting our example schematically as 'If p, then q,' then it will be said that q follows from p, typically either in the sense that p *entails* q or in the sense that p is a *cause* of q, though other important variations are possible. And it seems to be on these lines that Moore is thinking of the *if* in 'I can if I choose.'

But now, it is characteristic of this general sort of *if*, that from 'If *p* then *q*' we *can* draw the inference 'If not *q*, then not *p*,' whereas we can *not* infer either 'Whether or not *p*, then *q*' or '*q*' simpliciter. For example, from 'If I run, I pant' we *can* infer 'If I do not pant, I do not run' (or, as we should rather say, 'If I am not panting, I am not running'), whereas we can *not* infer either 'I pant, whether I run or not' or 'I pant' (at least in the sense of 'I am panting'). If, to avoid these troubles with the English tenses, which are unfortunately prevalent but are not allowed to matter, we put the example in the past tense, then from 'If I ran, I panted' it *does* follow that 'If I did not pant, I did not run,' but it does *not* follow either that 'I panted whether or not I ran' or that 'I panted' period. These possibilities and impossibilities of inference are typical of the *if* of causal condition: but they are precisely reversed in the case of 'I can if I choose' or 'I could have if I had chosen.' For from these we should not draw the curious inferences that 'If I cannot, I do not choose to' or that 'If I could not have, I had not chosen to' (or 'did not choose to'), whatever these sentences may be supposed to mean. But on the contrary, from 'I can if I choose' we certainly should infer that 'I can, whether I choose to or not' and indeed that 'I can' period: and from 'I could have if I had chosen' we should similarly infer that 'I could have, whether I chose to or not' and that anyway 'I could have' period. So that, whatever this *if* means, it is evidently not the *if* of causal condition.

This becomes even clearer when we observe that it is quite common *elsewhere* to find an ordinary causal conditional *if* in connexion with a *can*, and that then there is no doubt about it, as for example in the sentence 'I can squeeze through if I am thin enough,' which *does* imply that 'If I cannot squeeze through I am not thin enough,' and of course does *not* imply that 'I can squeeze through.' 'I can if I choose' is precisely different from this.

Nor does *can* have to be a very special and peculiar verb for *ifs* which are not causal conditional to be found in connexion with it: all kinds of *ifs* are found with all kinds of verbs. Consider for example the *if* in 'There are biscuits on the sideboard if you want them,' where the verb is the highly ordinary *are*, but the *if* is more like that in 'I can if I choose' than that in 'I panted if I ran': for we can certainly infer from it that 'There are biscuits on the sideboard whether you want them or not' and that anyway 'There are biscuits on the sideboard,' whereas it would be folly to infer that 'If there are no biscuits on the sideboard you do not want them,' or to understand the meaning to be that you have only to want biscuits to cause them to be on the sideboard.

The *if*, then, in 'I can if I choose' is not the causal conditional *if*. What of the *if* in 'I shall if I choose'? At first glance, we see that this is quite different (one more reason for refusing to substitute *shall* for *can* or *should have* for *could have*). For from 'I shall if I choose' we clearly cannot infer that 'I shall whether I choose to or not' or simply that 'I shall.' But on the other hand, can we infer, either, that 'If I shan't I don't choose to'? (Or should it be rather 'If I don't I don't choose to'?) I think not, as we shall see: but even if some such inference can be drawn, it would still be patently wrong to conclude that the meaning of 'I shall if I choose' is that my choosing to do the thing is sufficient to cause me inevitably to do it or has as a consequence that I shall do it, which, unless I am mistaken, is what Moore was supposing it to mean. This may be seen if we compare 'I shall ruin him if I choose' with 'I shall ruin him if I am extravagant.' The latter sentence does indeed obviously state what would be the consequence of the fulfilment of a condition specified in the *if*-clause—but then, the first sentence has clearly different characteristics from the second. In the first, it makes good sense in general to stress the 'shall,' but in the second it does not.[4] This is a symptom of the fact that in the first sentence 'I shall' is the present of that mysterious old verb *shall*, whereas in the second 'shall' is simply being used as an auxiliary, without any meaning of its own, to form the future indicative of 'ruin.'

I expect you will be more than ready at this point to hear

[4] In general, though of course in some contexts it does: e.g. 'I may very easily ruin him, and I *shall* if I am extravagant,' where 'shall' is stressed to point the contrast with 'may.'

something a little more positive about the meanings of these curious expressions 'I can if I choose' and 'I shall if I choose.' Let us take the former first, and concentrate upon the *if*. The dictionary tells us that the words from which our *if* is descended expressed, or even meant, 'doubt' or 'hesitation' or 'condition' or 'stipulation.' Of these, 'condition' has been given a prodigious inning by grammarians, lexicographers, and philosophers alike: it is time for 'doubt' and 'hesitation' to be remembered, and these do indeed seem to be the notions present in 'I can if I choose.' We could give, on different occasions and in different contexts, many different interpretations of this sentence, which is of a somewhat primitive and *loose-jointed* type. Here are some:

I can, quaere do I choose to?
I can, but do I choose to?
I can, but perhaps I don't choose to
I can, but then I should have to choose to, and what about *that?*
I can, but would it really be reasonable to choose to?
I can, but whether I choose to is another question
I can, I have only to choose to
I can, in case I (should) choose to,
and so on.

These interpretations are not, of course, all the same: which it is that we mean will usually be clear from the context (otherwise we should prefer another expression), but sometimes it can be brought out by stress, on the 'if' or the 'choose' for example. What is common to them all is simply that the *assertion*, positive and complete, that 'I can,' is linked to the *raising of the question* whether I choose to, which may be relevant in a variety of ways.[5]

Ifs of the kind I have been trying to describe are common

[5] If there were space, we should consider other germane expressions: e.g. 'I can do it or not as I choose,' 'I can do whichever I choose' (*quidlibet*). In particular, 'I can whether I choose to or not' means 'I can, but whether I choose to or not is an open question': it does *not* mean 'I can on condition that I choose and likewise on condition that I don't,' which is absurd.

enough, for example the *if* in our example 'There are biscuits on the sideboard if you want them.' I do not know whether you want biscuits or not, but in case you do, I point out that there are some on the sideboard. It is tempting, I know, to 'expand' our sentence here to this: 'There are biscuits on the sideboard *which you can* (*or may*) *take* if you want them': but this, legitimate or not, will not make much difference, for we are still left with 'can (or may) if you want,' which is (here) just like 'can if you choose' or 'can if you like,' so that the *if* is still the *if* of doubt or hesitation, not the *if* of condition.[6]

I will mention two further points, very briefly, about 'I can if I choose,' important but not so relevant to our discussion here. Sometimes the *can* will be the *can,* and the choice the choice, of legal or other *right,* at other times these words will refer to practicability or feasibility: consequently, we should sometimes interpret our sentence in some such way as 'I am entitled to do it (if I choose),' and at other times in some such way as 'I am capable of doing it (if I choose).' We, of course, are concerned with interpretations of this second kind. It would be nice if we always said 'I *may* if I choose' when we wished to refer to our rights, as perhaps our nannies once told us to: but the interlocking histories of *can* and *may* are far too chequered for there to be any such rule in practice.[7] The second point is that *choose* is an important word in its own right, and needs careful interpretation: 'I can if I like' is not the same, although the 'can' and the 'if' may be the same in both, as 'I can if I choose.' Choice is always between alternatives, that is between several courses to be weighed in the same scale against each

[6] An account on these lines should probably be given also of an excellent example given to me by Mr. P. T. Geach: 'I paid you back yesterday, if you remember.' This is much the same as 'I paid you back yesterday, don't you remember?' It does not mean that your now remembering that I did so is a condition, causal or other, of my having paid you back yesterday.

[7] Formerly I believed that the meaning of 'I can if I choose' was something like 'I can, I have the choice,' and that the point of the *if*-clause was to make clear that the 'can' in the main clause was the 'can' of right. This account, however, does not do justice to the role of the 'if,' and also unduly restricts in general the meaning of 'choice.''

other, the one to be *preferred*. 'You can vote whichever way you choose' is different from 'You can vote whichever way you like.'

And now for something about 'I *shall* if I choose'—what sort of *if* have we here? The point to notice is, that 'I shall' is not an assertion of *fact* but an expression of *intention*, verging towards the giving of some variety of undertaking: and the *if*, consequently, is the *if* not of condition but of *stipulation*. In sentences like:

I shall | marry him if I choose
I intend | to marry him if I choose
I promise | to marry him if he will have me

the *if*-clause is a part of the object phrase governed by the initial verb ('shall,' 'intend,' 'promise'), if this is an allowable way of putting it: or again, the *if* qualifies the *content* of the undertaking given, or of the intention announced, it does *not* qualify the giving of the undertaking. Why, we may ask, is it perverse to draw from 'I intend to marry him if I choose' the inference 'If I do not intend to marry him I do not choose to'? Because 'I intend to marry him if I choose' is not like 'I panted if I ran' in this important respect: 'I panted if I ran' does not assert anything 'categorically' about me—it does not assert that I did pant, and hence it is far from surprising to infer something beginning 'If I did not pant': but 'I intend to marry him if I choose' (and the same goes for 'I shall marry him if I choose') *is* a 'categorical' expression of intention, and hence it is paradoxical to make an inference leading off with 'If I do *not* intend.'

3. Our third question was as to when we are entitled or required to supply *if*-clauses with *can* or *could have* as main verb.

Here there is one thing to be clear about at the start. There are *two* quite distinct and incompatible views that may be put forward concerning *if*s and *can*s, which are fatally easy to confuse with each other. One view is that wherever we have *can* or *could have* as our main verb, an *if*-clause must always be understood or supplied, if it is not actually present, in order to complete the sense of the sentence. The other view is that the meaning of 'can' or 'could have' can be more clearly reproduced by *some other verb* (notably 'shall' or 'should have') with an *if*-clause appended to *it*. The first view is that an *if* is required to *complete* a *can*-sentence: the second view is that an *if* is required in the *analysis* of a *can*-sentence. The suggestion of Moore that 'could have' means 'could have if I had chosen' is a suggestion of the first kind: but the suggestion also made by Moore that it means 'should have if I had chosen' is a suggestion of the second kind. It may be because it is so easy (apparently) to confuse these two kinds of theory that Moore was tempted to talk as though 'should have' could mean the same as 'could have.'

Now we are concerned at this moment solely with the *first* sort of view, namely that *can*-sentences are not complete without an *if*-clause. And if we think, as Moore was for the most part thinking, about 'could have' (rather than 'can'), it is easy to see why it may be tempting to allege that it always requires an *if*-clause with it. For it is natural to construe 'could have' as a past subjunctive or 'conditional,' which is practically as much as to say that it needs a *conditional* clause with it. And of course it is quite true that 'could have' *may* be, and very often is, a past conditional: but it is *also* true that 'could have' may be and often is the *past* (*definite*) *indicative* of the verb *can*. Sometimes 'I could have' is equivalent to the Latin 'Potui' and means 'I *was* in a position to': sometimes it is equivalent to the Latin 'Potuissem' and means 'I *should have been* in a position to.' Exactly similar is the double role of 'could,' which is sometimes a conditional meaning 'should be able to,' but also sometimes a past indicative (indefinite) meaning 'was able to': no one can doubt this if he considers such contrasted examples as 'I could do it 20 years ago' and 'I could do it if I had a thingummy.' It is not so much that 'could' or 'could have' is ambiguous, as rather that two parts of the verb *can* take the same shape.

Once it is realized that 'could have' can be a past indicative, the general temptation to supply *if*-clauses with it vanishes: at least there is no more temptation to supply them with 'could have' than with 'can.' If we ask how a Roman would have said 'I could have ruined you this morning (although I didn't),' it is clear that he would have used 'potui,' and that his sentence is complete without any conditional clause. But more than this, if he had wished to add 'if I had chosen,' and however he had expressed that in Latin, he would still not have changed his 'potui' to 'potuissem': but this is precisely what he *would* have done if he had been tacking on some other, more 'normal' kind of *if*-clause, such as 'if I had had one more vote.'[8]

That is to say, the 'could have' in 'could have if I had chosen' is a past indicative, *not* a past conditional, despite the fact that there is what would, I suppose, be called a 'conditional' clause, that is an *if*-clause, with it. And this is, of course, why we can make the inferences that, as we saw, we can make from 'I could have if I had chosen,' notably the inference to 'I could have' absolutely. Hence we see how mistaken Moore was in contrasting 'I could have if I had chosen' with the 'absolute' sense of 'I could have': we might almost go so far as to say that the addition of the 'conditional' clause 'if I had chosen' makes it certain that (in Moore's language) the sense of 'could have' is the absolute sense, or as I should prefer to put it, that the mood of 'could have' is indicative.

It might at this point be worth considering in general whether it makes sense to suppose that a language could contain any verb such as *can* has been argued or implied to be, namely one that can never occur without an *if*-clause appended to it. At least if the *if* is the normal 'conditional' *if* this would seem very difficult. For let the verb in question be *to X:* then we shall never say simply 'I X,' but always 'I X if I Y': but then also, according to the accepted rules, if it is true that 'I X if I Y,' and *also* true

[8] If the *if*-clause is 'if I had chosen,' then I *was* able, *was* actually in a position, to ruin you: hence 'potui.' But if the *if*-clause expresses a genuine *unfulfilled condition,* then plainly I was *not* actually in a position to ruin you, hence not 'potui' but 'potuissem.' My colleague Mr. R. M. Nisbet has pointed out to me the interesting discussion of this point in S. A. Handford, *The Latin Subjunctive*, pp. 130 ff. It is interesting that although this author well appreciates the Latin usage, he still takes it for granted that in English the 'could have' is universally subjunctive or conditional.

(which it must surely sometimes be) that 'I do, in fact, Y,' it must surely follow that 'I X,' simpliciter, without any *if* about it any longer. Perhaps this was the 'possible complication' that led Moore to switch from the suggestion that 'I could have' (in one sense) has always to be *expanded* to 'I could have if' to the suggestion that it has always to be *analysed* as 'I should have if': for of course the argument I have just given does not suffice to show that there could not be some verb which has always to be *analysed* as something containing a conditional *if*-clause: suggestions that this is in fact the case with some verbs are common in philosophy, and I do not propose to argue this point, though I think that doubt might well be felt about it. The only sort of 'verb' I can think of that might always demand a conditional clause with it is an 'auxiliary' verb, if there is one, which is used solely to form subjunctive or conditional moods (whatever exactly they may be) of other verbs: but however this may be, it is quite clear that *can*, and I should be prepared also to add *shall* and *will* and *may*, are not in this position.

To summarize, then, what has been here said in reply to Moore's suggestions in his book:

(*a*) 'I could have if I had chosen' does not mean the same as 'I should have if I had chosen.'

(*b*) In neither of these expressions is the *if*-clause a 'normal conditional' clause, connecting antecedent to consequent as cause to effect.

(*c*) To argue that *can* always requires an *if*-clause with it to complete the sense is totally different from arguing that *can*-sentences are always to be analysed into sentences containing *if*-clauses.

(*d*) Neither *can* nor any other verb always requires a conditional *if*-clause after it: even 'could have,' when a past indicative, does not require such a clause: and in 'I could have if I had chosen' the verb is in fact a past indicative, not a past subjunctive or conditional.

Even, however, if all these contentions are true so far, we must recognize that it may nevertheless still be the case that *can*, *could*, and *could have*, even when used as indicatives, are to be analysed as meaning *shall*, *should*, and *should have*, used as auxiliaries of tense or mood with another verb (i.e. so as to make that other verb into a future or subjunctive), followed by a conditional *if*-clause. There is some plausibility,[9] for example, in the suggestion that 'I can do X' means 'I shall succeed in doing X, if I try' and 'I could have done X' means 'I should have succeeded in doing X, if I had tried.'

It is indeed odd that Moore should have plumped so simply, in giving his account whether of the necessary supplementation or of the analysis of 'could have,' for the one particular *if*-clause 'if I had chosen,' which happens to be particularly exposed to the above objections, without even mentioning the possibility of invoking other *if*-clauses, at least in some cases. Perhaps the reason was that *choose* (a word itself much in need of discussion) presented itself as well fitted to bridge the gulf between determinists and free-willers, which *try* might not so readily do. But as a matter of fact Moore does himself at one point give an analysis of 'I could have done X' which is different in an interesting way from his usual version, although confusible with it. At a crucial point in his argument, he chooses for his example 'The ship could have gone faster,' and the suggestion is made that this is equivalent to 'The ship *would* have gone faster *if her*

[9] Plausibility, but no more. Consider the case where I miss a very short putt and kick myself because I could have holed it. It is not that I should have holed it if I had tried: I did try, and missed. It is not that I should have holed it if conditions had been different: that might of course be so, but I am talking about conditions as they precisely were, and asserting that I could have holed it. There is the rub. Nor does 'I can hole it this time' mean that I shall hole it this time if I try or if anything else: for I may try and miss, and yet not be convinced that I could not have done it; indeed, further experiments may confirm my belief that I could have done it that time although I did not.

But if I tried my hardest, say, and missed, surely there *must* have been *something* that caused me to fail, that made me unable to succeed? So that I *could not* have holed it. Well, a modern belief in science, in there being an explanation of everything, may make us assent to this argument. But such a belief is not in line with the traditional beliefs enshrined in the word *can:* according to *them*, a human ability or power or capacity is inherently liable not to produce success, on occasion, and that for no reason (or are bad luck and bad form sometimes reasons?).

officers had chosen.' This may well seem plausible, but so far from being in line, as Moore apparently thinks, with his general analysis, it differs from it in two important respects:

(*a*) the subject of the *if*-clause ('her officers') is different from the subject of the main clause ('the ship'), the subject of the original sentence:

(*b*) the verb in the *if*-clause following 'chosen' is different from the verb in the main clause, the verb in the original sentence. We do not readily observe this because of the ellipsis after 'chosen': but plainly the verb must be, not 'to go faster,' but 'to make her go faster' or, for example, 'to open the throttle.'

These two features are dictated by the fact that a ship is inanimate. We do not wish seriously to ascribe free will to inanimate objects, and the 'could' of the original sentence is perhaps only justifiable (as opposed to 'might') because it is readily realized that some person's free will is in question.

If we follow up the lines of this new type of analysis, we should have to examine the relations between 'I could have won' and 'I could, or should, have won if I had chosen to lob' and 'I could, or should, have won if he had chosen to lob.' I will do no more here than point out that the difference between 'could' and 'should' remains as before, and that the sense of 'I could have won,' if it really is one, in which it means something of the sort 'I should have won if he had chosen to lob' or 'to let me win' (the parallel to the ship example), is of little importance—the 'if' here is of course the conditional *if*.

It is time now to turn to a second discussion of *if*s and *cans*. Quite recently my colleague Mr. Nowell Smith, in another little book called *Ethics*, also reaches a point in his argument at which he has to examine the sentence 'He could have acted otherwise,' that is, could have done something that he did not in fact do. His reason for doing so is that, unless we can truly say this of people, we might find ourselves unable to blame people for things, and this would be generally regretted. This reason is not unrelated to Moore's reason for embarking on his earlier discussion, and Nowell Smith's views show some resemblances to Moore's: perhaps this is because Nowell Smith, like Moore at the time he wrote his book, is willing, if not anxious, to come to terms with determinism.

Nowell Smith begins his discussion by saying (p. 274) that ' "could have" is a modal phrase, and modal phrases are not normally used to make categorical statements.' I am not myself at all sure what exactly a 'modal phrase' is, so I cannot discuss this assertion: but I do not think this matters, because he proceeds to give us two other examples of modal phrases, viz. 'might have' and 'would have,'[10] and to tell us first what they are not (which I omit) and then what they are:

> 'Would have' and 'might have' are clearly suppressed hypotheticals, incomplete without an 'if . . .' or an 'if . . . not . . .' Nobody would say 'Jones would have won the championship' unless (*a*) he believed that Jones did not win and (*b*) he was prepared to add 'if he had entered' or 'if he had not sprained his ankle' or some such clause.

Here (*a*) is actually incorrect—we can say 'Jones would (still) have won the championship, (even) if Hagen had entered'—but this does not concern us. (*b*), however, seems to be fairly correct, at least as far as concerns 'would have' (in the case of 'might have' it might well be doubted[11]). So we have it that, when Nowell Smith says that 'would have' is a 'suppressed hypothetical' he means that it requires the addition of an *if*-

[10] Also perhaps 'may have,' for he discusses 'It *might* have rained last Thursday' in terms that seem really to apply to 'It *may* have rained last Thursday.'

[11] I refrain here from questioning it in the case of 'would have.' Yet 'would' is agreed to be often a past indicative of the old verb *will*, requiring no *if*-clause: and I think myself that in, say, 'X would have hanged him, but Y was against it' 'would have' is likewise a past indicative—indeed it is from this sort of example that we can see how the past tenses of *will* have come to be used as auxiliaries of mood for forming the conditionals of other verbs.

To state what seem to be some grammatical facts (omitting all reference to the use of the words concerned in expressing wishes):

Could have is sometimes a past indicative, sometimes a past subjunctive of the verb *can*. When it is the main verb and is a subjunc-

clause to complete the sense. And he goes on to say that 'could have' sentences also (though not so obviously) 'express hypotheticals,' if not always at least in important cases, such as notably those where we say someone could have done something he did not actually do: in these cases 'could have . . .' is equivalent to 'would have . . . if . . . .'

It will be clear at once that Nowell Smith, like Moore, is not distinguishing between the contention that 'could have' *requires supplementation by* an *if*-clause and the quite different contention that *its analysis contains* an *if*-clause.[12] On the whole it seems plain that it is the second (analysis) view that he wishes to argue for: but the argument he produces is that 'could have' is (in important cases) like 'would have,' the point about which is that it needs an *if*-clause to complete it—as though this, which is an argument in favour of the *first* view, told in favour of the second view. But it cannot possibly do so: and in any event *could have* is liable, as we have already seen, to be in important cases a past indicative, so that the contention that it is like *would have* in requiring a conditional *if*-clause is unfounded.

Nevertheless, it must be allowed that Nowell Smith may still be right in urging that 'could have' *means* 'would have if' and that, as he eventually adds, 'can' means 'will if.' What has he to say in support of this?

---

tive, it does require a conditional clause with it. *Can* and its parts are *not* used as auxiliaries of tense or mood to form tenses or moods of other verbs.

Would have, whether or not it is used as a past indicative or subjunctive of the verb *will,* is now commonly used (*should have* in the first person) as an auxiliary for forming the past subjunctive of other verbs: hence if it is the main verb it does in general require a conditional clause with it.

[12] It is true that he uses two different expressions: 'would have' *is* a (suppressed) hypothetical, while 'could have' sentences *express hypotheticals.* But it does not look as if any distinction is intended, and if it is, the protracted initial analogy between 'could have' and 'would have' seems irrelevant and misleading. Moreover, discussing the (unimportant) case of 'It could have been a Morris,' he writes that 'it would be absurd to ask under what conditions it *could or would* have been a Morris' (my italics): this seems to show an indifference to the distinction that I am insisting on.

He propounds two examples for discussion, which I think do not differ greatly, so I shall quote only the first. Here it is:

> He could have read *Emma* in bed last night, though he actually read *Persuasion;* but he could not have read *Werther*, because he does not know German.

This is evidently of the same kind as Moore's 20-minute-mile example. The first thing that Nowell Smith urges is that such a 'could have' statement is not a categorical, or a 'straightforward' categorical, statement. And his argument in favour of this view is derived from the way in which we should establish its truth or falsity. No inspection of what the man actually did will, he says, verify directly that he could have done something else (here, read *Emma*) which he did not do: rather, we should, to establish this, have to show

> (*a*) that he has performed tasks of similar difficulty sufficiently often to preclude the possibility of a fluke, and (*b*) that nothing prevented him on this occasion. For example, we should have to establish that there was a copy of *Emma* in the house.

To refute it, on the other hand, we should have to show either 'that some necessary condition was absent' (there was no copy of *Emma*) or 'that the capacity was absent.' That is, let us say, we have to show on the one hand that he had both the ability and the opportunity to read *Emma*, or on the other hand that he lacked either the ability or the opportunity.

Nowell Smith seems, at least at first, to be less interested in the matter of opportunity: for he says that we can establish 'directly,' i.e., by considering what the facts at the time actually were, at least that he did *not* have the opportunity, that is, that something did prevent him, and he does not seem daunted by the obviously greater difficulty of establishing, in order to establish that he *could* have done it, the general negative that *there was nothing* to prevent him. At any rate, it is at first upon our manner of establishing that he had (or had not) the *ability* to do this thing that he did not do that Nowell Smith fastens in order to support his assertion that the 'could have' statement is not categorical. That the man had the *ability* to read *Emma* can *not,* he says, be established 'directly,' i.e., by observing what happened on that past occasion, but only by considering what prowess he has displayed in the face of similar tasks in the past on other occasions, or displays now when put to the test: the argument that we have perforce to use is an 'inductive' one (and, he adds, none the worse for that).

Now let us pass all this, at least for the sake of argument.[13] What interests us is to discover why Nowell Smith thinks that these considerations show that 'He had the ability to read *Emma*' is not a categorical statement. I confess I fail to follow the argument:

> The very fact that evidence for or against 'could have' statements must be drawn from occasions other than that to which they refer is enough to show that 'He could have acted otherwise' is not a straightforward categorical statement.

But do we really know what is meant by a 'straightforward categorical statement'? Certainly it is not the case that statements made on the strength of inductive evidence are in general not categorical—for example, the statement that the next mule born will prove sterile: this seems categorical enough. Perhaps this example should be ruled out as not in point, on the ground that here there *will some day* be 'direct' evidence relevant to the assertion, even if it is not available at the moment. Could the same, I wonder, be said of the inductive conclusion 'All mules are sterile'? Or is that not categorical? I know that this has been interpreted by some philosophers to mean 'If anything is a mule then it is sterile,' but I see no reason to support that curious interpretation.

The situation becomes still more puzzling when we remem-

[13] Yet I think it is not hard to see that we cannot establish 'directly,' at least in many cases, that something 'prevented' him: he was drugged or dazzled, which prevented him from reading, which establishes that he could not have read—but how do we know that being drugged or dazzled 'prevents' people from reading? Surely on 'inductive' evidence? And, in short, to be prevented is to be rendered unable.

ber that Nowell Smith is about to generalize his theory, and to assert, not merely that 'could have' means 'would have . . . if,' but also that 'can' means 'shall or will . . . if.' Suppose then that I assert 'I can here and now lift my finger,' and translate this as 'I shall lift my finger if . . .': then surely this will be 'directly' verified if the conditions are satisfied and I do proceed to lift the finger? If this is correct, and if the theory is indeed a general one, then there seems to be no point in insisting on the non-availability of 'direct' evidence, which is only a feature of certain cases. Incidentally, it is not in fact the case that to say 'He could have done it' is always used in a way to imply that he did not in fact do it: we make a list of the suspects in a murder case, all of whom we think could have done it and one of whom we think did do it. True, this is not Nowell Smith's case: but unless we are prepared to assert that the 'could have' in his case differs in meaning from that in the murder case, and so to rule out the latter as irrelevant, we are in danger of having to admit that even 'could have' sentences can be 'directly' verified in favourable cases. For study of the facts of that past occasion can prove to us that he did it, and hence that our original 'He could have' was correct.[14]

However, to proceed. Whether or not we should describe our conclusion here as 'categorical' it seems that it should still be a conclusion of the form 'he *could* have done so and so,' and not in the least a conclusion concerning what he *would* have done. We are interested, remember, in his abilities: we want to know whether he could have read *Emma* yesterday: we ascertain that he did read it the day before yesterday, and that he does read it today: we conclude that he could have read it yesterday. But it does not appear that this says anything about what he *would* have done yesterday or in what circumstances: certainly, we are now convinced, he *could* have read it yesterday, but

[14] There are, I should myself think, good reasons for not speaking of 'I can lift my finger' as being directly verified when I proceed to lift it, and likewise for not speaking of 'He could have done it' as being directly verified by the discovery that he did do it. But on Nowell Smith's account I think that these would count as direct verifications.

would he have, considering that he had read it only the day before? Moreover, supposing the view is that our conclusion is not of the 'could have' but of the 'would have if' form, nothing has yet been said to establish this, nor to tell us what follows the 'if.' To establish that he would have read it yesterday if . . . , we shall need evidence not merely as to his abilities and opportunities, but also as to his character, motives, and so on.

It may indeed be thought, and it seems that Nowell Smith does at least partly think this, that what follows the 'if' should be suppliable from the consideration that to say he could have, in the full sense, is to say not merely that he had the ability, which is what we have hitherto concentrated on, but also that he had the *opportunity*. For to establish *this*, do we not have to establish that certain *conditions* were satisfied, as for instance that there was a copy of *Emma* available? Very well. But here there is surely a confusion: we allow that, in saying that he could have, I do assert or imply that certain *conditions*, those of opportunity, *were satisfied:* but this is totally different from allowing that, in saying that he could have, I *assert something conditional*. It is, certainly, entirely possible to assert something conditional such as 'he could have read *Emma* yesterday if there had been a copy available,' *could* being then of course a subjunctive: but to say this sort of thing is precisely not to say the sort of thing that we say when we say 'He could have acted otherwise,' where 'could have' is an indicative—implying, as we now do, that there was no copy available, we imply that *pro tanto* he could *not* have acted otherwise. And the same will be true if we try saying 'He would have read *Emma* yesterday if there had been a copy available': this too certainly implies that he could not in fact have read it, and so cannot by any means be what we mean by saying that he could have read it.

In the concluding paragraph of his discussion, Nowell Smith does finally undertake to give us his analysis not merely of 'could have,' but also of 'can' (which he says means 'will if'). And this last feature is very much to be welcomed, because if an analysis is being consciously given of 'can' at least we shall at length be clear of confusions connected with the idea that 'could have' is necessarily a subjunctive.[15]

The argument of the last paragraph runs as follows. It is 'logically odd' to say something of this kind (I am slightly emending Nowell Smith's formula, but only in ways that are favourable to it and demanded by his own argument):

> Smith has the ability to run a mile, has the opportunity to run a mile, has a preponderant motive for running a mile, but does not in fact do so.

From this it follows directly, says Nowell Smith, that 'can,' means 'will if,' that is, I suppose, that 'Smith can run a mile' *means* 'If Smith has the opportunity to run a mile and a preponderant motive for running it, he will run it.'

It seems, however, plain that nothing of the kind follows.

This may be seen first by setting the argument out formally. Nowell Smith's premiss is of the form

> Not (p and q and r and not–s)

that is

> Logically odd (ability + opportunity + motive + non-action).

Now from this we can indeed infer

$$p \supset ((q \text{ and } r) \supset s),$$

that is that

> If he has the ability, then, if he has the opportunity and the motive, he will do it.

But we can*not infer* the converse

$$((q \text{ and } r) \supset s) \supset p,$$

[15] It must, however, be pointed out once again that if we are to discuss the assertion that somebody *can* (now) do something, the previous arguments that our assertions are not categorical because they are based on induction and cannot be verified directly, whether they were good or not, must now be abandoned: because of course it *is* possible to verify this 'directly' by the method Nowell Smith has specified in another connexion earlier, viz. by getting the man to try and seeing him succeed.

or in other words that

> If, when he has the opportunity and the motive, he does it, he has the ability to do it.

(I do not say this last is not something to which we should, when so put into English, assent, only that it does not follow from Nowell Smith's premiss: of course it follows merely from the premiss that he does it, that he has the ability to do it, according to ordinary English.) But unless this second, converse implication *does* follow, we cannot, according to the usual formal principles, infer that p is *equivalent* to, nor therefore that it means the same as, $(q \text{ and } r) \supset s$, or in words that ability *means* that opportunity plus motive leads to action.

To put the same point non-formally. From the fact that, if three things are true together a fourth must also be true, we cannot argue that one of the three things *simply means* that if the other two are true the fourth will be true. If we could argue indeed in this way, then we should establish, from Nowell Smith's premiss, not merely that

> 'He has the ability to do X' simply means that 'if he has the opportunity and the motive to do X, he will do X'

but also equally that

> 'He has the opportunity to do X' *simply means* that 'If he has the ability and the motive to do X, he will do X'

and likewise that

> 'He has a preponderant motive to do X' *simply means* that 'if he has the ability and the opportunity to do X, he will do X.'

For clearly we can perform the same operations on q and r as on p, since the three all occupy parallel positions in the premiss. But these are fantastic suggestions. Put shortly, Nowell Smith is pointing out in his premiss that if a man both can and wants to (more than he wants to do anything else), he will: but from this it does not follow that 'he can' *simply means* that 'if he wants to he will.' Nowell Smith is struggling to effect a transition from *can* to *will* which presents difficulties as great as those of the transition from *could* to *would:* he puts up his show of effecting it by importing the additional, and here irrelevant, concept of motive, which needless to say is in general very intimately connected with the question of what 'he will' do.

When, in conclusion, Nowell Smith finally sets out his analysis of 'Smith could have read *Emma* last night,' it is this:

> He would have read it, if there had been a copy, if he had not been struck blind, &c., &c., and if he had wanted to read it more than he had wanted to read (this should be 'do') anything else.

But so far from this being what we mean by saying he could have read it, it actually implies that he could *not* have read it, for more than adequate reasons: it implies that he was blind at the time, and so on. Here we see that Nowell Smith actually does make the confusion I referred to above between a statement which implies or asserts that certain conditions *were* fulfilled and a conditional statement, i.e. a statement about what would have happened if those conditions had been fulfilled. This is unfortunately a confusion of a general kind that is not uncommon: I need only mention the classic instance of Keynes, who confused asserting on evidence *h* that *p* is probable with asserting that on evidence *h p* is probable, both of which can be ambiguously expressed by 'asserting that *p* is probable on evidence *h*,' but only the former of which asserts that *p* is (really) probable. Here similarly there is a confusion between asserting on the supposition (or premiss) that he had a copy that he could/would have read it, and asserting that on the supposition that he had a copy he could/would have read it, both of which can be ambiguously expressed by 'asserting that he could/would have read it on the supposition that he had a copy,' but only the former of which asserts that he (actually) could have read it.

To some extent, then, we learn from studying Nowell Smith's arguments lessons similar to those that we learned in the case of Moore. But some are new, as for instance that many assertions about what a man *would have* done or *will do* depend, in critical cases, upon premisses about his *motives* as well as, or rather than, about his abilities or opportunities: hence these assertions cannot be what assertions about his abilities *mean.*[16]

On one point I may perhaps elaborate a little further. It has been maintained that *sometimes* when we say 'He could have done X' this is a conditional: it requires completion by an *if*-clause, typically 'if he had had the opportunity,' and so does *not* require us, if we are to establish its truth, to establish that he did in fact have the opportunity. Sometimes on the other hand it is a past indicative, implying that he did have the opportunity: in which case we do, to establish its truth, have to establish that certain conditions were satisfied, but the assertion is *not* to be described as a conditional assertion.

Now while I have no wish to retract this account in general or in all cases, I doubt whether it is the whole story. Consider the case where what we wish to assert is that somebody had the opportunity to do something but lacked the ability—'He could have smashed that lob, if he had been any good at the smash': here the *if*-clause, which may of course be suppressed and understood, relates not to opportunity but to ability. Now although we might describe the whole sentence as 'conditional,' it nevertheless manages to assert, by means of its main clause, something 'categorical' enough, viz. that he did have a certain opportunity. And in the same way Nowell Smith's 'He could have read *Emma,* if he had had a copy,' does seem to assert 'categorically' that he had a certain ability, although he lacked the opportunity to exercise it. Looking at it in this way, there is a temptation to say that 'could have' has, besides its 'all-in' *sense* several more *restricted senses:* this would be brought out if we said 'He could have smashed it, *only* he is no good at the smash' or 'He could have read *Emma but*

[16] Yet here it must be pointed out once more that it has not been shown that *all* assertions about what he would have done are so dependent, so that this particular argument against the analysis of 'could have' as 'would have if' is not conclusive: in particular, it does not dispose of the possible suggestion that 'could have' means 'would have if he had *tried,*' for here considerations of motive may be irrelevant.

he had no copy,' where, we should say, 'could have' is being used in the restricted senses of opportunity or of ability[17] only, and is a past indicative, not a past conditional.

This view might be reinforced by considering examples with the simple 'can' itself. We are tempted to say that 'He can' sometimes means just that he has the ability, with *nothing said* about opportunity, sometimes *just* that he has the chance, with nothing said about ability, sometimes, however, that he really actually *fully can* here and now, having both ability and opportunity. Now nobody, I think, would be tempted to say that 'can,' where it means one of the two lesser things, for example, 'has the opportunity,' i.e., 'can in the full sense if he has the ability,' is grammatically a subjunctive or conditional. Perhaps, then, it was not correct to describe 'He could have,' either, as always a conditional where it asserts ability or opportunity only, with nothing said about the other, or even where the other is denied to have existed.

The verb *can* is a peculiar one. Let us compare it for a moment with another peculiar verb, *know,* with which it shares some grammatical peculiarities, such as lack of a continuous present tense. When I say that somebody *knows* what the thing in my hand is, I may mean merely that he has the ability to identify it given the opportunity, or that he has the opportunity to identify it if he has the ability, or that he has both. What do we say about *know* here? Certainly we are not prone to invoke the idea of a conditional, but rather that of different senses, or perhaps the still obscure idea of the dispositional. I must be content here merely to say that I do not think that the old armoury of terms, such as 'mood' and 'sense,' is altogether adequate for handling such awkward cases. The only point of which I feel certain is that such verbs as *can* and *know* have each an all-in, paradigm use, around which cluster and from which divagate, little by little and along different paths,

[17] I talk here and throughout of 'ability' and 'opportunity' only: but I realize that other abstract nouns like 'capacity,' 'skill,' and even 'right' are equally involved. All these terms need listing and elucidating before we really get to grips with 'can.'

a whole series of other uses, for many of which, though perhaps not for all, a synonymous expression ('opportunity,' 'realize,' and so on) can be found.

It is not unusual for an audience at a lecture to include some who prefer things to be important, and to them now, in case there are any such present, there is owed a peroration. Why, in short, does all this matter? First, then, it needs no emphasizing that both *if* and *can* are highly prevalent and protean words, perplexing both grammatically and philosophically: it is not merely worth while, but essential, in these studies to discover the facts about *if*s and *can*s, and to remove the confusions they engender. In philosophy it is *can* in particular that we seem so often to uncover, just when we had thought some problem settled, grinning residually up at us like the frog at the bottom of the beer mug. Furthermore and secondly, we have not here been dissecting these two words in general or completely, but in a special connexion which perhaps no one will hold trivial. It has been alleged by very serious philosophers (not only the two I have mentioned) that the things we ordinarily say about what we can do and could have done may actually be consistent with determinism. It is hard to evade all attempt to decide whether this allegation is true—hard even for those who, like myself, are inclined to think that determinism itself is still a name for nothing clear, that has been argued for only incoherently. At least I should like to claim that the arguments considered tonight fail to show that it *is* true, and indeed in failing go some way to show that it is *not*. Determinism, whatever it may be, may yet be the case, but at least it appears not consistent with what we ordinarily say and presumably think. And finally there is a third point. Reflecting on the arguments in this lecture, we may well ask ourselves whether they might not be as well assigned to grammar as to philosophy: and this, I think, is a salutary question to end on. There are constant references in contemporary philosophy, which notoriously is much concerned with language, to a 'logical grammar' and a 'logical syntax' as though these were things distinct from ordinary grammarian's grammar and syntax: and certainly they do seem, whatever exactly they may be, different from traditional grammar. But grammar today is itself in a state of flux; for fifty years or more it has been questioned on all hands and counts whether what Dionysius Thrax once thought was the truth about Greek is the truth and the whole truth about all language and all languages. Do we know, then, that there will prove to be any ultimate boundary between 'logical grammar' and a revised and enlarged *Grammar?* In the history of human inquiry, philosophy has the place of the initial central sun, seminal and tumultuous: from time to time it throws off some portion of itself to take station as a science, a planet, cool and well regulated, progressing steadily towards a distant final state. This happened long ago at the birth of mathematics, and again at the birth of physics: only in the last century we have witnessed the same process once again, slow and at the time almost imperceptible, in the birth of the science of mathematical logic, through the joint labours of philosophers and mathematicians. Is it not possible that the next century may see the birth, through the joint labours of philosophers, grammarians, and numerous other students of language, of a true and comprehensive *science of language?* Then we shall have rid ourselves of one more part of philosophy (there will still be plenty left) in the only way we ever can get rid of philosophy, by kicking it upstairs.

IFS AND CANS

P. H. NOWELL SMITH

If someone were to ask what idea is expressed by the verb 'can' in all its moods and tenses, he might be told that it expressed power, potency or potentiality, capacity, capability or ability, contingency or possibility—all or some of these. But

From P. H. Nowell Smith, "Ifs and Cans," *Theoria*, XXVI, Part 2 (1960), pp. 85–101.

A reply to J. L. Austin: *Ifs and Cans*. British Academy Lecture, Oxford University Press, 1956.

this answer, though true enough, is unenlightening, and unenlightening just because it is so obviously true. If there are puzzles about 'can' there will be puzzles about these. Human actions, the things people actually do, are, we feel, ground-floor members of the world; their abilities are not. Philosophers have often felt that particular statements, expressed by sentences in the indicative mood with names of entities as subjects, are somehow paramount. We use the indicative mood to say flatly that something is or was or will be the case. Hypothetical and universal statements, by contrast, are suspect. This feeling has led some philosophers (for example some logicians who have been incautious about the relation between the logical constants of a language and those of a calculus) sadly astray. It is certainly wrong to say flatly that 'all mules are sterile' means the same as 'if anything is a mule, it is sterile' or 'nothing is both a mule and non-sterile'; but the idea that it is not sufficiently categorical to get in on the ground floor but requires to show its connections with true-blue categoricals about this and that mule before it can be admitted is not wholly erroneous. Likewise statements about the next mule are not wholly irreproachable, and the drive to analyze universal statements into hypotheticals and then treat these hypotheticals as truth-functional sets of particular categoricals is not wholly to be resisted.

There is a notorious connection between universal statements and statements made with 'can' which leads us to suspect that the latter, though in one sense categorical enough, are not wholly, flatly and irreducibly categorical. One of the many features which these two types of statement have in common is that, while they must always be backed in the end by statements as to what is or was the case, they always assert more than this. We can see Tom and Dick playing bridge, but we cannot see the class of all bridge-players, and in much the same way, though we can see someone playing bridge and perhaps see him manifesting his ability to play bridge, we cannot see his ability. Abilities are somehow parasitic on performances, if only because an ability to do something is an ability to *do* that thing.

This is one reason why philosophers have so often tried to analyze can-statements in terms of if-statements, a type of analysis which it is the main purpose of Austin's paper to defeat. Their attempts have often been complicated and confused by two factors. (i) They have, as Austin plainly shows, confused analysis with supplementation, the idea that 'X can do Y' must be *analyzed* into some statement in which the word 'can' does not occur (for example 'X will do Y, if he tries'), with the idea that 'X can do Y' is always *incomplete* as it stands, that it always means something of the form 'X can do Y, if . . . ,' a form in which the word 'can' is still present. (ii) The topic is usually raised in the context of free will and responsibility; and here it is usually 'could have' that requires analysis. On the face of it, it is much more plausible to maintain that 'could have' requires analysis in terms of or supplementation by an if-clause than the whole verb 'can' in all its moods and tenses does so. Hence philosophers (including myself) have confused considerations which might lead one to give an hypothetical analysis of 'could have' with those that make for an hypothetical analysis of 'can.'

On the first point, both in *Ethics* and in this paper I am concerned to argue that 'can' requires analysis in terms of 'if,' not that it requires supplementation. Moore was quite wrong when he said that 'I could have walked a mile in 20 minutes' means 'I *could* have walked a mile in 20 minutes, if I had chosen.' To avoid the second error I shall start here with 'can' and move to 'could have' later.

There are two points in Austin's paper which may be accepted from the start. (i) There are at least three senses of 'can,' which Austin calls the 'ability,' the 'opportunity' and the 'all-in' senses. (ii) The form 'could have' is often, not a subjunctive, but the past indicative of 'can' in any of these three senses. It means, not 'would have been able, if . . .' but categorically '*was* able.' In the first part of this paper I shall discuss the relations between the three senses of 'can.' Austin's view here is that there is "an all-in, paradigm use, around which cluster and from which divagate, little by little and along different paths, a whole series of other uses,"[1] among them 'ability' and 'opportunity.' In the second part of the paper I shall argue that, in all three senses, the whole verb 'can' requires to be analyzed in terms of 'does . . . , if . . . .'

I

My first thesis, then, is that the all-in 'can' (to be *fully* able) is a conjunction of ability and opportunity. These are umbrella-like words covering a host of things such as 'having the strength, skill, know-how, etc.' and 'being in a position to, having the means or equipment to, etc.' So my first thesis is still highly schematic in character. A full treatment would have to go into these differences and I suspect that it might emerge that ability and opportunity are not as clearly distinct *genera* as we usually take them to be.

That the all-in 'can' is a conjunction of ability and opportunity emerges, I think, from what Austin himself says about the case in which 'he could have done X' really is a conditional, requiring, to give its full sense explicitly, to be completed by an if-clause, typically 'if he had had the ability' or 'if he had had the opportunity.'[2] 'He could have smashed that lob, if he had been any good at the smash' is a conditional; yet, according to Austin, "it nevertheless manages to assert, by means of its main clause, something categorical enough, that he *did* have a certain opportunity." We must ask here which of the three senses of 'can' is being used in the main clause. It cannot be the 'can' of ability; for if it were, the whole sentence would read 'He would have had the ability, if he had had the ability,' and it is clearly not this tautology that we mean to assert. Nor can it be the 'can' of opportunity; for in that case the whole sentence would read 'he would have had the opportunity, if he had had the ability.' But according to Austin we assert categorically that he *did* have the opportunity, not that he *would* have had it if he had had the ability; the opportunity was there

[1] *Op. cit.*, p. 130.
[2] *Op. cit.*, p. 129.

whether or not he had the ability to make use of it. It must, then, if the statement is genuinely conditional, be the past subjunctive of the all-in 'can' that we are using here. For clarity we may re-write the sentence as 'he would have been fully able, if he had had the ability.' Now this certainly does imply, even though it does not state, something that is "categorical enough." For it implies that he actually had everything other than ability which is necessary for being fully able, that he had, among things, an opportunity to smash that lob.

These categorical implications of 'he could have done X, if he had had the ability' and of 'he could have done X if he had had the opportunity' lead Austin to suggest that they are not conditional sentences at all. He has already introduced us to an 'unorthodox' type of if-sentence, exemplified by 'there are biscuits on the sideboard if you want them,' which does not express a conditional and for which the ordinary logical rules for conditionals do not hold.[3] Perhaps, then, these sentences *just* assert respectively opportunity and ability, their if-clauses being of the unorthodox type. To reinforce this suggestion Austin tells us that 'he can' in the ability sense may be expressed by 'he can in the full sense if he has the opportunity' and that when 'he can' is used in this way no one would take it to be a subjunctive or conditional. If therefore, the 'could have' in 'he could have smashed that lob, if he had had the ability' is the past indicative tense of 'can,' that statement also will not be a conditional. This is true, but irrelevant. For it is not clear that 'could have' in the two hypothetical-seeming examples under discussion *must* be taken to be the past indicative of a restricted sense of 'can.' Why should it not be, what it certainly seems to be, the past subjunctive of the all-in 'can'? And, if this is what it is the statements will be genuine subjunctive conditionals equivalent to 'he would have been fully able, if he had had the ability' and 'he would have been fully able, if he had had the opportunity.'

[3] *Op. cit.*, pp. 113–5. The main features of these unorthodox cases are that they do not entail their contrapositives but do entail their own main clauses. From 'there are biscuits on the sideboard if you want them,' we cannot infer 'if there are no biscuits, you do not want them,' but we can infer 'there are biscuits on the sideboard.'

The question, then, is this: when we use these sentences are we *just* making categorical assertions of opportunity or ability—the if-clauses adding something indeed, but not imposing a condition—or are we making an hypothetical assertion, from which a categorical can indeed be deduced, but which cannot be identified with that categorical? It may be that these two come to the same thing for all practical purposes, just as 'q' and '$p \vee q : -p$' come to the same thing; but it is important to see whether or not they do. Suppose that there were another restricted sense of 'can' which we will call 't' and that it seems likely that 'he can (all-in)' means 'he has the ability and the opportunity and t.' There will now be a great difference between 'he would have been fully able, if he had had the opportunity' and the simple categorical 'he had the ability.' The categorical will still follow from the hypothetical; but the converse inference will not hold. From 'he had the ability' we cannot infer 'he would have been fully able if he had had the opportunity' since, if t were absent, the premise would be true and the conclusion false.

If Austin is prepared to identify 'he can do X, if he has the ability' with 'he has the opportunity to do X,' which at one point in his argument he actually does, it must be because he thinks (in my view rightly) that there is no further relevant sense, t. But if this and the corresponding identification of 'he can do X, if he has the opportunity' with 'he has the ability to do X' are correct, not only will the restricted categoricals follow from the relevant hypotheticals; we can also conclude that the all-in 'can' is a conjunction of ability and opportunity.[4]

Nevertheless, though ability and opportunity do add up to make the all-in 'can,' it would be wrong to say that the all-in

[4] If 'he has the ability' is equivalent to 'he is fully able, if he has the opportunity' and 'he has the opportunity' is equivalent to 'he is fully able, if he has the ability,' it follows truth-functionally that 'he is fully able' is equivalent to 'he has ability and he has opportunity.' Mr. P. T. Geach has pointed out to me that this conclusion can be reached without relying on the rules for the 'if' of material implication, which is certainly an unreliable procedure in an area in which 'ifs' are as slippery as they are here. We need rely only on the principle '$s \supset t . v \supset w : \supset : s.t \supset v.w$' which is valid for a greater variety of 'ifs,' including the counterfactual 'if.'

'can' is a *mere* conjunction of ability and opportunity; for these two are themselves conceptually related. Let us consider first what it is to have an opportunity. To say that someone has, here and now, an opportunity for doing X is not to say how things are in the world, though, to be sure, if you know about the activity X, you can deduce much about how things are. It is rather to say that the stage is *so* set that anyone who has, in general, the ability to do X is fully able to do it here and now. For example, to say that he was in a position to smash that lob is not to describe, even in outline, the relative positions of man, ball and net and the posture of the man. It says rather that man, ball and net were *so* placed in relation to each other and that the man's limbs were *so* disposed that if he has, in general, the ability to smash lobs, he could have smashed that one. But surely, it might be objected, the ability of the player makes no difference to the question whether there was an opportunity or not. Can I not conclude from the relevant statements about the positions of the objects concerned that there certainly was an opportunity to smash a lob, whether or not the player had the ability to smash it? Certainly, if I know about tennis, I can. But to describe the situation as an *opportunity* is to do more than merely to describe it; it is to say that the conditions for exercising a certain ability obtained. The description of the spatial relations remains true whether or not the player has any ability; but to see these relations as constituting an opportunity is to see them *as* conditions for the exercise of an ability. An opportunity is essentially an opportunity *for* someone who has an ability (which is why we can know exactly how we are placed without seeing in our situation an opportunity). If this is right, the concept of opportunity presupposes that of ability in the sense that, if there were no abilities, if everything in the world remained exactly as it is, nothing would constitute an opportunity.

In a somewhat different way the concept of ability includes that of opportunity. For an ability to do something is always the ability to do that thing in certain conditions without which the ability could not (logically) exist. Thus, if there are four men in a room where there are no cards, it may be that they can all play bridge in the sense that they have learnt and not forgotten. They cannot play bridge here and now; but this does not mean that their ability has deserted them, to return again when some cards arrive. It is rather that the ability they have is the ability to play-bridge-if-there-are-cards, not the remarkable ability to play-bridge-if-there-are-no-cards. The presence of cards, three other players, etc., may be collectively described as constituting an opportunity to play bridge, so that when we say of someone that he has the ability to play bridge we are saying that he has it *when* these conditions are fulfilled. It does *not* follow that when we assert ability we also assert or imply that the conditions *are fulfilled* here and now; the conditions are included in the description of the ability; for the ability is to do the thing in these conditions. It is the fact that an ability is always an ability to do-X-given-an-opportunity that makes it inevitable that, if we have any such concept as 'can' at all, we should have the triple concept of ability, opportunity and both together.

If this account of the relations between the three senses is correct in outline, Austin's picture of the 'all-in' use as the "paradigm use, around which cluster and from which divagate, little by little and along different paths, a whole series of other uses" is radically misleading. In the first place it is not the all-in, but the ability sense that is fundamental.[5] But I would not put too much emphasis on this point; it is not so much a question of getting one fundamental sense clear at the start and then seeing how other senses cluster round it, as of getting all three senses clear together by seeing how they fit in with each other. It is the word 'paradigm' that, as so often, gives

[5] As the etymological connection with 'know' would lead us to expect. Austin finds the same three senses in the case of 'know'; but while there is an ability-sense of 'know' we cannot use 'know' to assert opportunity without ability. A man cannot be said to know Chinese merely on the strength of his living in China and hence having many opportunities to speak it; nor, to take Aústin's example, could he be said to know what the thing in my hand is if he has an opportunity to identify it but lacks the ability.

a false impression; for it suggests that the all-in use provides a pattern or model to which the other uses, to a greater or lesser extent, conform. But, whatever the relations between the all-in and the other uses, it is not paradigmatic of them. The unravelling of a complex concept consists in showing how the elements that make it up (for example the different words which have the same stem, the different senses of a word, the different constructions into which it can enter) are related to each other. In particular we want to know which relations are logically necessary, which elements could not exist without some other. There is no doubt a good explanation for the fact that we use 'foot' both for a measure of length and for a part of the body; but, not only could we have different words for these two concepts, we could have either concept without the other. With 'can' the position is different; for we could not have either of the concepts of ability or opportunity unless we had both. Here we have to do, not with two related concepts, but with one complex concept. In a situation such as this it may be useful to exhibit one or more elements in the complex as fundamental, as giving the key to the others; but it is seldom or never the case that these key elements are paradigmatic of the others. To put the relation in this way is to suggest that, though they cannot be understood without it, it could be understood without them.

So far I have been concerned with the different senses of 'can.' There is no doubt whatever that Austin is right in saying both that this verb is used to make categorical statements and that 'could have,' being sometimes its past indicative tense, is also used to make categorical statements. In so far as the idea that 'can' requires analysis in terms of 'if' stems from the idea that 'could have' is subjunctive it is wholly mistaken. But I shall argue in this section that the central 'can' of ability is radically hypothetical, in all its moods and tenses, not in the sense that it must always be escorted by a spoken or unspoken 'if,' but in the sense that it can be analyzed in terms of 'if.'

I shall be concerned, in this section, solely with that use of 'can' which is relevant in connection with the freedom of the will, to the ascription of responsibility and to moral condemnation. In such cases we are always concerned, not with the question whether anyone can, in general, do or avoid something, but with the question whether he could or could not have done or avoided doing some particular thing that, as a matter of fact, he failed to do or did. This feature gives 'could have' a counter-factual air which tempts us to treat it as a past subjunctive, a temptation into which I certainly fell in *Ethics* with, as Austin shows, disastrous results. When we say, in preparation for an accusation of some kind 'he could have avoided doing that,' we are not saying anything conditional or subjunctive. We are saying categorically that he was both able and in a position to avoid doing what he did, and this is shown by the fact that if it can be shown that, as a matter of fact, he lacked either the ability or the opportunity, the accusation fails. Nevertheless it does not follow from the fact that 'could have' is a past indicative and used to make categorical assertions that these assertions may not require analysis in hypothetical terms; for it may be that the whole verb 'can' is susceptible of, or indeed requires analysis in terms of 'does . . . , if . . . .' Abilities are a sort of dispositional, and the idea of a dispositional does not seem to me, as it does to Austin, too obscure to be helpful. 'That chair is unstable' is categorical enough, compared with 'that chair would be unstable if one of its legs were an inch shorter than it is'; but it does seem to mean something like 'that chair would actually fall over, if *p*.' To be sure, when we call a chair unstable, we do not say precisely what it would do in precisely what conditions; we cannot spell out the analysis. But this only shows that the concept of instability in ordinary speech is inherently imprecise. Dispositional statements are used to connect an ill-defined, but not limitless set of occurrences with an ill-defined, but not limitless set of conditions.

Of all attempts to analyze 'can' in terms of what actually does or would happen, if something, Austin allows the greatest plausibility to 'he succeeds, if he tries.' This will certainly not do in all cases, since there are things that we can do without trying and in such cases 'trying' and 'success' are not in point. Neither this nor any other single analysis of all 'can'-statements is correct, but, I suggest, some analysis of this kind will always be found to work. I shall, however, limit my discussion to an example which Austin gives in connection with 'I shall succeed in doing X, if I try' as an analysis of 'I can do X.' The example is that of a golfer who misses a short putt, fails, and kicks himself because, things being exactly as they were, he could have holed it. "It is not," he says, "that I should have holed it if conditions had been different: that might of course be so, but I am talking about conditions as they precisely were, and asserting that I could have holed it. There's the rub. Nor does 'I can hole it this time' mean that I shall hole it this time if I try or if anything else: for I may try and miss, and yet not be convinced that I couldn't have done it; indeed further experiments may confirm my belief that I could have done it that time although I didn't. But if I tried my hardest, say, and missed, surely there *must* have been *something* that caused me to fail, that made me unable to succeed? So that I *could not* have holed it. Well, a modern belief in science, in there being an explanation of everything, may make us assent to this argument. But such a belief is not in line with the traditional beliefs enshrined in the word *can:* according to them, a human ability or power or capacity is inherently liable not to produce success, on occasion, and that for no reason (or are bad luck and bad form sometimes reasons?)."[6] Since this brings us to the edge of the determinist controversy, I propose to examine this example in some detail.

I. Austin notes that the facts alleged conflict with determinism but are in line with the traditional beliefs enshrined in the word 'can.' 'Determinism' he regards as the name for "nothing clear"; but it can be made clear enough for our purposes. For Austin, an ability is something that is inherently liable not to produce success, on occasion, and that for *no* reason; so we may, with sufficient clarity, say that a determinist is one who maintains that if an ability fails to produce success on some occasion there *must* have been a reason. Such a determinist has several lines of reply.

[6] *Op. cit.*, pp. 119–20n.

a) He might say that Austin's indeterminist belief is not, in fact, enshrined in our use of 'can'; ordinary language is quite non-committal on this point. Common sense, he will say, has a healthy habit of not coming down on one side or the other in a theoretical controversy which is not in practice decidable. If there *was* a reason for the failure of the ability on that occasion, we do not know it and have no hope of discovering it; so we shrug it off with the phrase 'it was just one of those things.' But it would be quite wrong to suppose that the use of this phrase implies a belief either that 'those things' have causes or that they do not; on this point traditional belief is silent.

b) He might argue that if our ordinary use of 'can' really does enshrine an indeterminist belief, so much the worse for it. You might as well argue that the heliocentric hypothesis is false on the grounds that it conflicts with the traditional beliefs enshrined in the phrase 'terra firma.' To be sure, he must now give up the claim that he is only analyzing 'can' as it is traditionally used. But this would not trouble him much. Our actual use of 'can,' he will now say, enshrines a false belief, and the sooner we get rid of it the better.

II. To accept the possibility of Austin's example and the interpretation he puts on it is to reject the thesis that 'he can' in this sort of case means 'he *always* does, if . . .'; but it invites, and I shall try to show that it requires, the thesis that 'he can' means 'he *usually* does, if . . . .' This would be a crucial, indeed a fatal change, if the issue were between determinism and indeterminism; but it is not; the issue is the possibility of an hypothetical analysis of 'can.' Let us agree for the moment that an ability is inherently liable not to produce success, on occasion, and that for no reason. It is also inherently liable to produce *success*, at least on most occasions. If you miss an occasional three-foot putt your ability to hole three-foot putts may not be in doubt; but if you miss too many, you lack the ability. 'He can,' then, implies 'he usually succeeds, if he tries'; and equally, though one success might be a fluke, 'he usually succeeds, if he tries' implies 'he can.' One might object that 'he usually succeeds, if he tries' is a much more guarded remark than 'he can,' expressing some doubt as to whether he can or not. But since 100% success is not, on Austin's view, required for the assertion of 'he can,' something less than 100% success must be sufficient if the assertion is ever to be made at all. There is, therefore, at least a material equivalence between 'he can' and 'he usually succeeds, if he tries' in this sort of case.

III. But, if there is a material equivalence, can we go further and assert a connection of meaning? It would certainly be odd to suggest that abilities are *causally* connected with successes.

It may well be that all human abilities are causally dependent on the possession of suitable muscles, nerves, brain cells and the like, and we learn from experience what equipment of this sort is required for each ability; but we do not learn from experience that if a man has a certain ability he will usually succeed when he tries or that he will not usually succeed if he lacks the ability. Austin talks of an ability as *producing* success or failure, as if it were a tool or a part of the body with which we do something and without which we cannot (contingently) do it. The metaphor of 'producing' can hardly be seriously intended; but the point is crucial. We can identify a niblick and then go on to say that it is used for getting out of bunkers; but we cannot identify the ability to get out of bunkers and then establish a contingent, but almost universal correlation between having this ability and actually getting out of bunkers. We do not, in short, learn by experience that people succeed in doing something if and only if they have the ability to do it.

Consider a contrasting case. I am looking out of the window and see that it is raining hard; I turn away for a moment and when I look back it is still raining. It would be ludicrous to suggest that it was not raining while my back was turned; for we know that rain is not that sort of thing. But, though ludicrous, the suggestion is not unintelligible, not logically absurd. Rain before and rain after is very good evidence; but it is not conclusive evidence. This is quite different from Austin's case, since in his case a run of successes before and after the one failure *conclusively* establishes the truth of the statement that he had the ability even on the occasion on which he failed. Why does Austin's golfer only say that further experiments may *confirm* his belief that he could have holed that putt? They prove it up to the hilt, since, given that n is large enough, a run of $n - 1$ successes *entails* the presence of an ability throughout the run. We are not arguing, as we are in the rain case, on the inductive grounds that rain is known to be the sort of thing that does not stop and start when people turn round. Abilities are by definition a sort of things that cannot suddenly stop and start, because they continue through periods of time in spite of failures; so the relation of evidence to conclusion in Austin's case is, like that of the evidence in the rain case to the conclusion 'the weather was foul the whole time I was in the room,' one of entailment.

But, it might be asked, might he not have retained his ability to hole putts of that sort throughout half an hour except at the one crucial moment? Not only did he fail, as we know; perhaps also he lacked the ability just then and there? It is important to see that this suggestion is ruled out by Austin's account, not as false, but as unintelligible. Statements of ability are statements to the effect that someone is usually, or would usually be successful in a series of attempts; and what could be meant by saying 'he was usually successful just then and there'? An ability endures through a period and can only be said to exist *at* a time in the sense that everything that endures may be said to exist at every time during its span of endurance. We may, then, say that he had the ability just then and there only in the sense that the time referred to by 'then and there' was within this span; and the evidence for his having had the ability just then and there in *this* sense is conclusive.

If Austin's indeterminism (abilities are liable not to produce success, on occasion, and that for no reason) is allowed, why should we not also allow this alternative account of the matter? Abilities, we say, are inherently liable to *desert* us, on occasion, and that for no reason. I lose my ability when I am drunk or tired or in a panic, and sometimes I *just* lose it for no reason at all. If both kinds of indeterminism were allowed, we should have to say that it was an open question which was the correct story to tell on some particular occasion; for the stories are critically different. It might be that he *could* have done it—this being one of the rare occasions on which his ability did not produce success; or it might be that he could *not* have done it—this being one of the rare occasions on which his ability deserted him. But it is clear that we cannot allow this choice of 'explanations'; for since, *ex hypothesi*, there is *no* difference between the two cases, we should never have any reason for preferring one to the other.

I conclude, then, that so far from being a reason for rejecting the possibility of an hypothetical analysis of 'can,' Austin's account of the case of the golfer actually confirms it. For, unless the idea of an ability *producing* success is taken more seriously than he intended—and I have given reasons for saying that it cannot—there is a logical equivalence, in this type of case, between 'he can' and 'he succeeds if he tries.' It is true that, if we accept Austin's account, we must rewrite the analysis as 'he usually succeeds, if he tries'; but this, while an important change, leaves the hypothetical analysis intact. One caution is necessary here. Philosophers who have offered analyses of this kind have often written as if they supposed that there was a *causal* connection between the consequent 'he does, or will, or succeeds' and the antecedent 'if he wants to, or chooses, or tries.' This is certainly incorrect.[7] There is a large number of verbs, including all those mentioned above and many others, which belong to the general area of *intentional action*. Many of the connections between them are, like that between ability and success, certainly not causal but, unlike that between ability and success, not logical either. What their status is I do not know; to find out would be to get to the heart of the matter.

IV

Austin was not, in his paper, directly concerned with questions of freedom and responsibility; but this is an area in which questions of the form 'could he have done it?' typically come up for an answer, and he touches on it when he says that

[7] On this point see Richard Taylor: 'I Can' in the *Philosophical Review*, January 1960, pp. 82–6.

the golfer kicks himself for missing the putt. There are cases in which everything else is beyond reasonable doubt and the question whether or not an ascription of responsibility or some accusation is called for turns solely on the question 'could he have done it?' or 'could he have avoided doing it?' No solution to the second-order philosophical question 'what do statements made with 'can' and 'could have' mean in these contexts?' can be considered satisfactory unless it succeeds in showing why the first-order questions should be considered relevant to ascriptions and accusations. The fact that they so obviously *are* relevant has sometimes blinded philosophers to the difficulty of seeing why this should be so and hence into giving theories of 'can' which will not explain it. This is the rock on which many theories founder. They give us senses of 'can' and 'could have' which may well be correct for other uses of these protean words, but which are such that they cannot explain why 'could have' questions are thought relevant to ascriptions and accusations. This is typically the case with theories of an intuitionist or introspectionist type, according to which both the meaning of 'I can' and the truth (on at least some occasions) of statements in the form 'I can' are held to be transparent.

Austin's theory would be immune from this criticism if it were not for the fact that the golfer reproaches himself for his failure. But it is not clear why he should do this, rather than cursing his luck. Certainly it was *he,* and not one of his team-mates, who missed the putt and, perhaps, thereby lost the match; and certainly he might lament the fact that his prowess was not greater than in fact it was. But, by the terms of the case, having tried as hard as he could and failed, he has nothing for which to reproach himself. We must distinguish (as philosophers are prone not to do) between the question 'Is determinism true?' and the question 'What, if any, is the bearing of departures, if any, from strict determinism on the freedom of the will, in that sense of freedom which is thought to be a necessary condition of responsibility?'. If we accept the terms of Austin's case, we must give a negative answer to the first question; but if we have no criterion for distinguishing cases in which an ability inexplicably fails to produce success (he could have done it, but did not) from cases in which the ability inexplicably lapses (he could not have done it), the indeterminism which we must accept will have no bearing whatever on freedom. The type of theory that I was criticizing in *Ethics* would say that, given the terms of Austin's case, it remained an open question whether or not the golfer could have holed the putt and hence whether or not he could be blamed for the consequent loss of the match. On Austin's view, as we have seen, the first question is no longer open, the evidence being sufficient to entail that he could have holed it; but we are obliged to construe 'he could have holed it' in such a way as to make the man as blameless for the loss of the match as he would have been if he had been unable to hole it. He is, of course, responsible for losing the match in the trivial sense already noticed, that it was he who missed the vital putt; but he would have been equally responsible in this sense if he had missed it through lack of ability. Even if Austin is right in giving an indeterminist account of abilities, he fails to show how and why ascriptions of responsibility may turn on the answers that we give to 'could have' questions.

In Austin's example as it stands no question of moral responsibility or moral appraisal comes up. How could it be made to come up? The player might have been bribed by the other side and have missed the putt on purpose, while pretending to try his hardest. Or, knowing that it was a critical shot in an important match, he may have been culpably negligent in its execution. (Negligence of this sort, thoughtlessness, lack of consideration, failure to see something in a situation that is morally relevant—all these, though different, belong in the same bag, and it is a bag which moral philosophers have not examined as carefully as they should; for nine tenths of our moral shortcomings will be found in it). But, to make moral assessment relevant at all, *something* of this kind must be introduced into the situation. I suggest that when, in preparation for a judicial or moral appraisal, we ask 'could he have helped it?' what we want to know is the answer to such questions as 'why did he do it?', 'why did he not succeed?', 'what prevented him?', 'but for what factor in the situation would he have done it?'. Some answers, notably lack of ability and lack of opportunity, exculpate, if not wholly at least to some degree; these are the answers that we summarize in the blanket phrase 'he could not help it'; other answers, notably 'he was bribed' and 'he just didn't care' have the opposite effect. The problem of the freedom of the will, in so far as this is not only a metaphysical problem but relevant to moral philosophy, is that of discerning some general feature that distinguishes the exculpatory from the non-exculpatory answers. To say that some things are in our power to do or not do and others not, though perhaps true, is wholly unenlightening. It merely restates the problem; and theories about what it is in our power to do cannot be acceptable unless they succeed in explaining why the question whether something is or is not in our power should be considered relevant to our moral status.

J. L. AUSTIN'S PHILOSOPHICAL PAPERS

RODERICK M. CHISHOLM

. . .

. . . At the beginning of "Ifs and Cans" (1956), Austin states that he intends to discuss two large questions:

(1) "Whenever . . . we say that we can do something, or could do something, or could have done something, is there an *if* in the offing—suppressed, it may be but due nevertheless to appear when we set out our sentence in full or when we give an explanation of its meaning?"

And (2) "if and when there *is* an *if*-clause appended to a main clause which contains a *can* or *could* or *could have,* what sort of an *if* is it? What is the meaning of the *if,* or what is the effect or the point of combining this *if*-clause with the main clause?"

From Roderick M. Chisholm, "J. L. Austin's Philosophical Papers," *Mind,* LXXIII, No. 289 (January, 1964), pp. 20–25.

With respect to the first of these questions, he notes that it is one thing to say (*a*) that categorical sentences beginning with "I can," "He could have," etc., carry with them an implicit *if*-clause which is always understood and capable of being supplied, and that it is quite another thing to say (*b*) that such sentences may be paraphrased or explicated by means of other sentences which contain *if*-clauses. If, for example, we said that "I can" means the same as "I can if I try" we would be affirming (*a*), and if we said that "I can" means the same as "I will succeed if I try," we would be affirming (*b*).

What Austin says about *ifs* in connection with (2) is very important, it seems to me. He points out that the *ifs* of such sentences as "I can if I choose," "There are biscuits on the sideboard if you want them," "I paid you back yesterday if you remember," and "You may exercise your rights if you want to," are not the *ifs* of causal (or other) conditions. For sentences of the form "if *p* then *q*," in which the *if* is the *if* of condition may be contraposed to "if not-*q* then not-*p*"; but none of the sentences just cited may be so contraposed. It is relevant to note that these non-conditional *if* sentences are not *if-then* sentences; even if we put the *if*-clause first, it would be unnatural to begin the other clause with *then*. Austin gives us a plausible positive account of the uses of these non-conditional *ifs* and shows how they may be used to express, or to assert, hesitation, doubt, or stipulation. For example, the *if* of "I shall marry him if I choose," provided the sentence is one in which the *shall* may be stressed, "qualifies the *content* of the undertaking given, or of the intention announced, it does *not* qualify the giving of the undertaking."

This account does not hold of all non-conditional *ifs*, however. There are some which are simply vulgarisms; *e.g.* "That's poisonous if you drink it" and "I hope you have a good time in Paris if I don't see you again." And there is another type of non-conditional *if* which Austin does not mention—those *ifs*, namely, that may be replaced by *even ifs*. "If it rains I will go," when the statement is intended in such a way that "even" may be inserted at the beginning, or "just the same" at the end, cannot be contraposed to "If I do not go it will not have rained."

Here, too, "then" is inappropriate. (The non-conditional "even if *p, q*" seems to be equivalent to "*q* whether or not *p*" and to "*q* and it is false that if *p* then not-*q*.")

Austin's first question—"When we say 'I can,' 'He could,' etc., is there an *if* in the offing?"—arises in connection with the treatment of the problem of free will (Austin says "the problem, so-called, of Free Will") in G. E. Moore's *Ethics*. Moore had answered the question affirmatively in trying to show that the thesis of determinism is compatible with saying that people can, or could, do things that they do not do. Moore said:

> There are certainly good reasons for thinking that we *very often* mean by "could" merely "would, *if* so and so had chosen." And if so, then we have a sense of the word "could" in which the fact that we often *could* have done what we did not do, is perfectly compatible with the principle that everything has a cause: for to say that, *if* I had performed a certain act of will, I should have done something which I did not do, in no way contradicts this principle.

Austin intimates that, in the course of this discussion, Moore made a "first-water, ground-floor mistake," but it is not clear to me just what the mistake is that Moore is supposed to have made.

It *would* be a mistake to say that the *ifs* in "I can if I choose" and "He could have if he had chosen" are conditional *ifs*, for, as Austin points out, these sentences cannot be contraposed and their *ifs* ordinarily perform quite a different function. In the first chapter of his *Ethics* Moore did repeatedly use such expressions as "can if I choose" and "could have if he had chosen," but in chapter six, in which the discussion of free will occurs (and from which the above quotation is taken) he does not use these expressions. He says there that "could" means "would, if so and so had chosen," and he says "I could have" means "if I had performed a certain act of will, I should have"; he does not suggest there that "can" and "could" are accompanied by implicit *if* clauses, much less that they are accompanied by *if*-clauses containing conditional *ifs*.

Moore's point, in showing that the thesis of free will might be reconciled with that of determinism, was to indicate that certain sentences in which "can" or "could" occur may be replaced by certain *if-then* sentences in which "can" or "could" do not occur. It was unfortunate that he used the particular verb "choose" in his *if*-clauses, for, as Austin notes, there are objections applying to "choose" which do not apply to other verbs which Moore might have used instead. (Note that Moore does use another verb in his example at the end of the passage quoted.) If Austin is right, *if*-clauses containing "choose" or one of its variants as the principal verb are almost always non-conditional, in the sense just described. Was Moore's mistake simply that of interpreting "choose" in a way in which it is not ordinarily interpreted? This would be a mistake, but not a "first-water, ground-floor mistake."[1]

What Austin took to be Moore's basic mistake may have been that of supposing that "can" may be expressed in terms of "will if," or "would if," and that the indicative "could have" may be expressed in terms of "would have if." This may well be a mistake, but Austin's objections to it can be met, I think. He considers two ways of rendering "can" in terms of "will if," etc., and he shows that one of these is unsatisfactory, but I do not think that he shows the other to be unsatisfactory.

The first of these is the account of "could have" in P. H. Nowell Smith's *Ethics*. Nowell Smith considers the sentence (*C*) "Smith could have read *Emma* last night" and says that what it means could also be expressed by (*W*): "Smith would have read *Emma* last night, if there had been a copy, if he had not been struck blind, etc., etc., and if he had wanted to read it more than he wanted to read anything else." (This statement, which has the form "if *p*, if *r*, and if *s*, then *q*," may also be put as "if *p* and *r* and *s*, then *q*.") Austin offers several objections, the most telling of which seems to me to be the follow-

[1] "Then you agree, I said, that the pleasant is the good and the painful evil. And here I would beg my friend Prodicus not to introduce his distinction of names, whether he is disposed to say pleasurable, delightful, joyful. However, by whatever name he prefers to call them, I will ask you, most excellent Prodicus, to answer in my sense of the words.

"Prodicus laughed and assented, as did the others." *Protagoras* 358.

ing: To establish *W* we need evidence, not merely as to Smith's abilities and opportunities, but also as to his character, motives, and the like; to establish *C* we do not need such evidence. But Austin also says this of *W:* So far from *W* being what we mean by saying Smith could have read the book, "it actually implies that he could *not* have read it, for more than adequate reasons: it implies that he was blind at the time, and so on." Unless I have seriously misunderstood Austin at this point, there would seem to be *two* mistakes underlying this remark. It is a mistake, first, to suppose that subjunctive conditionals, such as *W*, are necessarily contrary-to-fact—to suppose that they assert, imply, or presuppose that their antecedents are false. A man may assert *W*, for example, in the course of trying to decide whether its antecedent is true. ("Did he read *Emma* last night? I don't have the whole picture yet. But if there had been a copy . . . etc.") Or he may know that the antecedent is true and use the subjunctive in order to be non-committal. ("I'm not saying, one way or the other. But this much is true: if there had been a copy . . . etc.") And the second mistake is that of supposing that, from the fact that the antecedent of "if *p* and *r* and *s*, then *q*" is false, it follows that *p* is false and *r* is false and *s* is false.

There is still another possible way of expressing "can" in terms of "will if," or "would if," and expressing "could have" in terms of "would have if." Austin concedes that there is some plausibility in the "suggestion that 'I can do X' means 'I shall succeed in doing X, if I try' and 'I would have done X' means 'I should have succeeded in doing X if I had tried' "—plausibility, he says, "but no more," and he rejects the suggestion.

Among the objections to saying that "He can" means the same as "He will if he tries" are the following, all indicating possible cases in which "He can" is true and "He will if he tries" is not true. (i) A man who can do X may try to do X and because of an unexpected diversion or intrusion abandon the enterprise before he finishes; he gives up the puzzle because of a call to dinner. (Here we may say "He can but he wants his dinner" but not "He could if he did not want his dinner.") (ii) The man may try halfheartedly—*i.e.* he may not try as hard as he *can* try—and thus not complete the task. (iii) I can close my eyes, but it makes no sense to speak of me, now, *trying* to close my eyes. (iv) Austin suggests (this seems to be his principal objection to the formula) that "He can" is consistent with failure and "He will if he tries" is not. He says of the case where he misses a very short putt: "I may try and miss, and yet not be convinced that I could not have done it; indeed further experiments may confirm my belief that I could have done it that time although I did not." And finally (v) there may be things a man can do only if he does *not* try to do them. The golfer landed the ball at a certain place *p*; hence landing it at *p* was something which, at that time, he could do ("does" implies "can"); but had he tried to land the ball precisely at the place *p* where he did land it, then, in all probability, he would have failed.

These are valid objections to saying that "He can" means the same as "He will if he tries." But we may replace "He will if he tries" by a longer formula and then, I believe, they no longer apply. Suppose we say: "He can do X" means that there is something such that if he tried to do *it* then he would do X—*i.e.*, that there is something Y such that if he tried to do Y then he would do X.

Then (i) we may say, of the man who could do the puzzle but gave it up in order to have his dinner, that there was something—*e.g.* doing the puzzle without having dinner—which was such that, had he tried to do *that*, he would have done the puzzle. (ii) Or if doing the puzzle required only a little more effort than he cared to put into it, then there was something—putting more effort into the puzzle—which was such that had he tried to do it he would have done the puzzle. (iii) Perhaps it makes no sense to say of me, now, that I may try to close my eyes; but there are other things I can be said to try to do—I can try to look the way I do when I'm asleep—which are such that if I do try to do them I will close my eyes. (iv) If Austin's golfer really could have holed it that time, then there was something such that, had he tried to do it along with the other things he did do, then the absent condition (*e.g.* applying more pressure with the thumb) would have been supplied, and he would have holed the ball. And (v) we may say of the man who landed the ball at *p* and who would not have done it had he tried to do it, that there were things such that had he tried to do *them* he would have landed the ball at *p;* they were just the things he did try to do. (We cannot say, however, that landing it at *p* is something that he can do "at will," or something he "knows how to do," for landing it at *p* is not itself something he can do if he tries.)

But there is still another possible difficulty: the statements "He does X if and only if he tries to do Y" and "He *cannot try* to do Y" are inconsistent with "He can do X," but they are not inconsistent with our *analysans*—they are not inconsistent with "There is a Y such that if he tries to do Y he will do X." (There are, of course, many acts which one cannot even *try* to perform.) This is the serious difficulty, I think. If it is a genuine one, then it applies not only to the present formula, but also to those which Austin mentions and, in all probability, to any attempt to define "can" in terms of "will if." For any such attempt will presumably introduce a verb of which "he" may be made the subject; it will then be grammatically permissible to insert "can not" between the subject "he" and the verb; and then it will be possible to describe a situation in which the *analysans* is true and "He can" is false. To overlook this possibility *is* a "first-water, ground-floor mistake."

All of which confirms Austin's profound remark: "In philosophy it is *can* in particular that we seem so often to uncover, just when we had thought some problem settled, grinning residually up at us like the frog at the bottom of the beer mug."

THE PSYCHOLOGY OF EFFORT OF WILL

C. A. CAMPBELL

I should like to begin by emphasizing the word "psychology" in the title of this paper. My whole concern will be with the *experience* of making what we call "effort of will"—

From C. A. Campbell, "The Psychology of Effort of Will," *Proceedings of the Aristotelian Society*, XL (1940), pp. 50–69.

with its psychological nature, its psychological context, and its psychological antecedents. That psychological analysis of this experience must have an important bearing upon central problems of metaphysics, I am very far from doubting. But obviously we must first of all get a true view of the psychological facts before we can usefully study their metaphysical implications. As will become sufficiently clear, I think, from what follows, this is by no means so simple a matter as it has often been taken to be.

. . .

In the first place, we want a general description of the experiential situation in which effort of will is located, sufficient at least for purposes of identification. For the term effort of will is at times rather carelessly used, and is allowed to denote psychical processes which we should certainly not, on due reflection, identify with efforts of will.

There is some confusion, for example, between effort of will and the activity of willing. It is important to be clear that these are quite distinct phenomena. No doubt there is an activity of a sort involved in all willing or choosing; but to be conscious of that activity is not necessarily to be conscious of exerting effort of will. If I am considering how I may most enjoyably spend the evening, and choose, as the occupation which seems most attractive, to read the latest P. G. Wodehouse, I am, indeed, conscious of *choosing*, but it would be sheer nonsense to say that I am conscious of making an effort of will. I am choosing the course which is also the course towards which I feel that my desiring nature most strongly inclines me; and wherever that is the case—as it probably is in some 99 per cent of our choices—I think we must all agree that we are not conscious in our choosing of exerting what we call effort of will.

It is fairly evident, I think, that we are conscious of making an effort of will *only* when we choose a course that is contrary to the course towards which we feel that our desiring nature most strongly inclines us. The most obvious case, accepted by most writers on the subject as typical, occurs when, as we say, we succeed in "overcoming a temptation." What we mean when we so speak seems clear enough. The "temptation" consists in the fact that while believing a course X to be morally superior to a course Y, we are conscious of our desiring nature as inclining us more strongly to Y than to X. In William James's terminology, Y is felt by us to be "in the line of least resistance," relatively to our desiring nature. In choosing X we seem to ourselves to be acting in the line of greater resistance—not necessarily, as is more commonly said, in the line of *greatest* resistance[1]—and to be succeeding in doing so by virtue of making this so-called effort of will whereby we somehow reinforce the energy of the weaker desire.

So far nothing has been said with which any psychologist is likely seriously to quarrel. The trouble begins when we attempt a closer study of the psychological nature of this ostensibly new energy which is added to that of the weaker desire. Is it an unique form of energy, as the agent himself is apt to suppose, different in kind from that energy of the desires which is the dynamic of at least most of our choices, and the antecedents of which can be traced with some show of scientific rigour to determinate elements in the agent's psychical make-up of instincts, emotions, sentiments and the like? Or is it, despite first appearances, reducible to some specific manifestation of the energy of desire in a determinate context of circumstances which the psychologist can make plain to us? These are, broadly speaking, the alternatives between which the student of the problem has to choose.

There is not much doubt which of these alternatives has proved the more attractive to most psychologists. With James as almost the solitary exception, they have preferred the second alternative. Nor is this surprising. The psychologist is a scien-

[1] It is clear that we sometimes exert an effort of will in order to achieve an end recognised to be *higher* than that to which our desiring nature inclines us, but at the same time recognised not to be the *highest* end. In such cases it would seem that the latter, but not the former, end will be felt to be in the line of *greatest* resistance. The former end will be felt to be merely in the line of *greater* resistance—or perhaps just "resistance"—relatively to our desiring nature. The point, however, is not of first importance, and in dealing later with certain psychological theories I shall use whatever form of words their advocates prefer.

tist, and the scientist, as such, has a predilection for the discovery of as much law and order as possible in his subject-matter. Now, so long as choices are universally explicable in terms of desires, then, since desires themselves, in their various degrees of strength, are fairly intelligible, though often complex, products of determinate instincts, emotions and sentiments, there seems no serious obstacle in principle to regarding the psychical process of choice as a law-abiding member of a law-abiding system. If, on the other hand, choices can be influenced by some mysterious form of energy not reducible to that of desire, the causal continuity which the psychologist *qua* scientist desiderates is gravely threatened. It is thus not unnatural that the psychologist should be averse to the admission of this seemingly obstreperous element. He may even be commended, indeed, if he refuses to admit it until he has first tried out the alternative hypothesis for all that it is worth, and a little more.

And there is a further factor, I think, which has not been without its effect in determining the attitude of psychologists to our subject. Psychologists, until very recently, have also been philosophers, or, at the least, sufficiently interested in philosophy to be stirred by the prevailing currents of philosophic thought. Now in dealing with the problem of free will, the one thing upon which respectable philosophers of all parties have been agreed is that it is monstrous to admit as a subjective determinant of the will any element which has not intelligible roots in the character of the agent. An act of will which does not spring from the self's character, it is said, is obviously not the self's act at all. It is of no more use to the wise Libertarian than to the Determinist. This may fairly be said to have established itself as a philosophical cliché. It is also, as I believe, and as I have argued more than once elsewhere, a devastating error which has played havoc with the whole free will controversy. My purpose at the moment, however, is merely to point out that here, in the climate of philosophical opinion, there has been an additional encouragement to the psychologist to give a preference to one of the two rival hypotheses concerning the experience of will-effort. It is, I hope, not unfair to suggest that psychologists have often approached the analysis of the experience of will-effort with a rather definite expectation of finding that, even from the standpoint of psychology, there is nothing which lends countenance to the notion of a form of mental energy which, while not intelligibly rooted in character, can yet influence the act of choice.

One further word before commencing consideration of the more important of the psychological analyses which proceed along what, for the sake of a convenient label, we may call "Determinist" lines. We ought to be clear at the outset about the fundamental requirement which any such analysis must fulfil. If the explanation it offers is really going to *explain*, it must give an account of the psychical factors involved, and of their relationship, such that any person who faithfully constructs this complex experience in imagination is able to say "Yes, when these conditions are satisfied in my experience, I do find that I have the experience that I am accustomed to call 'effort of will.' " Otherwise, the psychologist is not explaining the experience, but merely explaining it away. His explanation is really a type of *ignoratio elenchi*. Whether or not any of the theories we are now about to examine are free from this fatal defect remains to be seen.

McDougall's View

It is natural to take one's start from the theory advanced by Professor McDougall in his *Social Psychology*. No one, so far as I know, has offered so thorough an analysis from the Determinist standpoint, and his conclusions are both well known and, apparently, widely approved.

. . .

Stripped to its barest essentials, McDougall's account of it is as follows. At first we do desire Y, the lower end, more strongly than we desire X, the higher end. But prior to our actual choice certain new desires intervene and ally themselves with the desire for X. These new desires are excited from within the self-regarding sentiment, which is defined by Mc-

Dougall as "the system of emotional and conative dispositions that is organised about the idea of the self, and is always brought into play to some extent when the idea of the self rises to the focus of consciousness."[2] The consequence of the increment of strength which the desire for X draws from these new desires—desires emanating from self-respect, pride, and the like—is that the desire for X is enabled to win the mastery over the desire for Y. It has become, in short, in virtue of these reinforcements, the stronger desire. Hence, so McDougall contends, the agent's choice of X becomes perfectly intelligible to us without our being obliged to acquiesce in the postulation of any mysterious new energy. Effortful volition is simply—to quote the definition at which McDougall eventually arrives—"the supporting or reinforcing of a desire or conation by the co-operation of an impulse excited within the self-regarding sentiment."[3]

Now without doubt this theory of McDougall's has a good deal of plausibility. For my part, I should not at all deny that the process described by McDougall, and supported by a wealth of aptly chosen examples, does very often take place. Indeed, I should even admit that McDougall has here accurately described the most common way in which a moral agent, confronted by a temptation, succeeds in choosing the right. The trouble is that this way is just *not* the way that the agent adopts in those cases in which he seems to himself to be exerting effort of will. The psychical process which McDougall describes could not, it seems to me, give rise to the experience of effort of will. For consider. What happens, according to McDougall is that the desire which was originally the weaker becomes now, through the co-operation of desires emanating from the self-regarding sentiment, the stronger desire. Hence it must now be X, the "higher" end, that is felt to be in the line of least resistance. But if X is now felt to be in the line of least resistance, how could one possibly suppose one's self to be *exerting an effort of will* in order to achieve it? Whatever else is involved in the

[2] *Social Psychology*, p. 213.
[3] *Ibid.*, p. 214.

experience of effortful willing, there is at least involved always the consciousness of acting contrary to the line of least resistance. Yet if McDougall's account be the true one, we are, after all, merely choosing what we most strongly desire, and we ought therefore to be conscious of acting not *against* but *in* the line of least resistance; unless, indeed, one cares to take refuge in the desperate assumption—to which I confess I can attach no intelligible meaning—that that which we most strongly desire may be felt by us as *not* that which we most strongly desire.

What McDougall has failed to see is that there are *two* ways—there is not just one way—in which a moral agent may seem to himself to overcome temptation. It is perfectly correct to say with McDougall that in a situation of moral temptation reflection upon the implications of the two opposed courses often brings into play new desires and aversions, more particularly desires and aversions emanating from the self-regarding sentiment, that these additional forces may have the effect of weighting the balance of the desiring situation in favour of the higher course, and that the agent is thereby enabled to choose the higher course. That is one way, and, as I have already granted, probably the most common way. The temptation in such cases is overcome, we may say, by ceasing to be a temptation. The lower end ceases to be felt by us as exerting a stronger attraction for our desiring nature than the higher end, and the willing of the latter accordingly takes place without any consciousness of effort. The other way in which we seem to ourselves to overcome temptation is by exerting effort of will. Whatever may be the ultimate analysis of this latter way, at least it seems certain that it cannot be coincident with that of the former way. McDougall has, as I think, confused the two, with the result that, having set out to explain what happens when we experience an effort of will in resisting temptation, what he actually gives us is an explanation of what happens when we resist a temptation without experiencing an effort of will.

Before we take final leave of McDougall's solution, it

will be worth our while to notice a brief "gloss" on that solution by Mr. Wisdom in his *Problems of Mind and Matter*.

Wisdom accepts in principle McDougall's account of what happens when we act in the line of greater resistance. It is always a matter of the reinforcing of the weaker desire by certain other desires. But Wisdom draws attention to a fact not explicitly noticed by McDougall, *e.g.*, that there are many cases in which the most careful introspection does not enable us to discover these new desires (or "motives," as Wisdom prefers to call them) whose introduction is, on McDougall's theory, supposed to determine the decision. We must even admit, he contends, that "we can sometimes be sure that the observable motives were not the complete cause of the decision."[4] Ought we then to conclude that in these cases some factor is operative other than the motive of desire? Wisdom sees no reason to embrace this dangerous alternative. McDougall's theory will still hold if we incorporate into it a recognition of the existence of *unobservable* desires. For "how do we know" asks Wisdom, "that there is not some other motive which is *unobservable* and which yet affects one's decisions and one's acts? We cannot know this unless we assume that every desire affecting decision can be detected by introspection. And no one will maintain this; especially in view of the evidence which the psycho-analysts provide for motives undiscoverable by introspection."[5]

The point seems to me fairly taken, and I imagine that McDougall would have accepted what Wisdom says here as a legitimate supplement to his own account. It is necessary to make clear, however, that, effective as Wisdom's appeal to sub-conscious desires is in rebutting one obvious criticism of McDougall's theory, it does not touch the particular criticism of it which I have just been advancing. The cardinal defect of McDougall's theory, I argued, was that whereas in exerting effort of will we seem to ourselves to be acting contrary to the line of least resistance, the process which McDougall de-

[4] *Mind and Matter*, p. 129.
[5] *Ibid.*

scribes would lead us to suppose ourselves to be acting along the line of least resistance. The use to which Mr. Wisdom puts the notion of the subconscious does nothing to meet this objection.

On the other hand—and this is why I have deemed it desirable to make reference to Wisdom's view—it is possible to conceive of an extended use of the notion of the subconscious which might seem to hold out promise of a way of escape. For where the new, reinforcing desires are unobservable by the agent, may not the increment of power which they bring be unobservable likewise? And if so, will it not be the fact, in such cases at any rate, that the agent will still *feel* that he is acting along the line of greater resistance whereas in *fact* he is acting along the line of least resistance?

The suggestion is at first sight attractive. It seems to me pretty certain, however, that it will not do. A sufficient, though by no means the sole, objection to it is this; that while we certainly have abundant evidence, as Wisdom claims, of the operation in us of desires of whose particular nature we are not at the time aware, no one, to the best of my knowledge, has found evidence that these or any other desires operate in us without their *impulsive tendency* being *felt.* On the contrary, the chief evidence for the existence of sub-conscious desires seems to be just that we do sometimes feel a strong impulsive tendency towards a certain end where introspection reveals no overt desire capable of explaining it. There is, I think, little need to dwell on the matter. Perhaps no one will seriously deny that sub-conscious desires, like any other desires, affect the felt balance of the desiring situation. What I referred to on a previous page as the "desperate assumption" that that which we most strongly desire may be felt by us as *not* that which we most strongly desire seems to me not to be rendered less desperate by an appeal to the sub-conscious.

Stout's View

Professor Stout's psychological explanation of effort of will is to be found in the chapter on Voluntary Decision in his

Manual of Psychology. His view has interesting points of difference from that of McDougall; but, like McDougall, he writes with the explicit aim of controverting the Libertarian interpretation sponsored by James, and he is equally convinced that action in the line of greater resistance does not, when carefully analysed, imply the introduction of any new psychical factor. His discussion of the topic is exceedingly brief, covering much less than three pages.[6]

The problem for Stout, as for McDougall, is what really happens when, as we say, we exert an effort of will and act against the line of least resistance? The key to the correct answer, he believes, lies in remembering that when a voluntary decision is once formed, "opposing conative tendencies either cease to operate, or they appear only as difficulties or obstacles in the way of carrying out our decision." "The disappearance of opposing tendencies, on the one hand," he proceeds, "or their persistence as obstacles, on the other, are the two alternatives which correspond to action in the line of least resistance and in the line of greatest resistance." In cases of hard, "effortful" volition, as when we voluntarily decide "in opposition to some present organic craving," the volition is felt as effortful because of the persistence of the opposing tendencies. For, in Stout's words, "the craving itself is maintained by organic conditions which continue to operate both in the very moment of decision and after the decision is made." In cases of easy, effortless volition, as when we decide "in favour of indulging the animal appetite," the volition is felt as effortless because (again in Stout's words) "the counter-motives tend to disappear altogether, instead of persisting as obstacles. They are not maintained by organic conditions, nor are they obtruded on the mind by any other circumstance."

This then, according to Stout, is all there is to the experience of effort of will. If he is right, there is evidently no reason to believe that in effortful willing the weaker desires triumph. The appearance to the contrary is due simply to our consciousness of the persistence of opposing tendencies, whereby we are

[6] *Manual of Psychology*, 5th Edition, pp. 639–641.

deluded into imagining that we are acting contrary to the line of least resistance. Accordingly there is no ground here at all for postulating the introduction of a new form of psychical energy.

I do not think, however, that this theory will suffice. It does not really seem to be the case that persistence of opposing tendencies as obstacles during and after decision causes a volition to be experienced as effortful. For, although it is true that in all effortful volition opposing tendencies persist as obstacles, it is also true that in many cases of effort*less* volition opposing tendencies *also* persist as obstacles.

To take an example. If I am fleeing from an angry bull, my aching limbs and panting lungs may cry out for rest long before I reach a place of refuge. I am acutely conscious that organic tendencies oppose themselves as obstacles to my volition to keep on the run. But I am certainly *not* conscious of having to exert an effort of will to keep on the run. My aversion to the prospect of what will happen to me if I desist is quite enough, and is felt to be quite enough, to determine me to continue my flight in despite of my physical cravings. A *muscular* effort, of course, I do exert. But muscular effort is very different from effort of will—a point to which I shall return. Effort of will, so far as I can see, there is none. Indeed, were anyone to suggest to me after such an adventure that it must have taken a great effort of will to keep moving, I might be pardoned for supposing him to be jesting.

Or take another instance. While listening with uncommon pleasure to a musical broadcast, I begin to feel thirsty. The thirst becomes acute, but I am aware that to get myself a drink will mean making a journey downstairs and interrupting my enjoyment of the recital. I continue to listen in, because much as I desire to quench my thirst, I desire still more to hear the music. "The craving itself is maintained," as Stout would put it, and I ought therefore, if his theory is correct, to be conscious of exerting effort of will and of acting in the line of greatest resistance. But in actual fact I am conscious of nothing of the sort. I am, and I know that I am, following my strongest desire, doing that to which my desiring nature in the given situation most strongly inclines me, and the continuing operation of opposing conative tendencies does not in the least lead me to imagine that I make or maintain my decision by exerting effort of will.

I must conclude, therefore, that Stout's account of the matter will not meet the facts. Experience of effortful volition is not reducible to experience of volition in the face of persisting obstacles. The psychological explanation of the characteristic of "effortfulness" is still to seek.

Thouless's View

Dr. R. H. Thouless in his *Social Psychology* has also devoted some little space to our problem. In the course of a general account of volition he tells us that "the difficulty in the explanation of volitional action lies in the fact that, of two impulses, it is often the one which appears the weaker that is voluntarily adopted."[7] He proceeds to consider, very briefly, the manner in which James and McDougall respectively have dealt with the difficulty and, in rejecting both of these accounts, to give us his own view of the matter.

That view appears to be that the problem is really meaningless in the terms in which it is usually formulated. James and McDougall both formulate the problem in terms of "strong" and "weak" impulses, and ask how we can choose the end of the weaker impulse. But, Thouless contends, such a formulation is open to the criticism "that the strength and weakness of impulses can in no wise be measured except by observing which of a pair of competing impulses finds expression in action."[8] The implication seems to be that it is nonsense to talk of stronger and weaker impulses unless we are simply meaning by the "stronger," that which in fact prevails, and by the "weaker," that which in fact does not prevail. But if that *is* what we are meaning, then, of course, *quaestio cadit*. There is no question of how the weaker impulse can triumph in a volition. For it never does.

[7] *Social Psychology*, p. 244.
[8] *Social Psychology*, p. 247.

Thouless's view, if I have interpreted it correctly, is certainly a paradoxical one. Unfortunately, it is stated with such brevity that the critic may do less than justice to the reasons which underlie it. But so far as I understand his position, it appears to me to be demonstrably false. Certainly we do not in practice wait until we have made our choice, and can thus observe "which of a pair of competing impulses finds expression in action," before pronouncing a confident judgment as to which of two competing impulses is the stronger. If I say that I want to hear a certain lecture this evening, but that I also want to go to the theatre, and that my desire to go to the theatre is the stronger of the two desires, this last clause has a perfectly intelligible meaning both for me and for my hearers. I mean that, so far as my desiring nature is concerned, I feel myself more strongly attracted to the theatre than to the lecture, so that, should my desiring nature as it stands be allowed to determine my choice, it is the theatre and not the lecture which I shall choose to attend. And it is hard to see how anyone can deny my ability to measure the relative strength of my desires, prior to action, in this sense.

Why should Thouless suppose that this is not a proper way of measuring the relative strength of desires? I am at a loss to find the answer. Of course we do not always know in advance—nor claim to know—which desire is the "stronger" in the sense of being the one that will in fact prevail. As we are well aware in many cases, other factors may intervene to influence us before the act of choice takes place. But we do know in advance, or certainly think we know, which desire is the stronger in the sense of being the one which will prevail *if* no further factor intervenes. Nor is there the slightest empirical evidence, so far as I can see, to suggest that we are ever mistaken in thinking that we know this. Surely we have here a perfectly valid meaning of the term "stronger desire," and a perfectly valid way of measuring it in advance?

I at any rate cannot regard it as seriously doubtful that we are able to measure in advance of action the relative strength of impulses in the way which James's and McDougall's formulation of the problem presupposes. It is true, of course, that there are rare occasions when we find it almost or quite impossible to say which of two competing impulses is the stronger. But that is not because we can apply to them no valid principle of measurement. It is because when we do apply to them our principle of measurement we find them to be approximately equal. We feel that the two ends exercise an equal attraction for us, so that (as we sometimes say on these occasions) "we do not know how to choose between them." That, so far as I can see, is the only kind of case in which there is a difficulty about knowing in advance which of two competing impulses is the stronger, and the difficulty is obviously completely compatible with the applicability of a valid principle of measurement.

This completes all that I think I can usefully say in this paper in the way of criticism of definitive theories. To complete the negative part of my programme, however, I must add a few words about certain mistaken views about effort of will which, although not as a rule supported by any explicit analysis, seem to be implied in a good many casual references to the subject.

I suspect, for example, that there is a certain amount of confusion of effort of will with both *muscular* effort and *intellectual* effort. It is not difficult to show that neither a volition involving the exertion of muscular effort nor a volition involving the exertion of intellectual effort is necessarily a volition involving effort of will. But I am not at all sure that this is always realised. I propose, therefore, to devote a little space to making clear that effort of will (as experienced) is distinct from either of these phenomena.

To take muscular effort first. If my child falls, and I pick her up, I am conscious of exerting muscular effort in picking her up. But it would be absurd to suggest that I am, in a normal case, exerting effort of will. In willing to pick her up I will to do what I most strongly desire to do, *i.e.,* I will along the line of least resistance. And that is precisely the kind of willing that is experienced as effort*less*. It is obvious, of course, that on occasion I do exert an effort of will in order to make a muscular effort. I may have to exert an effort of will, as well as muscular effort, in order to get out of bed on a December morning. And probably it is exclusive attention to cases of this sort that has led some persons to assume that the willing of a muscular effort is always a case of effort of will. But what such cases really indicate, of course, is simply that the willing of muscular effort is *sometimes* contrary to the line of least resistance, relatively to our desiring nature, just as *sometimes* it is along the line of least resistance.

The case of intellectual effort is amenable to parallel treatment. The chess-player is conscious of exerting intellectual effort in planning his next moves, but he would think it ridiculous if he were told that he had to exert an effort of will in making this intellectual effort. His zest for the game sustains the intellectual effort, and precludes any need for exerting an effort of will. Intellectual effort *may*, of course, like muscular effort, require an effort of will to initiate or sustain it, *e.g.*, when we are trying to read a difficult work which has little intrinsic interest for us, but which we feel we ought to master. Whether or not an intellectual effort does require an effort of will is, as in the case of muscular effort, simply a matter of whether or not it is felt to be against the line of least resistance.

There is one other thing which effort of will is *not*, of which we may remind ourselves before proceeding to the consideration of its positive features. It is not the activity characteristic of volition as such. That was made sufficiently clear, I think, at the beginning of my paper, and needs no further remark here.

I turn now to attempt what I can in the way of positive construction.

I may say at once that I am in substantial agreement with James's view of the matter. So far as I can see, effort of will, as we experience it, is an unique phenomenon, incapable of being analysed in terms of anything but itself. The attempts so to analyse it which we have surveyed seem manifestly to break down, and I can conceive of no other analysis which has a higher degree of plausibility.

But even if it be the case that effort of will is something unique, or *sui generis,* it does not, I think, follow that we are thereby precluded from saying anything at all about it save that it is just itself. Its uniqueness entails that we cannot define it in terms of anything other than itself, and that there is no more hope of explaining what effort of will is to anyone who has not experienced it than there is of explaining what colour sensa are to a blind man. But, given the requisite experience, there are important things that we can say about what is experienced, even if that *is* unique. For even if an experienced entity is not constituted in terms of other experienced entities, it may nevertheless have, as experienced, integral relations to other experienced entities. This, I believe, to be the case with effort of will. As I conceive it, the business of elucidating the psychological nature of effort of will can only consist in, negatively, the demarcation of it from certain other phenomena with which it might be confused, and, positively, in the ascertainment of the most fundamental of its integral relations to other elements in experience. The second of these tasks is our concern now.

Some of these relations we have already had occasion to observe in the course of our discussion of other theories. The relation of effort of will to our desires, *e.g.*, requires little further comment. We are, I hope, agreed that effort of will is always exerted against what is felt to be the existing "set" of our desiring nature. Not that there are *no* elements of our desiring nature directed to the end in whose service effort of will is exerted. Usually, and perhaps always, there are some so directed. All that I am interested to maintain is that the end to which effortful willing is directed is necessarily an end opposed to that to which our desiring nature at the time is felt to incline us most strongly.

Can we say anything positive about the nature of the end in whose service effort of will is made? I think that we can. If the end is opposed to that which we are conscious of most strongly desiring, why should we take an interest in its achievement at all? Only one answer seems possible, viz., that it is regarded by the agent as a *higher* end. There would appear to be two, and only two, grounds upon which we can take an interest in the achievement of an end. *Either* it must exercise an attraction for our desiring nature, *or* it must appeal to our sense of obligation. Now in the case of effort of will, the end we endeavour to achieve is felt as exercising less attractive force upon our desiring nature than the end we reject. If, then, we are taking sufficient interest in it to endeavour to achieve it, it would seem that this can only be because of the obligatory character which it wears for us. It must be regarded as the higher end, the end which has the greater authority for us though it has not the greater power. In a wide sense of the word "moral," a sense which admittedly begs certain large questions not directly relevant here, it seems true to say that effort of will has always a *moral* orientation.

Let us turn next to the relationship, for our experience, between effort of will and the *self*.

It is evident at once that this relationship is very different from the relationship between, say, desires, or emotions, and the self. We speak of the self "having" desires, or emotions: but it would be quite unnatural to speak of the self "having" an effort of will. We speak of the self *making* an effort of will. Clearly we regard ourself as the *author*, and not merely the *owner*, of our effort of will.

But it is necessary to try to ascertain, by introspecting as carefully as we can, the precise nature of this "authorship" with which we credit our self. What then do we find when we introspect our self making an effort of will? We find, certainly, that we regard our self as the "source" of the effort. But clearly the self is not taken to be its "source" merely in the sense that the effort is felt to "emanate" from it. We do not, as it were, suddenly find ourselves thinking "Hullo! Here I am making an effort of will!" On the contrary, we regard our self not as the blind origin of the effort, but as its *conscious originator*. For we are aware of the effort as issuing from our *conscious decision to exert it.* And we are further aware—or so at least I shall argue—that that decision of ours was a free or creative decision between genuinely open possibilities, in that we could have decided not to make the effort (or, in the appropriate circumstances,[9] to make it in less or in greater degree).

How can it be shown that these awarenesses concerning the relation of effort of will to the self are really inherent in the experience of making the effort, and that the relations in question may therefore be regarded as integral relations? It is obvious, of course, that they are not *explicitly* present, in the sense of being consciously formulated in the agent's mind. No one would claim that. But that they are implicitly present, requiring only the stimulus of the appropriate question in order to rise to explicit consciousness, may be shown, I think, without too great difficulty, by suitable introspective experiment. All that we require to do is to imagine ourselves exerting an effort of will, and then put to ourselves certain questions. In the first place, this question, "Can we, while making an effort of will, conceive it as even possible that the making of the effort does *not* issue from a decision on our part to make it?" I take it that anyone who carries out this not very complicated experiment will find, as I do, that one can*not* conceive this as even possible. But if so, if the experience of making an effort of will compels a negative answer to this question once it is asked, the situation seems not unfairly expressed by saying that implicit in the experience of making the effort is the consciousness that the effort issues from a decision on our part to make it.

Exactly the same procedure may be followed to elicit the presence of the second of the awarenesses mentioned above. We must ask ourselves in this case "Can we, while making an effort of will, conceive it as even possible that we could not have decided to refrain from making the effort?" And again, I take it, the only possible answer which the experiment can yield is the negative one. Wherefore, I submit, we are entitled to say that implicit in the experience of making the effort is

[9] It is quite obvious that there are such circumstances. But having formally noted the fact, I shall for the sake of simplicity ignore it in future references to the alternatives confronting moral decision in situations of temptation.

the consciousness that we could have decided to refrain from making it.

The phrase "could have decided to refrain" has, however, an ambiguity which has been repeatedly pointed out. It might mean "could have decided to refrain if certain elements in the situation, and particularly the agent's desires, had been different from what they were." Or it might mean "could have decided to refrain in the actual situation precisely as it was, with the agent's desires precisely as they were." Determinists have often suggested—usually without chapter and verse—that Libertarians fail to distinguish between these two meanings; that in consequence they allege as evidence in favour of Libertarianism the existence of a subjective certainty that one "could have decided to refrain absolutely," whereas in fact the only subjective certainty that exists is that one "could have decided to refrain *conditionally*"—which subjective certainty does not support Libertarianism at all. It becomes particularly important to point out, therefore, that the agent in the experience we are analyzing is certain that he "could have decided to refrain" in its absolute or unconditional meaning. To show that this is so, we must employ again our old technique. We must ask ourselves "Can we, while making the effort, conceive it as even possible that we could not have refrained from making it unless some factor or factors in the situation had been different?" For myself, I find that I cannot entertain this even as a possibility. Once the question is put to me, I find myself completely certain, while making the effort of will, that I could have decided to refrain from making it even if the situation had been different in no particular whatsoever. It is open to anyone, of course, to contend that my subjective certainty during the experience, and yours likewise (if, as I venture to presume, the results of our introspective experiments coincide) are illusory; that there are imperative metaphysical reasons—and perhaps reasons of other sorts also—for holding that an agent could not have decided otherwise than he did decide save in the weak, or conditional, sense of these words. This contention I should, in another context, vigorously dispute. But in the present context it is wholly beside the point. We are concerned here with the *psychology* of effort of will, and with that alone. And I maintain that, whether the belief be a true one or a false one, the agent in exerting effort of will does necessarily *believe* that he could have refrained from exerting it, in the strong, or unconditional, sense of these words.

FREEDOM AND RESPONSIBILITY

P. H. NOWELL SMITH

. . .

The Concept of 'Trying.' It might be thought that the libertarian could discover a criterion for distinguishing culpable weakness of will from non-culpable addiction in the concept of 'trying.' For the addict fails, try as he may, while the weak-willed man fails because he does not try hard enough. The concept of 'trying' is an important one for ethics since, whatever may be the case in a court of law, the question of moral blameworthiness often turns, not on what the agent did, but on what he tried or did not try to do. Morally we blame people, not for failing to live up to a certain standard, but for not trying hard enough to do so; and this is because, while we do not believe that they could always succeed, we do believe that they could always try. We must now see whether the introduction of this concept helps to save the categorical analysis.

We all know what it *feels* like to make an effort. These feelings are phenomena or occurrences that we experience in the same sort of way that we experience aches, pains, qualms, and twinges. And, if we take the introspective language of the libertarian seriously, it would seem that the question 'Did he try?' can be answered only by the man himself and that he answers it by observing whether or not one of these feelings occurred. The logical status of this question will be like that of 'Did it hurt?'. But on this view an effort is not something

From P. H. Nowell Smith, "Freedom and Responsibility," in *Ethics*. Harmondsworth, Middlesex: Penguin, 1954, pp. 285–290.

that a man *makes;* it is something that *happens* to (or inside) him; and it would be highly unplausible to make the question of his responsibility turn on the occurrence or non-occurrence of such a feeling. If 'making an effort' is to be relevant to responsibility, it must be thought of as something which a man can choose to do or not to do. The substitution of the active for the passive voice is an important advance; unfortunately it is fatal to the categorical interpretation of 'he could have acted otherwise.'

For 'trying' is now thought of as something that a man can choose to do or not to do, and the difficulties encountered in construing 'he could have acted otherwise' will emerge again in construing 'he could have tried to act otherwise.' On the libertarian analysis, if a man fails to act rightly, we must say either that his failure is inexplicable or that it was due to circumstances beyond his control—in which cases he is blameless—or that it was due to his not having tried as hard as he could have tried. For what exonerates is not 'I tried,' but 'I tried as hard as I could'; and, in order to distinguish the blameworthy man from the addict who literally couldn't help it because he tried as hard as he could, we must be in a position to answer the question 'Could he have tried harder than he did?'. But how can we answer this question? *Ex hypothesi* he did not try harder than he did; so that we must say either that his failure to try harder is inexplicable or that it was due to circumstances beyond his control—in which cases he is blameless—or that it was due to his not having tried to try as hard as he could have tried to try.

But this is absurd. In the first place 'try to try' is meaningless; and, if this be doubted, we must push the analysis one stage further. In fact he did not try to try harder than he did. But can he be justly blamed for this? Only if he could have tried to try harder. We must say either that his not having tried to try harder is inexplicable or that it was due to circumstances beyond his control—in which cases he is blameless—or that he failed to try to try harder because he did not try to try to try harder . . . and so on.

Libertarians sometimes speak in terms of our failure to make the best use of our stock of "will-energy"; but this usage gives rise to the same infinite regress. If using will-energy is thought of as something that we do not choose to do, but which just happens to us, it would appear to be irrelevant to responsibility; but if it is something that we can choose to do or not to do, we must be able to distinguish the man whose failure to use sufficient will-energy was due to circumstances beyond his control from the man who failed (culpably) to use it because he did not try hard enough to use it. And this involves answering the question 'Had he sufficient second-order will-energy to enable him to make more use of his first-order will-energy?'.

On these lines there is clearly no way out of the wood. The attempt to discover one is, I think, due to two mistakes. (a) It is noticeable that, on Campbell's analysis, a man's desires and even his character are continually referred to as 'it'; desires are thought of as forces which, sometimes successfully and sometimes unsuccessfully, prod a man into doing what he ought not, and his "character as so far formed" is the sum of these forces. Thus I am said to be able to choose whether or not to "let my desiring nature, my character as so far formed, have *its* way." And this is to treat all cases of 'doing what I want to do' on the model of the opium-addict, as the actions of a man who is a slave to his desires.

And since Campbell uses 'desire' for every motive except the sense of duty, his treatment presupposes that I can choose whether to act from a certain motive or not; and this is not so. If I am both hungry and thirsty I can choose whether to have a meal or a drink; but I cannot choose whether to act from hunger or thirst, unless this strange phrase is used simply as a (very misleading) synonym for 'choosing whether to eat or to drink.' In the same way, if I have a certain sum of money, I can choose whether to pay a debt or give my aunt a Christmas present. If I choose the former, my motive is conscientiousness; if the latter, it is generosity. And we might, therefore, say that I can choose whether to do the conscientious or the generous thing. But I cannot choose whether to act from conscientiousness or from generosity. What I do will depend on my character; and this 'cannot choose' is not a lamentable restriction on my freedom of action. For to say that my choice depends on my character is not to say that my character compels me to do what I do, but to say that the choice was characteristic of me. The creative 'self' that sits above the battle of motives and chooses between them seems to be a legacy of the theory that a man is not free when he does what he wants to do, since he is then the victim or slave of his desires; and it is postulated to avoid the unplausible doctrine that all action is involuntary.

(b) Campbell takes as a typical and, by implication, the only case of moral choice to which appraisals are relevant, that of a man who knows what he ought to do but is tempted to do something else. Now this, so far from being the only case, is not even the commonest or most important. For in the great majority of cases of moral difficulty what is difficult is not to decide to do what one knows he ought to do, but to decide what one ought to do. This sort of difficulty arises in three main types of case. (i) A humble and unimaginative person who accepts a customary code of morals without much question may find that two rules conflict; the voice of conscience is in this case ambiguous. (ii) A more self-confident, imaginative, and reflective person may wonder whether he ought, in the case before him, to do what the customary rule enjoins. He knows very well what the rule enjoins; but what prompts him to depart from it is not "part of his desiring nature," but a suspicion that the rule is one that, in this particular case, he ought not to follow. (iii) A man of fixed moral principles (whether or not they are those customarily adopted) may find himself in a radically new situation that is not catered for in his code. What is he to do? It is here, if anywhere, that the idea of an unpredictable 'creative' choice seems to make sense. He takes a leap in the dark, but just because it is a leap in the dark I doubt if we should be inclined to blame him if he leapt in what turned out to be the wrong direction.

Men who belong to a generation for whom the questioning of accepted principles has been no mere academic exercise and who have found themselves faced with momentous choices in situations not covered by their traditional rules will be less likely than their fathers perhaps were to suppose that the only sort of moral difficulty is that of resisting temptation.

If, in the first two of these three cases, a man decided that he ought to do something and did it, he might still be held to blame. For reasons given in chapter 17 conscientiousness is so valuable a motive that we should be chary of blaming a man who did what he honestly thought he ought to do, however misguided we thought him. But we should not necessarily excuse him, which we should have to do if all wrong-doing were failure to resist temptation. Integrity is not the only moral virtue, any more than it is the only virtue in an artist; and the belief that it is is one of the more regrettable consequences of the Romantic Movement. We blame people, not only for failing to live up to their moral principles, but also for having bad moral principles; and I shall examine the logic of this type of blame in the next chapter.

Perhaps the most crucial objection to the libertarian thesis lies in the sharp discontinuity which it presupposes between moral and non-moral choice and between moral and non-moral appraisal. It is not enough to admit that we can, within broad limits, predict what a man of known habits, tastes, and interests will do and to insist that our powers of prediction only break down in the small, but important area of moral choice. For it is not the extent of the area open to prediction that is at issue.

It is true that we can, within broad limits, predict what a man will choose from a menu, whether he will make a century to-day, or finish his cross-word puzzle; but we can also predict, again within broad limits only, whether or not he will resist the temptation to run away or to cheat at cards. Our reliance on the integrity of a bank clerk is not different from our reliance on his accuracy. In neither case do we believe that he 'must' or 'is compelled to' be honest or accurate; and what is paradoxical is not so much the libertarian's defence of moral freedom as his willingness to accept mechanical determinism as an explanation of non-moral action. For the rigid distinction between 'formed character' (where determinism reigns) and 'creative choice' (which is in principle unpredictable) it would be better to substitute a conception of continual modification of character in both its moral and its non-moral aspects. This not only does justice to the fact that we use both choosing and appraising language in the same way in moral and non-moral contexts, but it is closer to the facts. A man can grow more or less conscientious as time goes on, just as he can become better at tennis or more fond of Mozart.

INDEX

71 72 73 74 75 10 9 8